MENTAL ILLNESSES AND TREATMENTS

RESEARCH ON ONLINE/OFFLINE INTERVENTIONS IN MENTAL HEALTH

A CRITICAL REVIEW

MENTAL ILLNESSES AND TREATMENTS

Additional books in this series can be found on Nova's website under the Series tab.

Additional e-books in this series can be found on Nova's website under the e-book tab.

MENTAL ILLNESSES AND TREATMENTS

RESEARCH ON ONLINE/OFFLINE INTERVENTIONS IN MENTAL HEALTH

A CRITICAL REVIEW

LUCIANO L'ABATE

nova publishers
New York

Library of Congress Cataloging-in-Publication Data

ISBN: 978-1-63321-446-0

Library of Congress Control Number: 2014954118

Published by Nova Science Publishers, Inc. † New York

CONTENTS

DISCLAIMER

"The resources reviewed in this volume may help therapists, counselors, and other mental health clinicians to keep abreast of the rapidly evolving professional guidelines, research, treatments, innovations, and practices in the areas of tele-psychology, telehealth, and internet-based therapy (K. S. Pope)".

The information contained in this volume has been collected by and for the Coalition for Technology in Behavioral Science (CTiBS) as a public service. This Coalition is not responsible for nor can guarantee the helpfulness and usefulness of this information. The author would appreciate any additions and corrections to this draft from interested colleagues and readers.

ACKNOWLEDGMENTS

First of all, I want to acknowledge the important contribution of Marlene Maheu for her immense and continuous attention to the references in the original bibliography. Without her great leadership and strong support neither this work nor the Coalition for Technology in Behavioral Science would have gotten off the ground. Second, I am grateful for the gracious help received from Kenneth Drude, Reid Hester, David Luxton, Kenneth S. Pope, and Lee Ritterband, among many others, during the preparation of the bibliography used for this volume. Third, some of the references included here were taken from a Bibliography on Distance Counseling developed by a team consisting of Devan Coughlin, Jonathan D. Shy, James P. Sampson, Jr., and Janet G. Lenz (2010) from Florida State University and inserted here with the kind permission of Janet Lenz (12/18/2012).

Additionally, I want to acknowledge the personal communication received from Lee Ritterband (5/29/12): "There are two links that will likely provide most if not all of what is needed. The first is an incredibly comprehensive site of references related to this area of eHealth amazingly maintained by Azy Barak and his group at the University of Haifa: http://construct.haifa.ac.il~azy/refindx.htm. They spend hours every week keeping this bibliography up-to-date. The second is more focused on Internet interventions specifically (and beginning to include mHealth) and is a portal targeted for consumers to be able to see what online programs are available. It is maintained by colleagues at the Australian National University: http://beacon.anu.edu.au/." The third is a review of recommended online approaches that is by now outdated and limited in its scope (L'Abate, 2013d).

To include references contained in the first two bibliographies would render this task impossible to perform and to complete. Therefore, I have relied on those references available through members of the Coalition for Technology in Behavioral Science. Nonetheless, I want to acknowledge my dear friend Mrs. Louise Strait for helping to find and complete lost or incomplete references. Thank you Louise, you have been a real friend for many years.

BACKGROUND

The purpose of this research is to identify under what conditions will online interventions be more cost-effective than offline, face-to-face (F2F), talk-based (TB) ones. Given two types of interventions with equal outcomes, that is, same effectiveness, one would chose the least expensive one. Cost is usually measured by how much time Mental Health (MH) professionals spend in their practices: administering, monitoring, and feed-backing whatever information they receives from participants. The less professional time the lesser the cost, unless different levels of semi-quasi-professionals or para-professionals are used to administer structured Internet programs (L'Abate, 2001, 2002, 2013b)

This volume is the final, natural evolution and inevitable outcome of decades-long interest and involvement in distance or remote writing and enrichment rather than F2F talk (L'Abate, 1977, 1987; L'Abate & Rupp. 1981; L'Abate & Weinstein, 1987; L'Abate & Young, 1987), health promotion (L'Abate, 2007), self-help (Harwood & L'Abate, 2010), sickness prevention (L'Abate, 1990), social skills training (L'Abate & Milan, 1985), programmed distance writing (Hooper, L'Abate, Sweeney, Gianesini, & Jankowski, 2014; L'Abate, 1986, 1992, 2001, 2002, 2004a, 2004b, 2008, 2011a, 2011b, 2013b, 2013c, 2013d; L'Abate & De Giacomo, 2003), technology (L'Abate & Kaiser, 2012), and the laboratory method in clinical psychology (L'Abate, 2008) including written homework assignments (Kazantzis, Deane, Ronan, & L'Abate, 2005; Kazantzis & L'Abate, 2007; L'Abate, 2011, 2013b; L'Abate & Sweeney, 2011, in press).

These efforts were most of the time connected with specific models of Relational Competence Theory (Colesso, Cusinato, & L'Abate, 2013; Cusinato & L'Abate, 2012; L'Abate, 2013a; L'Abate, Cusinato, Maino, Colesso, & Scilletta, 2010) linking research with applications in clinical psychology, including prevention of mental illness (L'Abate, 1990), promotion of physical and mental health (L'Abate, 2007), and pre-para-post-therapeutic activities in mental health, including psychotherapy, crisis intervention, and rehabilitation (L'Abate, 2013d).

Finally, last but definitely not least, this volume, in many ways, is a follow-up to the ground-breaking, pioneering work of Marks, Cavanah, and Gega (2007), who, as shown in practically every chapter in this volume, set the foundations for reporting on research about most topics considered here. To avoid repetitious summaries, most of the research reviewed by Marks, Cavanah, and Gega (2007), will not be reported here. Nonetheless, we are grateful to those authors for outlining the many disadvantages of Computer-Aided Psychotherapy (CAP), such as technophobia, limited capacity to fulfill all the needs made by consumer, inability to detect subtle non-verbal and non-verbal cues, rigidity or inadequate flexibility, avoidance of relevant issue to focus on irrelevant ones, not all computer-driven users find psychotherapy acceptable, inability to deal with complications arising during the course of psychotherapy. Many other shortcomings listed by Marks et al., ignored the importance of programmed writing (L'Abate, 2011c, 2013b) approach that have solved in some ways the problem of matching a concrete problem with a specific solution and Pennebaker's expressive writing as a general way to deal with unexpressed traumas.

By the same token, Marks et al., (2007) listed the advantages and functions of CAP as interaction with a patient, linked to an identified computer with individuals, couples, and families, elimination of travel from one's home to a professional's office, increase in confidentiality, reduction of stigma, screening for suitability of online work, specification of which program goes with what kind of problem (L'Abate, 2013b).

Marks et al. (2007), however, emphasized the national origin (Australia, Holland, Sweden, UK, USA, etc.) of each piece of research they reviewed. This emphasis will be completely absent in this volume because each piece of research can evaluated on its own merits and not on its national origin. Indeed, I found this responsibility to be critical of every single contribution diminished considerably by the fact that each contribution in and of itself described the level of evidence used to report, such as testimonials without evidence, case studies, qualitative analyses, pilot studies without a control group, and, finally, controlled studies with experimental and control group comparisons as well as pre-post-evaluations and, in unfortunately too few cases, long-term follow-ups. Each summary will speak for itself. Nonetheless, in Appendix A I have added one chapter containing exemplary representatives from various countries outside the USA.

Four other relevant predecessors to the present volume were:

(1) Anthony, Nagel, and Goss' edited volume (2010) containing chapters covering most clinical, ethical, practical, and professional aspects of Internet interventions with little if any research coverage about results from these interventions;

(2) This latter aspect was covered extremely well by another important predecessor to this volume, namely: Gallego and Emmelkamp's (2012) chapter about the effectiveness of Internet psychological treatments in mental health disorders. These authors directly considered clinicians' resistance to the use of Internet resources, originally introduced by L'Abate (2001) and later by Sweeney and L'Abate (2011), such as: (1) fear of being replaced by a computer; (2) inadequate knowledge about the use of computers and interactive approaches to deal with the overwhelming number of mental health disorders; (3) inadequate information and training in the use of Internet-based interventions; (4) concerns about issues of confidentiality; (5) legal issues in dealing with patients at a distance rather than face-to-face (F2F); (6) worries about not being able to control the process of intervention at a distance, without having to see patients F2F; (7) non being able to see non-verbal cues (facial expression); (8) difficulty in dealing with crises through the Internet; and (9) questionable adherence to treatment and possibility of dropping-out from treatment. In short, this resistance and defenses to justify it could be condensed by a fear of losing the power of the personal presence and of the professional power to being one-up on patients through titles and the use of technical information or jargon not known to patients.

(3) In addition to the specific contribution by Gallego and Emmelkamp (2012), one must include: (a) the work by Cleary and DeLosh (2012) about wireless response systems in the

classroom; (b) animation and multimedia tutorials (Atkinson, Sabo, & Joseph, 2012); (c) the participatory web (Atkinson, 2012); (d) computer-based cognitive stimulation programs to remediate age related cognitive decline (Delahunt, Morton, & Mahncke, 2012); (e) uses of technology for and with children with autism spectrum disorders (Solomon, 2012); (f) mobile technologies in education and healthcare (Atkinson, Denham, & Quick, 2012); (g) using Virtual Reality for clinical assessment and intervention (Rizzo, Parsons, Kenny, & Buckwalter, 2012; (h) telehealth conferencing in the neurosciences (De las Cueras, 2012); and (i) workbooks as programmed interactive practice exercises (L'Abate, 2012).

(4) Professional practice was covered extremely well by Maheu, McMenamin, and Pulier's (2013) contribution about optimizing the use of technology in psychology in combination with best practice principles. Nonetheless, practitioners desirous to enter in the practice of tele-psychology should be conversant with Nelson and Lillis' (2013) recommendations for managing their practice in real time. As a general background for such a practice, practitioners should be conversant with social media (Barnett & Kolmes, 2013) and up-date their practice with smart-phones (Maheu, Pulier, & Roy, 2013).

I was responsible for integrating all the references and summaries into a more or less coherent whole manuscript and changing present verb dates to the past, changing English into American usage spelling, and adding editorial comments where necessary.

In the last chapter of this volume, I have added conclusions drawn from this enterprise to prognosticate about the present status and future perspectives for online interventions.

FOREWORD

Behavioral professionals are facing a serious, yet too-often neglected problem when considering outcome studies related to practicing via any of the advanced telecommunication technologies or other assistive technologies. The problem has to do with the evolution of the telehealth literature outside the evidence-base for the other behavioral sciences, otherwise known as the "allied" health fields. Telemedicine started with tele-radiology in the 1950's. In 1959, the first tele-psychiatric visit occurred in Nebraska and tele=psychiatry research has proliferated ever since. The problem is that most psychologists, social workers and counselors were unaware of the hundreds of millions of dollars of research in tele-psychiatry that was funded by not only the US government and private agencies, but others worldwide. When the Internet made its more public debut in the early 1990's the majority of allied health professionals considered the rapidly evolving Internet to be a completely new world, unexplored and unregulated. In an article published in 2000, Barry Gordon and I published results of a survey of online practitioners, in which the vast majority of respondents were unaware of legal or ethical mandates that related to their online work as clinicians (Maheu & Gordon, 2000).

Consumers began experiencing unprecedented opportunities to connect to both each other and to professionals, or those who claim to be professionals. They soon learned that online therapists don't follow traditional therapy protocols, and that getting help online can not only be less expensive, but available 24/7, often at low fees or for free, and the conventions of intakes, assessments, informed consent and other time-intensive procedures could be easily disregarded. They could get an immediate answer to an immediate problem, and all without leaving the privacy of their living or bed room.

They have since learned that when connecting with online therapists, they don't need to list the medications they take, report their current alcohol intake or provide a suicide history before asking a question about coping with an angry boss, reluctant spouse or depressed, cognitively impaired parent. They have learned that they can get help without undergoing an intake process that includes being forced to sit in the waiting room of a "mental health" facility, take the time or pay for an informed consent process that explains details that they don't think relevant in the moment, or take expensive psychological testing instruments prior to learning what to say to improve their marital relationship.

WHAT CONSUMERS DON'T KNOW CAN BE HARMFUL

Consumers may not know or understand that the research is strong for behavioral telehealth interventions, but those interventions are not the same as what usually occurs with online therapy. Traditional behavioral telehealth usually involves a treating professional who follows well-tested, controlled and prescribed protocols. It also often includes rigorous informed consent processes, full intakes, rigorous and standardized documentation, fully trained professionals, emergency support, etc. Referrals usually come from medical offices where the patient is known to the physician, and a full record is kept.

Online therapy often involves an informal exchange between a professional for quick chats and semi-professional relationships without full intakes, history-taking, releases and in many cases, without mandated reporting. (Some such relationships are anonymous, leaving the clinician without the ability to abide by mandated reporting rules). Regulatory boards have not been notably responsive to date, except for a few highly publicized cases. While it is clear that regulatory boards are becoming increasingly sensitized to the issues, it is also important to note that many online therapists have received significant training and do follow state as well as federal law. It is also fair to say that many others are unfamiliar with traditional models, and have not received any training in the differences between in-person care and online practice, or how to bridge the two worlds legally, ethically or clinically.

Online consumers then, may not know which type of service or practitioner they are accessing. Some may rely on professional's licensure for an assurance of professionalism. They deserve to be better educated about the issues. They also may not know enough to care that the professional was licensed 30 years ago, and is untrained for telephone or video-based practice.

Consumers also deserve to better understand the services they are purchasing from different types of professionals, and how training differs across disciplines. Most consumers don't know the differences in training or services between a psychologist and a psychiatrist, or a social worker and a clinical psychologist, or between a coach and a counselor. They deserve to have user-friendly information about any professional group they are encouraged to access.

THE PROFESSIONAL'S ROLE

While consumers have the right to request any number of services from their treating professionals, the professional's role is to make careful decisions about the types and locations of service delivery for each individual being served. Consumer protection is the professional's number one mandate. Unprepared professionals working with unprepared consumers in telemental health is a recipe for disaster.

One of the most serious dangers for online professionals is the lack of knowledge about training for best practices to understand and incorporate professional association guidelines. They may not be cognizant of the many issues consumers may need to know prior to being treated online.

TRADITIONAL BEHAVIORAL TELEHEALTH — CLIENT/PATIENT EXPERIENCE

Working in traditional behavioral or telemental health settings affords many benefits for risk management. Team members include the clinician, but can also include administrative assistants, nurses or physician assistants and information technology (IT) team members. Each of these professionals has the opportunity to make chart notations about their experience of the client/patient. Intake forms are completed in the waiting room, often under the watchful eye of an administrative assistant. Nurses often take vital signs and comments are entered into the patient record. Physicians, nurse practitioners or their representatives are responsible for management of the case. HIPAA requirements are explained and the patient consents to treatment. Release forms are signed and messages are sent to other involved health professionals.

Once the determination is made that a substance abuse, behavioral or mental health consult is needed, the client/patient is educated, often by a technical or other assistant. Information is shared about how the technology and support systems work, what they can expect, who they will see for their video consult and why. Proper expectations are set for the consult with a behavioral specialist, who is at a computer that might be hundreds of miles away. An appointment is set, often on another day. The client/patient returns to the clinic for that appointment with the behavioral specialist. Everyone involved understands mandated reporting and emergency treatment protocols. Such backup is available within the client/patient's local community with pre-identified personal or response teams.

TRADITIONAL BEHAVIORAL TELEHEALTH — PRACTITIONER'S EXPERIENCE

On the clinician's side, the professional is credentialed, trained in how to keep the client/patient record, and also trained in how to use the technology. Practitioners often don't need to be trained in the legal issues, because their institution handles requirements such of making sure the technology is HIPAA compliant, proper intake forms are signed, releases are sent, etc. Those legal requirements, for which they must exert effort, are understood and formally accepted in an agreement with the healthcare facility.

Both treatment protocols and technology protocols are understood by the clinician and carefully monitored by quality control staff. Mechanisms for mandated reporting are established and well-tested. Malpractice insurance is in place and has the advantage of a large system selecting the plan, a legal team to interpret its coverage, and the clout of the large organization is readily available to force payment of benefits when in question. There usually is a support team on standby to handle any unexpected technical failures with the video or other technology. Emergency back-up staff and processes are identified and available for unexpected emergencies.

The system works well. Scientific documentation for the effectiveness of using such professionals and video-based systems is well established. This large, interlocking system of checks and balances affords the practitioner many assurances and peace of mind when embarking on innovative forms of practice via technology.

Independent, Small Group and Clinic Practitioners

On the other hand, the experience of many independent or small group and clinic practitioners can be quite different. All too frequently, these professionals do not have an in-house system of checks and balances when working online. They have to cover all the bases, including:

- Following all relevant state and ethical requirements
- Authentication (verifying identity) of the consumer
- Establishing geographic location of all involved parties
- Intake/assessment
- Technology-related informed consent
- Understanding, developing and following appropriate protocols for both the technical and clinical interventions
- Consumer education and management
- Proper documentation and
- Emergency planning/intervention

Just as when a practitioner uses a telephone company to connect with a consumer, a professional using any video platform without the aid of a support staff at a distant site is responsible nonetheless. Such professionals need to understand how to handle all the required elements of a professional relationship and protect that client/patient from harm online — and all without assistance from supportive staff, large structures and the training afforded by such systems.

The Problem — Lack of Information

On the Internet, many practitioners are not only uncredentialed, many don't know where to go to get credentialed. Training is a serious problem. Many don't have any training to handle the many events that can easily go wrong online with a behavioral or mental health practice. Many don't know how to conduct a legal informed consent process, a distant intake or assessment. They often don't how where to find protocols for telemental health care or how to adapt what they find to their own clinical populations. They often don't know how to anticipate emergencies, prevent them or rally a local backup team when an emergency appears. Many also don't know how to properly bill for their services. They have not studied the many models for successful practice in over a dozen settings supported by the evidence base, and don't comprehend how to deliver comparable services to their own specialty populations.

The Solution — Training is Available to Remedy the Gaps

How this new breed of practitioner fares without guidance and the advantage of the evidence base is questionable. For example, if a patient arrives to an in-person session and smells of alcohol or has not bathed in weeks, the clinician's intake process is likely to differ substantially from an intake with a well-groomed, alert and sober client/patient. Likewise, a tremor in someone's hand can often be noticed upon the clinician's shaking hands prior to entering an office. Noting a hand tremor requires active inquiry when working online. If a new client/patient stumbles into a brick-and-mortar office, the clinician might be expected to conduct a gait analysis, that is, ask them to walk from one end of the office to the other to assess gait. Online, the gait analysis also needs to be actively pursued, because most clients/patients are seated at their monitors upon initial contact.

Many professionals seeking to work online often have good intentions, but misunderstand limitations imposed by licensure, assessment or reporting requirements. They often are unaware that it is their responsibility to know how regulations differ from state-to-state and internationally. They may not understand how much education the client/patient needs to make the contact without interruption, their expectations, and how to cover all that ground when online and charging a consumer by-the-minute for their services. They may agree to operate without the benefit of a full intake, informed consent or emergency backup when their state law mandates that they cover all these bases, and much more.

While the telephone or online platforms such as *Helpouts* are easy to use, delivering health care that is legal or ethical via these platforms isn't quick, easy or intuitive for most professionals.

These Limitations Can Be Easily Overcome by Careful Attention to Science

Most professionals delivering behavioral or mental health services in the United States do not work in well-established health care facilities with the needed systems in place to deliver telehealth. The worrisome reality of this professional community is that they:

- Do not know where to find the science behind the use of technology for clinical or educational purposes
- Haven't yet undergone graduate or professional training (CEU or CME training) related to technology in delivering behavioral or mental health care.
- Belong to professional membership groups that haven't yet identified easyu-to-0follow standards, guidelines or accompanying competencies for such training.
- Are licensed by state regulatory boards that are still struggling to understand the issues themselves.

Despite how burdensome these issues may seem, solutions have been developing for over six decades in the scientific literature, but we've had a lack of texts compiling this scientific body of work. I was involved in an initial attempt to compile and explain this information for all behavioral professionals in 2004 (Maheu et al.) A decade later, Dr. L'Abate has given close attention to updating references in this literature. They have documented the evidence as it exists, and exposed where it is lacking.

Why Are Scholarly Efforts Needed More Now than Ever?

Have the last 20 years of unregulated, unmitigated, improperly licensed online psychotherapy ruined it for everyone, or created a new way of serving consumers? We may never know for sure, but it is clear that traditional behavioral health care is being challenged. revolutionary online delivery models such as Google's *Helpouts,* which makes mental health services available for per-minute fee, or in flat-fee "packages" of 15, 30, or however many minutes deemed appropriate by the licensed professional.

The Mandate Remains to Do No Harm

When promised an answer sold in 15-minute packages online, consumers can reasonably expect to receive professional services from licensed professionals. Yet, online clinicians don't typically have good tools to screen or assess consumers they've not met in person, let alone give them answers in 15 minutes. The truth is that the unshowered, alcohol-laden or neurologically impaired, stumbling client/patient is difficult to accurately assess online. Without specialized training and local support services, online assessment via audio or video can involve more guesswork than professionalism.

Every now and again, a client/patient experiences a serious crisis or experiences a suicidal or homicidal emergency. Such patients are difficult enough to manage in a brick-and-mortar practice. They can quickly become unmanageable across a geographical distance. See a case in point: *Indeed, Skype Is Found to be Unacceptable for Telepsychiatry by Oklahoma Medical Board.*

Marlene M. Maheu, Ph.D.
mmaheu@telehealth.org
TeleMental Health Institute, Inc. & Arizona State University

REFERENCES

Maheu, M., & Gordon, B. (2000). Psychotherapy on the Internet: Legal, ethical and practice issues. *Professional Psychology: Research and Practice, 31*(5), 484- 489.

Maheu, M. M., Pulier, M. L., Wilhelm, F. H., McMenamin, J., & Brown-Connolly, N. (2004). *The mental health professional and the new technologies: A handbook for practice today.* Mahwah, NJ: Erlbaum.

Chapter 1

Basic Definitions, Testimonials, Evaluations, and Understudied Populations

> "I am convinced that digital learning is the most important innovation in education since the printing press (p. 54)... I strongly believe that by capitalizing on the strengths of online learning, we will make education more accessible, more effective and more affordable to more human beings than ever before
>
> *(L. Rafael Reif, President of MIT, TIME magazine, October 7, 2013, p. 55)*

The quote above can be applied just as well to interventions in mental health because the primary purpose of this chapter is to introduce various available definitions of what is now considered "online" psychological diagnoses and non-medical interventions. A secondary purpose of this chapter is to include non-empirically-based opinions, that is: testimonials that support the use of online diagnoses and interventions without any substantive evidence, that is: hype about online psychological work. They are included in this chapter in spite of their not being based on evidence as illustrations to compare them with the evidence presented in the other chapters of this volume. A tertiary purpose of this chapter was to introduce the importance of pre-post evaluation and follow up in both online and offline interventions. This chapter will include a self-explanatory Table 1.1 comparing online with offline interventions. Fourthly, special populations will be considered.

Foreseeable social and technological changes will force us to reevaluate our thinking about ethically appropriate ways to fulfill our mission of using psychology to advance human health and welfare in the twenty-first century (Koocher, 2007). Three categories of challenge related to societal and technological changes have become particularly evident. First, increasing patterns of delivering services over substantial distances by electronic means (i.e., telepsychology) demand consideration. Second, we must parse our ethical obligations to individuals, to groups, and to society at large as our influence working behind the scenes as "invisible" psychologists grows. Finally, as we witness the accelerating demise of psychiatry, we must take care not to follow a similar path. As we face new ethical challenges, we must continually ask ourselves where our responsibilities lie as individuals and as a profession. We must learn not to repeat the mistakes of the past and focus instead on optimizing the future for a science and practice of psychology focused on human health and welfare.

Rapidly expanding access to a wide array of electronically mediated modes of human communication has and will continue to change society (Koocher, 2009). Why should we not expect mental health services to change accordingly? Just as we contemplate and evaluate other advances in psychological assessment and intervention activities, we must consider the changes brought about by technology, including the good, the bad, and the risky. Current directions in videoconferencing and tele-mental health research provide a wonderful context to scratch a bit more beneath the surface of issues that will increasingly demand our attention as we move to serve people from greater distances than the founders of psychotherapeutic practice ever imagined.

Internet-based psychotherapeutic interventions have been used for more than a decade, but no comprehensive review and no extensive meta-analysis of their effectiveness have been conducted. Barak. Hen, Boniel-Nissim, and Shapira (2009) collected all of the empirical articles published up to March 2006 (n = 64) that examined the effectiveness of online therapy of different forms and performed a meta-analysis of all the studies reported in them (n = 92). These studies involved a total of 9,764 clients who were treated through various Internet-based psychological interventions for a variety of problems, whose effectiveness was assessed by different types of measures. The overall mean weighted effect size was found to be 0.53 (medium effect), which is quite similar to the average effect size of traditional, face-to-face therapy. Next, the authors examined interacting effects of various possible relevant moderators of the effects of online therapy, including type of therapy (self-help web-based therapy versus online communication-based etherapy), type of outcome measure, time of measurement of outcome (post-therapy or follow-up), type of problem treated, therapeutic approach, and communication modality, among others. A comparison between F2F and Internet intervention as reported on in 14 of the studies revealed no differences in effectiveness. The findings of this meta-analysis, and review of additional Internet therapy studies not included in the meta-analysis, provided strong support for the adoption of online psychological interventions as a legitimate therapeutic activity and suggested several insights in regard to its application. Limitations of the findings and recommendations concerning Internet-based therapy and future research were discussed.

The healthcare landscape in which independent practice of psychology is embedded has undergone significant change in the last three decades (Nordal, 2012). Following on those changes, the Affordable Care Act (ACA) was passed in 2010, with a goal of increasing access, improving patient outcomes, and curbing escalating healthcare costs, while providing 32 million more Americans with health insurance coverage. The partisan political climate in Washington, DC, and the serious budget deficit facing Congress, forecast an uncertain future for the ACA. Despite these uncertainties, there is considerable agreement by public and private payers, many healthcare systems, and employers about the need to improve America's healthcare system. The ACA encourages a healthcare system transformation that includes integration of behavioral healthcare into primary care settings and it is not clear what role psychologists will have in that evolving system. Additionally, mental and behavioral health services will be included in the Medicaid expansion program and state-based health insurance exchange plans. Critical issues affecting independent practitioners in the evolving healthcare system include access to program participation in Medicaid and health insurance exchange products, payment reform, new reimbursement structures, evolving practice models, acquisition of the skills necessary to practice in team-based primary care environments, and demonstration of psychology's value to the greater healthcare system. As these issues are addressed in the legislative, legal, and regulatory arenas, it is imperative that psychology's voice is heard. The implications of these changes for psychological practice and action steps for the profession are discussed.

Psychological assessment and intervention are extending from the clinic into daily life (Morris & Aguilera, 2012). Multiple forces are at play: Advances in mobile technology, constrained clinical care, and consumer demand for contextualized, non-stigmatizing, and low-cost alternatives are beginning to change the face of psychological assessment and interventions. Mobile, social, and wearable technologies are now enabling individuals to measure themselves and to integrate myriad forms of help and entertainment. The massive data sets generated by self-tracking of mood and passive sensing of voice, activity, and physiology may eventually reorganize taxonomies of mental health concerns. Compelling mobile therapies will also emerge, involving contextually appropriate, entertaining, and dynamic feedback to provide help in the context of daily life. The efficacy of such applications will be tested through citizen science as well as clinical trials. This article reviewed technical advances that can be applied to enhance assessment and intervention and dramatically increase access to psychotherapy. It is recommended that, in addition to exploring clinically oriented products, practitioners should support patients' use of direct-to-consumer applications in ways that align with therapeutic objectives.

Turnover in online communities is very high, with most people who initially post a message to an online community never contributing again. Joyce and Kraut (2006) evaluated whether responses that newcomers received to their first posts influence the extent to which they continue to participate. The data come from initial posts made by 2,777 newcomers to six public newsgroups. Joyce and Kraut (2006) coded the content and valence of the initial post and its first response, if it received one, to see if these factors influenced newcomers' likelihood of posting again. Approximately 61% of newcomers received a reply to their initial post, and those who got a reply were 12% more likely to post to the community again; their probability of posting again increased from 44% to 56%. They were more likely to receive a response if they asked a question or wrote a longer post. Surprisingly, the quality of the response they received—its emotional tone and whether it answered a newcomer's question—did not influence the likelihood of the newcomer's posting again.

Many healthcare organizations have embraced eHealth technologies in their efforts to promote patient-centered care, increase access to services, and improve outcomes (Hogan, Wakefield, Nazi, Houston, et al., 2011). Using the Department of Veterans Affairs (VA) as a case study, this paper presented two specific eHealth technologies, the Care Coordination Home Telehealth (CCHT) Program and the My HealtheVet (MHV) personal health record (PHR) portal with integrated secure messaging, and articulates a vision of how they might be implemented as part of a patient-centric healthcare model and used in a complementary manner to enhance access to care and to support patient-centered care. METHODS Based on our experience and ongoing work with both programs, we offer a series of recommendations for pursuing and ultimately achieving this vision. VA's CCHT and MHV programs are examples of an expanding repertoire of eHealth applications available to patients and healthcare teams. VA's new patient-centric healthcare model represents a significant shift in the way that services are delivered and a profound opportunity to incorporate eHealth technologies like the CCHT and MHV programs into clinical practice to increase access to care, and to ensure the responsiveness of such technologies to the preferences and circumstances of patients.

However, the field of Internet-supported therapeutic interventions has suffered from a lack of clarity and consistency (Barak, Klein, & Proudfoot, 2009). The absence of professional leadership and of accepted governing approaches, terminology, professional standards, and methodologies has caused this field to be diffused and unstructured. Numerous terms have been used to label and describe the activities conducted over the Internet for mental and physical health purposes: web-based therapy, e-therapy, cybertherapy, eHealth, e-Interventions, computer-mediated interventions, and online therapy (or counseling), among others. Following a comprehensive review, Bark et al., 2009) conceptualized Internet-supported interventions, using four categories based on prime practice approaches: web-based interventions, online counseling and therapy, Internet-operated therapeutic software, and other online activities (e.g., as supplements to face-to-face therapy). These authors provided a working definition and detailed description of each category, accompanied by numerous examples. These categories may now serve as guiding definitions and related terminologies for further research and development in this emerging field.

Questions have been raised about the internet's effect on mental health, although no principled review has yet tackled the issue. Bell (2007) aimed at examining the effect of the internet on mental health. Results of a literature review suggested that the internet is typically discussed as if it were a set of activities when it is actually a medium upon which various activities can occur. It is, therefore, neither "good" nor "bad" for mental health, although specific activities may have an influence. The standard of mental health information on the internet is probably equivalent to the mainstream media, although overall it still remains poor. The concept of "internet addiction" looks increasingly invalid, although it is likely that depressed or isolated individuals are more likely to focus on certain activities to excess. A number of "extreme communities" have formed online, such as pro-anorexia, pro-suicide, pro-amputation and likely-psychotic groups. These serve to provide support, outside a medical and social mainstream that finds their beliefs and behaviors unacceptable. A review of preliminary randomized controlled trials showed online therapy to be effective for many disorders. Therefore, mental health professionals are advised to lead the creation of online treatments and information. Clinical recommendations for the use of the internet were offered and will be implemented in the chapters of this volume.

Complementary and Alternative Medicine (CAM) has a long history of use with some modalities being in existence for thousands of years (Barnett & Shale, 2012). In recent years there has been a greater awareness of the many benefits of CAM for promoting health and wellness as well as for ameliorating a wide range of conditions and ailments treated by psychologists and other health professionals. One vision of the future of the practice of psychology includes each psychologist developing and maintaining competence in CAM and integrating it into each client's care as is relevant and appropriate. Support is provided for the belief that CAM will play an important role in the practice of psychology for years to come (L'Abate, 2013c). Relevant issues emphasized include an emphasis on Evidence Based Practice in Psychology, the needs and preferences of a rapidly diversifying society, and the increasing focus on health promotion, wellness, spirituality, and many non-Western traditions that are consistent with this approach. This article provided an overview of each of the 14 most widely used forms of CAM, discusses limitations in the current body of scientific evidence in support of CAM and makes recommendations for how psychologists should be integral in addressing them, highlights ethical issues that each psychologist will want to be cognizant of and address when integrating CAM into their practices, and makes recommendations for education, training, and practice.

In spite of the claims made above, Hughes (2008): "...found CAM treatments to be based on heterogeneous epistemologies and to suffer from poor records in empirical efficacy research" He "...argued that, given the likely incompatibility of CAM with clinical psychologist's positivist scientific ethos, CAM practices should not be integrated into clinical psychology at this time" (p. 657). This harsh conclusion might be tempered by what has happened to Internet technology and the increasing reliance on remote writing, as shown by the systematic review presented below.

The objective of a systematic review was to evaluate the effects of consumer use of online health information on decision-making, attitudes, knowledge, satisfaction and health outcomes and utilization (Bessell, McDonald, Silagy, Anderson, Hiller, & Sansom, 2002). Electronic databases searched included the Cochrane Controlled Trials Register, MEDLINE, PREMED-LINE (to 14 March 2001), CINAHL, Australian Medical Index, Health and Society, National Institutes of Health Clinical Trials Database and CenterWatch. All post-1995 comparative studies (including controlled studies, before and after studies, and interrupted time series analyses) of Internet users vs. non-Internet users and other communications mediums, and Internet characteristics such as e-mail vs. other communication mediums, were included.

Outcomes included consumer decision-making, attitudes, knowledge, satisfaction and measurable changes in health status or health utilization. One reviewer screened all papers then two reviewers independently assessed studies against the selection criteria and any discrepancies were resolved by discussion with a third reviewer. No attempt was made to combine the data for further statistical analysis. identified 10 comparative studies. Studies evaluated the effectiveness of using the Internet to deliver a smoking cessation program, cardiac and nutrition educational programs, behavioral interventions for headache and weight loss, and pharmacy and augmentative services. All studies showed some positive effects on health outcomes, although the methodological quality of many studies was poor. Despite widespread consumer Internet use to obtain health-care information, at that time (2002) there was almost a complete lack of evidence of any effects this process may have on health outcomes. Hopefully, the information contained in this volume will present sufficient evidence to help MH professionals decide to practice one way or another.

One major issue relating to the online/offline distinction relates to how and how much therapist feedback and involvement may occur. Too much therapist involvement may render the whole self-help enterprise irrelevant (Harwood & L'Abate, 2010). Too little involvement may reduce the efficacy of an intervention. By designating therapist involvement by the number of homework assignments completed, after each one, after two or more may be one way to determine the frequency of such an involvement.

As technology advances, psychologists increasingly have the opportunity to engage with patients or other users of psychological services via less traditional methods (Baker & Bufka, 2011). However, little guidance exists to prepare psychologists to navigate the legal, regulatory, reimbursement, and ethical issues that can arise when providing psychological services via technology. A review of relevant state and federal laws revealed inconsistencies even in the terminology used to describe provision of services via technology with some referring to "telehealth," others to "telemedicine," and others using additional terms. The following overview of laws, regulations, and existing guidelines in the area of telehealth and telemental health provides some preliminary guidance for psychologists as they attempt to meet the needs of their patients using available and emerging technologies. Specific issues addressed included the applicability of the HIPAA Privacy and Security Rules, informed consent and reimbursement by third party payers.

E-Mental Health

Lal and Adair (2014) conducted a review of the literature on e-mental health, including its applications, strengths, limitations, and evidence base. The rapid review approach, an emerging type of knowledge synthesis, was used in response to a request for information from policy makers. MEDLINE was searched from 2005 to 2010 by using relevant terms. The search was supplemented with a general Internet search and a search focused on key authors. A total of 115 documents were reviewed: 94% were peer-reviewed articles, and 51% described primary research. Most of the research (76%) originated in the United States, Australia, or the Netherlands. The review identified e-mental health applications addressing four areas of mental health service delivery: information provision; screening, assessment, and monitoring; intervention; and social support. Currently, applications are most frequently aimed at adults with depression or anxiety disorders. Some interventions have demonstrated effectiveness in early trials. Many believe that e-mental health has enormous potential to address the gap between the identified need for services and the limited capacity and resources to provide conventional treatment. Strengths of e-mental health initiatives noted in the literature include improved accessibility, reduced costs (although start-up and research and development costs are necessary), flexibility in terms of standardization and personalization, interactivity, and consumer engagement. In conclusion, E-mental health applications are proliferating and hold promise to expand access to care. Further discussion and research are needed on how to effectively incorporate e-mental health into service systems and to apply it to diverse populations

Ethics and Internet Interventions

The literature is replete with articles addressing how the electronic age has created new and improved ways to deliver health care services. This change, however, has raised many questions regarding how professionals can utilize this new technology in a fashion that is consistent with both ethics and law. In this article, Harris and Younggren (2011) attempted a point in time survey of the problems created by practicing psychotherapy in the digital age focusing on a conceptual overview of two specific areas. The authors reviewed various perceptions of the current state-based regulation of digital interstate practice by psychologists and provided an overview of some basic ethical and risk management principles to be addressed by practitioners before proceeding to offer these services given an uncertain regulatory environment.

Technologies such as smart-phones and digital cameras are an increasingly ubiquitous part of modern life, and the increasing convenience of these electronic tools provides psychotherapists with opportunities to incorporate these technologies into psychotherapy

(Eonta, Christon, Hourigan, Ravindran, Vrana, & Southam-Gerow, 2011). In the face of so much opportunity, psychotherapists must learn how to incorporate these tools effectively and responsibly. The authors present three case studies that demonstrated the use of digital technology to individualize and enhance the efficiency of existing evidence-based treatments. In the first, digital pictures were used to track the treatment progress of a client who compulsively hoards. In the second, a smart phone was used to record a personalized progressive muscle relaxation file for a client with agoraphobia, hypochondriasis, and generalized anxiety disorder. In the third, a smart phone was used to photograph and send pictures of in-session work to a client with trichotillomania and generalized anxiety disorder. The implications and ethical considerations of using technology in psychotherapeutic settings were explored, and practical strategies were provided for incorporating common digital technology into psychotherapeutic practice (Proudfoot, 2012).

Innovations in the production, storage, protection, and retrieval of digital information are occurring at breakneck speed (Devereaux & Gottlieb, 2012). With them can come perceived pressure to transition from paper to electronic records, because doing so may appear to offer benefits for improved patient care. At the forefront of this shift is the popularization of "cloud" computing. While "the cloud" has entered our everyday parlance from Internet-connected televisions to smart phones that track and control our finances, little has been written about how this technology functions and how it may expose practitioners to unforeseen and previously nonexistent risk. In this article we define "the cloud," discuss risks and benefits of its use, and provide questions for practitioners to ask when considering the appropriateness of maintaining patient records in this manner. Considerations were made in light of current federal legislation and recommendations, professional ethical standards and guidelines established by the American Psychological Association, and ethical decision-making practices. Different types of electronic connectivity and electronic medical records (EMR) that can be used in psychiatry. This article described various strategies to maintain patient confidentiality in EMR. It also presented case examples to illustrate and strategies to mitigate risk for practitioners considering their use (Dunne, Sarvet, Lambert, & Wertheimer, 2012). The internet gained popularity in the mid-nineties; its integration into psycho-social health care structures has been established in the meantime (Döring & Eichenberg, 2007). The mobile communication boom followed in the early years of the second millennium. Within a very short time, the cellular phone has become a personal multi-purpose tool. Against this background it seems obvious to investigate to what extent mobile media, beside the internet, can meaningfully support clinical practice. Current research and development status of clinical-psychological intervention with the aid of computer-based mobile media (Mobile Therapy, abbr. M-Therapy) was overviewed. Contrary to a desktop with internet access, where its use is limited to certain areas, wireless mobile media have the ability to instantly collect clinically relevant data, complete training units or organize contacts to therapists. Pilot projects and first evaluation studies showed that, for example, cellular phones, game consoles and handhelds are productive in psychological diagnostics, counseling, rehabilitation and therapeutic support. They are widely accepted and increase the effectiveness of therapy. Doring and Eichenberg (2007) discussed the media-specific opportunities and limitations of M-Therapy as well as its implications for clinical practice.

Trust is one of the most important constructs in psychology to explain interpersonal functioning and outcomes of interactions (Fletcher-Tomenius & Vossler, 2009). As with traditional F2F counseling it can be assumed that trust plays an important role in developing a working alliance in online counseling and therapy. However, due to the fact this is a relatively new field, most previous studies have only focused on the analysis of factors influencing the therapeutic relationship in a face-to-face context. This qualitative study therefore investigated how online counselors define and experience trust in online therapeutic environments and what affect the presence or absence of trust has on the therapeutic relationship online. Using Interpretative Phenomenological Analysis (IPA), semi-structured interviews were conducted with six online counselors who were accredited with the BACP and had at least three years post-qualification experience. Three main themes arose through the process of analysis: 1) The role of anonymity in trust online, 2) the impact of the medium of communication 3) similar issues to forming trust in face-to-face contexts. The findings have practical implications for the provision of mental health delivery systems.

Security Management

Psychologists increasingly rely upon "telepsychology" (e.g., e-mail and Internet-based client communications) despite the growing presence of threats to online security. However, practitioners may overestimate the benefits of electronic communications and underestimate their risks. Using the example of the availability heuristic as one cognitive bias, which may promote this imbalance, this article reviewed a number of resources for practitioners that provide enhanced security and confidentiality in the digital realm (Schwartz & Lonborg, 2011). Governmental, regulatory and professional bodies provide pertinent and detailed guidance that can achieve these goals. To illustrate this process, this article reviewed and augmented a number of safeguards (administrative, physical, and technical) within the HIPAA Security Rule. It also surveys opportunities for continuing education and credentialing that may enhance professional competence in electronic communications. It concluded with a list of recommendations for enhancing security and reducing the influence of the availability heuristic in tele-psychology. These recommendations ranged across several categories of professional practice: hardware and software management, confidentiality, informed consent, competence, consultation, and continuing education. This article may help practitioners reap the benefits of telepsychology while successfully enhancing confidentiality and security.

Internet Research

The field of Internet interventions is growing rapidly (Proudfoot, Klein, Barak, Carlbring, et al., 2011). New programs are continually being developed to facilitate health and mental health promotion, disease and emotional distress prevention, risk factor management, treatment, and relapse prevention. However, a clear definition of Internet interventions, guidelines for research, and evidence of effectiveness have been slower to follow. This article focused on the quality standardization of research on Internet-delivered psychological and behavioral interventions. Although the science underpinning Internet interventions is just starting to be established, across research studies there are often conceptual and methodological difficulties. The authors argue that this situation is due to the lack of universally accepted operational guidelines and evaluation methods. Following a critical appraisal of existing codes of conduct and guidelines for Internet-assisted psychological and health interventions, the authors developed a framework of guidelines for Internet intervention research utilizing aspects of facet theory (Guttman & Greenbaum, 1998). The framework of facets, elements, and guidelines of best practice in reporting Internet intervention research was then sent to several leading researchers in the field for their comment and input, so that a consensus framework could be agreed on. The authors outline 12 key facets to be considered when evaluating and reporting Internet intervention studies. Each facet consists of a range of recommended elements, designed as the minimum features for reporting Internet intervention studies. The authors proposed that this framework be utilized when designing and reporting Internet intervention research, so results across studies can be replicated, extended, compared, and contrasted with greater ease and clarity.

The new issue of the Association for Psychological Science's journal *Perspectives on Psychological Science* (January, vol. 9, #1) included an article: "No Appointment Necessary: Treating Mental Illness Outside the Therapist's Office," by Bethany Teachman. I shall quote various excerpts from this very important article.

Twenty-five years ago, it was generally assumed that the therapist relationship and face-to-face talk therapy were necessary elements of a successful (non-medicinal) treatment for mental illness. This idea had been made explicit back in the 1950s when Carl Rogers famously stated that two people being in psychological contact was one of the mandatory ingredients for psychotherapeutic change, and that change could only ensue if the client felt personally understood by the therapist (Rogers, 1957/1992). Even as late as 1997, Aaron T. Beck described "verbal mediation" in therapy as an essential ingredient for any effective anxiety therapy (Beck & Clark, 1997). Indeed, talk therapies have helped countless numbers of people who had been struggling, and there is now a long list of empirically supported, face-to-face therapist-based interventions (see APA Division 12's Web site on Research-Supported Psychological Treatments....). (Note, the focus here is on changing views toward psychotherapeutic interventions. Although the question of changing attitudes about the necessity of medication is also fascinating, it is outside the scope of this thesis. (Teachman, 2013).

In recent years, however, attitudes about the necessity of face-to-face talk therapy have been changing. Face-to-face talk therapy is not always required to effect sustained, meaningful psychological change *(emphasis mine). There are now a myriad of delivery methods for mental health services to reach people in need (see Kazdin & Rabbitt, 2013), from interactive computer programs to downloadable apps, including many that involve either minimal or zero therapist contact. Although there is a long history of (mostly untested) self-directed treatments, as the enormous market of self-help books makes clear, important advances have occurred in the last 15 years such that clinical science is now helping to determine when and how mental illness can be addressed outside the therapist's office.*

"More than two thirds of individuals struggling with a mental illness do not receive treatment (see Kessler et al., 2005), and rates of unmet need are even higher among minority populations (Wells, Klap, Koike, & Sherbourne, 2001). This means we need new approaches to meet the enormous burden of mental illness. To the extent we recognize that a therapist talking directly with a client is not always needed, we can greatly enhance access to treatments, opening up new lines of mental health communication, disseminating treatments far more widely, and potentially reducing costs while enhancing convenience (see Ritterband,

Thorndike, Cox, Kovatchev, & Gonder-Frederick, 2009)."

"I am in no way suggesting that face-to-face talk therapy is no longer needed. For many individuals, especially those who have not responded to other self-directed interventions and perhaps those with more severe problems (though this is not yet clear), therapy with a qualified clinician will be essential, but it is not required for everyone suffering with a mental illness."

For electronic reprint requests of this article please contact info: Bethany A. Teachman, Department of Psychology, University of Virginia, P.O. Box 400400, Charlottesville, VA 22904-4400 E-mail: bteachman@virginia.edu.

DEFINITIONS OF 'TELE' TERMS FROM RELEVANT RESOURCES*

American Psychological Association: Telepsychology Draft Guidelines

"Telepsychology is defined, for the purpose of these guidelines, as the provision of psychological services using telecommunication technologies.

Telecommunications is the preparation, transmission, communication, or related processing of information by electrical, electromagnetic, electromechanical, electro-optical, or electronic means (Committee on National Security Systems, 2010).

Telecommunication technologies include but are not limited to telephone, mobile devices, interactive videoconferencing, email, chat, text, and Internet (e.g., self-help websites, blogs, and social media). The information that is transmitted may be in writing, or include images, sounds or other data. These communications may be synchronous with multiple parties communicating in real time (e.g., interactive videoconferencing, telephone) or asynchronous (e.g., email, online bulletin boards, storing and forwarding information).

Technologies may augment traditional in-person care (e.g., psychoeducational materials online after an in-person therapy session), or be used as stand-alone services (e.g., therapy over videoconferencing). Different technologies may be used in various combinations and for different purposes during the provision of telepsychology services. For example, videoconferencing and telephone may also be utilized for direct service while email and text is used for non-direct services (e.g., scheduling). Regardless of the purpose, psychologists strive to be aware of the potential benefits and limitations in their choices of technologies for particular clients in particular situations. "

American Psychiatric Association

"Telepsychiatry, or telemedicine, is a specifically defined form of video conferencing that can provide psychiatric services to patients living in remote locations or otherwise underserved areas. It can connect patients, psychiatrists, physicians, and other healthcare professionals through the use of television cameras and microphones.

Telemedicine currently provides an array of services, including but not limited to diagnosis and assessment; medication management; and individual and group therapy. It also provides an opportunity for consultative services between psychiatrists, primary care physicians and other healthcare providers.“

Teleneuropsychology

Telemedicine refers to the use of electronic communications to deliver health-related services from a distance, and is particularly useful in bringing specialty services to remote and/or underserved areas. Despite the increasing use of videoconference technology in psychology, there are very few guidelines to direct practitioners as to the ethical practice and utilization of telemedicine, and even fewer resources for practitioners of tele-cognitive assessment or tele-neuropsychology. Several practical and ethical considerations that are relevant to the practice of telecognitive assessment and to assist practitioners in providing safe, ethical, and competent care to their patients by proposing some initial practice recommendations were outlined (Grosch, Gottlieb, & Cullum, 2011).

American Telemedicine Association: What Is Telemedicine

“What is Telemedicine? Formally defined, telemedicine is the use of medical information exchanged from one site to another via electronic communications to improve a patient’s clinical health status. Telemedicine includes a growing variety of applications and services using two-way video, email, smart phones, wireless tools and other forms of telecommunications technology.

Starting out over forty years ago with demonstrations of hospitals extending care to patients in remote areas, the use of telemedicine has spread rapidly and is now becoming integrated into the ongoing operations of hospitals, specialty departments, home health agencies, private physician offices as well as consumer’s homes and workplaces.

Telemedicine is not a separate medical specialty. Products and services related to telemedicine are often part of a larger investment by health care institutions in either information technology or the delivery of clinical care. Even in the reimbursement fee structure, there is usually no distinction made between services provided on site and those provided through telemedicine and often no separate coding required for billing of remote services. ATA has historically considered telemedicine and telehealth to be interchangeable terms, encompassing a wide definition of remote healthcare. Patient consultations via video conferencing, transmission of still images, e-health including patient portals, remote monitoring of vital signs, continuing medical education, consumer-focused wireless applications and nursing call centers, among other applications, are all considered part of telemedicine and telehealth.

While the term telehealth is sometimes used to refer to a broader definition of remote healthcare that does not always involve clinical services, ATA uses the terms in the same way one would refer to medicine or health in the common vernacular.

Telemedicine is closely allied with the term health information technology (HIT). However, HIT more commonly refers to electronic medical records and related information systems while telemedicine refers to the actual delivery of remote clinical services using technology. “

American Telemedicine Association Standards & Guidelines

"Telemental health is one of the most active applications of telehealth rendered in the United States. Mental health is particularly suited to the use of advanced communication technologies and the internet for delivery of care. By using advanced communication technologies, mental health professionals are able to widen their reach to patients in a cost-effective manner, ameliorating the maldistribution of specialty care. The following Guidelines are designed to aid in the development and practice of coherent, effective, safe and sustainable telemental health practices….

Telemental health, like telemedicine, is an intentionally broad term referring to the provision of mental health and substance abuse services from a distance. This guideline focuses on two-way, interactive videoconferencing as the modality by which telemental health services are provided. In the future, additional sections will be added to address the use of the internet and other asynchronous or social relationship environments for interactions between mental health professionals and their patients and families. The use of other modern technologies such as virtual reality, electronic mail, remote monitoring devices (home telehealth store and forward technology), chat rooms, and web-based clients are not included in this version of the telemental health guidelines. The ATA provides the core standards for telemedicine operations and provides overarching guidance for administrative, clinical, and technical standards

Telemental health, like telemedicine, is an intentionally broad term referring to the provision of mental health care from a distance. The prefix "tele" can refer to geographical, time, or even circadian distance when providing care across time zones. Telemental health (TMH) includes mental health assessment, treatment, education, monitoring, and collaboration. Patients can be located in hospitals, clinics, schools, nursing facilities, prisons and homes. TMH providers and staff include psychiatrists, nurse practitioners, physician assistants, social workers, psychologists, counselors, primary care providers and nurses. Thousands of clients and patients have experienced access to mental health care via telemental health technologies. The goal of the telehealth provider is to eliminate disparities in patient access to quality, evidence-based, and emerging health care diagnostics and treatments."

VHA Office of Telehealth Services

"The term Telehealth is defined as the use of Telehealth technologies to provide clinical care in circumstances where distance separates those receiving services and those providing services. The value VA derives from Telehealth is not in implementing Telehealth technologies alone, but how VA uses health informatics, disease management, care/case management and Telehealth technologies to facilitate access to care and improve the health of Veterans with the intent to provide the right care in the right place at the right time.

Telehealth in VHA is defined as: "The wider application of care and case management principles to the delivery of health care services using health informatics, disease management and telehealth technologies to facilitate access to care and improve the health of designated individuals and populations with the intent of providing the right care in the right place at the right time""

CMS: Telehealth

" Medicare pays for a limited number of Part B services that are furnished by a physician or practitioner to an eligible beneficiary via a telecommunications system. For eligible telehealth services, the use of a tele-communications system substitutes for an in-person encounter.

As a condition of payment, an interactive audio and video telecommunications system must be used that permits real-time communication between you, the physician or practitioner at the distant site, and the beneficiary, at the originating site. Asynchronous "store and forward" technology is permitted only in Federal telemedicine demonstration programs conducted in Alaska or Hawaii.

Ohio Psychological Association Communications and Technology Committee 2010

"Behavioral telehealth "refers to the use of psychotechnologies to provide behavioral health care services" (Maheu et al. 2005, p. 7).

E-therapy is 'a professional counselor or psychotherapist communicating with a client over the Internet for the purpose of mental health assistance or emotional help' (Pomerantz, 2002 as cited by Mallen & Vogel, 2005, p. 764) and is e-therapy is 'the process of interacting with a therapist online in ongoing conversations over time when the client and counselor are in separate or remote locations and utilize electronic means to communicate with each other' (Manhal-Baugus, 2001, p. 551 as cited by Mallen & Vogel, 2005, p. 764).

Online clinical practice refers to the "...use of psychotechnologies to deliver therapeutic dialogue at a distance" (Maheu et al. 2005, p. 8).

Online counseling is "...any delivery of mental and behavioral health services, including but not limited to therapy, consultation and psychoeducation, by a licensed practitioner to a client in a non-FtF [face to face] setting through distance communication technology such as the telephone, asynchronous e-mail, synchronous chat and videoconferencing" (Mallen & Vogel, 2005, p. 764).

Online therapy is "...any type of professional therapeutic interaction that makes use of the Internet to connect qualified mental health professionals and their clients" (Rochlen, Zack & Speyer, 2004, p. 270).

Telehealthis "...the transmission of images, voice and data between two or more health units via telecommunication channels, to provide clinical advice, consultation, education and training services" (Maheu et al., 2005, p. 7).

Telehealth is "...the use of telecommunications and information technology to provide access to health assessment, diagnosis, intervention, consultation, supervision, education, and information across distance" (Nickelson, 1998, p. 527).

Tele-medicine is "...the use of electronic signals to transfer medical data from one location to another"(Maheu et al. 2005 p.6).

Tele-psychology is the provision of non-face-to-face psychological services by distance communication technology such as telephone, e-mail, chat and videoconferencing. (CTC definition)

Other terms used to describe similar services include: telepsychiatry, behavioral e-care, behavioral e-health, cybertherapy, e-mail counseling, cyber-psychology, web counseling, e-health and, Internet psychotherapy."

Marks and Cavanah (2009), defined computer driven psychotherapy: "... as any computerized information technology that uses patient input to make at least some psychotherapy decisions" (p. 123). With this definition, these authors expressly eliminated video-conferencing, ordinary phone, and e-mail consultations, chat rooms, and support groups. They, however, acknowledged that the "divide" between what is computer-driven psychotherapy and other advances in technology is becoming "fuzzier" and "fazzier."

NCBI: Telemedicine or Telehealth or eHealth or Mobile Health

"Telemedicine: Delivery of health services via remote telecommunications. This includes interactive consultative and diagnostic services. Year introduced: 1993. *Subheadings:* classification economics ethics history instrumentation legislation and jurisprudence manpower methods organization and administration standards statistics and numerical data trends utilization Restrict to MeSH Major Topic.

Health Resources and Services Administration: Glossary

Telecommunications

The use of wire, radio, visual, or other electromagnetic channels to transmit or receive signals for voice, data, and video communications.

Teleconferencing

Interactive electronic communication between multiple users at two or more sites which facilitates voice, video, and/or data transmission systems: audio, audiographics, computer, and video systems.

Teleconsultation

The physical separation between multiple providers during a consultation.

Telediagnosis

The detection of a disease as a result of evaluating data transmitted to a receiving station from instruments monitoring a remote patient.

Telehealth

The use of electronic information and telecommunications technologies to support and promote long-distance clinical health care, patient and professional health-related education, public health, and health administration.

See also: http://www.hrsa.gov/ruralhealth/about/telehealth/

Telehealth is the use of electronic information and telecommunications technologies to support long-distance clinical health care, patient and professional health-related education, public health and health administration. Technologies include videoconferencing, the internet, store-and-forward imaging, streaming media, and terrestrial and wireless communications.

Telematics

The use of information processing based on a computer in telecommunications, and the use of telecommunications to permit computers to transfer programs and data to one another.

Telemedicine

The use of electronic communication and information technologies to provide or support clinical care at a distance. Included in this definition are patient counseling, case management, and supervision/preceptorship of rural medical residents and health professions students when such supervising/precepting involves direct patient care. The electronic medical record (EMR) is increasingly sought as the standard of documentation in health care. There has been relatively less experience with EMRs within mental health care. This article provided an overview of EMR use within health care and mental health care, with a particular focus on an implementation experience within an integrated health care setting (Steinfeld & Keyes, 2011). The potential for how an EMR can enhance effectiveness of mental health treatment in the communication, coordination, and delivery of mental health care is presented, along with how psychologists can help in the development and implementation of EMRs in mental health settings.

Telemental Health: Clinical, Technical, and Administrative Foundations for Evidence-Based Practice

State of West Virginia

"(B) As used in this section, the term "practice of telepsychology" means the use of electronic information and communication technologies to provide psychological services when distance separates participants and includes one or both of the following:"

State of Ohio

"Telepsychology" means the practice of psychology or school psychology as those terms are defined in divisions (B) and (E) of section 4732.01 of the Revised Code, including psychological and school psychological supervision, by distance communication technology such as but not necessarily limited to telephone, email, Internet-based communications, and videoconferencing.

American Psychological Association

Finally, this Association has defined Telepsychology "...for the purpose of [its] guidelines (American Psychologist, 2013, p. 792): "..as the provision of psychological services using telecommunication technologies. Telecommunication is the preparation, transmission, communication, or related processing of information by electrical, electromagnatic, electromechanical, or electronic means."

1) WHY ONLINE PRACTICE CAN BE HARMFUL -- PART III

by Marlene M. Maheu, Ph.D.

Many licensed behavioral healthcare providers and researchers are unaware of the legal and ethical codes that govern their use of technology. In fact, a Google search for these or related terms will return more than 1.5 million websites:

- online therapy
- online psychotherapy
- internet therapy
- etherapy
- online counseling
- online counseling
- internet therapy

Close examination of websites found by such a search will show that many professionals whose services are available online are operating without compliance with published mandates of their regulatory boards and professional associations. The current state of affairs has not improved dramatically since the year 2000, when an early study reporting such problems was published (Maheu & Gordon, 2000). Violations continue to include, but are not limited to:

- practicing over state lines without a license
- lack of an informed consent process of any type
- using technology that does not meet HIPAA requirements
- failing to collect identifying information needed for mandated reporting
- failing to collaborate with other treating professionals
- failing to arrange for emergency backup, etc.

SUMMARY

The College of Education of Augusta State University in Augusta, Georgia provided a summary of what e-therapy is: E-therapy is a term that has been coined to describe the process of interacting with a therapist online in ongoing conversations over time when the client and counselor are in separate or remote locations and utilize electronic means to communicate with each other. It is a relatively new modality of assisting individuals resolve life and relationship issues. E-therapy utilizes the power and convenience of the internet to allow simultaneous (synchronous) and time-delayed (asynchronous) communication between an individual and a professional. For the purposes of this paper, e-therapy is defined as a licensed mental health care professional providing mental health services via e-mail, video conferencing, virtual reality technology, chat technology, or any combination of these. It does not include self-help methods such as public bulletin boards or private listservs. E-therapy is not psychotherapy or psychological counseling per se since it does to presume to diagnose or treat mental or medical disorders. However, e-therapy is flexible enough to also address many difficulties which clients present to the online therapist. As in other types of therapy, such as bibliotherapy, occupational therapy, and rehabilitation therapy), e-therapy does assist a person in addressing specific concerns with specific skills. This article examines the following issues of e-therapy. First, the types of e-therapy and related services are described to provide a background for the article. Second, the ethical codes which have been adopted by three major professional organizations (American Counseling Association, National Board for Certified Counselors, and the International Society for Mental Health Online) pertaining to e-therapy are summarized for professional and consumer use. Finally, the practical, ethical, and legal issues of e-therapy services are discussed fully.

Mental health professionals planning to practice or already practicing online should be thoroughly familiar with these guidelines as well as laws pertaining to telehealth practice in their state.

*I am grateful to Erica Abel for collecting the foregoing information for the primary purpose of this chapter.

TESTIMONIALS

Here is a sample of early testimonials in favor of e-therapy and e-health interventions.

As a pioneer in this field, Barak (1999) reviewed various psychological applications in use on the Internet, with special emphasis given to their promises and advantages as well as to their shortcomings and problems. Specifically, 10 types of psychological Internet applications are reviewed: information resources on psychological concepts and issues; self-help guides; psychological testing and assessment; help in deciding to undergo therapy; information about specific psychological services; single-session psychological advice through e-mail or e-bulletin boards; ongoing personal counseling and therapy through e-mail; real-time counseling through chat, web telephony, and videoconferencing; synchronous and asynchronous support groups, discussion groups, and group counseling; and psychological and social research. Following a discussion of ethical and related concerns, a call is voiced for intensive research and international brainstorming.

Telehealth Projects

A literature review was carried out to identify the key challenges in the implementation of telehealth (Joseph, West, Shickle, D., Keen, et al., 2011) This was followed by a survey of organisations in England involved in telehealth projects in order to understand the challenges they faced. Ten of the 13 health or local authority organisations surveyed had telehealth projects and three were at the planning stage. The analysis revealed seven key challenges facing implementers of telehealth in England. Based on the findings from the literature review and the survey, a model was constructed and a checklist drawn up. The model contained the following elements: identifying issues, needs and partners; producing a strategy; securing funding; implementing changes; and monitoring and evaluating a telehealth project. The checklist was validated by using key informants from the organisations originally surveyed. The checklist may be useful to guide telehealth development and implementation in the future.

E-Design and Development

Given the wide reach and extensive capabilities of the Internet, it is increasingly being used to deliver comprehensive behavioral and mental health intervention and prevention programs. Their goals are to change user behavior, reduce unwanted complications or symptoms, and improve health status and health-related quality of life. Internet interventions have been found efficacious in addressing a wide range of behavioral and mental health problems, including insomnia, nicotine dependence, obesity, diabetes, depression, and anxiety. Despite the existence of many Internet-based interventions, there is little research to inform their design and development. A model for behavior change in Internet interventions has been published to help guide future Internet intervention development and to help predict and explain behavior changes and symptom improvement outcomes through the use of Internet interventions (Hilgart, Ritterband, Thorndike, & Kinzie, 2012).

An argument is made for grounding the development of Internet interventions within a scientific framework. To that end, the model highlights a multitude of design-related components, areas, and elements, including user characteristics, environment, intervention content, level of intervention support, and targeted outcomes. However, more discussion is needed regarding how the design of the program should be developed to address these issues. While there is little research on the design and development of Internet interventions, there is a rich, related literature in the field of instructional design (ID) that can be used to inform Internet intervention development. ID models are prescriptive models that describe a set of activities involved in the planning, implementation, and evaluation of instructional programs. Using ID process models has been shown to increase the effectiveness of learning programs in a broad range of contexts. ID models specify a systematic method for assessing the needs of learners (intervention users) to determine the gaps between current knowledge and behaviors, and desired outcomes (Hilgart, Ritterband, Thorndike, & Kinzie, 2012).

Through the ID process, designers focus on the needs of learners, taking into account their prior knowledge; set measurable learning objectives or performance requirements; assess learners' achievement of the targeted outcomes; and employ cycles of continuous formative evaluation to ensure that the intervention meets the needs of all stakeholders. The ID process offers a proven methodology for the design of instructional programs and should be considered an integral part of the creation of Internet interventions. By providing a framework for the design and development of Internet interventions and by purposefully focusing on these aspects, as well as the underlying theories supporting these practices, both the theories and the interventions themselves can continue to be refined and improved. By using the behavior change model for Internet interventions along with the best research available to guide design practice and inform development, developers of Internet interventions will increase their ability to achieve desired outcomes Hilgart, Ritterband, Thorndike, & Kinzie, 2012).

Clinicians Perceptions of Telemental Health

Equal access to mental health services is necessary for healthy individuals and communities. However, due to geographical distances and other barriers, some clients cannot easily access mental health professionals (Simms, Gibson, & O'Donnell, 2011). Technologies such as videoconferencing for clinical purposes (i.e., telemental health) may help to bridge these gaps to connect clients and clinicians at geographically diverse locations. However, despite its potential utility, telemental health has not been widely adopted in Canada. This study is an exploratory investigation into mental health professionals' attitudes toward telemental health, factors that affect the frequency with which they use this technology, and their perceptions of individual characteristics that make clients more or less suitable candidates for telemental health. This study has a particular focus on remote and rural and Operational Stress Injury (OSI) contexts. One hundred sixty mental health workers across Canada participated in an online survey, and 25 mental health workers from Operational Stress Injury clinics across Canada participated in in-person interviews. The data were examined using qualitative and quantitative analysis methods. Findings suggest that mental health workers have overall positive attitudes toward the use of telemental health—particularly for clients in remote and rural locations. Additionally, receiving training in telemental health, being in the mental health field for longer, and perceiving the technology as easy to use are associated with more frequent use of telemental health. Finally, clinicians reported specific client characteristics that they perceive to make some clients unsuitable candidates for telemental health. Implications of these findings and directions for future research are discussed.

E-Empowerment

The provision of health care over the Internet is rapidly evolving and potentially beneficial means of delivering treatment otherwise unsought and unobtainable (Ritterband, Gonder-Frererick, Cox, Clifton, et al., 2003). Internet interventions are typically behavioral treatments operationalized and transformed for Web delivery for the purpose of symptom improvement. The literature on the feasibility and utility of Internet interventions is limited, and there are even fewer outcome study findings. Ritterband et al., (2003) reviewed empirically tested Internet interventions and provided an overview of the issues in developing and/or using them in clinical practice. Future directions and implications were also addressed. Although Internet interventions will not likely replace face-to-face care, there is little doubt that they will grow in importance as a powerful component of successful psycho-behavioral treatment.

Amichai-Hamburger, McKenna, and Tal (2008) focused on the concept of empowerment and the ways in which the Internet is being utilized as an empowering tool. This analysis ranges from the personal to the global levels and the consequences of that empowerment were also discussed. They proposed a four-level model that serves to explain what we term E-empowerment and the effects that can be observed at each of the four levels, ranging from (1) the personal; (2) the interpersonal; (3) group; and (4) citizenship. The potential for future development of E-empowerment was also discussed.

The Importance of Pre-Post Evaluation in Offline/Online Interventions

With the advent of the Internet, delivered assessment applications are likely to make a difference in clinical psychology and in health care in general. The purpose of this paper was to present an overview of the authors' experience regarding Internet administration of diagnostic interviews, questionnaires, and information processing tests (Andersson, Ritterband, & Carlbring, 2008). A conclusion was reached that psychiatric assessments via the Internet are not yet to be recommended, but that questionnaire assessments are likely to generate equivalent or even superior data quality than traditional paper and pencil administration. Finally, the use of Internet-delivered tests of information processing is commented upon. Although these tests have been influential in theory development in clinical psychology, large-scale dissemination of tests has been slowed down by the need for laboratory facilities. Internet administration can provide new opportunities to administer tests from the patient's own home.

The current study was conducted to determine whether participants responded differently to online questionnaires presenting all items on a single webpage versus questionnaires presenting only one item per page, and whether participants prefer one format over the other (Thorndike, Carlbring, Smyth, Magee, Gonder-Frederick, Ost,, & Ritterband, 2009). Of participants seeking self-help treatment on the Internet (for depression, social phobia, or panic disorder), 710 completed four questionnaires (Beck Depression Inventory, Beck Anxiety Inventory, Quality of Life Index, Montgomery-Åsberg Depression Rating Scale) on the Internet on two occasions. The questionnaires were either presented with one questionnaire on one webpage (e.g., BDI on one webpage) or on multiple web-pages (e.g., BDI on 21 web-pages with one item each). Results suggested that the four web questionnaires measure the same construct across diagnostic group (depression, social phobia, panic), presentation type (single versus multiple items per page), and order of presentation (which format first). Within each diagnostic group, factor means for all questionnaires were equivalent across presentation method and time. Furthermore, factor means varied as expected across samples (e.g., depressed group scored higher on BDI), providing evidence of construct validity. The majority of participants in each diagnostic group preferred the single item per page format, even though this format required more time.

Table 1.1. Comparisons of differences between offline and offline media of communication and healing

	Off line	Online
Contacts between professionals and participants	Face-to-face (F2F)	F2F contacts not present unless Skype or equivalent visual channels are used
Identification of Participants through encryptions	None	Questionable or Anonymous unless verified 100% visual channels or
Medium of Communication	Talk	Writing
Costs	High	Lower than F2F interventions*
Impression Management	Necessary	Questionable
Non-verbal behavior	Visible	Present on Skype or on other visual channels

*To be evaluated throughout the course of this volume.

ASSESSMENT

Collaborative (or therapeutic) assessment is an empirically supported procedure that involves the client as an active participant in the assessment process (Smith, Fagan, Wilson, Chen, et al., 2011). Clients discussed data they provide with the assessor in a collaborative manner designed to provide insights and assist in setting mutually agreeable treatment goals. Internet-based procedures allow for ongoing (including daily) tracking of psychological variables and provision of immediate graphic feedback to therapists, clients, and clinical supervisors. As an example, the authors described one such system: Evidence-Based Assessment System for Clinicians that contains more than 30 brief and empirically validated assessment instruments that can be completed via the Internet or smartphone. They also provided examples from a stress management intervention demonstrating how single-client data from a Web-based daily stress and coping diary tied to the Evidence-Based Assessment System for Clinicians were utilized to provide clients with individualized feedback, assess progress, identify idiographic patterns of cognitions, affect, and coping strategies, and test clinical hypotheses. Internet- and computer- based technological advances can improve service delivery and help bridge the gap that currently exists between science and practice.

Vecchione, Alessandri, and Barbaronelli (2012) investigated equivalence of a five-factor measure of personality across two groups applying for jobs, who completed the same questionnaire using either a paper-and-pencil (n=429) or a web online answer format (n=651). The data were collected using the Big Five Questionnaire-2 BFQ-2), which is a measure of the Big Five Factor Model of personality traits. Multiple-group confirmatory factor analysis was used to test the equivalence of factor covariance and mean structure of the BFQ-2. Findings suggested that the Five Factor Model scales have the same measurement unit and origin across applicants using different administration modes. However, latent means were slightly higher for applicants who responded in a web and unproctored condition than for applicants who completed a paper-and-pencil version of the same test. Practical implications for personality assessment were discussed.

Assessment of Disruptive Behavior

Distinguishing between disruptive and normative behavior is a challenging task. How to best assess for disruptive behavior in children and adolescents is a significant question encountered by many professionals. The purpose of this review was to summarize the existing research regarding reliable and valid tools for assessing disruptive behavior disorders (McKinney & Morse, 2012). Following a summary of these various tools available to clinicians, recommendations for the assessment of disruptive behavior disorders were suggested. These recommendations included ideal situations where comprehensive assessments may be conducted as well as situations where resources may be limited. *Clinicians must conduct as thorough of an assessment as feasible so that accurate diagnoses and recommendations may be made to inform treatment.* (italics author's to emphasize the importance of pre-and-post intervention assessment and follow-up (L'Abate, 2014).

Web-Based Assessment and Monitoring

Telehealth and other technological innovations have become increasingly more popular in the practice of psychotherapy and the training of psychotherapists (Harwood, Pratt, Beutler, Bongar, et al., 2011). From the use of e-mail and online therapy to virtual reality (VR) technology and to patient and clinician interactive web-based systems, technology has resulted in a number of improvements, such as financial savings and time reductions. Additionally, technology has allowed clinicians to reach more people and provide potential patients with greater access to information about their presenting problem(s) and available treatments. The self-help movement in psychotherapy has also benefited from technological advances. This article summarized some of the key developments in the field and underline some of the ethical and clinical implications of these technological applications in clinical psychology. It will briefly describe different approaches to telehealth and extract from extant research literature suggestions for future research in areas of overlap between technology and psychology. Some of these implications were illustrated by reference to the establishment of a web-based assessment and monitoring system designed to capitalize on the strengths of telehealth procedures in facilitating improved treatment outcomes.

SPECIAL POPULATIONS

In this section, we shall include special populations in need of specific mental and physical health that deserve particular attention from the MH community.

School Counseling American Indian

This article provided an abbreviated description of a qualitative study of the Succeeding in School (SIS) program, an Internet-based intervention designed to help students reflect on key elements of academic and career success (Zyromski, Bryant, Deese, & Gerler, 2008). The

American School Counselor Association's National Standards call for school counselors to focus on the academic, career, and personal/social development of students. Strengths- Based School Counseling (Galassi & Akos, 2007) suggests that school counselors should implement that call through promoting context-based development for all students, promoting individual student strengths, and promoting strengths-enhancing environments. Students used the SIS program to identify personal strengths and characteristics, as well as strengths enhancing aspects of their environment useful for achieving academic and career success.

American Indians

Mental health issues are a serious concern for many American Indian Veterans, especially for post-traumatic stress disorder and related psychiatric conditions. Yet, acquiring mental health treatment can be a challenge in Native communities where specialized services are largely unavailable (Brooks, E., et al. (2012). Consequently, telehealth is increasingly being suggested as a way to expand healthcare access on or near reservation lands. In this study, we wanted to understand the factors affecting the diffusion of telehealth clinics that provided mental health care to rural, American Indian Veterans. The authors surveyed 39 key personnel and stakeholders who were involved in the decision-making process, technological infrastructure, and implementation of three clinics. Using Roger Everett's Diffusion Theory as a framework, they gathered information about specific tasks, factors hindering progress, and personal reactions to telehealth both before and after implementation.

Many participants expressed initial concerns about using telehealth; however, most became positive over time. Factors that influenced participants' viewpoint largely included patient and staff feedback and witnessing the fulfillment of a community health need. The use of outside information to support the implementation of the clinics and personal champions also showed considerable influence in the clinics' success. The findings presented here address critical gaps in our understanding of telehealth diffusion and inform research strategies regarding the cultural issues and outcomes related to telemental health services. Information contained in this report serves as a long overdue guide for developing telemental health programs and policies among American Indians, specifically, and rural populations in general.

Assessing Senior Citizens Wellness

The development of ongoing assessment tools to monitor older adult health and wellness can support improved quality of life and independence (Demiris, Thompson, Boquet, Le, Chaudhuri, & Chung, 2012). These technologies have often been employed within private residences. Our work describes a telehealth kiosk system implemented within a community setting, which reduces the costs of installing and maintaining individual systems. Though user acceptance of telehealth systems has been studied within the context of home residences, this has yet to be addressed for community-based systems. Older adults in a retirement community were recruited to use a telehealth system including assessment of vital signs and cognitive performance. With a series of focus groups (N = 12, average age 79.3 years), we examined user perceptions of the telehealth kiosk, addressing issues of usability, effectiveness and privacy. Older adults were favorable towards the collection of health monitoring information, recognizing the utility of these data sources. There were issues of usability, especially regarding ergonomics of the telehealth kiosk. We found no concerns over privacy, with some participants expressing increased preference for the social interactions afforded through the community setting. Understanding the social, technical and human factors involved with a community-based telehealth system can inform the design of cost-effective health monitoring systems.

Post deployment Military Community

Practicing psychologists and other health professionals are facing a growing patient population of United States military service members with significant psychological and behavioral health concerns returning from war zones in Afghanistan and Iraq. Some of these issues are new and unfamiliar to many health providers. Furthermore, because of a military culture of self-reliance, strength, and the perceived stigma of seeking mental health services, a second and substantial population of service members-in-need is choosing not to consult health professionals at all. The Internet and other networked multimedia technologies now offer a rich expert resource for providers, and an anonymous, less stigmatizing venue for self-management for service members and their families. Over the last 2 years the U.S. Defense Department's National Center for Telehealth & Technology has developed afterdeployment.org, a Web-based set of resources, tools, and aids for service members, veterans, and their families. afterdeployment.org provides education and skills-development exercises aimed at overcoming challenges to the adjustment process after a deployment. The Website also provides health professionals with a comprehensive resource to serve as an adjunct to face to face treatment of individuals in the military community (Bush, Bosmajian, Fairall, McCann, & Ciulla, 2011).

Rural MH

The Leon County Health Resource Commission sought to increase access to mental health services for their rural community (Wendel, et al. 2011). The commission formed a network of partners who collaborated to increase free transportation to mental health services outside the community and developed a telehealth-based counseling program through a counseling psychology training program. Learning opportunities emerged during the development and implementation of these activities for both the students and the community in how to successfully utilize and sustain this service. This article describes the telehealth counseling model, presents lessons learned in the process, and presents recommendations for others interested in utilizing similar strategies.

Gibson, O'Donnell, Coulson, and Kakepetum-Schultz (2011) conducted an online survey and interviews amongst mental health workers in Canada who reported experience in working with rural and remote First Nations (although not necessarily telemental health). Sixty-three respondents (of the 164) to the online survey reported experience in working with clients in remote and rural First Nations. Only 16 of the online survey respondents with remote and rural First Nations experience reported having received training in videoconferencing use.

When asked how frequently they used videoconferencing with clients, 51% reported never using it, 19% used it once every few months and 10% reported using it a few times a month. Approximately 50% of participants reported finding it useful. Approximately 38% found the technology easy or very easy to use, and 15% found it very difficult. Individual in-depth interviews were also conducted with professionals who had First Nations telemental health experience specifically (n = 5). A quantitative data analysis was used to explore their perceptions of usefulness and ease of use of telemental health, as well as the relationships among these constructs. Advantages, disadvantages and challenges in using the technology were identified from the qualitative data. Promising ways forward include incorporating traditional practices and the Seven Teachings into telemental health services.

The objective of this article was to discuss, using two case examples, the potential utility of Internet-based depression information and automated therapy programs in rural regions (Griffiths & Christensen, 2007). Systematic review of evaluations of two Australian web-based mental health programs: MoodGYM and BluePages Depression Information. Setting: Community, school, university. Participants: A total of 12 papers and reports derived from nine separate studies of MoodGYM and BluePages involving sample sizes ranging from 78 to 19 607 people. Outcome measures: Depressive symptoms, anxiety symptoms, dysfunctional thoughts, depression literacy, stigma, help seeking and cost-effectiveness. Results: Internet-based applications were effective in reducing depressive symptoms and stigmatizing attitudes to depression and in improving depression literacy. School-based programs also showed promise in decreasing depressive symptoms. Depression self-help and information programs can be delivered effectively by means of the Internet. As accessibility of F2F mental health services in rural areas is poor and as there is a strong culture of self-reliance and preference for self-managing health problems among rural residents, the Internet might offer an important platform for the delivery of help for depression in rural regions. Consideration should be given to developing programs tailored to rural settings and future research should evaluate the efficacy and effectiveness of such programs in rural settings.

The provision of services to informal caregivers, such as family, friends, and neighbors, in rural areas provides unique challenges for professional psychologists (Clancy Dollinger and K. Chwalisz (2011). The Telehelp Line for Caregivers, a clinical telehealth multi-component intervention for rural caregivers is described. Supportive services and resources through the Telehelp Line for Caregivers were provided during structured telephone counseling sessions. Caregiver knowledge, problem-solving skills, and help-seeking behavior and affect were the major components addressed. An eight-session structured telephone intervention and a call-in helpline was available. All components were available but tailored to individual participants based on caller presenting concerns and assessed needs. The benefits of a telehealth intervention for rural caregivers are addressed, as well as issues related to the applicability of telehealth services in professional practice.

> "With more psychologists and clients using social networking sites, practitioners face ethical concerns they may have never considered before. Offering guidance are rural psychologists, who have confronted small- World confidentiality concerns for decades (Lannin & Scott, 2014, p. 57).

In Hawai'i, rural residents suffer disproportionately from poor health and mental health outcomes (Chung-Do, Helm, Fukunda, Alicata, Nishimura, & Else, 2012). Hawai'i's island geography makes rural health service disparities especially compelling. Physician workforce shortages are projected to increase, despite 30 years of programs aimed at recruiting physicians to rural areas. Telepsychiatry has been shown to be a feasible way to provide a variety of health services to individuals living in rural areas with limited access to healthcare. The University of Hawai'i Rural Health Collaboration (UHRHC) was established by the Department of Psychiatry to address the need for workforce development and rural access to mental health services across the State of Hawai'i by using telepsychiatry. Partnerships with community health clinics have been formed to provide patient care and consultation-liaison services through telepsychiatry technology. In addition, UHRHC focuses on workforce development in its residency training curriculum by utilizing a service-learning approach to rural mental health. Evaluation of these efforts is currently underway, with preliminary evidence suggesting that UHRHC is a promising strategy to increase access to critical mental health services and reduce health disparities in rural Hawai'i.

The purpose of this article was to provide information to improve the quality of care of veterans living in geographically isolated areas who require treatment for mental health issues (Wynn & Sherrod, 2012). Because interactive care solutions are currently hot topics in the health care community, they should be viewed as possible strategies to meet the needs of this specialty group of veterans. An intervention using a mobile clinic and clinical video telehealth reduces distance barriers by making it possible for mental health specialists to come to rural veterans instead of the veteran attempting to find a way to get to the practitioner, who may be located in a clinic or hospital many miles away. This article focuses on an alternate strategy-telehealth in mobile clinics-as a possible solution to the mental health crisis of veterans in rural areas.

Young People

One third of young Americans experience mental health difficulties, often without seeking help. More than 90% use the Internet. Reach Out (www.reachout.com.au), an Australian Internet-based service, is discussed in relation to the role it could play in reducing stigma and increasing help seeking in young Americans aged 16–25 years (Burns, Durkin, & Nicholas, 2009).

College Psychotherapy: Cases are presented to illustrate effects of online communication by students in psychotherapy in a university counseling center (Baron, Bierschwale, & Bleiberg, 2006). In the first, a student's use of instant messaging to convey suicide threats exaggerated the level of the danger. In the second, a student used e-mail messages to his therapist to modulate the expression of feelings prior to psychotherapy sessions. In the third, the exchange of e-mail messages by the student and the therapist between scheduled sessions, served to sustain the therapeutic work. Acceptance of the potential of this technology to enhance clinical work, along with awareness of the dangers, is recommended.

More recently, instead of just cases, O'Neal (2014) reported about the successful growth of campus psychological counseling going online at the University of Florida with hundreds of participating students who improved at a higher rate than students who received F2F counseling as usual.

Students: It is recognized that young people experience difficulties in accessing mainstream mental health services particularly because of the stigma that remains associated with mental health problems. (Horgan & Sweeney, 2010). One potential solution is to use the many websites available offering information and support for mental health problems, such support and information could be offered by Psychiatric Nurses. However, young peoples' usage and views on using the Internet for this purpose has yet to be examined. This quantitative descriptive study aimed to elicit the views of 922 University students, aged between 18 and 24 years, on using the Internet for mental health information and support. Data were collected using a 30-item self-designed questionnaire and analysed using descriptive statistics. The findings indicated that 72.4% of participants used the Internet several times a day. In addition, 30.8% had previously searched for mental health information online, predominantly on depression. While it was found that 68% of participants indicated that they would use the Internet for mental health support if they needed to, 79.4% would still prefer face to face support. It is concluded that young people are willing to use the Internet for mental health information and that it represents a viable source of support for this age group.

Senior Citizens

Despite the benefits associated with a physically active lifestyle, many older adults are insufficiently active to achieve health gain, and also exhibit decreased activity levels with age. Insufficient physical activity in this population is associated with increased morbidity, mortality and demand on health care services and expenditure (clinical training, and our responsibilities as providers of clinical care will be addressed. (Garrett & Latham. 2006). There is a clear need for effective intervention to encourage physical activity in older adults. The aim of this paper is to describe the development and participant evaluation of a randomized controlled trial of TeleWalk, a telephone-based motivational counseling intervention to encourage physical activity in adults aged 65 years and older. Participants (N = 186, mean age 74 ± 6 years) were recruited through their General Practitioner (primary care physician) and randomized to either receive eight telephone counseling sessions and related printed materials over 3 months (intervention group) or participate in outcome assessments only (control group). Intervention group participants were mailed an anonymous evaluation questionnaire on intervention completion. A high response rate was achieved (70%). All respondents (100%) agreed or strongly agreed that a good overall level of service and support was provided, and that the counselor was understanding and supportive. Nearly all respondents agreed or strongly agreed that the service was professional, the counselor advice was helpful and motivating and the information provided was relevant (97, 95 and 89%, respectively). Most (87%) agreed or strongly agreed that the telephone calls encouraged them to be physically active. Among the participants who received printed material, most agreed or strongly agreed that these encouraged them to become or remain active. Findings from this evaluation can be used to inform such interventions and ensure their relevance to community-dwelling older adults.

Technological advances in telehealth systems are primarily focused on sensing and monitoring. However, these systems are limited in that they only rely on sensors and medical devices to obtain vital signs (Lee, Helal, Anton, DeDeugd, et al., 2012). New research and development are urgently needed to offer more effective and meaningful interactions between patients, medical professionals and other individuals around the patients. Social networking with Web 2.0 technologies and methods can meet these demands, and help to develop a more complete view of the patient. Also many people, including the elderly, may be resistant to change, which can reduce the efficacy of telehealth systems. Persuasive technology and mechanisms are urgently needed to counter this resistance and promote healthy lifestyles. In this paper, we propose the participatory and persuasive telehealth system as a solution for these two limitations. By integrating connected health solutions with social networking and adding persuasive influence, we increase the chances for effective interventions and behavior alterations.

Despite the benefits associated with a physically active lifestyle, many older adults are insufficiently active to achieve health gain, and also exhibit decreased activity levels with age. Insufficient physical activity in this population is associated with increased morbidity, mortality and demand on health care services and expenditure. There is a clear need for effective intervention to encourage physical activity in older adults. The aim of this paper is to describe the development and participant evaluation of a randomized controlled trial of TeleWalk, a telephone-based motivational counseling intervention to encourage physical activity in adults aged 65 years and older. Participants (N = 186, mean age 74 ± 6 years) were recruited through their General Practitioner (primary care physician) and randomized to either receive eight telephone counseling sessions and related printed materials over 3 months (intervention group) or participate in outcome assessments only (control group). Intervention group participants were mailed an anonymous evaluation questionnaire on intervention completion. A high response rate was achieved (70%). All respondents (100%) agreed or strongly agreed that a good overall level of service and support was provided, and that the counselor was understanding and supportive. Nearly all respondents agreed or strongly agreed that the service was professional, the counselor advice was helpful and motivating and the information provided was relevant (97, 95 and 89%, respectively). Most (87%) agreed or strongly agreed that the telephone calls encouraged them to be physically active. Among the participants who received printed material, most agreed or strongly agreed that these encouraged them to become or remain active. Findings from this evaluation can be used to inform such interventions and ensure their relevance to community-dwelling older adults.

Urban Telepsychiatry

Psychiatry is a particularly good specialty to provide by telemedicine. The psychiatric interaction translates very well to the interactive video medium and typically does not require any peripheral medical devices for the consultation compared with other specialties (Spaulding, Cain, & Sonnenschein, 2011). Although telemedicine is most often thought of as strictly a rural health tool for solving health care shortages, it has sometimes been used to improve access to many health specialists in urban areas of the United States. An urban infrastructure can be more supportive of telehealth from technical and clinical support perspectives, particularly in special or emergent situations. This article highlights the Kansas practice and reviews other urban applications of tele-psychiatry.

Technology Interventions for Aging, African-American, and Hispanic/Latino Clinical Populations. Symposium Presented at the Annual Meeting of the American Psychological Association, August 7th, 2014. Washington, D.C.

Technology for the purpose of clinical interventions is available in various forms including telehealth, videoconferencing, mobile applications, and telephone assisted services. The use of such technologies for diverse populations is beginning to be explored and holds promise of extending the reach of clinical interventions to traditionally underserved populations. The symposium describes examples of use of technology with older adults who have dementia, their caregivers, as well as African-American and Hispanic/Latino populations. We begin with the communication technology of videoconferencing and its potential to create greater access to care to older adults in nursing homes and similar facilities. Key aspects of legal and ethical considerations for telepsychology are also briefly outlined. We also address the role of telehealth for family caregivers of older adults with dementia, with special attention to African-Americans. Racial and ethnic minorities are populations most negatively affected by shortages of health services and we discuss the evidence of telehealth-based, cognitive-behavioral interventions for caregivers of older adults with chronic illnesses. Mobile applications, apps, are discussed in terms of their potential to also transform clinical service delivery for underserved patient populations. The Hispanic/Latino U.S. population is projected to triple to 128 million by 2050 and this group is examined as an example of the transformative potential of mobile app use for clinical populations. For rural community patient populations, a telephone assisted outreach program for veterans is described for access-related outcomes including reduced travel burden and cost savings. The program addressed geriatric mental health services veterans with dementia and their caregivers.

TITLE: Advanced Technologies for Risk Management in TeleGerontology
AUTHOR: Marlene M. Maheu, Ph.D.
PRESENTER INFORMATION: Marlene M. Maheu, Ph.D., TeleMental Health Institute, Inc. San Diego, CA.
Marlene.maheu@gmail.com

As with all disciplines, psychology is in the process of "re-tooling" to adapt to the demands of the information age. Not only can clinicians reach previously isolated patients, but, as controlled studies show, they can enhance effectiveness. Five decades of research confirms that many technologies can be efficiently used for psychotherapy, supervision, assessment and adjunctive treatments. These communication technologies include telephones, email, chat rooms, cell phones and text-massaging, Internet-based software and videoconferencing. None has enjoyed as much research as the use of video-conferencing in telehealth.

Further impetus is being given to psychologists by the U.S. government's health care reform legislation, which includes mandates under the Affordable Care Act to: reduce costs, deliver effective care and increase access to more consumers.

As psychologists then, our task is to not only examine the evidence base for effective interventions, but adapt our skill set to meet the needs of populations who are currently underserved, such as that of older adults. Videoconferencing technologies offer hope to the majority of older patients who have never met with psychologists, but who can be more appropriately assessed and given access care in ways that reduce travel to medical and mental health offices. These new approaches to care delivery can help to more closely monitor outcomes and intervene earlier in the trajectory of both physical and mental health challenges. This presentation will give a sample of how some companies have adapted their video-based equipment to meet the specific needs of older adults in nursing homes and similar facilities. Key aspects of legal and ethical considerations for tele-psychology will also be briefly outlined.

TITLE: Telehealth-Based, Cognitive-Behavioral and Spiritual Counseling for Minority Caregivers of Older Adults with Dementia: Key Issues and Initial Outcomes

AUTHOR: Robert L. Glueckauf, Ph.D.
PRESENTER INFORMATION: Robert L. Glueckauf, Ph.D., Florida State University, College of Medicine, Tallahassee, FL 32306-4300 robert.glueckauf@med.fsu.edu

The vast majority of adults with dementia receives ongoing care in the home from family caregivers and significant others. Although the federal government (i.e., U.S. Alzheimer's Project Act) has called for the dissemination of evidence-based interventions to enhance the well-being and health of dementia family caregivers, a substantial gap exists between caregiver needs and available services. The populations most negatively affected by this shortage of services are racial and ethnic minorities, especially African-Americans. Two developments have increased the prospects of meeting the mental and physical health needs of underserved dementia caregivers: (a) recent evidence supporting the efficacy of telehealth-based, cognitive-behavioral intervention for distressed minority dementia caregivers, and (b) engagement of volunteers from faith-based organizations in providing cognitive-behavioral interventions to adults with chronic illnesses. The objectives of this presentation are as follows: (1) summarize the key findings of research incorporating faith-based, volunteer workers in the delivery of cognitive-behavioral skills and support interventions, (2) discuss the rationale for and requirements of integrating spirituality into the framework of telehealth-based, cognitive-behavioral intervention for minority dementia caregivers, (3) discuss key factors in determining the successful engagement of faith-based volunteer workers in the delivery of cognitive-behavioral interventions for minority dementia caregivers, and (4) summarize the initial findings of Glueckauf et al.'s recent grant-funded clinical trial on the effects of telephone-based, cognitive-behavioral and spiritual counseling intervention for African-American dementia caregivers and their implications for future research.

TITLE: Mobile App Use for Culturally Diverse, and Aging Populations: Transformative Technology Potential for Clinical Practice

AUTHOR: Yvette N. Tazeau, Ph.D.
PRESENTER INFORMATION: Yvette N. Tazeau, Ph.D., ynt consulting, P.O. Box 20684, San Jose, CA 95160 ynt@yntconsulting.com

It is no longer a forecast: there are two stark demographic trends for the year 2050 - people in the U.S. will be older, and more Latino. The Hispanic population will triple to 128 million, and adults age 65 and older will comprise nearly 20 percent of the population. Reports from science and business tell about another important trend – Baby-Boomers and Hispanics are adopting smartphone usage faster than any other groups. What do these trends portend for clinicians and the use of mobile health technology? The presentation will review general patterns of smartphone and app usage in these populations. The potential to reach under-served populations' health needs through technology will be highlighted. The talk will also focus on the various categories of mobile health tools, and the innovations of digital devices in areas such as treatment administration, social engagement, wearable tech, aging in place, remote monitoring, data collection, and family connectivity. Increasingly, it is the patient, caregiver of the patient, or service setting provider who is approaching the clinician and asking for a recommendation of a mobile technology tool. Thus, also discussed will be how clinicians can consider usage of and recommendations for technology solutions in clinical practice. A review of the pitfalls of science struggling to keep up with commercial ventures of tech-enabled health, such as for efficacy and privacy matters will be addressed. Finally, resources to stay abreast of mobile technology use in health will be provided.

TITLE: Maximizing Rural Health Outreach through Technology: Translating Evidence-Based Treatments for Dementia Caregivers

AUTHORS: Michelle M. Hilgeman, Ph.D., A. Lynn Snow, Ph.D., Branka Primetica, MSW, David M. Bass, Ph.D., Sylvia Colon-Lindsey, M.D., Rebecca S. Allen, Ph.D., Mark E. Kunik, M.D.

PRESENTER INFORMATION: Michelle M. Hilgeman, PhD; Research & Development (151), Tuscaloosa VA Medical Center, 3701 Loop Road East, Tuscaloosa, AL, United States, 35404; Michelle.Hilgeman@va.gov

The remote delivery of healthcare services through telecommunications technology is of particular importance for vulnerable populations in rural communities. The Veterans Health Administration (VHA) Office of Rural Health supports clinical demonstration projects at the local VA level to increase access to quality specialty care such as geriatric mental health services. Through this mechanism, innovative care delivery systems are piloted at the local level before being adopted more broadly. The Telephone Assisted Dementia Outreach (TADO) Program is a new clinical pilot program developed to provide individualized, evidence-based, telephone-delivered dementia care services to: distressed Veterans with dementia, caregivers of Veterans with dementia, and Veterans who are serving as caregivers for persons with dementia. Clinical services are supported by a computerized care consultation information system (CCIS) that guides the clinician through an initial assessment of common stressors (e.g., arranging services, capacity to provide care, depression and anxiety, driving, dyadic relationship strain). Triggered domains are then used to prioritize health care information delivery, activation of informal support networks, utilization of community resources, and other coaching and support.

Clinical program evaluation data from the first 83 families are available; the majority are Veterans with dementia (92.7%), though six (7.2%) are Veteran caregivers for a loved one with dementia. Veterans range in age from 41-93 (M = 77.6 years old). Measures of distress including caregiver burden, patient symptoms of depression, and quality of life are completed at the introduction of services and at 3 months. Access-related outcomes include reduced travel burden (i.e., 1,977.6 miles saved) and potential cost savings for the hospital in unissued travel reimbursement (i.e., $387,195.66 for the first 50 Veterans). Implications for translating evidence-based protocols into rural care settings will be discussed with emphasis on the benefits of telephone-delivered services and the use of computerized clinical tools like the care consultation information system.

CONCLUSION

There is no doubt that computers and MH interventions are going to revolutionize the way these services will be delivered in this century. The major issue will be one of training MH professionals and especially clinical psychologists to up-date themselves with new skills and new techniques that cannot longer be practiced F2F.

SECTION I. INTERNALIZATIONS

Chapter 2

ADDICTIONS

The purpose of this chapter is to review whatever offline/online research is available about addictions. According to Marks et al., (2007):

Seven CP systems to lower alcohol intake, mostly for non-heavy drinkers, were evaluated in 11 studies including seven Randomized Control Trials (RCTs). Of the nine systems..... five were on PC, three on the net, and one on both. ... In a RCT of problem drinking volunteers with above-average socioeconomic status, education and motivation, net DinkingLess (DL) plus a minimally moderated online discussions board cut drinking more than net-information without a discussion board. The effects are unclear on DL per se versus an online discussion board. Cost-effectiveness studies were not found of CP with alcohol reduction (p. 138).

Three Computer Aided Psychotherapy (CP) systems for drug misuse were reported, in one RCT' and one two-schools comparisons in young people, and in a beta-test, one open study and two RCTs in poor undereducated American women who used it just once post-partum in an obstetric hospital. The young people studies found short-term changes in attitude so far. In the post-partum women, at four-month follow-up, self-rated drug misuse supported by urine analysis was less in women who had been randomized to use the full system than to use only its assessment part (64% versus 84%). (p. 138).

In their review of internet-based treatments for substance abuse, Gallego and Emmelkamp (2012, pp. 409-410) noted that a great many studies about alcohol abuse, were carried out with student populations, limiting any possible conclusion and generalized to patient populations. Nonetheless, studies not already contained in their review will be included here. For instance, long-term use of benzodiazepines remains common, and conveys significant risk (Parr, Kavanaugh, Young, & Mitchell, 2011). Providing psychological intervention in association with gradual dose reduction increases cessation rates above dose reduction alone, but appropriate psychological support is difficult to obtain. This study was undertaken to assess the outcomes of an uncontrolled case series of an Internet-based cognitive-behavior therapy for benzodiazepine cessation. Users of benzodiazepines for >3 months who wanted to reduce or cease benzodiazepines participated in the trial. They completed online assessments and accessed 13 newsletters on managing withdrawal symptoms and developing alternate ways to cope with life events. Therapist assistance was provided by email. Follow up was at 3 and 6 months and feedback was obtained via comments and emails. Program ratings and emailed comments of the program were positive.

Thirty-two people registered for the program and 14 (44%) completed a 6 month follow up. Of these, eight (57%) reduced weekly intake by at least half, including five (36%) who ceased use. Shorter duration of use and birth outside Australia predicted greater percentage reductions at 3 months, while being living with a partner and being in paid employment predicted reductions at 6 months. While results were encouraging, controlled research is required to confirm the efficacy of the program, and engagement of both users and prescribers needs further attention.

Early interventions that reduce the societal burden of mental health problems in the aftermath of disasters and mass violence have the potential to be enormously valuable (Ruggiero, Resnick, Acierno, Coffey, et al., 2006) Internet-based interventions can be delivered widely, efficiently, and at low cost and as such are of particular interest. The authors described the development and feasibility analysis of an Internet-delivered intervention designed to address mental health and substance-related reactions in disaster-affected populations. Participants (n = 285) were recruited from a cohort of New York City-area residents that had been followed longitudinally in epidemiological research initiated 6 months after the terrorist attacks of September 11, 2001. The intervention consisted of 7 modules: posttraumatic stress/panic, depression, generalized anxiety, alcohol use, marijuana use, drug use, and cigarette use. Feasibility data were promising and suggested the need for further evaluation.

A variety of obstacles (e.g., lack of transportation, less availability of treatment in rural districts) contribute to underutilization of treatment among patients with substance use disorders, warranting the need to develop innovative strategies for enhancing access to treatment for these patients. The telehealth in-home-messaging-device is a small message-delivering and monitoring device connected via landline phone to a secure server that provides assessment and disease self-management education to patients in their homes. Santa Ana, Stallings, Rounsaville, and Martino, S. (2011) described the development of a Substance Use Disorder telehealth management program (SUD program) for use on this device and a feasibility pilot of the program with six outpatient veterans with substance use disorders referred by their primary medical care providers. These patients indicated that the SUD program was acceptable, easy to use, and helpful toward addressing their substance use problems. Home telehealth technology may be an innovative and feasible approach for providing substance abuse evidence-based treatment either as an adjunct to specialty treatment for substance use disorders or as a stand-alone intervention within primary care for a larger number of patients who may otherwise not access traditional treatment services.

Traditional therapies for addictions are underutilized and characterized by high attrition rates suggesting they may not meet the needs of a proportion of individuals with addiction-related problems including problem drinking, smoking, substance use and problem gambling (Gainsbury & Blaszczynski, 2011). Internet-based therapy has emerged as a new treatment modality for psychological disorders and health issues and this review is the first attempt to summarize and evaluate the evidence of the effectiveness of Internet therapy for addictions. Extensive literature searches were conducted to identify studies meeting the criteria of delivering structured Internet-based treatment programs for addictions that incorporated a component of trained therapist interaction. Only nine studies met criteria for inclusion with seven representing a randomized controlled trial. These included seven papers reporting on tobacco-cessation programs, one Internet-based therapy for pathological gambling, and one treatment program for substance abuse. A range of therapeutic models, treatment components and outcome measures was included across these studies. Positive treatment effects were reported following completion of therapy and at longer-term follow-up. The review concluded that Internet-based therapies for addictions are effective in achieving positive behavioral changes but that more research is required to determine the comparative effectiveness of various Internet-based therapies and their components.

Technology-based interventions such as those delivered by telephone or online may assist in removing significant barriers to treatment seeking for cannabis use disorder. Little research, however, has addressed differing technology-based treatments regarding their comparative effectiveness, and how user profiles may affect compliance and treatment satisfaction (Rooke, Gates, Norberg, & Copeland, 2014). This study addressed this issue by examining these factors in online (N =225) versus telephone (N =160) delivered interventions for cannabis use, using data obtained from two previously published randomized controlled trials conducted by the current authors. Several differences emerged including stronger treatment effects (medium to large effect sizes in the telephone study versus small effect sizes in the Web study) and lower dropout in the telephone intervention (38% vs. 46%). Additionally, around half of the telephone study participants sought concurrent treatment, compared with 2% of participants in the Web study. Demographics and predictors of treatment engagement, retention and satisfaction also varied between the studies. Findings indicate that both telephone and Web-based treatments can be effective in assisting cannabis users to quit or reduce their use; however, participant characteristics may have important implications for treatment preference and outcome, with those who elect telephone-based treatment experiencing stronger outcomes. Thus, participant preference may shape study populations, adherence, and outcome.

Addicted individuals are usually resistant to seek and use professional help. Consequently, I am introducing this chapter with Motivational Interviewing as a necessary approach to deal with addicted individuals as well as other individuals resistant to psychological interventions.

Motivational Interviewing

The objectives of this article were to examine the relationship between participant preference and satisfaction with live interactive video, telephone, or face-to-face motivational interviewing sessions with problem drinkers (Baca & Manuel, 2007). Participants completed a satisfaction questionnaire after each motivational interviewing counseling session utilizing an abbreviated Likert scale. The participants were asked what mode they would have preferred, their satisfaction with their counselor, and their satisfaction with overall counseling. Results: When asked to choose a long-distance mode of communication, televideo was preferred more than 2:1 over telephone. Also those with televideo experience were significantly more likely to choose televideo as a preferred long-distance mode of choice. Findings supported the acceptability of 2 forms of long-distance communication, telephone and televideo, which might reasonably be studied in the future in rural areas (with some preference for televideo) to reduce heavy drinking and alcohol-related problems.

Over the past decade interest in brief motivational interventions aimed at reducing problem drinking also has increased. As a result, brief motivational interventions have been evaluated in a number of diverse clinical settings. These included emergency rooms, inpatient medical programs, as a prelude to inpatient or outpatient substance abuse treatment, as a mail order, self-help program, and within general clinical practice (see Bien, Miller & Tonigan, 1993 and Heather, 1995 for past and by-now updated reviews).

One of the largest trials of a brief motivational intervention was Project MATCH. The results of Project MATCH indicated that Motivational Enhancement Therapy (MET), consisting of four sessions over a 12-week period, compared favorably to both cognitive-behavioral therapy (CBT) and twelve-step facilitation (TSF). Additionally, it was more cost effective given that both the CBT and TSF conditions required three times as many sessions over the same 12-week period (Project MATCH Research Group, 1997; Project MATCH Research Group, 1998).

Therapeutic Feedback

The common elements of effective brief interventions are characterized by the acronym FRAMES (Miller & Sanchez, 1994). Feedback is personalized, Responsibility for changing is left with the individual, Advice to change is given (carefully), a Menu of options for changing is offered, the therapist uses an Empathic style, and Self-efficacy is emphasized. The personalized feedback usually compares the individual's drinking and related consequences to that of the general population and/or drinkers in treatment for their alcohol problems.

Years ago, Agostinelli, Brown, and Miller (1995) reported that personalized feedback significantly reduced consumption in a population of heavy drinking college students relative to controls. What is unusual about this finding is that the intervention was not conducted face-to-face, but through the mail. This outcome suggests that feedback about drinking given in an individualized, non-threatening manner, continues to be a promising approach even when the format does not involve a face-to-face, in-person exchange. Given the effectiveness of mailed feedback, another potentially effective alternative is to use computers (PCs). If a software program requiring little or no input from healthcare providers can motivate drinkers to change, the potential savings in healthcare and social costs from reduced heavy drinking could be substantial. Also, reductions or elimination of heavy drinking in clients who are in treatment for other problems improves their outcomes in these other areas.

Enhanced schedules of counseling can improve response to routine opioid-agonist treatment, although it is associated with increased time demands that enhance patient resistance and non-adherence (King, Stoller, Kidorf, Kindbom, et al., 2009). Internet-based counseling can reduce these concerns by allowing patients to participate from home. This study assesses treatment satisfaction and response to Internet-based (CRC Health Group's e-Getgoing) group counseling for partial responders to methadone maintenance treatment. Patients testing positive for an illicit substance (n = 37) were randomly assigned to e-Getgoing or onsite group counseling and followed for 6 weeks. Patients in both conditions responded favorably to intensified treatment by achieving at least 2 consecutive weeks of abstinence and 100% attendance to return to less-intensive care (e-Getgoing: 70% vs. routine: 71%, ns). Treatment satisfaction was good and comparable across conditions. E-Getgoing patients expressed a preference for the Internet-based service, reporting convenience and increased confidentiality as major reasons. Integrating Internet-based group counseling with on-site treatment services could help expand the continuum of care in methadone maintenance clinics.

Drinking

Interest in assessing and treating a variety of psychological conditions with software programs is increasingly rapidly. This report briefly reviews a Windows and web application for problem drinkers called the Drinker's Check-up (DCU). The DCU is a single session, brief motivational intervention. It can be used as a stand-alone intervention by therapists without expertise in substance abuse or as a prelude to alcohol treatment services. It is the first app to provide integrated assessment, feedback, and assistance with decision-making for individuals having problems with alcohol. In its randomized clinical trial, 61 problem drinkers were randomly assigned to either immediate treatment or a 4-week wait list control group. Outcomes strongly support the experimental hypotheses and long-term effectiveness of the program. Overall, participants reduced the quantity and frequency of drinking by 50%, and had similar reductions in alcohol-related problems that were sustained through 12-month follow-up (Hester, Squires, & Delaney, 2005).

The College Drinker's Check-up (CDCU) is an adaptation of the DCU for young adults. Its effectiveness was evaluated in two randomized clinical trials (Hester, Delaney, and Campbell , 2012). In Experiment 1, Hester and colleagues randomized 144 students to either the CDCU or an assessment-only control group with follow-ups at 1 and 12 months. In Experiment 2, these researchers randomized 82 students to either the CDCU or a delayed-assessment control group with follow-up at 1 month.

In Experiment 1, participants in both groups significantly reduced their drinking at both follow-ups. Compared to the control group, the CDCU group reduced their drinking significantly more at 1 and 12 months on three drinking measures at $\alpha < .05$. Using a more conservative, Bonferroni-adjusted criterion yielded one significant difference in a measure of heavier drinking at the 1 month follow-up. The mean between-group effect sizes were $d = .34$ and .36 at 1 and 12 months, respectively.

In Experiment 2, compared to the delayed assessment control group, the CDCU group significantly reduced (by the Bonferroni-adjusted criterion) their drinking on all consumption measures. These results supported the effectiveness of the CDCU with heavy drinking college students when used in a clinical setting. In addition, the significant reductions in typical drinking in the control group in Experiment 1 and not in Experiment 2 combined with comparable baseline characteristics suggests that the control group in Experiment 1 demonstrated assessment reactivity.

The United States military has high rates of alcohol misuse and alcohol-related problems, necessitating effective treatment programs that minimize participant burden. Web-based interventions have shown promise as efficient treatment options for college students and adults but have not been widely used in the military. This study evaluated the efficacy of two Web-based alcohol interventions, adapted from civilian programs, for active duty United States military personnel (Pemberto, Williams, Herman-Stahl, Calvin, Bradshaw, Bray, Ridenhour, Cook, Hersch, Hester, & Mitchell, 2011).

Two Web-based alcohol interventions, Alcohol Savvy (AS) and DCU, described above, were adapted for use among military populations. The interventions were evaluated using a convenience sample of 3,070 active duty military personnel at 8 installations. Following a baseline survey, participants were assigned to one of three treatment conditions: (1) AS; (2) DCU; or (3); control (no program participation). Follow-up surveys were completed by 1,072 participants 1 month following baseline, and 532 participants 6 months following baseline.

At one-month follow-up, participants who completed the DCU intervention had significant reductions in multiple measures of alcohol use relative to controls. Positive outcomes were found for average number of drinks consumed per occasion, frequent heavy episodic drinker status, and estimated peak BAC. This study expands the literature on the effectiveness of Web-based interventions for alcohol misuse. Findings indicate that Web-based programs (DCU in particular) can significantly decrease several indicators of alcohol use in U.S. military personnel.

Another web app developed by Hester and colleagues is Moderate Drinking is: (www.moderatedrinking.com). In a randomized clinical trial experimental group participants were given access to the web app combined with the use of the online resources of Moderation Management (MM) (www.moderation.org). The control group accessed the online resources of MM alone (Hester, Delaney, & Campbell, 2011). The authors randomly assigned 80 problem drinkers to either the experimental or control group with follow-ups at 3, 6, and 12 months. Seventy-five participants (94%) had outcome data at one or more follow-up points and 59 (73%) were assessed at all three follow-ups. Comparing baseline measures to the average outcomes at follow-ups indicated a significant overall reduction in both groups in alcohol-related problems and consumption variables. Compared to the control group, the experimental group had better outcomes on percent days abstinent (PDA). There was an interaction between intensity of drinking at baseline and treatment in determining outcomes assessing drinking. Less heavy drinkers in the experimental group had better outcomes on log Mean BAC per drinking day compared to the control group. Heavier drinkers did not differentially benefit from the MD program on this measure. Mixed model analyses in general corroborated these outcomes. These outcome data provided partial evidence for the effectiveness of the MD web application combined with MM, compared to the effectiveness of the resources available online at MM by themselves.

Overcoming Addictions (OA) is an abstinence-oriented, cognitive behavioral, web app based on the program of SMART Recovery. SMART Recovery is an organization that has adapted empirically supported treatment strategies for use in a mutual help framework with in-person meetings, online meetings, a forum, and other resources. The aim of this research (Hester, Lenberg, Campbell, & Delaney, 2013) was to evaluate the effectiveness of OA and SMART Recovery (SR) with problem drinkers who were new to SMART Recovery. The experimental hypotheses were: (1) All groups will reduce their drinking and alcohol/drug-related consequences at follow-up compared to their baseline levels, (2) The OA condition will reduce their drinking and alcohol/drug-related consequences more than the control group (SR), and (3) The OA+SR condition will reduce their drinking and alcohol/drug-related consequences more than the control group (SR only).

The authors recruited 189 heavy problem drinkers primarily through SMART Recovery's website and in-person meetings throughout the United States. They randomly assigned participants to (1) OA alone, (2) OA+ attend SMART Recovery meetings (OA+SR), or to (3) attend SMART Recovery meetings (SR) only. Baseline and follow-ups were conducted via GoToMeeting sessions with a Research Assistant (RA) and the study participant. (Hester, Lenberg, Campbell, and Delaney (2013). They interviewed significant others to corroborate the participant's self-report. Primary outcome measures included percent days abstinent (PDA), mean drinks per drinking day (DDD), and alcohol/drug-related consequences.

The intent-to-treat analysis of the 3-month outcomes supported the first hypothesis but not the others. Participants in all groups significantly increased their percent days abstinent from 44 to 72% (P<.001), decreased their mean drinks per drinking day from 8.0 to 4.6 (P<.001), and decreased their alcohol/drug-related problems (P<.001). Actual use relationships were found, for the OA groups, between SR online meetings and improvement in PDA (r=.261, P=.033). In addition, in the OA groups, the number of total sessions of support (including SR & other meetings, counselor visits) was significantly related to PDA (r=.306, P= 012) and amount of improvement in alcohol-related problems (r=.305, P=.012). In the SR only group, the number of face-to-face meetings was significantly related to all three dependent variables, and predicted increased PDA (r=.358, P=.003), fewer mean DDD (r=-.250, P=.039) and fewer alcohol-related problems (r=-.244, P=.045), as well as to the amount of improvement in all three of these variables. Six-month follow-ups have been completed and the results are currently being analyzed. These results support our first experimental hypothesis but not the second or third. All groups significantly increased their PDA and decreased both their mean DDD and their alcohol-related problems, which indicates that both interventions being investigated were equally effective in helping people recover from their problem drinking.

Commenting on the results between online and offline interventions Reid Hester (personal communication, 10/15/13) suggested that "...if you look at the within group effect sizes in the experimental groups, they compare favorably to those reported for similar face-to-face interventions." Given the same results, therefore, one needs to look at comparative costs between online and offline interventions, as discussed in the final Chapter 16 of this volume. Hopefully, these comparisons will be found throughout the various chapters of this volume.

THE DRINKER'S CHECK-UP

Interest in assessing and treating a variety of psychological conditions with software programs is increasingly rapidly. This report briefly reviewed a new software program for problem drinkers called the Drinker's Check-up (DCU) (Squires & Hester, 2004). The DCU utilizes the latest in PC and web-based technology, and is based on the principles of brief motivational interventions. It can be used as a stand-alone intervention by therapists without expertise in substance abuse or as a prelude to alcohol treatment services. It is the first software program to provide integrated assessment, feedback, and assistance with decision-making for individuals having problems with alcohol. Preliminary data from an on-going clinical trial of the DCU as a stand-alone intervention indicate that it is an effective clinical intervention for a wide range of problem drinkers (Squires & Hester, 2004).

The use of software programs for the assessment and treatment of various psychological conditions represents an exciting prospect for the mental health field. Rather than being viewed as a threat to the interpersonal nature of helping professions, or dismissed as far-fetched, computer-based interventions hold the potential to aid clinicians and their clients in a number of valuable ways. For example, computer programs that engage clients in a creative, interactive manner may serve to foster client interest in any number of areas, and may help to stimulate earlier self-exploration of salient therapeutic topics. Computer programs also may be an effective way to offer low-cost, preliminary treatments to a greater number of clients (Squires & Hester, 2004).

Sixty-one problem drinkers were randomly assigned to either immediate treatment or a 4-week wait list control group (Hester, Squires, & Delaney, 2005). Treatment consisted of a computer-based brief motivational intervention, the Drinker's Check-up (DCU). Outcomes strongly support the experimental hypotheses and long-term effectiveness of the program. Overall, participants reduced the quantity and frequency of drinking by 50%, and had similar reductions in alcohol-related problems that were sustained through 12-month follow-up. The DCU seems to be effective in enhancing problem drinkers' motivation for change.

Research on the reliability and validity of computer-based interventions has produced promising results (e.g., Miller et al., 2002; Squires & Hester, 2002), and demonstrates that software programs can offer an effective clinical option in the treatment of various psychological problems (see Wright & Bloom, 1997 for a review). One problem area in particular that has been addressed with some success by computer programs is that of problem drinking. Servan-Schreiber (1986) concluded that "...patients suffering from...alcohol or drug abuse tend to report more information to a computer interviewer than to its human counterpart" (p. 197). In corroboration of this conclusion, Kobak and colleagues (1997) reported that the rate of detection of alcohol abuse using a computer-based screening was twice that of face-to-face screening, and some computer-based interventions have been evaluated within treatment settings for addictive behaviors.

The Computerized Lifestyle Assessment (CLA; Skinner, 1994) was one of the first programs to address problem drinking by assessing drinkers and providing feedback. The CLA assesses behavior in a number of domains and provides feedback to both the individual and his or her healthcare provider on lifestyle strengths, areas of concern, and risks. These domains include, but are not limited to, use of alcohol, tobacco, and other drugs. Importantly, Skinner reported that patients and staff were accepting of a computer-based assessment and feedback program. He has also documented the effectiveness of the CLA in screening and case finding (Skinner, 1994). However, the alcohol component of the CLA is limited to a relatively brief screening procedure, not a comprehensive assessment. As a result the feedback provided to clients is also limited. In related work, Cunningham and colleagues have developed a brief (2 page) screen available on the Internet for problem drinkers and report initial feedback from a survey of its users (Cunningham, Humphreys, & Koski-Jannes, 1999). Fourteen percent of the first 1,729 users responded to their survey and generally expressed interest in and satisfaction with the screening and feedback they received. As with Skinner's CLA, however, the program is a screening procedure rather than a program that provides an in-depth assessment, objective feedback, and help with decision-making.

There is also evidence of the effectiveness of PC-based interventions from a recent controlled clinical trial of the Behavioral Self-Control Program for Windows (BSCPWIN). Developed to assist already motivated clients with a goal of moderation, twelve month follow-up results provided strong support for the hypothesis that computer-based treatment can be effective. Examination of effect sizes with other clinical trials of self-control training delivered in-person suggest that a computer-based modality can be as effective as face-to-face treatment (Hester & Delaney, 1997).

Given the efficacy of treatment-oriented software and of brief interventions, Hester and colleagues concluded that there could be substantial value in developing a computer-based brief motivational intervention for problem drinkers. To pursue this, they applied for and received funding from NIAAA under the Small Business Innovative Research (SBIR) program. The Windows-based program they developed, and tested in a controlled clinical trial, is the Drinker's Check-up (DCU). The DCU, like other brief motivational interventions, is designed for individuals ambivalent about changing their drinking (which includes the majority of heavy drinkers who aren't in treatment). It provides a comprehensive assessment of drinking (and drug use) and seeks to motivate the user to change his or her behaviors using the FRAMES elements discussed earlier, and strategies developed since the CLA (e.g., Decisional Balance exercises).

The DCU consists of integrated Assessment, Feedback, and Decision Making modules that allow the user to undergo not just a comprehensive assessment, but also provides structured (individualized) feedback, and is sensitive to the individual's level of readiness for change. At the start of the Decision Making module, after the client has gone through the assessment and feedback modules, the program branches depending on where the individual indicates he or she is in considering change. If the individual is "Not at all Ready" and has taken all the assessment instruments, then he or she is given the options of printing their feedback summary and the lists they created in the program to that point, or viewing the Project MATCH pamphlet Alcohol and You before exiting the program. If the individual is "Unsure," the program proceeds with a more detailed exploration of issues surrounding readiness. If, however, the individual is "Really Ready to Change" the program proceeds directly with negotiating goals of change and helping the user develop a change plan.

The target population encompasses a wide range from at-risk drinkers (e.g., binge drinking college students) to individuals with alcohol dependence (e.g., individuals presenting for treatment at specialized alcohol treatment programs). For more details about the software and current results of the on-going clinical trial, see Squires & Hester (2002) and our web site at www.behaviortherapy.com.

Case Illustrations

For the present chapter, Squires and Hester (2004) presented case data regarding 3 of 61 individuals who have participated in, and completed 12-month follow-up evaluations for our clinical trial of the DCU (personal communication, 11/11/13). Once enrolled in the study, all participants use the software program on a PC at our offices in Albuquerque, NM, and are then followed-up either 1, 2 and 12 months (immediate treatment group), or at just 1 and 12 months (delayed treatment group) depending on random group assignment. To enroll in the study, participants must not already be receiving other treatment services for their drinking problems. However, once enrolled they are free to seek whatever services they wish. The only treatment they receive through the study is the DCU. In addition to evaluating the program's stand-alone efficacy, we also are evaluating the DCU in a second study where it is offered as an adjunct to other alcohol treatment. (Those results will not be discussed here, however.) Ultimately, we expect the program to be useful in both contexts. Preliminary data from the stand-alone trial indicate that even when the program is the only treatment received, there are significant reductions in drinking and associated problems at all follow-up intervals. We decided to outline 3 cases to demonstrate the effects of the program across a diverse sample of participants--a Caucasian male in his thirties, a middle-aged Native American male, and a Caucasian female in her late 60's.

Presenting Problems/Client Descriptions

Because participants in their clinical trial of the DCU consider their drinking problems significant enough to seek help (as evidenced by the fact that they self-refer in response to an advertisement for the program run in a local newspaper), structured clinical interviews are not conducted since formal diagnosis would add little in the way of additional value to the participant. In fact, many study participants specifically mentioned that they were attracted to the non-traditional qualities of the program. Based on anecdotal evidence, however, we estimate that between 90-95 percent of the total study sample did meet criteria for DSM (DSM-IV; American Psychiatric Association, 1994) alcohol abuse or dependence at the time of enrollment. Two of the three cases that will be profiled here were clearly alcohol dependent, while the third likely met criteria for alcohol abuse.

Each of the three individual's whose cases will be profiled gave explicit permission for details of their participation to be published. However, names and other identifying information have been altered to protect their confidentiality. Descriptions of presenting problems were compiled from assessment instruments contained within the Assessment Module of the DCU after the client used the program for the first time, and during subsequent follow-up appointments using a Follow-up Drinker's Check-up program (FDCU). The FDCU parallels the Assessment Module of the DCU and allows data to be collected on up to three follow-up points. Additionally, when each participant completed the 12-month follow-up, they were asked to briefly describe the impact, if any, they felt as though the program had on their drinking. Consumption is reported in standard drinks (SD) where 1 SD = a 12oz. (355 ml.) beer, a 5 oz. (125ml.) glass of wine, or 1 ½ oz. (45ml.) 80 proof (40 percent) spirits.

Case 1, "Jim"

Jim entered the study as an unemployed 37 year-old white male with Type I diabetes. According to the Brief Drinker Profile (BDP) that is a part of the Assessment Module of the DCU, he reported taking his first drink at 12 years of age, first became intoxicated when he was 17, and indicated that his drinking began to cause noticeable problems for him at age 30. Based on information from his baseline assessment in the DCU, Jim was a steady pattern drinker, meaning that he was consuming the same types of alcoholic beverages (beer) in roughly similar quantities from week-to-week. In a typical week, Jim would consume a case of beer (24, 12oz beers) over 12 hours, 3 times a week. This level of consumption put Jim in the 98th percentile of American males. In other words, only two percent of the population reports drinking more than he did. Jim's estimated peak blood alcohol concentration when he consumed 24, 12oz. beers over 12 hours was 350mg%, or .35. This is 4 times the legal limit of .08 in New Mexico, and indicates a very high level of tolerance to alcohol. In addition to his drinking, Jim also reported using illicit drugs within 3 months of entering the study. Specifically, Jim reported using marijuana, cocaine or crack, hallucinogens, and phencyclidine (PCP).

Jim's score on the screening instrument (the Alcohol Use Disorders Inventory Test; AUDIT) given at the beginning of the program was 28. This score was in the very high range, suggesting that relative to other adults, he was experiencing a significant number of negative consequences within the previous 12-months. This was also confirmed with the Drinker Inventory of Consequences (DrInC) for the 3-months prior to entering the study. Information from the Severity of Alcohol Dependence Questionnaire, Community Sample (SADQ-C) indicated that Jim's impaired control over drinking was in the medium to high range relative to other drinkers. Lastly, from the Stages of Change Readiness and Treatment Eagerness Scale (SOCRATES), Jim scored medium to high on the recognition subscale (indicating that he realized that his drinking was problematic), high on the ambivalence subscale (indicating that he was feeling unsure of whether or not he really wanted to change), and, ironically, high in taking steps range (indicating that he was already taking steps to change). Though ironic given his stated ambivalence, his score on this subscale is intuitive given the fact that he had taken the time to seek out our study.

Case 2, "Nathan"

Nathan came to the study as an unemployed, 45 year-old Native American male who reported being homeless for 60 of the 90 days preceding his intake. Nathan had a long history of problematic alcohol use beginning when he was 15 years old, and reported a substantial family history of relatives with alcohol-related problems including his father, brother, 2 grandparents, and 3 uncles. At baseline, Nathan reported an episodic pattern of drinking with intermittent periods of abstinence. For the 30 days prior to going through the DCU, Nathan reported drinking roughly 46 standard drinks in a typical week. However, this figure was averaged across several heavy drinking episodes where Nathan consumed as many as 25 drinks over a single 16-hour period. His estimated peak blood alcohol concentration (BAC) for this type of episode was 429mg% (.429). This indicated a very high tolerance to alcohol, as this high a BAC level is lethal for most people. In addition to his drinking, Nathan also reported regular marijuana use during the 30 days preceding his use of the program.

Nathan's score on the AUDIT of 22 was in the high range, and information from the DrInC indicated medium to high consequences across several areas for the 3 months prior to entering the study. Not surprising given his level of consumption and tolerance, Nathan's score on the SADQ-C indicated a high level of impaired control of drinking. On the SOCRATES, Nathan was low to medium with respect to problem recognition, medium to high on ambivalence about changing, and, ironically like Jim above, medium to high on taking steps.

Case 3, "Lisa"

Lisa entered the study as a 67 year-old Caucasian female. Between the time when she was enrolled and her first appointment, Lisa was diagnosed with breast cancer. Despite the obviously difficult nature of that time for her, she nonetheless decided to continue her participation in the study. At baseline, Lisa reported a steady drinking pattern consisting of 17 drinks per week on average (consisting of wine and other spirits). This put her in the 96th percentile for women. Her estimated peak weekly BAC was 59mg% (.059). Lisa was 18 years old when she took her first drink, and indicated that this was also the age when she first became intoxicated. She indicated that alcohol had never caused her any major problems, and demonstrated little to no evidence of tolerance to alcohol.

Lisa had an unremarkable history of illicit drug use, and only indicated using marijuana experimentally when she was much younger. She had no immediate family history of drinking problems. Her score on the AUDIT of 21, however, was in the high range, indicating that she may have been experiencing at least some negative consequences associated with her drinking, although her total score on the DrInC indicated low, and very low consequences for both lifetime and for the 3 months prior to entering the study. Her score on the SADQ-C indicated that she had low to medium impaired control over drinking. Finally, Lisa's scores on the SOCRATES indicated that relative to others seeking treatment for alcohol problems, Lisa's level of recognition (of problems related to the use of alcohol) was relatively low. Her level of ambivalence was also low, as were her score on the "taking steps" subscale. Overall, despite the fact that Lisa came into the study as a moderately heavy drinker, she reported few major functional problems, and did not consider her drinking habits to be in dire need of change. However, the fact that she did self-refer to the study would indicate that there was at least some intrinsic motivation for her to do so.

Case Formulation

Despite significant differences in initial case presentation across the 3 individuals outlined above, all were self-referred respondents to a treatment study with a fixed protocol for anyone interested in learning more about their drinking. As a result, traditional, ideographic, case formulation was not utilized to establish individual treatment plans. Each of the 3 participants used the DCU program one time for about 2 hours, and were in the group that presented for only 2 distal follow-up appointments at 1 and 12 months to assess outcomes.

Course of Treatment

As discussed briefly above, the DCU consists of integrated Assessment, Feedback, and Decision Making modules. Each aspect of the program will now be described in greater detail.

Assessment Module

When drinkers begin the DCU, they are first asked to complete the Alcohol Use Disorders Identification Test (AUDIT) prior to registration. This allows new users to screen themselves and make an informed decision as to whether it might be worth their time to go through the program. Based on Project MATCH data, the program then provides feedback on whether they scored low, medium, high, or very high in terms of their risk and experienced alcohol-related consequences. Individuals who score as having mild problems or higher (8+) on the AUDIT are advised that they might benefit from using the program and are invited to proceed. Registration is then necessary to personalize the program's interactive responses to the user. Registration requires the user's first name, a password, age, gender, weight and height. The latter are used to calculate peak blood alcohol concentrations (BACs) in the Feedback Module. Because the entire program (Assessment, Feedback, and Decision Making) will take, on average, one to two hours to complete, the user has the option of exiting the program at any time after having registered and returning at a later point to resume working on it. In practice, however, all clients went through the program from start to finish in one session.

Once new users complete the registration process, the Assessment Module is prefaced with an initial decisional balance exercise. In face-to-face brief motivational interventions, a decisional balance is often used as a way to acknowledge ambivalence that may be present in individuals with alcohol problems when they consider changing. The decisional balance exercise compares the "good things and the not-so-good things" (Miller & Rollnick, 2002) of drinking. Acknowledging that there are things about drinking that the individual likes (the "good things") makes it easier for them to consider and explore the consequences of their drinking (the "not so good things"). In this exercise, users can choose from lists of positive and negative things about drinking or type in their own. When they submit the information, it is saved and brought up later in the Decision Making Module.

On the main page of the Assessment Module is a list of questionnaires the user could choose to take. These include the Brief Drinker Profile (BDP), the Drinker Inventory of Consequences, the Severity of Alcohol Dependence Questionnaire, Community Sample (SADQ-C), or the Stages of Change Readiness and Treatment Eagerness Survey (SOCRATES). References for these instruments can be found in Squires & Hester (2002). When the program is used as an adjunct to other treatment, the health care provider can recommend that a client complete a particular instrument (or combination of instruments) which then show up on the main page highlighted in red. In the web application all questionnaires are highlighted. Once an assessment instrument has been completed, a check mark appears on the screen next to it. By clicking on the check mark in the Windows application, the user can receive immediate feedback for that instrument, or they can wait until they complete all applicable assessments and enter the Feedback Module, which is what most people did.

Feedback Module

The Feedback Module has the most potential for generating resistance and defensiveness in users because they often receive information that is discrepant with their views of their drinking. For instance, in face-to-face brief motivational intervention feedback sessions it is common for clients to express disbelief when told how their drinking compares to the overall U.S. adult population. Minimizing resistance requires a delicate balance between empathic responses to their reactions while not dismissing or invalidating the results. The program accomplishes this by providing a number of automatic links to different forms where it can respond to the most common reactions. Here is an example of the program's response to a user reacting to his or her quantity/frequency feedback by indicating that the results are "higher than I expected":

> "It can be surprising and (for some) discouraging to see that they fall higher on the alcohol use scale than they expected. Some people think there might be a mistake in the way results are calculated. (Feel free to review your answers in the BDP questionnaire.) Remember that you are being compared to other men for the entire U.S. adult population. Also, it is not uncommon for people to socialize with others who drink the same as --or more-- than they do. Think about which, if any, of these reactions apply to you."

The program also anticipates discrepancies between feedback from different instruments (e.g., heavy drinking compared to the general population but low levels of problems relative to individuals in treatment) and provides links to appropriate responses. In structuring the feedback process, the program offers users a "Guided Tour" option on the main feedback page that will literally "walk" them through feedback specific to each of the assessments they complete. Users can also select feedback from specific instruments as well.

Decision Making Module

Once the user has completed the Feedback Module, they can begin the Decision Making Module. This module starts with a "Readiness Ruler." The Readiness Ruler is presented as a slide bar control with a pointer the user clicks and drags along a continuum from "Not at all Ready" to "Really Ready to Change." The program then branches depending on where the individual indicates he or she is in considering change. If the individual is "Not at all Ready" and has taken all the assessment instruments, then he or she is given the options of printing their feedback summary and the lists they created in the program (e.g., the initial decisional balance exercise) or viewing the Project MATCH pamphlet Alcohol and You before exiting the program. If the individual is "Unsure," the program proceeds with a second, more detailed Decisional Balance exercise. If the individual is "Really Ready to Change" the program skips this second decisional balance exercise and proceeds directly with negotiating goals of change and helping the user develop a change plan.

The Decisional Balance Exercise

This is a computerized version of what is used in Guided Self-Change. It asks the user to consider the importance of various aspects of the feedback he or she has received and to rank the order of their importance. These reasons for changing are compared to what the user likes about his or her drinking (the "good things" from the initial decisional balance exercise). This results in a two-column form that contrasts the reasons for changing versus the reasons for not changing. The user is asked to consider whether the reasons for changing outweigh the reasons for not changing. Once completed, the program again asks the individual to decide whether he or she is ready to change. If the individual is still undecided, the program respectfully asks the user to consider what he or she has learned in the program and to talk about it with close family members and his or her therapist, if appropriate. It also asks the user to consider a series of questions found to be related to long-term sobriety (Fletcher, 2001). In the event that the user is not working in conjunction with a treatment provider, the program also invites the individual to return and reconsider after having given the matter some thought. If the individual still decides not to change, he or she is offered the same exit option discussed in the previous paragraph. If, however, the decision to change is made, the program then proceeds with negotiating goals of change.

Negotiating Goals of Change

Consistent with the FRAMES components of brief motivational interventions, the DCU offers individuals a menu of options for both how they are going to change their drinking and how they can accomplish that goal. Although abstinence is the safest way to avoid alcohol-related problems, it is often a goal rejected by individuals with less severe alcohol-related problems. In addition, empirical data show that moderate drinking is an achievable goal for many such drinkers. Therefore, an exploration of this goal is appropriate. If the individual chooses moderation as a goal of change, the program offers to take him or her through a section that defines moderate drinking, contraindications to it, and an offer to take the Michigan Alcoholism Screening Test (MAST) to determine their long-term chances of success with moderation. Hester and colleagues included the MAST because of its ability to predict success with moderate drinking 2-8 years after training (Miller, Leckman, Delaney, & Tinkcom, 1992).

Developing Alternatives and a Plan of Change

Once a user has chosen a goal of change, the program offers to help them figure out how they will achieve and maintain those changes. This section begins with a variation of Miller's New Roads exercise (Miller & Pechacek, 1987) and then proceeds to the Change Plan worksheet used in Project MATCH. At the end of the program users are presented with a link to a page on our web site (www.behaviortherapy.com) that provides resources to help them achieve their goals. In addition to listing therapists who work with clients seeking to moderate their drinking, we also link to Moderation Management and Self-Management and Recovery Training (SMART) and to other self-help materials. Lastly, once the user has completed the program, whether or not they have chosen to change, a summary of each of the worksheets and feedback from all completed assessments automatically prints so that they have a hard-copy reference of their work with the program.

Outcome and Prognosis

Case 1, "Jim"

As you may recall, at baseline, Jim was a steady pattern drinker, and was consuming 72 standard drinks per week with an estimated peak BAC of 350mg% (.35). While Jim reported being abstinent at the 1-month follow-up, for the 30 days prior to his 12-month follow-up, Jim reported continued steady pattern drinking, but at the much lower rate of 24 standard drinks per week. His corresponding peak BAC had also reduced substantially to 143mg% (.14) based on consumption of 6, 12oz. beers over a two-hour period of time.

With respect to Jim's level of dependence on alcohol, his SADQ-C score continued to indicate that he had a medium to high level of impaired control over drinking, but that the consequences associated with use were dramatically lower across a number of areas (interpersonal, physical, etc.) outlined by the DrInC. In addition, his score on the AUDIT dropped from 28 (very high) at baseline, to 19 (high) at 12-month follow-up.

When Jim was asked to describe the impact, if any, he felt as though the program had on his drinking, he responded that the program helped him to think both more openly, and critically, of his drinking, and the negative role that it was having on his life. When asked about the period of abstinence present at the 1-month follow-up, and why he resumed drinking by the 12-month follow-up, Jim responded that he began drinking again after the events of September 11th. He also reported resuming his use of chewing tobacco at the same time (he had initially quit both drinking, and use of tobacco after using the program). Despite the fact that Jim continues to drink, he began seeing a therapist to address his continued use of alcohol, and had attended two appointments at the time of the 12-month follow-up.

Case 2, "Nathan"

At baseline, Nathan, reported being homeless for two-thirds of the 90 days prior to entering the study, and was drinking episodically with heavier episodes of 25 standard drinks in a single day. At 12-month follow-up, Nathan had been abstinent for 7 months. Even at the 1-month follow-up, he had dramatically reduced his intake to 14 standard drinks over an entire month (2 beers over 2 hours, a total of 7 times) with an estimated peak BAC of only 3mg% (.03), down from a staggering 429mg% (.429). In addition, he reported no homeless days for the 3 months prior to the 12-month follow-up, and was living with his sister, while looking for work.

Because Nathan reported being abstinent for 7 months prior to the 12-month follow-up, information from the AUDIT, DrInC, and SADQ-C where not applicable at 12-month follow-up. Data from the SOCRATES, however, indicated that Nathan was very low with respect to ambivalence about changing, compared to a medium level of ambivalence at baseline. His scores on recognition and taking steps were similar at 12-month follow-up to those at baseline.

While Nathan's progress in reducing his drinking (among other changes) was remarkable, data from the two follow-up periods fail to tell the whole story. When asking Nathan what, if any, role the program played in his changes, Nathan revealed that within a couple of months of the 1-month follow-up, he had actually resumed a drinking level similar to that at baseline. However, during one of his heavy binges, Nathan was hit by a car and hospitalized for several days. Nathan reported that while he was in the hospital he frequently thought about the information he learned from the DCU and realized that if he didn't make some permanent changes he would remain at high risk for other injuries, or even death. He stated that the program helped him to consider aspects of his drinking that he hadn't previously thought of, and indicated that the long-term effect of the information gained through the program helped him to make the eventual commitment to abstinence. In addition to living with his sister while he searched for employment, Nathan was also attending Alcoholics Anonymous and other related support groups weekly at the time of his 12-month follow-up, and reported feeling much better physically.

Case 3, "Lisa"

As you may recall, Lisa had just been diagnosed with breast cancer the week of her first appointment to use the program. At baseline, she reported a steady pattern of 17 standard drinks per week with a corresponding estimated peak BAC of 59mg% (.059). At 12-month follow-up, Lisa's consumption had not changed appreciably. She continued to consume 14 standard drinks per week. However, her estimated peak BAC had increased from 59mg% to 91mg% (.091) indicating a higher intensity (rate) of drinking.

Lisa's score on the AUDIT also indicated an increase in alcohol-related problems as it went from the very low range to a score of 17 (high) by 12-month follow-up. Associated drinking-related consequences as reported on the DrInC did not, however, indicate significant problems across the 3 months prior to her 12-month follow-up. In fact, despite evidence to the contrary, she also reported less impaired control over drinking than she did at baseline, and her ambivalence about change score increased from the low range at baseline and 1-month follow-up, to medium at 12 months.

When asking Lisa about the impact (if any) the program had for her, she indicated (not surprisingly) that the last year had been very difficult for her. In addition to having been diagnosed with, and treated for, breast cancer, she had also lost her daughter suddenly. While she reported having made concerted efforts to change her drinking, including an attempt to quit "cold turkey," she was simply unable to make the kinds of changes that she wanted to.

She said that she had originally expected the software program to be more directive or problem solving, but that even though it wasn't what she had expected, it did help to open her eyes to the extent of her drinking-related issues. At the time of the 12-month follow-up, Lisa had begun seeing a therapist to address both emotional and addiction issues. Figure 1 illustrates progress for each of the 3 cases described in terms of average weekly consumption across the 3 assessment periods.

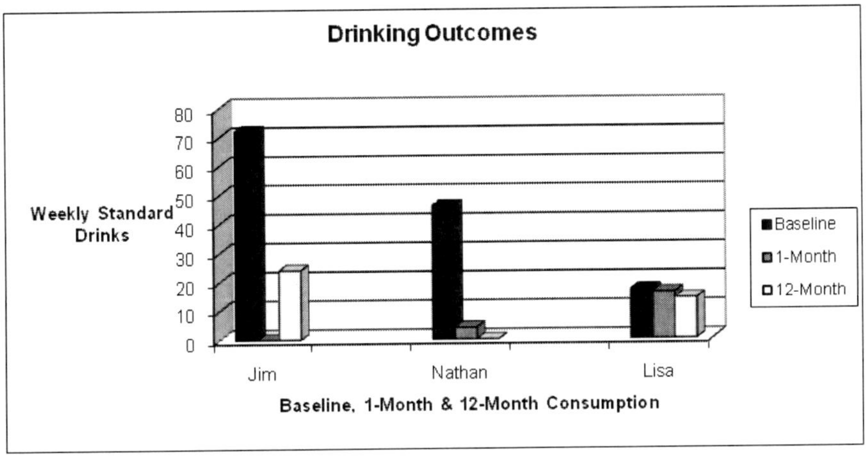

Figure 2.1. Drinking Outcomes.

Clinical Issues and Summary

These three case illustrations are examples of the range of drinkers Hester and colleagues saw in their clinical trial of the DCU. Outcomes range from relatively unchanged (Lisa) to remarkable (Nathan). For Jim, the DCU initially motivated him to become abstinent. He relapsed after the terrorist attacks of September 11, but at 12-month follow-up his consumption level and peak BACs were a third of his baseline drinking. We are encouraged that he has begun seeing a therapist to address his drinking, which is still putting him at risk for further alcohol-related problems. Similarly, Lisa, whose drinking was relatively unchanged, has begun seeing a therapist to deal with her emotional and alcohol-related issues. Nathan also was pursuing support but from a mutual help group, A.A. Each has taken additional steps to either make further gains or to maintain them. We think that the DCU acted as a catalyst for these clients, motivating them to change. It also resulted in their seeking additional assistance. Rather than replacing therapy or therapists, it would seem that the DCU facilitated their seeking professional or mutual help group assistance.

As Hester and colleagues collected the 12-month follow-up data on the clients in their study, they were struck by the positive outcomes both in drinking and alcohol-related consequences they saw overall. (Current outcome data will be available on their web site at www.behaviortherapy.com.) Most heavy drinkers who were motivated enough to contact them for a confidential evaluation and feedback of their drinking derived benefit from using the DCU. It increased their motivation for change. The authors do not know what percentage of the heavy drinking population at large fit this category, but research clearly shows that both heavy and moderate problem drinkers can benefit from brief motivational interventions whether the goal is abstinence or moderation. To have software programs that can motivate such individuals is exciting.

In their initial research application, Hester proposed to develop a web application, also called the Drinker's Check-up. Hester have developed that application (www.drinkerscheckup.com) and see it as a cost-effective way to reach many problem drinkers. If your clinical practice is typical of most, approximately one quarter of your clients may be drinking heavily enough that their drinking is interfering with their progress in treatment for other concerns. Providing clients that have drinking problems, whether this is the focus of treatment or not, with a brief motivational intervention such as the DCU can improve the quality of their lives and reduce barriers to progress for other presenting problems as well.

Smoking

According to Marks et al., (2007):

"Seven stop-smoking CP systems were evaluated in ten studies including five RCTs. A phone-IVr system recruited via worksite and media ads. The other systems were net-based and invited website visitors to register with stop-smoking sites giving tailored information, education, email prompts and support and in some cases an online discussion group and other peer support. The systems were tested in four RCTs and four non-RCTs. Subjects mostly enrolled without a diagnostic screen and most dropped out prematurely. How to retain a higher proportion is still unclear. Study durations ranged from 1 to 12 months. In two RCTs having computer-information controls, smoking fell more by three months with CP, though only a small minority were abstinent. Huge numbers of smokers can access net stop-smoking systems. As only a small minority of all smokers actually use such systems, formal cost-effectiveness studies are needed to judge the overall value of the gains achieved (p. 137).

Smoking

Tobacco use is prevalent among people living with bipolar disorder. Prochaska, Reyes, Schroeder, Daniels, et al., (2011) examined tobacco use, attempts to quit, and tobacco-related attitudes and intentions among 685 individuals with bipolar disorder who smoked $\geq$ 100 cigarettes in their lifetime. Data were collected online through the website of the Depression and Bipolar Support Alliance, a mood disorder peer-support network. The sample was 67% female, 67% aged 26 to 50, and 89% Caucasian; 87% were current smokers; 92% of current smokers smoked daily, averaging 19 cigarettes/day (SD = 11). The sample began smoking at a mean age of 17 years (SD = 6) and smoked a median of 7 years prior to bipolar disorder diagnosis. Among current smokers, 74% expressed a desire to quit; intent to quit smoking was unrelated to current mental health symptoms [$\chi^2(3) = 5.50$, $p = 0.139$]. Only 33% were advised to quit smoking by a mental health provider, 48% reported smoking to treat their mental illness, and 96% believed being mentally healthy was important for quitting. Ex-smokers (13% of sample) had not smoked for a median of 2.7 years; 48% quit 'cold turkey.'

Most ex-smokers (64%) were in poor or fair mental health when they quit smoking. At the time of the survey, however, more ex-smokers described their mental health as in recovery than current smokers [57% versus 40%; $\chi^2(3) = 11.12$, $p = 0.011$]. Most smokers living with bipolar disorder are interested in quitting. The Internet may be a useful cessation tool for recruiting and potentially treating smokers with bipolar disorder who face special challenges when trying to quit and rarely receive cessation treatment from their mental health providers.

Smoking Cessation

Tobacco use remains widespread in every nation in the world. Worldwide, >1.3 billion people use tobacco products (McDaniel & Stratton, 2006). Many smokers who attempt to quit need cessation assistance such as education, motivation, counseling, and pharmacologic treatments, but many lack access to these resources because of geographic isolation, economic constraints, and cultural barriers. As global Internet use continues to grow, Internet-based smoking cessation programs are a promising strategy for reaching smokers world-wide. The purpose of this article was to examine Internet-based initiatives to assist smokers to quit. The advantages and disadvantages of this type of forum, the likely effectiveness in achieving smoking cessation, and the impact on clinical and cost outcomes are discussed. The primary advantage of Internet-based smoking cessation initiatives is their potential public health reach. Disadvantages included the potential for privacy and security breaches, concerns about inferior quality of information, and failure of websites to utilize online technologies. Internet-based smoking cessation programs can extend the clinical encounter, in essence allowing the provider to offer 'virtual' support to the patient who is attempting to quit smoking. The potential of Internet technology to reach large numbers of smokers and provide reliable information for quitting is only beginning to be realized. Few studies have rigorously examined the question of efficacy, and many questions remain unanswered.

To illustrate the important features of Internet-based smoking cessation initiatives, this review evaluated existing online programs. A smoking cessation program was defined as a structured, multi-component treatment plan specifically designed to aid in quitting. Twelve websites were identified from an Internet search (using an Internet search engine) that met our criteria. The interactive capabilities of Internet applications show great promise for customizing a smoking cessation plan 'on-the-fly' for individuals seeking support in quitting, but few websites offer programs that incorporate tailored approaches. Thus, patients should look to healthcare providers to help them understand the benefits and limitations of Internet-based information resources for smoking cessation.

This important study described a novel approach to the identification of the motivation processes in text data extracted from an internet support group (ISG) for smoking cessation (Johnsen, Vambheim, Wynn, & Wangberg, 2014). Based on the previous findings that a prevention focus might be more relevant to maintaining behavior change, it was hypothesized that: (1) language use (i.e., the use of emotional words) signaling a promotion focus would be dominant in the initiating stages of the ISG, and (2) that the proportion of words signaling a prevention focus would increase over time (*See T. E. Higgins' work on this distinction, author*). Data were collected from the ISG site, spanning four years of forum activity and were analyzed using the Linguistic Inquiry and Word Count application (*See James Pennebaker's work on this method, L'Abate & Sweeney, 2011*).The first hypothesis—of promotion focus dominance in the initial stages—was not supported during year one. However, for all the other years measured, the data showed that a prevention failure was more dominant compared with a promotion failure. These results indicated that content analysis could be used to investigate motivational and language-driven processes in ISG. Understanding the interplay between self-regulation, lifestyle change, and modem communication channels could be of vital importance in providing the public with better care services and interventions.

To test the feasibility and efficacy of an internet program for smoking cessation during and after inpatient treatment in rehabilitation centers (Haug, Meyer, & John, 2011). A total of 7574 consecutively admitted inpatients from three German rehabilitation centers were assessed for smoking status. Daily smokers or former daily smokers who regularly used the internet and e-mail were proactively invited for study participation. Out of 749 eligible patients, 477 (64%) participated in the study and were randomly assigned to an intervention or an assessment only control group based on the calendar week of admission. Patients of the intervention group had the possibility to use an internet program for smoking cessation for a period of six months. The program provided at least one but up to seven individual counseling sessions through a computer expert system, informational websites and a message board. At six-months follow-up, seven-day point prevalence smoking abstinence was twice as high in the intervention group as in the control group (OR=2.0; CI 1.1-3.8; p=.02). Apparently, proactive recruitment of smokers in combination with the provision of an internet program for smoking cessation allowed for an inexpensive and effective smoking cessation support during and after inpatient rehabilitation treatment.

The objective of this study was to evaluate the effectiveness of individually tailored smoking cessation advice letters as an adjunct to telephone counseling and generic self-help materials (Sutton & Gilbert, 2007). The design consisted of a randomized controlled trial in the UK Quitline. Participants were a total of 1508 current smokers and recent ex-smokers. The control group received usual care (telephone counseling and an information pack sent through the post). The intervention group received in addition a computer-generated individually tailored advice letter. Main outcome measures All outcomes were assessed at 6-month follow-up. The primary outcome measure was self-reported prolonged abstinence for at least 3 months. Secondary outcomes were self-reported prolonged abstinence for at least 1 month and 7-day and 24-hour point-prevalence abstinence. For the sample as a whole, quit rates did not differ significantly between the two conditions. However, among the majority (n = 1164) who were smokers at baseline, quit rates were consistently higher in the intervention group: prolonged abstinence for 3 months, 12.2% versus 9.0% [odds ratio (OR) = 1.40, 95% confidence interval (CI) = 0.96–2.04, P = 0.080); prolonged abstinence for 1 month, 16.4% versus 11.3% (OR = 1.53, 95% CI = 1.09–2.15, P = 0.013); 7-day point-prevalence abstinence, 18.9% versus 12.7% (OR = 1.59, 95% CI = 1.15–2.19, P = 0.004); 24-hour point-prevalence abstinence, 20.9% versus 15.4% (OR = 1.45, 95% CI = 1.07–1.96, P = 0.015). The results for the smokers are encouraging in showing a small but useful effect of the tailored letter on quit rate. Versions of the tailoring program could be used on the web and in general practices, pharmacies and primary care trusts.

Dallery, Raiff, and Grabinski (2013) evaluated an Internet-based contingency management intervention to promote smoking cessation. Participants in the contingent group (n = 39) earned vouchers contingent on video confirmation of breath carbon monoxide (CO) ≤ 4 parts per million (ppm). Earnings for participants in the noncontingent group (n = 38) were independent of CO levels. Goals and feedback about smoking status were provided on participants' homepages. The median percentages of negative samples during the intervention in the noncontingent and contingent groups were 25% and 66.7%, respectively. There were no significant differences in absolute CO levels or abstinence at 3- and 6-month follow-ups. Compared to baseline, however, participants in both groups reduced CO by an estimated 15.6 ppm during the intervention phases. The results suggested that the contingency for negative COs promoted higher rates of abstinence during treatment, and that other elements of the system, such as feedback, frequent monitoring, and goals, may reduce smoking.

Smoking Cessation-Videoconferencing

An article providing an historical background on smoking research and smoking cessation offline is available (DeAngelis, 204). In spite of this background, large-group behavioral smoking cessation interventions are effective for helping people quit smoking, but have not been evaluated using videoconferencing technology for rural and remote participants who have no access to in-person cessation programs (Carlson, Lounsberry, Maciejewski, Wright, Collacutt, Taenzer, 2012). The objectives of this study were to provide and evaluate an evidence-based group smoking cessation program for rural/remote smokers wishing to quit through a Telehealth videoconferencing link at their local Health Centre. Methods: From September 2005 through April 2008, eight separate eight-session, 4 month long smoking cessation group programs were offered both in person to urban participants in Calgary and at up to six rural sites simultaneously via Telehealth videoconferencing. Quit rates were assessed at program completion, 6 and 12 month follow-up. Participants also provided evaluations of the program and technology. Results: 554 smokers participated in the program: 370 in Calgary and 184 at various remote sites. Sixteen Telehealth sites participated from across Alberta and one site from the Northwest Territories. After program completion, continuous abstinence rates using the most conservative intent-to-treat method were 27.5% in Calgary and 25.5% for the rural Telehealth sites. Quit numbers were much higher using only Available Data at 39.2% for Calgary and 37.2% for the rural sites. Similar rates were maintained over the 12-month follow-up. Program evaluations were positive. Conclusions: It is possible to offer effective smoking cessation to small groups of patients in rural or remote locations through Telehealth videoconferencing technology, which produces quit rates similar to in-person groups.

Substance Abuse

The purpose of this multisite clinical trial was to evaluate the effectiveness of a web-based version of the Community Reinforcement Approach, plus motivational incentives, within community-based, outpatient substance abuse treatment (Campbell, Miele, Nunes, McCrimmon, & Chitza, 2012). . This ongoing study is being conducted within the National Drug Abuse Treatment Clinical Trials Network, funded by the National Institute on Drug Abuse. Midway through the enrollment of 500 participants, the study is being implemented in 10 treatment programs across the United States. Information is provided on design, sample, intervention and technology, and preliminary lessons learned.

Drug craving has purportedly been linked to relapse and to substance use. For over two decades, cue reactivity has been a viable method to assess craving and physiological reactions to drug stimuli (Bordnick, Graap, Copp, Brooks, & Ferrer, 2005). However, traditional cue reactivity has faced the following limitations: austere situations or stimuli, lack of complex cues, lack of standardization, and limited generalization outside of the lab setting. In order to improve cue methodologies, a virtual reality (VR) nicotine cue reactivity assessment system (VR-NCRAS) was developed and tested in a controlled experimental trial. Ten nicotine dependent smokers were exposed to VR smoking cues and VR neutral cues in a standardized, timed, computer controlled experiment. Subjective craving and physiological responses were recorded and compared across VR-NCRAS stimuli. Subjective cigarette craving increased significantly and corresponding physiological reactivity was observed in response to VR smoking cues. VR neutral cues did not result in subjective or physiological changes consistent with craving. Implications of these findings on substance abuse research and treatment were discussed.

Virtual Reality Approaches

Virtual reality (VR) cue environments have been developed and successfully tested in nicotine, cocaine, and alcohol abusers. Aims in the current article include the development and testing of a novel VR cannabis cue reactivity assessment system (Bordnick, Copp, Traylor, Graap, Carter, Walton, & Ferrer, 2009). It was hypothesized that subjective craving levels and attention to cannabis cues would be higher in VR environments with cannabis cues compared to VR neutral environments. Twenty non-treatment-seeking current cannabis smokers participated in the VR cue trial. During the VR cue trial, participants were exposed to four virtual environments that contained audio, visual, olfactory, and vibrotactile sensory stimuli. Two VR environments contained cannabis cues that consisted of a party room in which people were smoking cannabis and a room containing cannabis paraphernalia without people. Two VR neutral rooms without cannabis cues consisted of a digital art gallery with nature videos. Subjective craving and attention to cues were significantly higher in the VR cannabis environments compared to the VR neutral environments. These findings indicate that VR cannabis cue reactivity may offer a new technology-based method to advance addiction research and treatment.

The use of virtual reality (VR) programs in behavioral science research has been gaining prominence over the past several years. In the field of substance abuse, VR cue reactivity programs have been successfully tested for feasibility in nicotine and cocaine dependent samples (Bordnick, Traylor, Copp, Graap, Carter, Ferrer, & Walton, 2008). Seeking to expand VR applications in alcohol cue research, a novel VR alcohol cue reactivity assessment system incorporating visual, auditory, and olfactory stimuli was developed and tested. In a controlled trial, 40 non-treatment-seeking drinkers with alcohol use disorders were exposed to VR alcohol cue environments. Subjective craving, attention to alcohol cues, and level of presence (realism of experience) in VR were assessed across the environments. Overall, subjective craving for alcohol increased across the VR alcohol-related cue environments versus VR neutral cue environments. Participants reported high levels of presence in VR, indicating that the environments were perceived as realistic and compelling. These initial findings support the use of VR based cue reactivity environments for use in alcohol cue-based treatment and research.

Internet Addictions

Many today suffer from an imbalance between life and life on the screen (Essig, T. (2012). When extreme, such as excessive gaming, clinicians retreat to familiar explanations, such as "Internet addiction." But the addiction concept is of limited value, limiting both research and treatment options. This article discusses an alternative. Pathological overuse is seen as a failed solution in which people become entrapped by technology's promise of delivering that which only life can offer, such as the grand adventure simulated in World of Warcraft. A two-part treatment approach of such "simulation entrapment" is described in which both the original problem and the entrapment are treated, the former by traditional psychodynamic psychotherapy and the later by highlighting differences between the technologically mediated experience and traditional experiences of being bodies together. The case of a college student suffering from pathological shame with excessive gaming as the failed solution is offered as an illustration.

Problem Gamblers

This paper reported on one of the first ever studies to evaluate the effectiveness of an online help and guidance service for problem gamblers (Wood & Griffiths, 2007). The evaluation utilized a mixed methods design in order to examine both primary and secondary data relating to the client experience. In addition, the researchers posed as problem gamblers in order to obtain first-hand experience of how the service works in practice. A total of 80 participants completed an online evaluation questionnaire, and secondary data were gathered from 413 distinct clients who contacted an advisor. It was concluded that the service appears to be one of the few genuinely international guidance and 'counseling' services available to problem gamblers. Gambling online was the most preferred form of gambling and gambling location of GamAid clients. The service also appears to be favored by females more than any other comparable service. Overall, the vast majority of clients were very positive about their experience of using GamAid, although there were some minor technical difficulties. In light of the findings, the utility of using online guidance and therapeutic services was discussed.

Conclusion

Given the high drop-out rates and issues of non-compliance and avoidance of F2F TB approaches, internet-based interventions might seem more cost-effective to treat addictions. These interventions will not require tiresome F2F TB approaches that eventually may lead to high drop-out rates in the therapists themselves. This possibility leads to conclude that one cannot expect therapists trained in F2F therapy to be able to transfer to the Internet without proper and appropriate training. This issue will be discussed in Chapter 15 of this volume.

Chapter 3

ANXIETY AND PANIC DISORDERS

The purpose of this chapter is to include research on anxiety and panic disorders related to a process of internalization rather than externalization (See Chapter 6 for the latter process). Here is a paraphrase of Marks et al., (2007) findings about phobic/panic disorder:

"More computer psychotherapy (CP) systems have appeared for phobic and panic disorders than any other mental health problem. Since 1979 at least 18 CP systems for phobia/panic disorders were developed.....quite apart from immersive virtual reality (VR) displays which were not reviewed as they promote exposure therapy like photos, films, videos, etc. but do not make CP decisions or save therapist's time, though this may change soon .... The CP systems were evaluated in at least 12 open studies and 26 RCTs, mostly for panic with agoraphobia and some for social flying, spider, dental-injection, examination or mixed phobias. CP systems for phobia/panic vary hugely in mode and site of access., assumed educational level of users, therapy tasks taken on, and amount of therapist time saved. They were studied in single or larges case series, group comparisons and RCTs of varying sophistication. The CP was accessed on desktop or PC systems, CD-ROMs, DVDs, handheld devises to help homework between F2F sessions, vicarious or direct display systems and increasingly in recent years, the internet" (p. 23).

For a variety of general anxiety and emotional problems, Marks et al., *(2007) found:"... 14 computer psychotherapy systems... Only two were on the net. They were tested in a beta test, six open studies, one nonrandomized controlled study, and ten RCTs. The system functions ranged from simple teaching of relaxation to complex enhancement of counseling and stress management. Some of the systems might save therapist time. None has yet proved reliably valuable for general anxiety and emotional problems in the way which has been attained by certain computer psychotherapy systems for different clinical problems where effective therapy components have been better specified" (p. 73).*

Gallego and Emmelkamp (2012), in their review chapter, provided seven controlled studies on mixed anxiety (p. 399), six studies on PTSF (p. 400), twelve studies on panic disorder (p. 401), and ten studies on social phobia. There may be an overlap between studies included in Gallego and Emmelkamp's chapter and those included in this chapter. The Internet is increasingly used to deliver treatment programs for common mental disorders.

However, little is known about the acceptability of online interventions. The present study used an online survey to explore levels of acceptability of Internet-based treatment programs for anxiety and depression (Gun, Titov, & Andrews, 2011). Visitors to websites operated by the Clinical Research Unit for Anxiety and Depression (CRUfAD), were invited to complete an online questionnaire during 16 weeks in 2008. Of 1543 people who began the survey, 1104 (72%) Australian health professionals and lay people completed it. Internet treatment programs for people with mild or moderate symptoms were more acceptable than programs for people with severe symptoms. There were no differences between health professionals and non-health professionals in acceptability ratings. As expected, previous users of Internet treatments reported significantly greater acceptability and preference for Internet treatments than non-users. Conclusions: Respondents rated Internet-based treatment programs as acceptable, with higher ratings from previous users. In order to facilitate implementation, program developers need to implement strategies for increasing knowledge about the efficacy and effectiveness of such programs, and engage therapists and consumers in establishing ethical and professional guidelines for their safe and responsible use.

The Swedish National Board of Health and Welfare (2010) recently issued guidelines on the diagnosis and treatment of anxiety and depression (Carlbring, Andersson, & Kaldo, 2011). This government agency, part of the Ministry of Health and Social Affairs, recommended three approaches of equal merit in the treatment of moderate depression: Internet-based cognitive behavioral therapy (CBT), standard CBT, and selective serotonin reuptake inhibitor (SSRI) medication. Internet-based CBT (iCBT) was also advocated for several other psychiatric conditions, although usually after SSRI treatment or standard CBT. It is clear that Internet-based treatment is here to stay. However, a number of issues need to be considered before optimal treatment can be provided for the ordinary patient. There are several program development issues that these companies need to consider. In addition to specific content and the way it is presented, we need to establish the best way for patients to enter the program and the best type of guidance. Internet-based treatment has several risks, including the danger of patients failing to understand the instructions or, even worse, misinterpreting key concepts, thereby carrying out the exercises incorrectly, with the treatment ending in failure and discouragement.

Finally, possibly the two most important issues of the day are the tailoring of the treatment and the prediction of response. Regarding the first issue, most Internet-based treatment programs that have been tested are specific to one diagnosis, and a patient presenting with panic disorder would, therefore, be offered the panic disorder program. The second most pressing issue is to find reliable predictors of which patients are most likely to benefit from Internet-based treatment. This would enable us to offer unsuitable patients another treatment option immediately instead of allowing them to try and then fail with Internet-based therapy, leaving them with a sense of worthlessness and hopelessness. Another area in need of expansion is the testing of mediator and moderator effects. Even though there are step-by-step guides, there still is much confusion regarding this. Essentially, it means that we should move beyond the testing of only direct effects and also include the analysis of indirect effects.

Previous studies on Internet-based treatment with minimal to moderate therapist guidance have shown promising results for a number of specific diagnoses (Carlbring, Maurin, Törngren, Linna, Eriksson, Sparthan, & Andersson, 2011). The aim of this study was to test a new approach to Internet treatment that involves tailoring the treatment according to the patient's unique characteristics and comorbidities. A total of 54 participants, regardless of specific anxiety diagnosis, were included after an in-person, semi-structured diagnostic interview and randomized to a 10 week treatment program or to a control group. Treatment consisted of a number of individually-prescribed modules in conjunction with online therapist guidance. Significant results were found for all dependent measures both immediately following treatment and at 1 and 2 year intervals. Mean between-group effect size including measures of anxiety, depression and quality of life was Cohen's d = 0.69 at post-treatment, while the mean within-group effect size was d = 1.15 at post-treatment and d = 1.13 and d = 1.04 at 1 and 2 year follow-up respectively. The tentative conclusion drawn from these results is that tailoring the Internet-based therapy can be a feasible approach in the treatment of anxiety in a homogeneous population.

This study evaluated the efficacy of a brief version of an internet-administered transdiagnostic CBT protocol, the Wellbeing Program (Titov et al., 2011), designed to treat three anxiety disorders and major depression within the same program (Dear, Titov, Schwencke, Andrews, Johnston, Craske, & McEvoy, 2011). This brief version included the same core CBT skills as the original, but condensed the materials from 8 to 5 online lessons, reduced the duration of treatment from 10 to 8 weeks and did not include an online forum. Thirty-two individuals with a principal diagnosis of major depression, generalized anxiety disorder, panic disorder or social phobia received CBT-based online educational lessons, homework assignments, weekly contact from a clinical psychologist and automated emails. Eighty-one percent of participants completed the lessons within the 8 week program. Post-treatment and 3-month follow-up data were collected from 28/32 and 31/32 participants respectively. Participants improved significantly on the Depression Anxiety and Stress Scales - 21 Item, Patient Health Questionnaire - 9 Item, and Generalized Anxiety Disorder - 7 Item scales, with corresponding within-group effect sizes (Cohen's d) at follow-up of 1.05, .73, and .95, respectively. Participants rated the procedure as highly acceptable with gains of a similar magnitude as those found for the original program, but less time was spent per participant by the clinician in the present trial (mean = 44.61 min, SD = 34.45) compared to the original program (mean = 84.76 min, SD = 50.37). These results provided additional support for the efficacy of trans-diagnostic iCBT in the treatment of anxiety and depressive disorders and indicate that a brief version may be of benefit.

The development of e-mental health interventions to treat or prevent mental illness and to enhance wellbeing has risen rapidly over the past decade. This development assists the public in sidestepping some of the obstacles that are often encountered when trying to access traditional face-to-face mental health care services (Klein, Meyer, Austin, & Kyrios, 2011). The objective of this study was to investigate the post treatment effectiveness of five fully automated self-help cognitive behavior e-therapy programs for generalized anxiety disorder (GAD), panic disorder with or without agoraphobia (PD/A), obsessive-compulsive disorder (OCD), posttraumatic stress disorder (PTSD), and social anxiety disorder (SAD) offered to the international public via Anxiety Online, an open-access full-service virtual psychology clinic for anxiety disorders. METHODS: We used a naturalistic participant choice, quasi-experimental design to evaluate each of the five Anxiety Online fully automated self-help e-therapy programs. Participants were required to have at least subclinical levels of one of the anxiety disorders to be offered the associated disorder-specific fully automated self-help e-therapy program. These programs are offered free of charge via Anxiety Online.

A total of 225 people self-selected one of the five e-therapy programs (GAD, n = 88; SAD, n = 50; PD/A, n = 40; PTSD, n = 30; OCD, n = 17) and completed their 12-week post treatment assessment (Klein, Meyer, Austin, & Kyrios, 2011). Significant improvements were found on 21/25 measures across the five fully automated self-help programs. At post-assessment the authors observed significant reductions on all five anxiety disorder clinical disorder severity ratings (Cohen d range 0.72-1.22), increased confidence in managing one's own mental health care (Cohen d range 0.70-1.17), and decreases in the total number of clinical diagnoses (except for the PD/A program, where a positive trend was found) (Cohen d range 0.45-1.08). In addition, we found significant improvements in quality of life for the GAD, OCD, PTSD, and SAD e-therapy programs (Cohen d range 0.11-0.96) and significant reductions relating to general psychological distress levels for the GAD, PD/A, and PTSD e-therapy programs (Cohen d range 0.23-1.16). Overall, treatment satisfaction was good across all five e-therapy programs, and post treatment assessment completers reported using their e-therapy program an average of 395.60 (SD 272.2) minutes over the 12-week treatment period. Overall, all five fully automated self-help e-therapy programs appear to be delivering promising high-quality outcomes; however, the results require replication (all single, first-time positive results require replication, italics author).

Supporting Highly Stressed Individuals

The purpose of the study was to examine the contribution made by dimensions of session-impact factors (depth and smoothness), end-of-session factors of client's mood (positivity and emotional arousal), and several textual variables (use of positive and negative emotional words; helper's and client's writing lengths) to perceived helpfulness of emotional support conversations carried on by trained, paraprofessional helpers through an Internet chat with highly distressed individuals (Barak & Bloch, 2006). Two studies were conducted at an Israeli, exclusively online emotional support service for suicidal and highly distressed people who have undergone various negative experiences (SAHAR). Study 1 compared 40 chat conversations deliberately indicated by clients as having been helpful at the termination stage of session with 40 other conversations, using expert judgments of session-impact factors, as well as objective word counts for textual variables. Study 2 examined correlations between helpers' evaluation of the sessions' helpfulness to clients in 60 (other) chat support conversations and session-impact factors and textual variables.

The findings of Study 1 showed that all four impact factors significantly differentiated between helpful and other conversations, while textual variables did not. In Study 2, the results showed that all four session-impact factors positively correlated with session helpfulness, yielding multiple R = 0.54, as well as the length of helper's and client's writing. The implications of these studies are similar to offline counseling sessions: deep, smooth conversations that yield positive responses and arouse clients' emotions in online support are more helpful than shallow, bumping conversations that leave clients emotionally indifferent. Longer writing, by both helpers and clients, seems to be an important factor, as well.

Anxiety Disorders and Cognitive Behavioral Therapy

Internet-delivered cognitive behavior therapy commonly consists of disorder-specific modules that are based on F2F manuals. A recent development in the field is to tailor the treatment according to patient profile, which has the potential to cover comorbid conditions in association with anxiety and mood disorders. However, it could be that the patients themselves are able to decide what modules to use. Andersson, Estling, Jakobsson, Cuijpers, and Carlbring (2011) tested this possibility in an open pilot trial with 27 patients with mixed anxiety disorders. Modules were introduced with a brief description, and patients could choose which modules to use. The exception was the two first modules and the last, which involved psycho-education and relapse prevention. The treatment period lasted for 10 weeks. Results showed large within-group effect sizes, with an average Cohen's d of 0.88. In a structured clinical interview, a majority (54%) had significantly improved 10 weeks after commencing treatment. Only one person dropped out. On the basis of results of this preliminary study, the authors suggested that the role of choice and tailoring should be further explored in controlled trials and that patient choice could be incorporated into Internet-delivered treatment packages.

Fear of Public Speaking

The present research was a randomized controlled trial in which the effects of a Dutch version of «Talk to me», an Internet-based cognitive-behavioral treatment for fear of public speaking were investigated (Gallego, Emmelkamp, van der Kooij, & Mees, 2011). Forty one participants with a formal diagnosis of social phobia were assigned at random to either «Talk to me», or a waiting list control group. The group treated by an Internet-based cognitive-behavioral treatment resulted in significant improvement from pre-test to pos-test on all social phobia measures and in social and work impairment. Talk to me was significantly more effective than the control group on a number of measures: fear and avoidance to the target behaviors, fear of public speaking and work impairment. Regarding to the effect size (Cohen-d) for the measures related to social phobia the Internet treatment had a high within-group (d= 1.13) and between-groups effect size (d= .86). Results achieved with the Talk-to-me program are comparable to results of face-to-face treatment of social phobia. Finally, it is important to emphasize that Talk to me was well accepted by the participants.

Several randomized controlled studies have shown the efficacy of Internet-based self-help treatments. These studies have centered their attention on axis I (efficacy) of the Guidelines for Empirically Validated Treatments, although there are a few studies that also take into account axis II (effectiveness). The aim of the present work was to test the acceptability of an Internet-based self-help program for fear of public speaking and to compare its acceptability with the same treatment administered by a therapist (Botella, Gallego, Garcia-Palacios, Banos, Quero, & Alcaniz, 2009). Fifty-two participants suffering from social phobia were randomly selected to take part in one of these treatments. All participants reported being satisfied with the treatment received, and results did not show significant differences between both treatments. These outcomes were maintained at 12-month follow-ups.

This study described the use of a cognitive-behavioral computer-administered self-help program with minimal therapist contact for public speaking anxiety (Anderson, Zimand, Schmertz, & Ferrer, 2007). Participants (N = 10) with social phobia, as measured by a structured clinical interview, completed the self-help program in an open clinical trial. The program was delivered via a CD-ROM during individual sessions at an outpatient clinic, including 4 sessions of psycho-education/cognitive therapy and 4 sessions of exposure therapy using a virtual audience presented on a computer screen. A therapist was available in another room to answer questions and to debrief for up to 10 minutes after each session. Participants completed standardized self-report questionnaires assessing social anxiety at pretreatment, post-treatment, and 3-month follow-up. Participants also completed measures of computer usability. Results showed decreases on all self-report measures of social anxiety from pre- to post-treatment, which were maintained at follow-up (n = 8). Participants also reported that they were satisfied with treatment, that they felt improved after treatment, and that the computer program was user-friendly. This study provides preliminary evidence that a computer-administered cognitive-behavioral-based program that includes minimal therapist contact may reduce public speaking anxiety and suggests that further research with a controlled design is needed.

Agoraphobia & Panic Disorder VRE

The main goal of this study was to offer data about the efficacy of virtual reality exposure (VRE) in the treatment of panic disorder with or without agoraphobia (PDA) (Botella, García-Palacios, Villa, Baños, Quero, Alcañiz, & Riva, 2007). The study was a between-subject design with three experimental conditions (VRE group, in vivo exposure [IVE] group and waiting-list [WL] group) and repeated measures (pre-treatment, post treatment and 12 month follow-up). The treatment programs lasted 9 weekly sessions. Thirty-seven patients meeting DSM-IV criteria for PDA participated in this study. The improvement achieved using virtual exposure was superior to a WL condition and similar to that achieved using IVE. These results supported the efficacy of VRE in the treatment of PDA at short and long term. The advantages of VRE for the treatment of PDA regarding cost-benefit issues are described.

Panic Disorder CBT via Videoconferenzing

Delivering psychotherapy by videoconference could significantly increase the accessibility of empirically validated treatments. The aim of this study was to compare the effectiveness of cognitive-behavior therapy (CBT) for panic disorder with agoraphobia (PDA) when the therapy is delivered either F2F or by videoconference (Bouchard, Paquin, Payeur, & et al. (2004). A sample of 21 participants was treated either F2F or by videoconference. Results showed that CBT delivered by video-conference was as effective as CBT delivered F2F. There was a statistically significant reduction in all measures, and the number of panic-free participants among those receiving CBT by videoconference was 81% at post-treatment and 91% at the 6-month follow-up. None of the comparisons with F2F psychotherapy suggested that CBT delivered by videoconference was less effective. These results were confirmed by analyses of effect size. Participants reported the development of an excellent therapeutic alliance in videoconference as early as the first therapy session. The importance of these results for treatment accessibility was discussed. Hypotheses were proposed to explain the rapid creation of strong therapeutic alliances in videoconferencing (see Chapter 16 of this volume for further research on the therapeutic alliance, Author)

This controlled study evaluated an Internet-delivered self-help program plus minimal therapist contact via e-mail for people suffering from panic disorder (Carlbring, Westling, Ljungstrand, Ekselius, & Andersson, 2001). Out of the 500 individuals screened using the self-administered diagnostic instrument Composite International Diagnostic Interview in shortened form (World Health Organization, 1999), 41 fulfilled the inclusion criteria. These participants were randomized to either treatment via the Internet or to a waiting-list control. The main components of the treatment were psycho-education, breathing retraining, cognitive restructuring, interoceptive exposure, in vivo exposure, and relapse prevention. From pre- to post-test self-help, participants improved significantly more on almost all dimensions. The results from this experiment generally provide evidence for the continued use and development of self-help programs for panic disorder distributed via the Internet.

Social Phobia

Internet-based self-help for social phobia with minimal therapist support via email have shown efficacy in several controlled trials by independent research teams. The role and necessity of therapist guidance is, however, still largely unclear. The present study compared the benefits of a 10-week web-based unguided self-help treatment for social phobia with the same intervention complemented with minimal, although weekly, therapist support via email (Berger, Caspar, Richardson, Kneubühler, Sutter, & Andersson, 2011). Furthermore, a third treatment arm was included, in which the level of support was flexibly stepped up, from no support to email or telephone contact, on demand of the participants. Eighty-one individuals meeting diagnostic criteria for social phobia were randomly assigned to one of the three conditions. Primary outcome measures were self-report measures of symptoms of social phobia. Secondary outcome measures included symptoms of depression, interpersonal problems, and general symptomatology. Measures were taken at baseline, post-treatment, and at 6-month follow-up. Data from a telephone-administered diagnostic interview conducted at post-treatment were also included. Results showed significant symptom reductions in all three treatment groups with large effect sizes for primary social phobia measures (Cohen's $d = 1.47$) and for secondary outcome measures ($d = 1.16$). No substantial and significant between-groups effects were found on any of the measures (Cohen's $d = 00–.36$). Moreover, no difference between the three conditions was found regarding diagnosis-free status, clinically significant change, dropout rates, or adherence measures such as lessons or exercises completed. These findings indicate that Internet-delivered treatment for social phobia is a promising treatment option, whether no support is provided or with two different types of therapist guidance.

Sixty-four individuals with social phobia (social anxiety disorder) were assigned to a multimodal cognitive-behavioral treatment package or to a waiting list control group (Andersson, Carlbring, Holmstrom, Sparthan, Furmark, Nilsson-Ihrfelt, & Ekselius, 2006). Treatment consisted of a 9-week, Internet-delivered, self-help program that was combined with 2 group exposure sessions in real life and minimal therapist contact via e-mail. Results were analyzed on an intention-to-treat basis, including all randomized participants. From pre- to posttest, treated participants in contrast to controls showed significant improvement on most measured dimensions (social anxiety scales, general anxiety and depression levels, quality of life). The overall within- and between-groups effect sizes were Cohen's d = 0.87 and 0.70, respectively. Treatment gains were maintained at 1-year follow-up. The results from this study support the continued use and development of Internet-distributed, self-help programs for people diagnosed with social phobia.

Internet-delivered guided cognitive behavior therapy for social anxiety disorder has been found to generate promising short-term results, up to one year post treatment . No study has however documented longer follow-up periods. In this 30-month follow-up Carlbring, Nordgren, Furmark, and Andersson (2009) contacted 57 participants from the original study of which 77.2% (44/57) responded to the Internet-administered outcome measures and 66.7% (38/57) completed a telephone interview. Results showed large pretreatment to follow-up within-group effect sizes for the primary outcome measures (Cohen's d 1.10–1.71), and a majority (68.4%; 26/38) reported improvements in the interview. The findings suggest that the long-term effects seen in previous live treatment CBT trials can occur in Internet-delivered treatment as well.

Internet-based cognitive behavior therapy (CBT) has been shown to be a promising method to disseminate cognitive behavior therapy for social anxiety disorder (SAD). (Hedman, Furmark, Carlbring, Ljotsson, et al., 2011). Several trials have demonstrated that Internet-based CBT can be effective for SAD in the shorter term. However, the long-term effects of Internet-based CBT for SAD are less well known. The authors' objective was to investigate the effect of Internet-based CBT for SAD 5 years after completed treatment. They conducted a 5-year follow-up study of 80 persons with SAD who had undergone Internet-based CBT. The assessment comprised a diagnostic interview and self-report questionnaires. The main outcome measure was the Liebowitz Social Anxiety Scale-Self-Report (LSAS-SR). Additional measures of social anxiety were the Social Interaction Anxiety Scale (SIAS) and the Social Phobia Scale (SPS). Attrition rates were low: 89% (71/80) of the participants completed the diagnostic interview and 80% (64/80) responded to the questionnaires.

Mixed-effect models analysis showed a significant effect of time on the three social anxiety measures, LSAS-SR, SIAS, and SPS ($F(3,98\text{-}102) = 16.05 - 29.20$, $P < .001$) indicating improvement. From baseline to 5-year follow-up, participants' mean scores on the LSAS-SR were reduced from 71.3 (95% confidence interval [CI] 66.1-76.5) to 40.3 (95% CI 35.2 - 45.3). The effect sizes of the LSAS-SR were large (Cohen's d range 1.30 - 1.40, 95% CI 0.77 - 1.90). Improvements gained at the 1-year follow-up were sustained 5 years after completed treatment. Apparently, Internet-based CBT for SAD is a treatment that can result in large and enduring effects.

The present study (Shyness 7) had two aims: Firstly, to replicate an earlier trial showing that a self-guided Internet treatment for social phobia is efficacious, and secondly, to examine whether the addition of self-guided motivational enhancement strategies improves completion rates and clinical outcomes (Titov, Andrews, Schwencke, Robinson, et al., 2010). A randomized controlled trial (RCT) of self-guided Internet-based cognitive behavioral treatment (iCBT), or iCBT plus self-guided motivational enhancement strategies (iCBT+MS), was conducted. An intention-to-treat and last observation carried forward model was used for data analyses. The participants consisted of 108 volunteers with social phobia. The iCBT intervention consisted of two online lessons about symptoms and treatment of anxiety disorders and six lessons about management of social phobia (the Shyness program) with complex automated reminders.

The motivational intervention was based on traditional techniques including understanding and exploring ambivalence about change using a cost–benefit analysis, developing and resolving discrepancy between values and symptoms, and enhancing self-efficacy for change. The main outcome measures were the Social Interaction Anxiety Scale and Social Phobia Scale. More iCBT+MS group participants completed the eight lessons than iCBT group participants (75% versus 56%, respectively), but there were no between-group differences in outcome measures at post-treatment or at 3 month follow up. Large mean within-groups effect sizes (Cohen's d) for the two social phobia measures were found for both the iCBT and iCBT+ MS groups (1.1 and 0.95, respectively), which were sustained at 3 month follow up (1.06 and 1.07, respectively). Both iCBT and iCBT+MS group participants reported that the procedures were highly acceptable. Both self-guided versions of the Shyness program were reliably efficacious, confirming that people with social phobia may significantly benefit from a highly structured self-guided intervention. The addition of motivational techniques increased completion rates but did not improve clinical outcomes or acceptability.

SOCIAL ANXIETY

Guided Internet-based cognitive-behavioral self-help (ICBT) has been proven to be effective for social anxiety disorder (SAD) by several independent research groups. However, as the proportion of clinical significant change has room for improvement, new treatments should be developed and investigated. A novel treatment is attention bias modification (ABM).(Boettcher, Hasselrot, Sund, Andersson, et al., 2014). This study aimed at evaluating the combination of ABM and ICBT. We compared two groups, one group receiving ICBT and ABM targeting attentional avoidance and the other group receiving ICBT and control training. ABM and control training tasks were both based on the dot-probe paradigm. A total of 133 participants, diagnosed with SAD, were randomised to these two groups. The attention training group (N = 66) received 2 weeks of daily attention training followed by 9 weeks of ICBT. The control group (N = 67) received 2 weeks of daily control training, also followed by 9 weeks of ICBT. Social anxiety measures as well as the attention bias were assessed at pre-assessment, at week 2, and at post-treatment. Results showed no significant differences between the attention training group and the control group. Both groups improved substantially on social anxiety symptoms from pre- to post-assessment (d[sub]within[/sub] = 1.39–1.41), but showed no change in attention processes (d[sub]within[/sub] = 0.10–0.17). In this trial, the attention modification training failed to induce differential change in attention bias. Results demonstrated that the applied ABM procedure with its focus on the reduction of attentional avoidance was ineffective in the Internet-based setting. The results do not suggest that adding ABM targeting attentional avoidance to ICBT results in better outcomes than ICBT alone.

Cognitive Behavioral Therapy

Mewton, Smith, Rossouw, and Andrews (2014) provided a summary of research into internet-delivered cognitive-behavioral therapy (CBT) for anxiety disorders. The authors included 37 randomized controlled trials that examined the efficacy of CBT programs in adults (aged over 18 years), as compared with waiting list or active control. The included studies were identified by Medline searches and from reference lists, and only published data were included. Seven trials of CBT for generalized anxiety disorder, panic disorder, and social phobia were identified. Two trials for obsessive-compulsive disorder were identified, whilst one trial each was identified for hypochondriasis, specific phobia (spiders), and post-traumatic stress disorder. Finally, there were five trials that focused on transdiagnostic therapy for either a range of comorbid anxiety disorders or comorbid anxiety and depression. Between-group effect sizes were moderate to large for all disorders, and ranged from .30 to 2.53. iCBT was found to be commensurate with F2F CBT whether delivered individually or in group format. Guidance may not be necessary for iCBT to be effective for immediate gains, but may be more important in long-term maintenance of symptom improvement and maximizing patient adherence. The clinical experience of the individual providing guidance does not appear to impact treatment outcomes. Future research needs to focus on the optimal level of guidance required to generate maximum patient benefits, whilst balancing the efficient use of clinical time and resources. Evidence-based contraindications for iCBT should also be developed so that the choice of treatment modality accurately reflects patient needs. Further research should be conducted into the effective elements of iCBT, as well as the extent to which therapy enhances and advanced technology can be accommodated into established iCBT frameworks.

CBT Health Anxiety/Hypochondrisis

Hypochondriasis, characterized by severe health anxiety, is a common condition associated with functional disability. Cognitive-behavioral therapy (CBT) is an effective but not widely disseminated treatment for hypochondriasis (Hedman, Andersson, Andersson, Ljotsson, et al., 2011). Internet-based CBT, including guidance in the form of minimal therapist contact via email, could be a more accessible treatment, but no study has investigated internet-based CBT for hypochondriasis. The aim of this study was to investigate the efficacy of internet-based CBT for hypochondriasis. : A randomised controlled superiority trial with masked assessment comparing internet-based CBT (n = 40) over 12 weeks with an attention control condition (n = 41) for people with hypochondriasis. The primary outcome measure was the Health Anxiety Inventory. This trial is registrated with ClinicalTrials.gov (NCT00828152). Participants receiving internet-based CBT made large and superior improvements compared with the control group on measures of health anxiety (between-group Cohen's d range 1.52-1.62). Internet-based CBT seems an efficacious treatment for hypochondriasis that has the potential to increase accessibility and availability of CBT for hypochodriasis.

CB Group Therapy Social Anxiety

Cognitive behavioral group therapy (CBGT) is an effective, well-established, but not widely available treatment for social anxiety disorder (SAD). (Hedman, Andersson, Ljotsson, Andersson, et al., 2011). Internet-based cognitive behavior therapy (ICBT) has the potential to increase availability and facilitate dissemination of therapeutic services for SAD. However, ICBT for SAD has not been directly compared with in-person treatments such as CBGT and few studies investigating ICBT have been conducted in clinical settings. Our aim was to investigate if ICBT is at least as effective as CBGT for SAD when treatments are delivered in a psychiatric setting. These researchers conducted a randomized controlled non-inferiority trial with allocation to ICBT (n=64) or CBGT (n=62) with blinded assessment immediately following treatment and six months post-treatment. Participants were 126 individuals with SAD who received CBGT or ICBT for a duration of 15 weeks. The Liebowitz Social Anxiety Scale (LSAS) was the main outcome measure. The following non-inferiority margin was set: following treatment, the lower bound of the 95 % confidence interval (CI) of the mean difference between groups should be less than 10 LSAS-points.

Both groups made large improvements. At follow-up, 41 (64%) participants in the ICBT group were classified as responders (95% CI, 52%-76%). In the CBGT group, 28 participants (45%) responded to the treatment (95% CI, 33%-58%). At post-treatment and follow-up respectively, the 95 % CI of the LSAS mean difference was 0.68-17.66 (Cohen's d between group=0.41) and -2.51-15.69 (Cohen's d between group=0.36) favoring ICBT, which was well within the non-inferiority margin. Mixed effects models analyses showed no significant interaction effect for LSAS, indicating similar improvement across treatments (F=1.58; df=2, 219; p=.21). ICBT delivered in a psychiatric setting can be as effective as CBGT in the treatment of SAD and could be used to increase availability to CBT.

Generalized Anxiety Disorder

This RCT (N=131) compared three groups: Clinician-supported (CL) vs. Coach-supported (CO) vs. waitlist control (Control). Individuals met DSM-IV criteria for a principal diagnosis of generalized anxiety disorder (GAD), social phobia (SP) or panic disorder with or without agoraphobia (Pan/Ag).(Johnston, Titov, Andrews, Spence, et al., 2011). Treatment consisted of an 8-lesson/10 week iCBT program with weekly contact from a Clinician or Coach, and follow-up at 3-months post-treatment.

Outcomes for the pooled treatment groups (CL+CO) were superior to the Control group on measures of anxiety, depression and disability, were associated with medium to large effect sizes (Cohen's d=.76-1.44) (response rate=89-100%), and were maintained at follow-up. Significant reductions were found on disorder-specific outcomes for each of the target diagnoses, and were associated with large effect sizes. CO participants achieved similar outcomes to CL participants at post-treatment, yet had significantly lower symptom severity scores on general anxiety, panic-disorder, depression and disability at follow-up (d=.45-.46). Seventy-four percent of CO and 76% of CL participants completed the program. Less than 70 minutes of Clinician or Coach time was required per participant during the program. This trans-diagnostic iCBT course for anxiety appears to be efficacious, associated with significant change for three target disorders, and is efficacious when guided by either a Clinician or Coach.

Anxiety Prevention

This project aims to conduct a medium-term follow-up to assess the efficacy of a preventive cognitive behavioural intervention delivered via the Internet to individuals at risk of developing anxiety disorders (Kenardy, McCafferty, & Rosa, 2006). Previous work on immediate outcome indicated that the program was effective in reducing depression and anxiety-related cognitions. Forty-two university students with elevated anxiety sensitivity who were randomised either to an Internet-based program over a period of 6 weeks or a waiting list control were followed up at 6 months after intervention. As with the outcome immediately after intervention, significant treatment effects were found for anxiety-related cognitions and symptoms of depression. Long-term outcomes were related to program component satisfaction.

Agoraphobia and Panic Disorder

This study compared Panic Online (PO), an internet-based CBT intervention, to best-practice face-to-face CBT for people with panic disorder with or without agoraphobia (Kiropoulos, Klein, Austin, Gilson, et al., 2008). Eighty-six people with a primary diagnosis of panic disorder were recruited from Victoria, Australia. Participants were randomly assigned to either PO (n=46) or best practice face-to-face CBT (n=40). Effects of the internet-based CBT program were found to be comparable to those of face-to-face CBT. Both interventions produced significant reductions in panic disorder and agoraphobia clinician severity ratings, self-reported panic disorder severity and panic attack frequency, measures of depression, anxiety, stress and panic related cognitions, and displayed improvements in quality of life. Participants rated both treatment conditions as equally credible and satisfying. Participants in the face-to-face CBT treatment group cited higher enjoyment with communicating with their therapist. Consistent with this, therapists' ratings for compliance to treatment and understanding of the CBT material was higher in the face-to-face CBT treatment group. PO required significantly less therapist time than the face-to-face CBT condition.

Generalized Anxiety Disorder

It has been proposed that a persistent and pervasive tendency to avoid risks is involved in the development and maintenance of clinically significant anxiety. Few studies, however, have examined the clinical implications of risk-aversion, and particularly the association between risk-aversion and treatment outcome. The current study investigated how risk-aversion in specific domains (Social and Recreational) related to treatment outcome in a clinical sample of patients with generalized anxiety disorder (GAD) undergoing internet-delivered cognitive-behavioral therapy (CBT). Lorian, Titov, and Grisham (2012) hypothesized that: (1) risk-taking would increase as a result of treatment and (i2) risk-taking would mediate changes in symptom severity and impairment as a result of treatment. Individuals recruited online (N = 44) meeting diagnostic criteria for GAD were randomized to the treatment (n = 24) or control group (n = 20). Participants completed measures of symptom severity, impairment and risk-taking before and after treatment. Results partially confirmed the authors's hypotheses, demonstrating that participants in the treatment group significantly increased social and recreational risk-taking scores relative to the control group and risk-taking mediated treatment outcome for depression, but not for anxiety symptoms. The results of this study suggested that social and recreational risk-avoidance decreases following CBT treatment, and this change may mediate treatment outcome for depression. Clinical implications of these findings were discussed.

Panic Disorder

Guided self-help via Internet is a promising way of treating panic disorder (PD).(Nordgreen, Standal, Mannes, Haug, et al., 2010). The present study examined the effects of a self-help program via Internet with weekly therapist contact for PD after disseminated to a new country. Predictors of outcome were also examined. The study was an open trial with 27 participants with PD with or without agoraphobia as their primary diagnose. Medium to large effects on PD-symptoms were reported after treatment and at 6 months follow-up, with smaller effects on secondary outcome measures, i.e., depression, interpersonal problems, and sleep problem. The attrition rate of 30% in present study was higher than in Swedish studies. Predictor analysis showed that participants with longer duration of PD-symptoms had less improvement on all outcome measurers, whereas higher age predicted more improvement. The guided self-help program remained effective when disseminated to a new country, but the high attrition rate needs to be addressed in future studies.

Anxiety & Phobias

Virtual reality exposure therapy (VRET) is an increasingly common treatment for anxiety and specific phobias (Parsons & Rizzo, 2008). Lacking is a quantitative meta-analysis that enhances understanding of the variability and clinical significance of anxiety reduction outcomes after VRET. Searches of electronic databases yielded 52 studies, and of these, 21 studies (300 subjects) met inclusion criteria. Although meta-analysis revealed large declines in anxiety symptoms following VRET, moderator analyses were limited due to inconsistent reporting in the VRET literature. This highlights the need for future research studies that report uniform and detailed information regarding presence, immersion, anxiety and/or phobia duration, and demographics.

Subclinical Anxiety

This study evaluated the efficacy of a spiritually integrated treatment (SIT) for subclinical anxiety in the Jewish community (Rosmarin, Pargament, Pirutinsky, & Mahoney, 2010). One hundred and twenty-five self-reported religious Jewish individuals with elevated levels of stress and worry received SIT (n=36), progressive muscle relaxation (PMR, n=42), or a waitlist control condition (WLC, n=47). SIT and PMR participants accessed Internet-based treatment on a daily basis for a period of 2 weeks. All participants completed self-report assessments at pre-treatment (T1), post-treatment (T2), and 6-8-week follow-up (T3). SIT participants reported large improvements in primary (stress and worry) and secondary (depression and intolerance of uncertainty) outcomes, and moderate improvements in spiritual outcomes (positive/negative religious coping; trust/mistrust in God). SIT participants reported greater belief in treatment credibility, greater expectancies from treatment and greater treatment satisfaction than PMR participants. SIT participants also reported better improvements in both primary outcomes (stress and worry), one of two secondary outcomes (intolerance of uncertainty), and two of four spiritual outcomes (positive religious coping and mistrust in God) compared to the WLC group, whereas PMR and WLC participants did not differ on most outcomes. Results of this investigation offered initial support for the efficacy of SIT for the treatment of subclinical anxiety symptoms among religious Jews. Results further suggested that it is important to incorporate spiritual content into treatment to help facilitate the delivery of psychotherapy to religious individuals.

Anxiety and Depression

Disorder-specific cognitive behavioral therapy programs delivered over the internet (iCBT) with clinician guidance are effective at treating specific anxiety disorders and depression. The present study examined the efficacy of a trans-diagnostic iCBT protocol to treat three anxiety disorders and/or depression within the same program (the Wellbeing Program). (Titov, Dear, Schwencke, Andrews, et al., 2011). Seventy-seven individuals with a principal diagnosis of major depression, generalized anxiety disorder, panic disorder, and/or social phobia were randomly assigned to a Treatment or Waitlist Control group. Treatment consisted of CBT-based online educational lessons and homework assignments, weekly email or telephone contact from a clinical psychologist, access to a moderated online discussion forum, and automated emails. Eighty one percent of Treatment group participants completed all 8 lessons within the 10 week program. Post-treatment data were collected from 34/37 Treatment group and 35/37 Control group participants, and 3-month follow-up data were collected from 32/37 Treatment group participants. Relative to Controls, Treatment group participants reported significantly reduced symptoms of anxiety and depression as measured by the Depression Anxiety and Stress Scales-21 item, Patient Health Questionnaire-9 item, and Generalised Anxiety Disorder-7 item scales, with corresponding between-groups effect sizes (Cohen's d) at post treatment of.56,.58, and.52, respectively. The clinician spent a mean time of 84.76 min (SD = 50.37) per person over the program. Participants rated the procedure as highly acceptable, and gains were sustained at follow-up. These results provide preliminary support for the efficacy of trans-diagnostic iCBT in the treatment of anxiety and depressive disorders.

PANIC DISORDER

Guided Internet-based cognitive behavior therapy (ICBT) for panic disorder has been shown to be efficacious in several randomized controlled trials. However, the effectiveness of the treatment when delivered within routine psychiatric care has not been studied. The aim of this study was to investigate the effectiveness of ICBT for panic disorder within the context of routine psychiatric care. Hedman, Ljótsson, Rück, Bergström, et al., (2013) conducted a cohort study investigating all patients (n = 570) who had received guided ICBT for panic disorder between 2007 and 2012 in a routine care setting at an out- patient psychiatric clinic providing Internet-based treatment. The primary outcome measure was the Panic Disorder Severity Scale-Self-report (PDSS- SR). Results: Participants made large improvements from screening and pretreatment assessments to post-treatment (Cohen's d range on the PDSS- SR = 1.07–1.55). Improvements were sustained at 6-month follow-up. Conclusion: This study suggested that ICBT for panic disorder is as effective when delivered in a routine care context as in the previously published randomized controlled trials.

SNAKE PHOBIA

In this study, Andersson, Waara, Jonsson, Malmaeus, et al., (2013) compared guided Internet-delivered self-help with one-session exposure treatment (OST) in a sample of snake phobic patients. A total of 30 patients were included following a screening on the Internet and a structured clinical interview. The Internet treatment consisted of four weekly text modules which were presented on a web page, a video in which exposure was modelled, and support provided via Internet. The OST was delivered in a three-hour session following a brief orientation session. The main outcome was the behavioural approach test (BAT), and as secondary measures questionnaires measuring anxiety symptoms and depression were used. Results showed that the groups did not differ at post-treatment or follow-up, with the exception of a significant interaction for the BAT in favour of the OST. At post-treatment, 61.5% of the Internet group and 84.6% of the OST group achieved a clinically significant improvement on the BAT. At follow-up, the corresponding figures were 90% for the Internet group and 100% for the OST group (completer sample). Within-group effect sizes for the Snake Phobia Questionnaire were large (d = 1.63 and d = 2.31 for the Internet and OST groups, respectively, at post-treatment). It is concluded that guided Internet-delivered exposure treatment is a potential treatment option in the treatment of snake phobia, but that OST probably is better.

CONCLUSION

There is no question that Cognitive-Behavior Therapy (CBT) seems the most successful treatment for anxiety disorders. This conclusion is evident since research about other comparable forms of treatments does not seem available. Nonetheless, other recommended programs based on programmed distance writing about anxiety are available (L'Abate, 2011c). Furthermore, through programmed distance writing, additional anxiety-specific treatments are available (L'Abate, 2013c).

Chapter 4

DEPRESSION

According to Marks et al., (2007):

"Since 1990 at least nine computer psychotherapy (CP) systems for depression were published... They include(d) five PC systems, an IVR system, and three net systems. Interactivity of the systems ranged from limited tin CP bibliotherapy with users who mostly had above average education, to complex interactivity of some other CP systems in less highly educated users. CP systems for depression were evaluated in at least 12 open studies, a nonrandomized controlled study, and nine primary RCTs. Subjects studied variously included inpatients, outpatients, primary care patients, and unscreened website visitors. NICE recently recommended the most published system, PC-based Beating the Blues, for managing depression in the English National Health Service, and it is in commercially licensed use around the UK. Across CP studies improvement for depression ranged from slight to large. Attrition was dramatic in net users who were unsupported (ODIN, 1 MoodGYM study).

As expected, uptake and completion rates tended to we lower in field studies than in RCTs. Most waitlist and TAU RCT designs did not exclude potential placebo effects. Outcome was unimpaired when CP (Good Days Ahead) was given after f2fCBT with total therapist time cut from 450 to 250 minutes. It remains unclear what (p. 85) GDA might achieve with less substantial therapist time. In an especially instructive RCT, interactive CP (net MoodGYM) did no better than non-interactive information (net BluesPages) with similar live phone support to a total of one hour.

CP results were disappointing to modest where it gave cognitive restructuring but no behavioral activation instructions (ODIN, OD1). Some uncertainties about which aspects of CP per se are therapeutic for depression mirror our uncertainties about which aspects of f2f psychotherapy improve mood, given that diverse forms of brief f2f psychotherapy helped depression in RCTs (e.g., behavioral activation alone, CBT. Interpersonal therapy, problem-solving, mindful meditation) (p. 89).

Gallego and Emmelkamp (2012, p. 404) reviewed ten studies conducted on depression, some of which are included here and some were also reviewed by L'Abate (2013c).

Behavioral Activation

Spates, Kalata, Ozeki, Stanton, et al., (2012) presented preliminary findings from the use of a novel computer program that implements an evidence-based psychological intervention to treat depression based on behavioral activation (BA) therapy. The program is titled "Building a Meaningful Life through Behavioral Activation.". The findings derived from an open trial with moderately to severely depressed individuals (N=15) in an intention to treat sample. Hierarchical linear modeling (HLM) analyses revealed significant change over time over the Beck Depression Inventory (Second Edition) scores. Revised Hamilton Depression Rating Scores, and significant contribution to BDI-II score variance by particular age over time, change over time in negative automatic thoughts, and change over time in BA scores. Piecewise HLM analyses revealed that significant change over time was associated uniquely with active treatment and not during 3 weeks of baseline measurement. In addition to treatment-associated significant change on all dependent measures over time, effect sizes were in the moderate to large range. Limitations were a small sample size, nonrandomized control, research-recruited patients instead of purely treatment-seeking patients, possible rating bias by independent assessors who had knowledge that participants had received active treatment in the open trial, and the influence of additional services received in the post acute-treatment phase by some participants could have contributed to maintenance of gains reported for that period.

Care Management

The objective of this study was to test the feasibility, acceptability, and preliminary clinical outcomes of a method to leverage existing home healthcare telemonitoring technology to deliver depression care management (DCM) to both Spanish- and English-speaking elderly homebound recipients of homecare services (Sheeran, Rabinowitz, Lotterman, Reilley, et al., 2011). Three stand-alone, nonprofit community homecare agencies located in New York, Vermont, and Miami participated in this study. Evidence-based DCM was adapted to the telemonitor platform by programming questions and educational information on depression symptoms, antidepressant adherence, and side effects. Recruited patients participated for a minimum of 3 weeks. Telehealth nurses were trained on DCM and received biweekly supervision. On-site trained research assistants conducted in-home research interviews on depression diagnosis and severity and patient satisfaction with the protocol. An ethnically diverse sample of 48 English- and Spanish-only–speaking patients participated, along with seven telehealth nurses. Both patients and telehealth nurses reported high levels of protocol acceptance. Among 19 patients meeting diagnostic criteria for major depression, the mean depression severity was in the "markedly severe" range at baseline and in the "mild" range at follow-up. Results of this pilot support the feasibility of using home care's existing telemonitoring technology to deliver DCM to their elderly homebound patients. This was true for both English- and Spanish-speaking patients. Preliminary clinical outcomes suggested improvement in depression severity, although these findings require testing in a randomized clinical trial. Implications for the science and service of telehealth-based depression care for elderly patients are discussed.

Depression in Chinese Australians

Although depression can be treated effectively with Cognitive Behavior Therapy (CBT), only a small percentage of Chinese Australians access evidence-based treatment due to practical and cultural barriers (Choi, Zou, Titov, Dear, Li, Johnston, & Hunt, 2012). The present study examined the efficacy and acceptability of an Internet delivered CBT (iCBT) program to treat Chinese Australians with depression. The Chinese depression iCBT program (the Brighten Your Mood Program) is a culturally adapted version of the clinically efficacious Sadness iCBT Program. Fifty-five Chinese Australians with depression were randomly allocated to either an immediate treatment group or to a waitlist control group. Treatment consisted of an 8 week program with 6 CBT online educational lessons, homework assignments, additional resources presented in Chinese and English, and weekly telephone support with Mandarin/Cantonese-speaking support personnel. An intention-to-treat model was used for data analyses.

Seventeen of twenty-five (68%) treatment group participants completed all lessons within the timeframe. Compared to controls, treatment group participants reported significantly reduced symptoms of depression on the Chinese versions of the Beck Depression Inventory (CBDI) and Patient Health Questionnaire-9 item (CB-PHQ-9). The within- and between-group effect sizes (Cohen's d) were 1.41 and 0.93 on the CBDI, and 0.90 and 0.50 on the CB-PHQ-9, respectively. Participants rated the procedure as acceptable, and gains were sustained at three-month follow-up. This study, however, included several subclinical participants and some measures that have not been previously validated with Chinese Australians. Results provided preliminary support for the efficacy and acceptability of an iCBT program at reducing symptoms of depression in Chinese Australians.

Depression and Individual Differences

The purpose of this study was to evaluate whether patients differ in their response to treatments (Button et al. (2012). There is obvious clinical utility in establishing patient characteristics that are associated with differential treatment responses (i.e., are effect modifiers or moderators of treatment response). Factors that moderate response to cognitive behavioral therapy (CBT) remain unclear. This study investigated whether factors prognostic of general depression outcome generally are also moderators of response to online CBT in a sample of depressed patients recruited through UK general practices. The method consisted of a secondary analysis of a randomized controlled trial, internet-based psychotherapy for depression. A total of 297 patients referred from 55 UK general practices and suffering from depression were randomly allocated to receive either online CBT or waiting list control. Treatment effect was measured by comparing depression score at 4 months between randomization groups. Treatment effect modification was assessed using regression analyses focusing on interactions between treatment effect and putative moderator variables. Results showed that pretreatment severity and marital status moderated treatment response. More severe patients, and patients who were separated, widowed, or divorced, benefited most from the intervention. Weak evidence suggested that treatment effectiveness diminished with increasing recent adverse life events. No evidence was found to suggest that educational attainment, age, and history of depression-moderated treatment response. In conclusion, it looks like secondary analyses of trials comparing two or more treatments allow factors that may moderate treatment response to be distinguished from more general prognostic indicators, although caution is needed in interpreting such exploratory analyses.

Major Depressive Disorder

Major depressive disorder (MDD) is projected to rank second on a list of 15 major diseases in terms of burden in 2030. The major contribution of MDD to disability and health care costs is largely due to its highly recurrent nature. Accordingly, efforts to reduce the disabling effects of this chronic condition should shift to preventing recurrence, especially in patients at high risk of recurrence. Given its high prevalence and the fact that interventions are necessary during the remitted phase, new approaches are needed to prevent relapse in depression (Bockting, et al., 2011). The best established effective and available psychological intervention is cognitive therapy. However, it is costly and not available for most patients. Therefore, the authors compared the effectiveness and cost-effectiveness of self-management supported (SMS) by online CT accompanied by SMS based telemonitoring of depressive symptomatology, i.e., Mobile Cognitive Therapy (M-CT) versus treatment as us usual (TAU).

Remitted patients (n = 268) with at least two previous depressive episodes will be recruited and randomized over (1) M-CT in addition to TAU versus (2) TAU alone, with follow-ups at 3, 12, and 24 months. Randomization will be stratified for number of previous episodes and type of treatment as usual. Primary outcome is time until relapse/recurrence over 24 months using DSM-IV-TR criteria as assessed by the Structured Clinical Interview for DSM-IV Axis I Disorders (SCID). For the economic evaluation the balance between costs and health outcomes will be compared across strategies using a societal perspective. Discussion Internet-based interventions might be helpful in empowering patients to become their own disease managers in this lifelong recurrent disorder. This is, as far as the authors were aware of, the first study that examines the (cost) effectiveness of an E-mental health program using SMS monitoring of symptoms with therapist support to prevent relapse in remitted recurrently depressed patients.

The objective of this investigation was to identify whether Internet-based cognitive behavior therapy (CBT) can prevent relapse in persons with partially remitted major depression after previous treatment (Holländare, Johnsson, Randestad, M., Tillfors, M., et al., 2011). Seventy-one women and 13 men (N = 84) with partially remitted major depression after treatment were randomly assigned to either 10 weeks of Internet-based CBT or to a control group. Self-help material was used in combination with e-mail contact with a personal therapist. Monthly self-ratings of depressive symptoms were made, and diagnostic interviews were conducted before and after the treatment period, as well as 6 months later. Significantly fewer participants in the CBT group experienced relapse (4/38 or 10.5%) compared with those in the control group (14/37 or 37.8%). The difference in relapse rates between groups occurred early in the study period and was still apparent after 6 months. A trend towards a larger reduction in depressive symptoms was observed at post-treatment in the participants who received CBT compared with controls. Reduction in depressive symptoms reduced the risk of relapse. A trend towards a higher remission rate was found in the CBT group at the 6 month follow-up. Internet-based CBT seems promising in preventing relapse in persons with partially remitted major depression after previous treatment.

Internet-delivered psychological treatment of major depression has been investigated in several trials, but the role of personalized treatment has been less investigated (Vernmark, Lenndin, Bjärehed, Carlsson, et al., 2010). Studies suggested that guidance is important and that automated computerized programs without therapist support are less effective. Individualized e-mail therapy for depression has not been studied in a controlled trial. Eighty-eight individuals with major depression were randomized to two different forms of Internet-delivered cognitive behavior therapy (CBT), or to a waiting-list control group. One form of Internet treatment consisted of guided self-help, with weekly modules and homework assignments. Standard CBT components were presented and brief support was provided during the treatment. The other group received e-mail therapy, which was tailored and did not use the self-help texts i.e., all e-mails were written for the unique patient. Both treatments lasted for 8 weeks. In the guided self-help 93% completed (27/29) and in the e-mail therapy 96% (29/30) completed the post treatment assessment. Results showed significant symptom reductions in both treatment groups with moderate to large effect sizes. At post-treatment 34.5% of the guided self-help group and 30% of the e-mail therapy group reached the criteria of high-end-state functioning (Beck Depression Inventory score below 9). At six-month follow-up the corresponding figures were 47.4% and 43.3%. Overall, the difference between guided self-help and e-mail therapy was small, but in favor of the latter. These findings indicated that both guided self-help and individualized e-mail therapy can be effective.

Patient Engagement Strategies

Computerized, Internet-delivered interventions can be efficacious; however, uptake and maintaining sustained client engagement are still big challenges. Whiteside, Lungu, Richards, Simon, et al. (2014) saw the development of effective engagement strategies as the next frontier in online health interventions, an area where much creative research has begun. The authors also argued that for engagement strategies to accomplish their purpose with novel targeted populations, they need to be tailored to such populations (i.e., content is designed with the target population in mind). User-centered design frameworks could provide a theoretical foundation for increasing user engagement and uptake by including users in development. However, deciding how to implement this approach to engage users in mental health intervention development is challenging.

The aim of this study was to get user input and feedback on acceptability of messaging content intended to engage suicidal individuals. In March 2013, clinic intake staff distributed flyers announcing the study, "Your Feedback Counts" to potential participants (individuals waiting to be seen for a mental health appointment) together with the Patient Health Questionnaire. The flyer explained that a score of two or three ("more than half the days" or "nearly every day" respectively) on the suicide ideation question made them eligible to provide feedback on components of a suicide prevention intervention under development. The patient could access an anonymous online survey by following a link. After providing consent online, participants completed the anonymous survey. Thirty-four individuals provided data on past demographic information. Participants reported that they would be most drawn to an intervention where they knew that they were cared about, that was personalized, that others like them had found it helpful, and that included examples with real people. Participants preferred email invitations with subject lines expressing concern and availability of extra resources. Participants also provided feedback about a media prototype including a brand design and advertisement video for introducing the intervention. This study provided one model (including development of an engagement survey, audience for an engagement survey, methods for presenting results of an engagement survey) for including target users in the development of uptake strategies for online mental health interventions.

POSITIVE PSYCHOTHERAPY AND DEPRESSION

Positive psychotherapy (PPT) contrasts with standard interventions for depression by increasing positive emotion, engagement, and meaning rather than directly targeting depressive symptoms. Seligman, Rashid, and Parks (2006) tested the effects of these interventions in a variety of settings. In informal student and clinical settings, people not uncommonly reported them to be "life-changing." Delivered on the Web, positive psychology exercises relieved depressive symptoms for at least 6 months compared with placebo interventions, the effects of which lasted less than a week. In severe depression, the effects of these Web exercises were particularly striking. This address reported two preliminary studies: In the first, PPT delivered to groups significantly decreased levels of mild-to-moderate depression through 1-year follow-up. In the second, PPT delivered to individuals produced higher remission rates than did treatment as usual and treatment as usual plus medication among outpatients with major depressive disorder. Together, these studies suggest that treatments for depression may usefully be supplemented by exercises that explicitly increase positive emotion, engagement, and meaning. *Apparently, this approach ignored completely the positive reframing practice of paradoxial psychotherapy developed decades earlier* (Weeks & L'Abate, 1982).(Author's note).

SELF-HELP TREATMENT

Background Internet-based self-help treatment with minimal therapist contact has been shown to have an effect in treating various conditions. The objective of this study was to explore participants‘ views of Internet administrated guided self-help treatment for depression (Bendelin, Hesser, Dahl, Carlbring, Nelson, & Andersson, 2011). Methods In-depth interviews were conducted with 12 strategically selected participants and qualitative methods with components of both thematic analysis and grounded theory were used in the analyses. Three distinct change processes relating to how participants worked with the treatment material emerged which were categorized as (a) Readers, (b) Strivers, and (c) Doers. These processes dealt with attitudes towards treatment, views on motivational aspects of the treatment, and perceptions of consequences of the treatment. The authors concluded that their findings corresponded with existing theoretical models of F2F psychotherapy within qualitative process research. Persons who take responsibility for the treatment and also attribute success to themselves appear to benefit the most. Motivation, therefore, is a crucial aspect of guided self-help in the treatment of depression.

Self-Help Plus Therapist Guidance

Internet-delivered self-help for depression with therapist guidance has shown efficacy in several trials (Berger, et al., 2011). Results from meta-analyses suggested that guidance is important and that self-help programs without support are less effective. However, there are no direct experimental comparisons between guided and unguided internet-based treatments for depression. The present study compared the benefits of a 10-week web-based unguided self-help treatment with the same intervention complemented with weekly therapist support via e-mail. A waiting-list control group was also included. Seventy-six individuals meeting the diagnostic criteria of major depression or dysthymia were randomly assigned to one of the three conditions. The Beck Depression Inventory (BDI-II) was used as the primary outcome measure. Secondary outcomes included general psychopathology, interpersonal problems, and quality of life. Sixty-nine participants (91%) completed the assessment at post treatment and 59 (78%) at 6-month follow-up.

Results showed significant symptom reductions in both treatment groups compared to the waiting-list control group. At post-treatment, between-group effect sizes on the BDI-II were $d = .66$ for unguided self-help versus waiting-list and $d = 1.14$ for guided self-help versus waiting-list controls. In the comparison of the two active treatments, small-to-moderate, but not statistically significant effects in favor of the guided condition were found on all measured dimensions. In both groups, treatment gains were maintained at 6-month follow-up. These findings provided evidence that internet-delivered treatments for depression can be effective whether support is added or not. However, all participants were interviewed in a structured diagnostic telephone interview before inclusion, which prohibits conclusions regarding unguided treatments that are without any human contact.

Depression and Social Resources

Bessière, Kiesler, Kraut, and Boneva (2008) examined how people's different uses of the Internet predict their later scores on a standard measure of depression, and how their existing social resources moderate these effects. In a longitudinal US survey conducted in 2001 and 2002, almost all respondents reported using the Internet for information, and entertainment and escape; these uses of the Internet had no impact on changes in respondents' level of depression. Almost all respondents also used the Internet for communicating with friends and family, and they showed lower depression scores six months later. Only about 20 percent of this sample reported using the Internet to meet new people and talk in online groups. Doing so changed their depression scores depending on their initial levels of social support. Those having high or medium levels of social support showed higher depression scores; those with low levels of social support did not experience increases in depression. Their results suggested that individual differences in social resources and people's choices of how they use the Internet may account for the different outcomes reported in the literature.

Suicide Prevention

Suicide has reached such epidemic proportions, especially in the military and in rural areas, to receive a federally funded Suicide Prevention Resource Center that offers training, publications, and specialization (Clay, 2014a, 2014b). For instance, Gros, Veronee, Strachan, Ruggerio, and Acierno (2011) described the case of a US veteran from the war in Afghanistan with post-traumatic stress disorder (PTSD). The patient was undergoing treatment at home via telehealth as part of a research trial. In week six, he presented with severe suicidal ideation and required emergency hospitalization. Through a series of immediate enhanced communications (i.e., by videoconference) between the patient, patient's family, treatment team and local resources, the patient's symptoms were assessed to identify suicidality and an intervention was successfully carried out, involving the development of a safety plan and eventual transportation to an inpatient unit at the local Veterans Administration Medical Center, where he was hospitalized for three days. This case demonstrated the value of telehealth in identifying and treating severe psychiatric symptoms in addition to supporting the safety of these procedures to address suicidality.

Luxton, June, and Kinn (2011) reported on current and emerging technologies for suicide prevention. Technology-based programs discussed included interactive educational and social networking websites, email-based outreach, and programs that use mobile devices and texting. The authors described innovative applications, such as virtual worlds, gaming, and text analysis that are currently being developed and applied to suicide prevention and outreach programs. Luxton, June, and Kinn (2011) also discussed the benefits and limitations of technology-based applications and discussed future directions for their use (see also Chapter 16 of this volume).

The Internet, therefore can be efficiently exploited to help people in severe emotional distress, including those contemplating suicide (Barak, 2007). Based on this premise and guided by various psychological principles that characterize Internet communication and behavior, on the one hand, and by factors related to the provision of emotional support, on the other, an Israeli project with the Hebrew acronym SAHAR was established. The idea behind SAHAR was to initiate an anonymous, confidential online environment that would attract people in a crisis situation and offer them a listening ear, mental support, and warmth, provided by anonymous, skilled helpers. At the heart of this exclusively online service is a content-rich Hebrew website (http://www.sahar.org.il) that provides relevant and continuously updated information for people in need. Accessed through the site, SAHAR offers, in addition, personal communication to users through synchronous and asynchronous support. For group communication, SAHAR provides online forums (a chat room will soon be launched). The website is accessed more than 10,000 times a month, or 350 times a day, a considerable number relative to Israel's small population. Approximately 1000 personal contacts with SAHAR itself take place, each month, of which at least a third of the distressed users are clearly suicidal. The forums receive over 200 new messages a day. SAHAR on numerous occasions has participated in rescue operations of individuals who threatened to commit suicide or were actually in the process of trying. In many other cases, a supportive conversation or a referral to appropriate help resources prevented hasty decisions by highly distressed, desperate people contemplating suicide. Feedback by users also indicates the success of SAHAR as a unique psychological application on the Internet.

Clinical Outcomes in Veterans

The study assessed clinical outcomes of 98,609 mental health patients before and after enrollment in telemental health services of the U.S. Department of Veterans Affairs between 2006 and 2010 (Godleski, Darkins, & Peters, 2008). The study compared number of inpatient psychiatric admissions and days of psychiatric hospitalization among patients who participated in remote clinical videoconferencing during an average period of six months before and after their enrollment in the tele-mental health services. Between 2006 and 2010, psychiatric admissions of tele-mental health patients decreased by an average of 24.2% (annual range 16.3%–38.7%), and the patients' days of hospitalization decreased by an average of 26.6% (annual range 16.5%–43.5%). The number of admissions and the days of hospitalization decreased for both men and women and in 83.3% of the age groups. This four-year study, the first large-scale assessment of tele-mental health services, found that after initiation of such services, patients' hospitalization utilization decreased by an average of approximately 25% (decreasing considerably hospitalization costs, N/Es).

The Department of Veterans Affairs (VA) encompasses one of the largest tele-mental health networks in the world, with over 45,000 videoconferencing and over 5,000 home tele-mental health encounters annually (Godleski, Nieves, Darkins, & Lehmann, 2008). Recently, the VA designated suicide prevention as a major priority, with telehealth modalities providing opportunities for remote interventions. Suicide risk assessments, using videoconferencing, are now documented in the literature, as are current studies that find tele-mental health to be equivalent to face-to-face treatment. Remote assessment of suicidality, however, involves complex legal issues: licensing requirements for remote delivery of care, legal procedures for involuntary detainment and commitment of potentially harmful patients, and liability questions related to the remote nature of the mental health service. VA best practices for remote suicide risk assessment include paradigms for establishing procedures in the context of legal challenges (licensing and involuntary detainment/commitment), for utilizing clinical assessment and triage decision protocols, and for contingency planning to optimize patient care and reduce liability.

Telephone Tracking and Depression

Telephone helplines are frequently and repeatedly used by individuals with chronic mental health problems and web interventions may be an effective tool for reducing depression in this population (Farrer, Christensen, Griffiths, & Mackinnon, 2011). To evaluate the effectiveness of a 6 week, web-based cognitive behavior therapy (CBT) intervention with and without proactive weekly telephone tracking in the reduction of depression in callers to a helpline service. Method: 155 callers to a national helpline service with moderate to high psychological distress were recruited and randomized to receive either Internet CBT plus weekly telephone follow-up; Internet CBT only; weekly telephone follow-up only; or treatment as usual. Results: Depression was lower in participants in the web intervention conditions both with and without telephone tracking compared to the treatment as usual condition both at post intervention and at 6 month follow-up. Telephone tracking provided by a lay telephone counselor did not confer any additional advantage in terms of symptom reduction or adherence. Conclusions: A web-based CBT program is effective both with and without telephone tracking for reducing depression in callers to a national helpline.

VIDEOCONFERENCING FOR DEPRESSION IN SENIOR CITIZENS

Depression affects up to 25% of older adults (Lazzari, Egan, & Rees, 2011), Under-detection and subsequent under-treatment of depression in older adults has been attributed in part to difficulties in older adults being able to access treatment. This uncontrolled pilot study, N = 3, explored the acceptability and efficacy of a brief behavioral activation treatment delivered via videoconferencing to 3 participants, aged 64 to 73 years, diagnosed with major depressive disorder. The results indicated that a 5-session behavioral activation treatment delivered via videoconferencing produced clinically significant and reliable decreases in depression. The results also showed clinically significant and reliable decreases in negative affect and clinically significant and reliable increases in positive affect. Treatment gains were maintained at 1-month follow-up. Videoconferencing can be a valuable and effective tool in increasing accessibility to psychological treatment for older adults.

DEPRESSION AND ANXIETY

Spek, Cuijper, Nyklicek, Riper, et al., (2006) studied to what extent internet-based cognitive behavior therapy (CBT) programs for symptoms of depression and anxiety are effective through a meta-analysis of 12 randomized controlled trials. The effects of internet-based CBT were compared to control conditions in 13 contrast groups with a total number of 2334 participants. A meta-analysis on treatment contrasts resulted in a moderate to large mean effect size [fixed effects analysis (FEA) d=0.40, mixed effects analysis (MEA) d=0.60] and significant heterogeneity. Therefore, two sets of post hoc subgroup analyses were carried out. Analyses on the type of symptoms revealed that interventions for symptoms of depression had a small mean effect size (FEA d=0.27, MEA d=0.32) and significant heterogeneity. Further analyses showed that one study could be regarded as an outlier. Analyses without this study showed a small mean effect size and moderate, non-significant heterogeneity. Interventions for anxiety had a large mean effect size (FEA and MEA d=0.96) and very low heterogeneity. When examining the second set of subgroups, based on therapist assistance, no significant heterogeneity was found. Interventions with therapist support (n=5) had a large mean effect size, while interventions without therapist support (n=6) had a small mean effect size (FEA d=0.24, MEA d=0.26). In general, effect sizes of internet-based interventions for symptoms of anxiety were larger than effect sizes for depressive symptoms; however, this might be explained by differences in the amount of therapist support.

Guided Internet-Delivered Therapy

Guided internet-delivered cognitive behavior therapy (ICBT) has been found to be effective in the treatment of mild to moderate depression, but there have been no direct comparisons with the more established group-based CBT with a long-term follow-up (Andersson, Hesser, Veilord, Svedling, et al., 2013). Participants with mild to moderate depression were recruited from the general population and randomized to either guided ICBT (n = 33) or to live group treatment (n = 36). Measures were completed before and after the intervention to assess depression, anxiety, and quality of life. Follow-ups were conducted at one-year and three-year after the treatment had ended. Results: Data were analyzed on an intention-to-treat basis using linear mixed-effects regression analysis. Results on the self-rated version of the Montgomery–Åsberg Depression Scale showed significant improvements in both groups across time indicating non-inferiority of guided ICBT, and there was even a tendency for the guided ICBT group to be superior to group-based CBT at three year follow-up. Within-group effect sizes for the ICBT condition at post-treatment showed a Cohen's d = 1.46, with a similar large effect at 3-year follow-up, d = 1.78. For the group CBT the corresponding within-group effects were d = 0.99 and d = 1.34, respectively. This study was small with two active treatments and there was no placebo or credible control condition. Apparently, guided ICBT is at least as effective as group-based CBT and long-term effects can be sustained up to 3 years after treatment.

Complicated Grief

The present study investigates the efficacy of an Internet-based cognitive-behavioral therapy program for bereaved people suffering complicated grief (Wagner, Knaevelsrud, & Maercker, 2006). The program combined established methods of psychotherapy with new technology– therapists and patients communicated exclusively by e-mail. Bereaved individuals diagnosed with complicated grief (n = 55) were randomly assigned to either the treatment group or a waiting list control condition. The 5-week intervention consisted of three modules: (1) exposure to bereavement cues; (2) cognitive reappraisal; and (3) integration and restoration. The Impact of Event Scale (IES), a failure to adapt scale, and the depression and anxiety subscales of the Brief Symptom Inventory (BSI) were used to assess treatment outcomes. Participants in the treatment group (n = 26) improved significantly relative to participants in the waiting condition on symptoms of intrusion, avoidance, maladaptive behavior, and general psychopathology, and showed a large treatment effect. Follow-up results show that this improvement was maintained after 3 months.

Suicide Prevention

Computerized, Internet-delivered interventions can be efficacious; however, uptake and maintaining sustained client engagement are still big challenges. Whiteside, Lungu, Richards, Simon, et al. (2014), saw the development of effective engagement strategies as the next frontier in online health interventions, an area where much creative research has begun. They also argued that for engagement strategies to accomplish their purpose with novel targeted populations, they need to be tailored to such populations (i.e., content is designed with the target population in mind). User-centered design frameworks provide a theoretical foundation for increasing user engagement and uptake by including users in development. However, deciding how to implement this approach to engage users in mental health intervention development is challenging. Objective: The aim of this study was to get user input and feedback on acceptability of messaging content intended to engage suicidal individuals. Methods: In March 2013, clinic intake staff distributed flyers announcing the study, "Your Feedback Counts" to potential participants (individuals waiting to be seen for a mental health appointment) together with the Patient Health Questionnaire. The flyer explained that a score of two or three ("more than half the days" or "nearly every day" respectively) on the suicide ideation question made them eligible to provide feedback on components of a suicide prevention intervention under development. The patient could access an anonymous online survey by following a link. After providing consent online, participants completed the anonymous survey.

Thirty-four individuals provided data on past demographic information. Participants reported that they would be most drawn to an intervention where they knew that they were cared about, that was personalized, that others like them had found it helpful, and that included examples with real people. Participants preferred email invitations with subject lines expressing concern and availability of extra resources. Participants also provided feedback about a media prototype including a brand design and advertisement video for introducing the intervention. Conclusions: This paper provides one model (including development of an engagement survey, audience for an engagement survey, methods for presenting results of an engagement survey) for including target users in the development of uptake strategies for online mental health interventions.

The Internet can be efficiently exploited to help people in severe emotional distress, including those contemplating suicide. Based on this premise and guided by various psychological principles that characterize Internet communication and behavior, on the one hand, and by factors related to the provision of emotional support, on the other, an Israeli project with the Hebrew acronym SAHAR was established (Barak, 2007). The idea behind SAHAR was to initiate an anonymous, confidential online environment that would attract people in a crisis situation and offer them a listening ear, mental support, and warmth, provided by anonymous, skilled helpers. At the heart of this exclusively online service is a content-rich Hebrew website (http://www.sahar.org.il) that provides relevant and continuously updated information for people in need. Accessed through the site, SAHAR offers, in addition, personal communication to users through synchronous and asynchronous support. For group communication, SAHAR provides online forums (a chat room will soon be launched). The website is accessed more than 10,000 times a month, or 350 times a day, a considerable number relative to Israel's small population. Approximately 1000 personal contacts with SAHAR itself take place, each month, of which at least a third of the distressed users are clearly suicidal. The forums receive over 200 new messages a day. SAHAR on numerous occasions has participated in rescue operations of individuals who threatened to commit suicide or were actually in the process of trying. In many other cases, a supportive conversation or a referral to appropriate help resources prevented hasty decisions by highly distressed, desperate people contemplating suicide. Feedback by users also indicates the success of SAHAR as a unique psychological application on the Internet.

Luxton, June, and Kinn (2010) reported on current and emerging technologies for suicide prevention. Technology-based programs discussed included interactive educational and social networking websites, email-based outreach, and programs that use mobile devices and texting. The authors described innovative applications, such as virtual worlds, gaming, and text analysis that are currently being developed and applied to suicide prevention and outreach programs. Luxton, June, and Kinn also discussed the benefits and limitations of technology-based applications and discuss future directions for their use.

CONCLUSION

There does not seem any question about Internet interventions for depression fast becoming a major avenue of service delivery. Furthermore, a variety of depression-related interactive practice exercises or workbooks (L'Abate, 2011c) need evaluation under controlled conditions. These interventions need to occur within a stepped-care context, where Internet interventions occur before more expensive F2F treatments (O'Donohue & Draper, 2011) The latter plus medication may be appropriate whenever a less expensive approach fails.

Chapter 5

EATING DISORDERS

Marks et al., (2007) traced 13 CP systems to diverse eating problems:

"The systems were evaluated in at least 30 studies, including 18 RCTs and 5 non-RCT group comparisons. They were variously designed to just monitor eating behavior or to cut therapist time or to prevent, improve or maintain benefits regarding eating disorders. Study durations ranged from a mere six days to five years, but most lasted about two months and reported short-term outcome. System types and aims varies hugely. At the simple end were wristwatch or handheld computers or a scale linked to a PDA or semi-automated phone SMSs in order to prompt users to rate eating behavior on site and perhaps to exercise or do other CP homework or to eat at a normal rate. At the more complex end were multisession, multimedia, interactive standalone or net systems offering brief education about eating attitudes and behavior in high school girls or college women or overweight adults and a CD-ROM guiding eight consecutive CBS sessions in a clinic for bulimia. Computer-aided monitoring alone did not improve eating disordered behaviors. Some CP studies reported benefits for eating problems. Even more significant, effects seemed fairly modest, take-up was low and dropout rates were high. The (p. 109) most evaluated system, net. Student Bodies, improved eating disorders but evidence for improved behavior was more tentative. In a big RTC (n=480) with a waitlist design, netSB plus online discussion groups were followed by less onset of eating problems in certain at-risk students, but the role of netSB per se remains unclear. The RCTs usually had control/contrast groups lacking an expectation of improvement (e.g., on a waitlist) or lacking the bulletin board, email, phone or other f2f support which after accompanied CP, thus precluding conclusions about the value of CP per se as opposed to differential support and/or expectations of improvement across groups. Adding online discussion groups or email guidance seemed to add value to such CP. In contrast, one hour of F2F therapist support did not add value when CD-ROM guidance was given in a clinic" (p.113).

Internet-based treatments for eating disorders were reviewed by Gallego and Emmelkamp (2012, p. 410). They found that treatment adherence was low in most studies, ranging from 26% to 82%, not a very acceptable rate. New communication technologies offer novel possibilities for the prevention of mental illness, in which geographical and psychosocial distances often hamper help-seeking.

This paper introduced ES[S]PRIT, an Internet-based eating disorders (ED) prevention program for university students (Bauer, Moessner, Wolf, Haug, & Kordy, 2009). The program followed a stepped-care approach combining various support components of increasing intensity. These components comprise psycho-education, symptom monitoring, supportive feedback, peer support, and professional online counseling. Participants who develop substantial ED symptoms during their participation are referred to the University Student Counselling Center. These authors outlined the underlying concepts and various components of the program and reported first experiences with the approach in a sample of German college students. Finally, potentials of the approach were highlighted and the need for further research was stressed.

A cross-cultural comparison of a cognitive–behavioral, Internet-based, 8-week prevention program for eating disorders (StudentBodies™) evaluated in the USA and in Germany was performed by Beintner, Jacobi, and Taylor (2012). Six US and four German randomized controlled trials with a total (N) of 990 female high school and college students were included in the review. Two of the US and two of the German trials explicitly addressed high risk samples in a selective prevention approach. Effect sizes for main outcomes (disordered eating, weight and shape concerns) were calculated at post-intervention and at follow-up. The intervention was associated with moderate improvements in eating disorder-related attitudes, especially reductions of negative body image and the desire to be thin. The reported effects remained significant at follow-up. No clear differences between US and German samples could be found on any of the outcome measures at post-intervention. In conclusion, StudentBodies™ seems equally suitable and effective for American and German students.

Women reporting initial eating disorder (ED) symptoms are at highest risk for the development of an eating disorder (Jacobi, Volker, Trockel, & Taylor, 2012). Preventive interventions should, therefore, be specifically tailored for this subgroup. To adapt and evaluate the effects of the Internet-based prevention program "Student Bodies™" for women with symptoms of disordered eating and/or sub-threshold eating disorder (ED) syndromes. Method: 126 women, reporting sub-threshold ED symptoms (high weight and shape concerns and below threshold bingeing, purging, chronic dieting or several of these symptoms) were randomly assigned to a Student Bodies™+ (SB+) intervention or a wait list control group and assessed at pre-intervention, post-intervention, and 6-month follow-up. "Student Bodies™" was adapted to be suitable for sub threshold EDs. Main outcome measures were attitudes and symptoms of disordered eating. Pre-follow-up data were analyzed by ANCOVAS with mixed effects.

At 6-month follow-up, compared to participants in the control group, participants in the intervention group showed significantly greater improvements on ED-related attitudes. Intervention participants also showed 67% (95% CI = 20–87%) greater reductions in combined rates of subjective and objective binges, and 86% (95% CI = 63–95%) greater reduction in purging episodes. Also, the rates of participants abstinent from all symptoms of disordered eating (restrictive eating, binge eating and any compensatory behavior) were significantly higher in the intervention group (45.1% vs. 26.9%). Post-hoc subgroup analyses revealed that for participants with binge eating the effect on EDE-Q scores was larger than in the pure restricting subgroup. Conclusion: The adapted "SB+" program represents an effective intervention for women with sub threshold EDs of the binge eating subtype.

One hundred and ten people in an university population responded to emailed eating disorder questionnaires (Robinson & Serfaty, 2008). Ninty-seven fulfilling criteria for eating disorders (bulimia nervosa (BN), binge eating disorder (BED), EDNOS) were randomized to therapist administered email bulimia therapy (eBT), unsupported Self directed writing (SDW) or Waiting list control (WLC). Measures were repeated at 3 months. Diagnosis, Beck depression inventory (BDI) and Bulimia investigatory test (BITE) scores were recorded. Follow-up rate was 63% and results must be interpreted cautiously. However significantly fewer participants who had received eBT or SDW fulfilled criteria for eating disorders at follow up compared to WLC. There was no significant difference between eBT and SDW in the analysis of variance (ANOVA), although in separate analyses, eBT was significantly superior to WLC ($p < 0.02$) and the difference for SDW approached significance ($p = 0.06$). BDI and BITE scores showed no significant change. For eBT participants there was a significant positive correlation between words written and improvement in BITE severity score. BN, BED and EDNOS can be treated via email.

Anorexia Nervosa

Anorexia nervosa (AN) poses a major burden on families. Carers (e.g., parents or partners) of people with AN are often highly distressed and may inadvertently respond in ways that can contribute to the maintenance of the disorder, e.g., through high levels of over-involvement and criticism [also known as expressed emotion (EE)]. This study aimed to evaluate the efficacy of a novel web-based systemic cognitive-behavioural (CBT) intervention for caregivers of people with AN, designed to reduce caregivers distress and teach skills in how to offer effective support (Grover, Naumann, Mohammad-Dar, Glennon, et al., 2011). Carers of people with AN (n=64) were randomly allocated to either the web-intervention, overcoming anorexia online, with limited clinician supportive guidance (by email or phone), or to ad-hoc usual support from the UK patient and carer organization Beat. Carer outcomes were assessed at post-treatment (4 months) and follow-up (6 months). Compared with the control intervention, web-based treatment significantly reduced carer anxiety and depression (primary outcome) at post-treatment, with a similar trend in care givers' EE. Other secondary outcomes did not favor the online intervention. Gains were maintained at follow-up. This seems the first ever study to use an online CBT program to successfully reduce carer distress and improve carers' ability to support the person with AN.

Technological advancements allow new approaches to psychotherapy via electronic media (Fichter, Quadflieg, Misslmuller, Lindner, Osen, Huber, Wunsch-Lieteritz, 2012). The eating disorder literature currently contains no studies on internet intervention in anorexia nervosa (AN). This study presents a RCT on an internet-based relapse prevention program (RP) over nine months after inpatient treatment for AN. The sample comprised 258 women, randomized to the RP or treatment as usual (TAU). Expert- and self-ratings were evaluated by intent-to-treat analyses. Concerning age, age at onset and comorbidity, both groups were comparable at randomization. During the RP, the intervention group gained weight while the TAU group had minimal weight loss. RP completers gained significantly more body weight than patients in the TAU condition. Group-by-time comparisons for eating-related cognitions and behaviors and general psychopathology showed a significantly more favorable course in the RP program for "sexual anxieties" and "bulimic symptoms" (interview), and "maturity fears" and "social insecurity" (EDI-2). General psychopathology showed no significant group-by-time interaction. Important factors for successful relapse prevention were adherence to the intervention protocol and increased spontaneity. Considering the unfavorable course and chronicity of anorexia nervosa (AN), internet-based relapse prevention in AN following inpatient treatment appears a promising approach. Future internet-based programs may be further improved and enhanced.

Binge Eating

Binge eating disorder (BED) is a common and under-treated condition with major health implications. Cognitive behavioral therapy (CBT) self-help manuals have proved to be efficient in BED treatment (Carrard, Crépin, Rouget, Lam, Golay, & Van der Linden, 2011). Increasing evidence also support the use of new technology to improve treatment access and dissemination. This is the first randomised controlled study to evaluate the efficacy of an Internet guided self-help treatment programme, based on CBT, for adults with threshold and sub threshold BED. Seventy-four women were randomised into two groups. The first group received the six-month online program with a six-month follow-up. The second group was placed in a six-month waiting list before participating in the six-month intervention. Guidance consisted of a regular e-mail contact with a coach during the whole intervention. Binge eating behavior, drive for thinness, body dissatisfaction and interoceptive awareness significantly improved after the Internet self-help treatment intervention. The number of objective binge episodes, overall eating disorder symptoms score and perceived hunger also decreased. Improvements were maintained at six-month follow-up. Dropouts exhibited more shape concern and a higher drive for thinness. Overall, a transfer of CBT-based self-help techniques to the Internet was well accepted by patients, and showed positive results for eating disorders psychopathology.

A significant percentage of obese patients suffer from binge eating disorder (BED), with negative consequences on psychological health, quality of life, weight loss treatment and maintenance (Isabelle, Christelle, et al., 2011). CBT), delivered in traditional or self-help format, is effective in reducing BED symptoms. To improve dissemination, a self-help treatment program composed of eleven CBT based modules was implemented on the Internet and evaluated in a population of adult obese patients with BED. Method: Forty-two obese BED patients wait listed for a multi-disciplinary obesity treatment took part in the study. Twenty-two patients completing the six-month online guided self-help treatment program were compared to a control group of twenty patients without intervention. Both groups were evaluated before and after six months of Internet self-help treatment or waiting list. A follow-up evaluation was carried out six months later. Results: Participants in the online self-help treatment program showed higher binge eating abstinence rates, lower EDE-Q shape and weight concerns, and improved TFEQ disinhibition of eating and hunger scores compared to the control group. They also scored better on psychological health and quality of life measures after intervention, and gains were maintained at follow-up. No effect was found regarding BMI. The number of modules completed was correlated with a better quality of life improvement at post evaluation. Participants rated the program as useful and easy to use. Conclusion: The Internet seems to be a valuable tool for disseminating CBT for BED obese patients. Acceptance of new technology was good in this population. Further research is needed with a larger sample to corroborate these results.

BULIMIA NERVOSA

The present study investigated the efficacy of self-help based on cognitive behavior therapy in combination with Internet support in the treatment of bulimia nervosa and binge eating disorder (Ljotsson, Lundin, Mitsell, Carlbring, et al., 2007). After confirming the diagnosis with an in-person interview, 73 patients were randomly allocated to treatment or a waiting list control group. Treated individuals showed marked improvement after 12 weeks of self-help compared to the control group on both primary and secondary outcome measures. Intent-to-treat analyses revealed that 37% (46% among completers) had no binge eating or purging at the end of the treatment and a considerable number of patients achieved clinically significant improvement on most of the other measures as well. The results were maintained at the 6-month follow-up, and provide evidence to support the continued use and development of self-help programs.

The purposes of this study were to evaluate the use of an online guided self-treatment program for bulimia nervosa (BN) and to determine predictors of outcome (Carrard, Fernandez-Aranda, Lam, Nevonen, Liwowsky, et al., 2011). Data were collected in four European countries where the program was simultaneously used. Method: One hundred and twenty-seven BN or sub threshold BN female patients (mean age of 24.7 years) participated in a 4-month intervention using a CBT based online-guided self-help program. Contact during the treatment period included weekly e-mails with a coach. Measures included the Eating Disorders Inventory-2 (EDI-2) and the Symptom Check List-Revised (SCL-90R). Results: Severity of eating disorders symptoms and general psychopathology improved significantly. Twenty-three per cent of patients were symptom free at the end of treatment. The dropout rate was 25.2%. A better score of general psychological health was a predictor of a better outcome. Conclusions: This study encourages further developments and research on innovative therapy approaches, particularly for those disorders such as BN, with difficult therapy and unclear prognosis.

The sustainability of treatment effects is a major challenge in clinical practice. As in most other mental disorders, patients with eating disorders frequently experience relapses following treatment termination. This calls for feasible maintenance strategies that can be implemented in clinical routine at reasonable cost and effort for both treatment providers and patients. This article introduces an Internet-based intervention for maintenance support of patients with bulimia nervosa (BN) and related eating disorders not otherwise specified (EDNOS).(Gulec, Moessner, Mezei, Kohls, et al., 2011). The program comprises several online components for psychoeducation, self-help, peer support, and professional counseling. In the present pilot study, 22 women had access to the program for 4 months. The intervention proved feasible and well accepted, and participants‘ satisfaction with the program was high. Adherence to the various program components was overall acceptable. Patterns of utilization support the assumption that patients with eating disorders have heterogeneous needs for support following treatment termination. The study confirms the potential of flexible and individually tailored Internet-based interventions for the optimization of care for these patients.

Even with the best available treatment, most bulimia nervosa (BN) sufferers are not symptom free at the end of therapy and, for those who have achieved remission, risk of relapse is high (Robinson, Perkins, Bauer, Hammond, et al., 2006). Thus, there is a need for aftercare or relapse prevention interventions after therapy. It is not yet known what type of intervention should be delivered, and how to suit patient needs while being mindful of cost and time constraints of service providers. This pilot study was conducted to explore the feasibility, acceptability, and efficacy of a text messaging (short messaging service [SMS])-based intervention in the aftercare of BN patients who had received outpatient psychotherapy.

Little is known about what determines uptake and acceptability of internet-based treatments in eating disorders, and users' experience with such treatments. Sánchez-Ortiz, House, Munro, Treasure, et al., (2011) investigated these factors in participants of a randomized controlled trial of an internet-based cognitive- behavioral treatment (iCBT) package (Overcoming bulimia online). Nine participants were interviewed using purposive sampling. The content of interviews were analyzed using thematic analysis. Additionally, participants received questionnaires about their impressions of iCBT. Participants talked about their experience of using iCBT, its impact and compared it to other treatments. Questionnaire responses echoed themes identified in the interviews. iCBT was received positively as a way of fitting treatment into busy lives. Comments on the layout of some of the package content and the practitioner support offered were identified as areas that could be modified or improved.

Email has been progressively used as a means for providing therapeutic guidance and support for cognitive behavioral treatment (CBT) self-care programs. Many aspects of the use of email in self-care need to be explored such as the content of therapists' emails. Such information would optimize the delivery of self-care treatments (Sánchez-Ortiz, Munro, Startup, Treasure, et al., 2011). To date no study has looked at the content of the therapists' emails. The authors analyzed the content of emails (n = 712) sent by therapists to participants (n = 71) of a randomized controlled trial (RCT) of internet-based CBT with email support for bulimic disorders. 14.7% of the emails therapists sent contained at least one CBT comment, while 95.4% had at least one supportive comment and 13.6% had at least one technical comment. The mean time spent on providing email support to each participant across the complete program was 45 minutes. Emails sent by therapists were mainly supportive in content, with only a small amount of time being required by therapists to provide email support. (italics author's, n/e).

Bulimic eating disorders are common among female students, yet the majority do not access effective treatment. Internet-based cognitive-behavioral therapy (iCBT) may be able to bridge this gap (Sánchez-Ortiz, Munro, Stahl, House, et al., 2011). Seventy-six students with bulimia nervosa (BN) or eating disorder not otherwise specified (EDNOS) were randomly assigned to immediate iCBT with e-mail support over 3 months or to a 3-month waiting list followed by iCBT [waiting list/delayed treatment control (WL/DTC)]. ED outcomes were assessed with the Eating Disorder Examination (EDE) at baseline, 3 months and 6 months. Other outcomes included depression, anxiety and quality of life. Students who had immediate iCBT showed significantly greater improvements at 3 and 6 months than those receiving WL/DTC in ED and other symptoms. iCBT with e-mail support is efficacious in students with bulimic disorders and has lasting effects.

CONCLUSION

The results of most recent studies present a seemingly rosier picture than those reported by Marks et al., (2007) about low adherence rates. Within a stepped-care therapeutic context, one would conclude that Internet-related interventions for eating disorders should be the very first step before moving on to more expensive interventions requiring F2F contacts and inclusion of family members in the whole intervention process, as suggested by models of psychopathology reviewed by Hooper et al., 2014).

SECTION II. EXTERNALIZATIONS

Chapter 6

EXTERNALIZATIONS

The purpose of this chapter is to include as many studies that are available for disorders of externalizations, when individuals blame and put responsibility for their behavior on sources outside of the self. Originally, these disorders were included in the by-now-outdated Cluster B in the Psychiatric Association Diagnostic and Statistical Manual. These disorders are characterized by narcissistic acting out, disruptive, and in its extremes, out-and-out criminal behavior. A pioneer study with inmates using distance, programmed writing was initiated years ago but without controls or long-term follow-up (L'Abate, Reed, & McMahan, 2001). Nonetheless, that study showed that it is indeed possible to work at a distance with motivated inmates, especially if workbooks are specifically created to deal with externalizing behaviors (Hooper et al., 2014; L'Abate, 1992, 2011c, 2013b). It is relevant to note that no externalizing disorders were included in Marks et al., (2007) and Gallego and Emmelkamp's (2012) reviews.

ANGER MANAGEMENT

Therapist adherence to a manualized cognitive-behavioral anger management group treatment (AMT) was compared between therapy delivered via videoconference (VC) and the traditional in-person modality, using data from a large, randomized controlled trial comparing the effectiveness of AMT for veterans with combat-related PTSD (Morland, Greene, Grubbs, Kloezman, et al., 2011). Therapist adherence was rated for the presence or absence of process and content treatment elements. Secondary analyses were conducted using a repeated measures ANOVA. Overall adherence to the protocol was excellent ($M = 96\%$, $SD = 1\%$). Findings indicate that therapist adherence to AMT is similar across delivery modalities and VC is a viable service delivery strategy that does not compromise a therapist's ability to effectively structure sessions and manage patient care.

CYBERBULLYING

For a short background article on offline bullying the reader could consult Novotney (2014). For a more technical review article on offline bullying the reader could consult a chapter by its name in Hooper, L'Abate, Sweeney, Gianesini et al. (2014). Cyberbullying among adolescents has been a major focus of attention in mainstream media and has been documented to have many negative effects, as evidenced by several highly publicized suicides of teens who had been bullied online (Alvarez, 2012). The growing body of research about cyberbullying has rarely considered, however, the practice of cyberbullying between intimate partners. This article focuses on the frequency, types, and effect of cyberbullying between intimate partners in teen dating relationships. Alvarez also examined the use of cyber tools (electronic forms of communication) as mechanisms of power and control in relationships for both the target and the perpetrator. Suggested methods of prevention and intervention for adults working with teens who are experiencing cyberbullying in dating relationships were discussed.

VIOLENCE

This article reported on a 4-year therapeutic intervention combining in-person and email communication with a 13-year-old Greek-Cypriot teenager who witnessed and later was the victim of severe domestic violence (Georgiades, 2008). The intervention is based on an empowerment philosophy and solution-focused strategies, and its usefulness is evaluated by three standardized measures at five time points between the years 1999 and 2003. Pertinent cultural and ethical dynamics of the interventional context are highlighted. The intervention may have helped to produce better perpetrator–youth relations, remission of the client's depression and post-traumatic stress symptoms, and improvement in his academic performance. Implications and limitations were discussed.

CONCLUSION

A surprising conclusion from the very meager research available on externalizing disorders is a very inadequate number of studies attempting to deal with them. Contrary, to only clinical reports and workbooks to deal with many externalizing disorders, provided by L'Abate (1992, 2011c, 2013b), this population would be ideal for computer-driven Internet interventions. Unfortunately, many penal institutions seem resistant to the use of online interventions, apparently for fear of abuse and distortions in the process. Clearly, this population is in dire need of online interventions with workbooks especially designed to improve cognitive functions and decrease one of the major characteristics of externalizations, that is: impulsivity (L'Abate, 2011c, 2013b, 2013c).

SECTION III. CHILDREN, YOUTH, AND FAMILIES

Chapter 7

CHILDREN AND FAMILIES

According to Marks et al., (2007):

"Computer psychotherapy (CP) for childhood phobias, anxiety, depression, headache, brain injury, autism, encopresis was developed in at least seven systems.... They were tested in at least three open studies and Five RCTs lasting from just one session to 35 weeks. The systems ranged widely from simple presentation of a set of stimuli with progress to another level of answers were correct, through to multi-module, multi-media CD-ROM and net systems guiding a broad range of therapy tasks. Some CP systems were implemented as enhancements of TAU while others were part of joint CP plus live therapy either f2f or by videoconferencing. In various RCTs CP allowed f2f therapy time to be cut without impairing anxiety or headache reduction, and improved encopresis, parents' management of brain-injured progeny's behavior, and taught autistic children to recognize emotions in cartoons and stories.

Results seem(ed) promising for the use of CP in a variety of mental health problems in children. Of six children's interactive asthma education systems (none in the net) used the personal or case vignettes and games. All had an RCT and one a pilot (p. 187) study too. Of the RCTs, five were in asthma clinics and one in ordinary school classes. Comparisons were with usual care, non-asthma computer games, or educational booklets. The systems generally increased asthma knowledge in children and parents, improved asthma management and where measured, cost savings from fewer emergency room visits. Children and parents were generally satisfied with the systems. Overall, CP for managing childhood asthma had [shown] encouraging results"(p. 188),

Since, Marks et al. (2007) review, there have been significant workforce shortages for psychologists with expertise in evidence-supported therapies with children, particularly in nonmetropolitan areas. Nonetheless, no studies with children, youth, and their families were reported in the otherwise excellent review by Gallego and Emmelkamp (2012). Tele-psychology, or psychology services delivered by real-time videoconferencing, helps bridge this access gap (Nelson, Bui, & Velasquez, 2011). This article (Nelson et al., 2011), first reviewed the tele-psychology literature and then built on early tele-psychology guidance for the current practice environment. The practicalities of tele-psychology implementation and the lessons drawn from the more well-established tele-psychiatry practice were described.

The authors also provided an update to pioneering interdisciplinary telehealth principles presented a decade ago.

Several novel technologies have long been used in pediatric psychology (Van Allen, Davis, & Lassen, 2011). From using electronic pill-count bottles to track child adherence to pill-taking regimens to using bed alarms for night time enuresis, psychologists have relied on technology in their work with children who are ill. Much of the recent technology literature in pediatric psychology has focused on the use of the Internet and other Web-based technologies. This article thoroughly reviews the literature regarding telehealth in the field of pediatric psychology, more specifically the application of televideo or teleconferencing in various populations of children and adolescents with chronic illnesses, followed by the authors' clinical and research applications of telehealth in pediatric psychology. The review concludes with a summary of study findings and future directions in the field for clinicians and researchers alike.

In an introduction to a series of articles edited by Ritterband and Palermo (2009) revealed some of the diversity of this young field of eHealth in pediatric psychology The eHealth interventions developed and tested show great promise and may even have some significant advantages over traditional forms of care. For example, Internet interventions may lower barriers associated with face-to-face treatments, such as eliminating the need to travel to receive specialized care, the inconvenience of scheduling appointments, and missing work/school. Internet interventions also have the potential for wide-scale dissemination as they are capable of providing treatment to much greater numbers of people. This could be of particular importance in areas with limited resources or in the event that mass resources are needed.

eHealth interventions may also have the potential to reduce health disparity, particularly disparity caused by geographical isolation. In the United States, there are large and persistent racial, ethnic, and socioeconomic disparities in health across the life course (Harris, Gordon-Larsen, Chantala, & Udry, 2006; National Center for Health Statistics, 2002), with increasing economic and racial inequality (Lenfant, 1996). Although the reduction and ultimate elimination of these health disparities has been identified as a major public health goal (Satcher, 2000), these health disparities remain a steady trend in the US health system. Internet interventions and other technologies can be used to increase access to care by offering a method of treatment that is not restricted by geographical location, work schedule, or the availability of insurance. For example, the Askins et al. paper in this series, which focused on the use of PDAs to deliver problem-solving skills training to Spanish-speaking mothers, demonstrates the potential of using an eHealth treatment to provide care to an underserved group.

The eHealth field of pediatric psychology is still in its infancy and must address numerous challenges. Feasibility and efficacy trials, particularly related to pediatric-based Internet interventions, are showing promising results, but few studies have begun to examine how these programs might fare in the "real world" (Ritterband et al., 2008). Further, empirical support and validation is necessary as we move from efficacy to effectiveness trials. This research will be critical to establishing these types of programs as truly viable treatment options. However, if future research is able to build on the pioneering work presented here and continues to find results that support this treatment modality, Internet interventions may have the potential to reach more children and their families than would otherwise be served through more traditional forms of care. As we stated at the outset, we believe it is important for clinicians and researchers to be apprised of how eHealth technologies are being used in pediatric psychology and to consider these developments when thinking about provision of care in the future.

Tele-psychiatry is emerging as a valuable means of providing mental health care in juvenile justice settings. Youth in the juvenile justice system have high levels of psychiatric morbidity. State and local juvenile justice systems frequently struggle to provide specialized psychiatric care, as these systems have limited resources and often operate in remote locations. Case studies in the use of tele-psychiatry to provide improved care in juvenile corrections in 4 states are described, along with a review of advantages and disadvantages of tele-psychiatry in these settings (Kaliebe, Heneghan, and Kim, 2011).

In addition to tele-psychology and tele-psychiatry (L'Abate & Kaiser, 2012), neuroscience research is making rapid gains toward identifying associations between atypical brain development and mental health problems in children (South, Wolf, & Herlihy, 2012). The goal of such research was to identify risk and protective factors that affect treatment outcome, to personalize treatment to meet specific individual needs. In this review, the authors discussed the potential for developmental neuroscience research to directly inform professional practice in child and adolescent psychology. Beginning with the case presentation of an 11-year-old girl with multiple developmental difficulties, we highlight research using animal models along with studies of genetics and human neuroimaging that target three different dimensions: (a) face processing in autism; (b) response inhibition and impulsive behavior; and (c) the problems caused by anxiety that can cut across all child mental health conditions. The authors noted that neuroscience research necessarily depends on dimensional rather than categorical diagnostic approaches and discuss the benefits as well as some drawbacks to the clinical utility of dimensional definitions. As the technology to study brain development continues to improve, the need for basic researchers and practicing clinicians to communicate effectively with each other becomes all the more critical.

"Not accepting new patients," is a phrase too frequently heard by frantic parents in search of behavioral health treatment for their children (Ward-Zimmerman & Cannata, 2012). There are simply not enough services available to meet the need. The American Academy of Pediatrics (AAP) has endorsed primary care physicians (PCPs) as critical to ameliorating this state of affairs by promoting skill development for their membership to prevent, assess, and treat children's mental health issues. Health care reform initiatives are calling for the establishment of patient-centered medical homes (PCMHs) where the physician is responsible for ensuring comprehensive and well-coordinated care that includes mental health. These movements offer opportunities for psychologists to collaborate with PCPs, capitalizing on psychologists' specialized expertise. While there has been increasing discussion of collaborative health care models, much of this work is focused on the treatment of adults. This article draws on the authors' experiences developing a pediatric behavioral health and primary care colocation program in Connecticut and the lessons learned from more than a decade of partnering. The overarching lesson is that psychologists can facilitate practice transformation in pediatric primary care to improve early mental health detection, intervention, and referral. This article highlights knowledge, skill sets, and considerations for psychologists wishing to establish effective partnerships with pediatric primary care to improve behavioral health service delivery.

Increasingly, young people are using various forms of technology in the service of communicating with others, and many have noted the possibility of various dire consequences of this phenomenon, including sexting, cyberbullying, online harassment, and Internet addiction (Farber, Shafron, Hamadani, Wald, & Nitzburg, 2012). In their own survey of over 300 adolescents, these authors found that texting and face-to-face communication were considered the most "convenient" forms of communication, while face-to-face communication and phone conversations were perceived as most likely to lead to "feeling understood" and "feeling intimate." Face-to-face communication and texting were perceived as most likely to result in feeling regret for sharing too much information. By choosing to communicate through technology, many young people, including our patients, can continue to be social and, at the same time, keep a somewhat safer emotional distance.

In line with the wider trend of offering support via the Internet, many counseling and referral services for children have introduced online chat, often in addition to a traditional telephone service. A comparative study was conducted between the telephone service and the confidential one-on-one online chat service of the Dutch Kindertelefoon. The design included a concise pretest and a posttest (n = 902). The study also comprised a follow-up test (n = 213), which included the Strengths and Difficulties Questionnaire. Children experienced a higher sense of well-being and a reduced severity of their problems after consulting the Kindertelefoon. The results were slightly more favorable for the chat service than for the telephone service. The follow-up survey showed that many of the children who contact the Kindertelefoon suffer from relatively severe emotional problems. Both telephone and web-based support improved the children's well-being and decreased their perceived burden of problem. The results of this study underline the need for closer cooperation between child helplines and mental health and child welfare services.

CHILDHOOD ANXIETY

Seventy-two clinically anxious children, aged 7 to 14 years, were randomly allocated to clinic-based, cognitive-behavior therapy, the same treatment partially delivered via the Internet, or a wait list control (WL). Children in the clinic and clinic-plus-Internet conditions showed significantly greater reductions in anxiety from pre- to post treatment and were more likely to be free of their anxiety diagnoses, compared with the WL group. Improvements were maintained at 12-month follow-up for both therapy conditions, with minimal difference in outcomes between interventions. The Internet treatment content was highly acceptable to families, with minimal dropout and a high level of therapy compliance.

AUTISM SPECTRUM DISORDERS

Effective training of caregivers is an integral part of top-quality treatment programs for individuals with autism spectrum disorders (ASD.(Jang, Dixon, Tarbox, Granpeesheh, et al., 2012). However, traditional caregiver training can be time consuming and costly. The development of Web-based electronic training programs (e.g., "eLearning") may extend training to rural areas, thereby increasing accessibility and improving efficiency. The eLearning approach has been shown to be effective and efficient in various disciplines and industries, but studies evaluating eLearning programs for training parents of children with

ASD are limited. The purpose of this study was to evaluate the effectiveness of an eLearning program for training family members of children with ASD in the principles and procedures of applied behavior analysis treatment. A total of 28 family members participated in this randomized, waitlist-controlled, between-groups study. Differences in change scores between groups were significant, with the trained group substantially outperforming the waitlist control group at post-test. The control group then received training and also demonstrated significant gains post training.

This article described an evolution of training programs to use first-person interaction in virtual reality (VR) situations to teach safety skills to children with autism spectrum disorder (ASD) and fetal alcohol spectrum disorder (FASD).(Strickland, McAllister, Coles, & Osborne, 2007). Multiple VR programs for children aged 2 to 9 were built and tested between 1992 and 2007. Based on these results, a learning design evolved that uses practice in virtual space with guidance and correction by an animated character, strategic limitations on allowed actions to force correct patterning, and customization of worlds and responses to simplify user controls. This article describes program evolution by comparing design details and results as variations in behavioral responses between disorders, differences in skill set complexity between different safety skills being taught, and improved technology required changes in the virtual training methodology. A series of research projects are summarized in which the VR programs proved effective for teaching children with ASD and FASD new skills in the virtual space and, where measured, most children generalized the actions to the real world.

ENCOPRESIS

Since 1995, Borowitz and Ritterband (2001) have maintained a tutorial about chronic childhood constipation and encopresis on their web site. The tutorial is directed at parents and older children and includes a feedback form comprised of six multiple-choice questions and a free-text comment field. Between 1 January 1998 and 30 April 2000, these authors received 1,142 completed feedback forms. The vast majority of respondents identified themselves as parents or guardians of a child with constipation or encopresis. All respondents felt the tutorial was clear and easy to understand. 98% of respondents felt the tutorial helped them understand why children develop constipation and/or encopresis and 91% of respondents felt the tutorial made them better able to take care of a child suffering from constipation and/or encopresis. More than 99% of respondents felt this type of tutorial was a good way to teach people about health problems. 74% of participants sent us comments about the tutorial. Most often, the comments expressed thanks for having this information available in clear and understandable language, however a significant number of people inquired about a particular child's difficulties or asked a general question not clearly pertaining to a particular child. The results of this study indicate that many people are searching the Internet for information concerning childhood encopresis and that the World Wide Web can provide families with useful information about this common pediatric problem.

This study evaluated the benefits of enhanced toilet training delivered through the Internet for children with encopresis (Ritterband, Cox, Walker, Kovatchev et al., (2003). Twenty-four children with encopresis were randomly assigned to the Internet intervention Group (Web) or no Internet intervention group (No-Web). All participants continued to receive routine care from their primary care physician. The Web participants demonstrated greater improvement in terms of reduced fecal soiling, increased defecation in the toilet, and increased imprompted trips to the toilet ($ps<.02$). Both groups demonstrated similar improvements in knowledge and toileting behaviors. Internet interventions may be an effective way of delivering sophisticated behavioral interventions to a large and dispersed population in a convenient format.

The objective of this investigation was to evaluate whether parental worry about their children's health predicts usage of a pediatric Internet intervention for encopresis (Magee, Ritterband, Thorndike, Cox, & Borowitz, 2008). Thirty-nine families with a child diagnosed with encopresis completed a national clinical trial of an Internet-based intervention for encopresis (www.ucanpooptoo.com). Parents rated worry about their children's health, encopresis severity, current parent treatment for depression, and parent comfort with the Internet. Usage indicators were collected while participants utilized the intervention. Regression analyses showed that parents who reported higher baseline levels of worry about their children's health showed greater subsequent intervention use ($\beta = .52$, $p = .002$), even after accounting for other plausible predictors. Exploratory analyses indicated that this effect may be stronger for families with younger children. Characteristics of individuals using Internet-based treatment programs, such as parental worry about their children's health, can influence intervention usage, and should be considered by developers of Internet interventions.

The Internet is a significant source of medical information and is now being shown to be an important conduit for delivering various health-related interventions. Ritterband, Ardalan, Thorndike, Magee, Saylor, Cox, Sutphen, and Borowitz, (2008) examined the utility and impact of an Internet intervention for childhood encopresis as part of standard medical care in a "real world" setting. Patients diagnosed with encopresis were given a Web-based information prescription to use an Internet intervention for pediatric encopresis. A total of 22 families utilized the intervention between July 2004 and June 2006. A chart review and phone interview were undertaken to collect user characteristics; defecation-related information, including frequency of soiling, bowel movements (BMs) in the toilet, and amount of pain associated with defecation; and information on computer/Internet usage. Three questionnaires were used to examine the utility of, impact of, and adherence to the Internet intervention. Program utilization was obtained from a data tracking system that monitored usage in real time.

Overall, parents rated the Internet intervention as enjoyable, understandable, and easy to use. They indicated that the Internet intervention positively affected their children, decreasing overall accidents and increasing child comfort on the toilet at home. Of the 20 children who initially reported fecal accidents, 19 (95%) experienced at least a 50% improvement, with a reduction of accident frequency from one fecal accident per day to one accident per week. Although it was not clear whether this improvement is directly related to the use of the Internet intervention, patient feedback suggested that the program was an important element, further establishing Internet interventions as a viable and desirable addition to standard medical care for pediatric encopresis.

To those authors' knowledge, this is the first time a pediatric Internet intervention has been examined as part of a "real world" setting. This is an important step toward establishing Internet interventions as an adjunctive component to treatment of pediatric patients in a clinical setting, particularly given the positive user feedback, possible cost savings, and significant potential for large-scale dissemination.

Encopresis is a significant medical problem for millions of children. Despite its prevalence, poor treatment success rates indicate that it is often difficult to treat. The goal of this study (Ritterband, Thorndike, Lord, Borowitz, Walker, Ingersoll, Sutphen, & Cox, 2013) was to evaluate an Internet intervention for encopresis (UCanPoopToo) with children from across the US. A 2 (Group) × 3 (Time) RCT was used to evaluate the efficacy of UCanPoopToo. Participants were randomized to a treatment-as-usual (TAU) or TAU + UCanPoopToo group. Assessments were completed at baseline (Pre), 4–6 weeks following baseline (Post), and one year follow-up (Post12). At baseline, the TAU and TAU + UCanPoopToo retrospectively reported a median 9 and 8 accidents, respectively, over the previous two weeks. Using prospective online diary data, the TAU group reported a median 8 accidents at Post and 3 accidents at Post12, compared to the TAU + UCanPoopToo group report of a median 4.5 accidents at Post and 1 accident at Post12. At Post12, a significant difference was found between success rates (≤1 accident/2 weeks) of 28% for the TAU group and 64% for the TAU + UCanPoopToo group. At Post12, a significant difference was also found between cure rates (0 accidents/2 weeks) of 20% for the TAU group and 50% for the TAU + UCanPoopToo group. This study supports the use of an Internet intervention for encopresis. Increasing the ability for clinicians to refer their patients to evidence-based Internet interventions has meaningful implications for clinical practice as it extends the reach of treatment options for patients and enables provision of interventions otherwise unavailable.

Rural Obesity in Children

Pediatric obesity occurs most frequently in underserved communities where families have difficulty accessing healthcare (Megan, Irby, Boles, & Skelton, 2012). Disproportionate obesity rates in rural children denote significant disparities warranting innovative solutions. However, intensive, tertiary-care treatment options outlined in recent expert recommendations may not be available to families living in rural areas. Telemedicine may be useful for providing pediatric obesity treatment to rural families. The aim of this study was to assess the impact of a new outreach program (TeleFIT), which placed telemonitors in four rural satellite clinics to increase access to a pediatric obesity clinic (Brenner Families In Training [FIT]). Before TeleFIT began, of five patients from rural counties enrolled in treatment over a 1-year period, all dropped out by their third visit. Within the first year of TeleFIT, the number of rural patients increased nearly threefold (to 14) and increased again in the second year by an additional 16 new patients (n=35). Preliminary outcomes indicate comparable attrition rates and improvement in weight status compared with patients in conventional treatment. Telemedicine allows rural families to access intensive obesity treatment from local pediatric offices, eliminating geographic barriers. Systems delivering state-of-the-art care in rural areas have tremendous potential for reducing health disparities in rural populations. Further research is needed to test the efficacy of such interventions.

The objective of this study was to determine health care provider needs related to pediatric obesity management in rural California and to explore strategies to improve care through telehealth (Shaikh, Nettiksimmons, & Romano, 2011). This study consisted of a cross-sectional survey of health care providers who treated children and adolescents at 41 rural clinics with existing telehealth connectivity. Most of the 135 respondents were family physicians at designated rural health clinics serving low-income families. Respondents had practiced in rural areas for an average of 10 years. Most providers rated their self-efficacy in managing pediatric obesity as 2 or 3 on a 5-point scale. The barriers most frequently reported by health care providers were lack of local weight management programs, lack of patient motivation, and lack of family involvement in treatment. Providers reported that the resources they would find most helpful were readily accessible patient education materials, strategies to link patients with community treatment programs and training in brief, focused counseling skills. Three-quarters of providers already used telehealth for distance learning. Providers reported very high interest in participating in continuing education on pediatric obesity delivered by telehealth, specifically Internet communication with specialists, web-based education, and interactive video case-conferencing. In conclusion, rural health care providers face several barriers related to pediatric obesity management. Targeted interventions provided via telehealth to rural health care providers may enhance the care of obese children and adolescents. The results of this study provide directions and priorities for the design of appropriate interventions.

Phobias

Cognitive behavior therapy (CBT) has been shown to be an effective treatment for specific phobia in youth, but not all affected seek or receive treatment. Internet-delivered CBT could be a way to increase the availability of empirically supported treatments (Vigerland, Thulin, Ljótsson, Svirsky, et al. (2013). An open trial was conducted to evaluate Internet-delivered CBT for children with specific phobia. Children (N = 30) aged 8–12, and their parents, with a principal diagnosis of specific phobia were recruited through media advertisement. Participants received six weeks of Internet-delivered CBT with therapist support. The treatment was aimed for the parents and the children, with the first part being only for the parents. The primary outcome measure was the Clinician Severity Rating (CSR), and secondary measures included clinician-rated global functioning and child- and parent-reported anxiety and quality of life. All assessments were made at pretreatment, post-treatment, and three-month follow-up. At post-treatment, there were significant reductions on the CSR, with a large within-group effect size (Cohen's d = 1.0) and 35% of children no longer meeting criteria for specific phobia. Self-report measures from parents and children showed significant effects on anxiety, with small to moderate effect sizes. Effects were maintained at three-month follow-up. Results showed that Internet-delivered CBT with therapist support for children with specific phobia has the potential to reduce symptom severity. Randomized controlled trials are needed to further evaluate this treatment format.

Children and Youth

Contributors to this special issue of The Journal of Clinical Psychology: In Session have given us a wide range of ideas about technology use among children and adolescents, illustrated with rich clinical material (Rosegrant, 2012). Of the many interesting issues they raise, the author briefly discussed four that are particularly salient: the interaction of technology with personality and development; the concept of Internet addiction; the importance of adult guidance and limit setting; and technology and clinical creativity. Taken as a whole, these papers suggested that while technology can certainly contribute to and help create pathology, it can also contribute to growth, and that in either case technology interacts with fundamental human needs and developmental processes.

CHILD AND ADOLESCENTS VIDEOCONFERENCING

Ciccia, Whitfor, Krumm, & McNeal (2011) studied the feasibility of low-cost videoconferencing (using Skype) in urban community health clinics for speech, language and hearing screening of children up to six years of age. During a two-year study, screening services were provided via videoconferencing at two community clinics in an inner city area of Cleveland, Ohio. In total, 411 screenings were completed. Of these, 358 children (87%) received hearing screenings, 377 (92%) received tympanometry screening and 263 (64%) received speech and language screening only. A total of 151 children were aged three years or under (37%). The reliability of pure tone hearing screening (n = 7), DPOAE screening (n = 51) and speech-language screening (n = 10) was 100%. Typanometry screenings (n = 55) were 84% reliable. Families reported a high level of satisfaction with both the technology and with the videoconferencing. The results indicate that low-cost videoconferencing for screening of speech, language and hearing development in very young children in urban community health clinics is feasible, reliable and strongly supported by the community.

Children and adolescents living in rural areas have difficulty accessing psychological services due to a lack of psychologists and other behavioral health professionals, especially those with expertise in treating youth (Duncan, Velasquez, & Nelson, 2014).Telepsychology helps bridge this access gap. This article extended evidence supporting videoconferencing for psychological assessment and treatment in adults to support telepsychological treatment for youth. In addition, the basic components needed to begin and sustain a telepsychological practice are explored. Finally, a case example of an adolescent presenting with depression and disordered eating illustrates the practice of, and ethical standards needed for, telepsychology. Future technologies and applications around tele-psychology were also discussed.

CHILDREN, COUPLES AND FAMILIES

Internet Addiction

Excessive and potentially addictive use of the Internet among children and adolescents has emerged as a major concern in recent times (King, Defabbro, Griffith, & Gradisar, 2012). Internet addiction is often conceptualized as an impulse control disorder, with features similar to pathological gambling. However, there remains considerable debate about the core components, etiological processes, course, and maintaining factors of the disorder. This article presents a case study of a 16-year-old male with generalized pathological Internet use.

Critical issues relevant to case conceptualization, assessment, and choice of therapy were examined. Although the evidence base seemed limited in this emerging area of clinical psychology, the authors provided a summary of empirically supported cognitive-behavioral techniques for Internet addiction.

This article explored the inevitable phenomenon of online therapy provided by professional counselors (Pollock, 2006). Advantages of Internet counseling were examined from clients' and counselors' perspectives. Disadvantages were discussed, particularly in the area of asynchronous communication without the benefit of nonverbal cues. The possibility of providing marriage and family counseling via the Internet was considered. Through perusal and extrapolation of the current literature available on Internet counseling, this article speculated on the potential usefulness of this venue in the 21st century and the need for more research.

Overweight Children

Interactive technologies have the potential to increase the reach and frequency of practical clinical interventions that assist the parents of overweight and at-risk children to promote healthy lifestyle behaviors for their families (Estabrooks, Shoup, Gattshall, Dandamudi, Shetterly, & Xu, 2009). A practical RCT evaluated the relative effectiveness of three interventions to support parents of overweight or at-risk children to change the home environment to foster more healthful child eating and activity behaviors, thereby reducing child BMI and BMI z-scores. A secondary purpose was to determine the patterns of use and potential dose effect for the highest-intensity intervention. Setting/participants: Parent-and-child (aged 8–12 years) dyads (N=220) who received care from Kaiser Permanente Colorado were assigned randomly to one of the three Family Connections (FC) interventions: FC-workbook, FC-group, or FC-interactive voice response (IVR) counseling. Main outcome measures: Child BMI z-scores, as well as symptoms of eating disorders and body image, were assessed at baseline, 6 months, and 12 months. Results: The BMI z-scores of children assigned to the FC-IVR intervention were the only ones that decreased from baseline to 6 months (0.07 SD) and from baseline to 12 months (0.08 SD, $p<0.05$). Children whose parents completed at least six of the ten FC-IVR counseling calls had decreased BMI z-scores to a greater extent than children in the FC-workbook or FC-group interventions at both 6 months ($p<0.05$) and 12 months ($p<0.01$). No intervention increased child symptoms of eating disorders or body dissatisfaction at any time point. Conclusions: This trial demonstrated that automated telephone counseling can support the parents of overweight children to reduce the extent to which their children are overweight.

Low-income Families

This article outlined the development and usability–feasibility testing of an automated text-messaging adjunct to cognitive–behavioral therapy (CBT) for depression in a public sector clinic serving low-income patients (Aguilera & Muñoz, 2011). The text-messaging adjunct is aimed at increasing homework adherence, improving self-awareness, and helping track patient progress. Daily text messages were sent to patients, inquiring about their mood. Additional daily messages corresponded to themes of a manualized group CBT intervention. These included (1) thought tracking (both positive and negative), (2) tracking of pleasant activities, (3) tracking of positive and negative contacts, and (4) tracking of physical well-being. Aguilera and Muñoz (2011) tested the adjunct in 2 CBT groups (1 English & 1 Spanish) consisting of 12 patients total during and after treatment. Participants responded at a rate of 65% to text messages, and they reported overall positive experiences. The authors proposed that text messaging has the potential to improve mental health care broadly, and among low-income populations specifically, with cost-effective means.

Sexual Abuse

The training of physicians, nurse examiners, social workers and other health professional on the evidentiary findings of sexual abuse in children is challenging (Frasier, Thraen, Kaplan, & Goede, 2012). The objective of this study was to develop peer reviewed training cases for medical examiners of child sexual abuse, using a secure web based telehealth application (TeleCAM). Methods: Sixty de-identified cases developed by 2 child abuse pediatricians, were stratified by availability of information (minimal, moderate, comprehensive) for both positive and negative child sexual abuse findings. These cases were narrowed to a set of 30 cases through an expert peer review process using pediatricians with extensive expertise in the evaluation of child sexual abuse. A previously studied secure web-based telehealth application TeleCAM which contains a child abuse workflow, was used to develop, disseminate and review cases. A series of Free Margin agreement statistics are used to select those cases with the highest rates of agreement. A final set of 30 cases are stratified equally by availability of information and for both positive and negative findings. Mantel Haenszel Chi-square was used for trend analysis of the ordered categorical variables. Results: The highest degrees of inter-rater reliability was found in cases with moderate to comprehensive information. Cases with minimal data had poor kappa agreement indicating that availability of differing levels and types of information contribute to variability in diagnostic findings. These final cases will be further studied with medical examiners in various settings utilizing TeleCAM as the application for dissemination.

School Mental Health

The provision of mental health services in schools has been one effective strategy for reaching out to a greater number of youth to identify and provide treatment for mental health issues (Grady, Lever, Cunningham, Stephan, 2011). With the increasing challenges related to shortages in child and adolescent psychiatrists, it is critical to develop models of care that can maximize a full range of mental health services for all children and adolescents who need them. Telehealth offers an innovative distance technology strategy to effectively and efficiently provide access to psychiatric services in schools. Telepsychiatry has the potential to better link and enhance the provision of health services, and can be particularly beneficial in addressing geographic distance and/or capacity issues. This article describes the clinical, educational, and administrative uses of telemental health in the school environment with mental health professionals and staff.

Youth Special Needs

In recent years an increasing number of people under psychological distress turn to computer-mediated communication for support. A related development is the increasing number of computer-mediated support groups in which people meet, share interests, and exchange socio-emotional support through text-based messages on computer networks. To date, a few policy makers and researchers have addressed the phenomenon of social-emotional support through electronic communication for populations with special needs. This paper presents a conceptual framework developed to characterize an electronic socio-emotional support process for people with special needs (Spigelman, Reiter, & Weiss, 2009). The electronic socio-emotional support framework is based on a review of the literature as well as the results of a pilot study, which examined the use of an electronic mentoring intervention program based on mutual self-disclosure and friendship between mentors and youth with special needs. The implications of the electronic socio-emotional support framework for people with special needs are discussed.

Parent–Child Interaction Therapy (PCIT)

Parent–Child Interaction Therapy (PCIT) training was provided to therapists working with parents of children with disruptive behavior problems (Wilsie & Brestan-Knight, 2012). Therapists uploaded video-recordings of selected sessions using a web-based tool for video sharing and review, the Video Analysis Tool (VAT). Trainers utilized the VAT for consultation to improve treatment fidelity. Clinical practice benefits include the ability to provide targeted, specific feedback to the trainees soon after a session and to disseminate PCIT to a larger, global audience.

Videoconferencing Children and Youth

Although tele-psychiatry can increase access to care for underserved populations, its use presents challenges to practicing culturally competent care, especially when high degrees of cultural disparity exist between the psychiatrist and the patient and/or family (Savin, Glueck, Chardavoyne, & Novins, 2011). Psychiatrists delivering care from a distance may be challenged to understand the health beliefs and practices of the local community as well as the social and community settings of clients from different cultural backgrounds. Similarly, because providing services via tele-psychiatry typically requires the involvement of different health care organizations, bridging distinct institutional cultures can challenge the effective delivery of services. Cultural awareness and sensitivity from the tele-psychiatrist are prerequisites for helping culturally diverse and remote-dwelling patients to access quality care. This article elucidates cultural challenges encountered in the practice of tele-psychiatry and offers suggestions for how to deal with them.

CONCLUSION

The evidence included in this chapter indicates how and how much the Internet can add to improve existing mental health needs of children and their families. The need for more controlled studies using programmed distance writing is clear, especially with children (Hooper et al., 2014).

We cannot longer rely solely on F2F talk-based paradigm after reading how helpful online interventions can be with children and their families.

Chapter 8

YOUTH

The purpose of this chapter is to review online interventions with youth or young adults. Despite the high prevalence of mental health concerns, few young adults access treatment. While much research has focused on understanding the barriers to service access, few studies have explored unbiased accounts of the experiences of young adults with mental health concerns (Marcus, Westra, Eastwood, & Barnes, 2012). It is through hearing these experiences and gaining an in-depth understanding of what is being said by young adults that improvements can be made to interventions focused on increasing access to care. The objective of this study was to move beyond past research by using an innovative qualitative research method of analyzing the blogs of young adults (18–25 years of age) with mental health concerns to understand their experiences. The authors used an enhanced Internet search vehicle, DEVONagent, to extract Internet blogs using primary keywords related to mental health. Blogs (N = 8) were selected based on age of authors (18–25 years), gender, relevance to mental health, and recency of the entries. Blogs excerpts were analyzed using a combination of grounded theory and consensual qualitative research methods. Two core categories emerged from the qualitative analysis of the bloggers accounts: I am powerless (intrapersonal) and I am utterly alone (interpersonal). Overall, the young adult bloggers expressed significant feelings of powerlessness as a result of their mental health concerns and simultaneously felt a profound sense of loneliness, alienation, and lack of connection with others. The present study suggested that one reason young adults do not seek care might be that they view the mental health system negatively and feel disconnected from these services. To decrease young adults' sense of powerlessness and isolation, efforts should focus on creating and developing resources and services that allow young adults to feel connected and empowered. Through an understanding of the experiences of young adults with mental health problems, and their experiences of and attitudes toward receiving care, the authors provided some recommendations for improving receptivity and knowledge of mental health care services for youth and young adults.

Engaging adolescents is one of many challenges facing Child and Adolescent Mental Health Services today. However, taking advantage of the technology available can bring professionals a step closer to their patients by providing an alternative means of interaction. In this article, Mehta and Calhoun (2006) explored the use of e-mail as a method of engaging adolescents. The advantages and disadvantages of e-mailing patients were discussed along with recommendations for its safe use.

Mental health interventions for young people are increasingly being delivered online. This is occurring due to an assumption that young people prefer online interventions because they address some of the well-established help-seeking barriers (Bradford & Rickwood, 2014). A self-report questionnaire investigating preferences for mental health care delivery was administered to a nonclinical sample of 231 young people aged 15-19. The strongest help-seeking intention in response to a scenario describing symptoms of depression was for face-to-face services, followed by not seeking help at all. Only 16% expressed a preference for online treatment. Conclusion The assumption that a majority of young people will prefer online delivery of mental health treatment was not supported, although boys showed a stronger relative preference for online modes.

Internet has become increasingly common in adolescents‘ daily lives and also in health care. However, there is still need to explore how nurses perceive its use as a part of adolescents' treatment (Kurki, Kovivunen, Anttila, Hätönen, et al., 2011). This qualitative study aimed to explore how nurses perceive the usefulness of Internet in adolescents' outpatient care in mental health. The data were collected among nurses (n=12) working in two psychiatric adolescent outpatient clinics in university central hospitals in Finland. The data were collected in focus group interviews and analysed using inductive content analysis. The analysis showed that Internet use could promote the care process of adolescents with depression by supporting their self-reflection and self-management, enhancing nurses' understanding of adolescents' daily lives and facilitating nurse-adolescent interaction. Disadvantages identified among nurses were fear of role changes in the nurse-adolescent interaction, changes in the intervention, when Internet might be a third party in the face-to-face interaction and negative effects of Internet on adolescents. Facilitators in the use of Internet were nurses' positive attitude to Internet, knowledge and experiences of Internet usage. Nurses' negative attitude to Internet and lack of training and instructions were seen as barriers in promoting the successful utilization of Internet among adolescents with depression in outpatient care.

The purpose of this article was to examine the needs and views of adolescents regarding the development of online support for mental health problems (Havas, de Nooijer, Crutzen, & Feron, 2011). Semi-structured qualitative focus group interviews were conducted with ten groups of Dutch adolescents (n=106), aged 12-19 years, from four urban secondary schools offering different levels of education in the Southeastern part of The Netherlands. Interviews were verbally transcribed and analyzed with Nvivo, using a classification based on the research questions. Participants reported that they searched on the internet to get information or help for some mental health problems. They also expressed the need for a youth healthcare website offering information, self-tests and anonymous help. They had different ideas about the layout of such a website, which were related to their educational level. Reliability of such a website was an important issue. Practical implications related to adolescents' reporting a distinct need for online information and help for mental health problems. Youth healthcare organizations could meet this need by creating an innovative additional assistance method. These organizations should cooperate with website developers, taking into account that adolescents with different levels of education have different preferences regarding the interventions for online information and help. This article provided a conclusive examination of the needs and views of adolescents regarding development of online support for mental health problems.

Bailey, Yager, and Jenson (2002) discussed the use of computer technology in the practice of good psychiatry, with reference to other historical technological innovations that have been incorporated by clinicians and patients. Two clinical vignettes were presented to illustrate the Internet both as a feature of the psychiatric landscape and as a tool for psychiatric intervention. The 1st case described the computer-facilitated enhancement of social life for a 15-yr-old male patient with social phobia. The 2nd case described email as an adjunctive treatment tool in the outpatient management of a 17-yr-old female with anorexia nervosa. These cases were used to illustrate the point that new technologies can yield examples of classic psychotherapeutic phenomena and dilemmas. Suggestions for future usage, clinical issues, ethical matters, and the limitations of computer technology in delivering psychiatric care were discussed.

BIPOLAR DISORDER

Despite efforts that have been made to develop and evaluate psychosocial interventions for youth with bipolar spectrum disorders (BPSDs), there has been limited evidence regarding treatment delivery and consumer experiences in clinical settings (Chung, Vesco, Resko, Schiman, & Fristad, 2012). Two parallel web-based surveys were conducted to assess clinicians' experiences with providing psychosocial treatments to youth with BPSD, and caregivers' experiences with accessing and receiving care for their youth with BSPD. Clinicians who were members of the American Psychological Association's Division 53 listserv were invited to report on (1) their training in and knowledge of BPSD among youth; (2) types of treatments they had provided and their perceived effectiveness; (3) treatment-related challenges; and (4) further training opportunities or resources they desire. Caregivers who were members of the Balanced Mind Foundation listserv were invited to participate in a separate survey. They were asked to report on both negative and positive experiences they had in their most recent experience with accessing and receiving psychosocial treatment for their youth with BPSD. Overall, the majority of clinician respondents reported receiving training in providing psychosocial treatments to youth with BPSD, though most reported desiring further training and greater access to resources (e.g., treatment manuals, workshops, case consultation). Caregivers indicated overall positive experiences with psychosocial treatments for their youth with BPSD. Positive experiences included those associated with nonspecific factors of therapy, and negative experiences included content-related factors and barriers to accessing treatments. Implications for enhancing treatment delivery and overall experience of psychosocial interventions among youth with BPSD were discussed.

BRAIN INJURY

The objective of this study was to examine the efficacy of teen online problem solving (TOPS) in improving executive function (EF) deficits following traumatic brain injury (TBI) in adolescence (Wade, Walz, Carey, Williams, et al., 2010). Families of adolescents (aged 11–18 years) with moderate to severe TBI were recruited from the trauma registry of 2 tertiary-care children's hospitals and then randomly assigned to receive TOPS (n = 20), a cognitive-behavioral, skill-building intervention, or access to online resources regarding TBI (Internet resource comparison; n = 21). Parent and teen reports of EF were assessed at baseline and a post-treatment follow-up (mean = 7.88 months later). Improvements in self-reported EF skills were moderated by TBI severity, with teens with severe TBI in the TOPS treatment reporting significantly greater improvements than did those with severe TBI in the Internet resource comparison. The treatment groups did not differ on parent ratings of EF at the follow up. Findings suggested that TOPS may be effective in improving EF skills among teens with severe TBI.

The objective of this preliminary report was to evaluate the efficacy of a Web-based treatment program to improve adolescent and family psychosocial functioning following traumatic brain injury (TBI). (Wade, Walz, Carey, & Williams, 2008, 2009). Participants were the families of 9 adolescents with TBI (2 severe and 7 moderate) injured less than 24 months ago participated in this study. The intervention consisted of a Web-based family treatment program designed to enhance family problem solving and adjustment, as well as reduce adolescent behavioral and social problems that are common sequelae of moderate-to-severe TBI was used as intervention. The program consisted of 10 core sessions and up to 4 supplemental sessions, each consisting of self-guided Web exercises followed by a videoconference therapy session. Significant improvements were found in parent-reported adolescent internalizing behaviors, self-reported adolescent depressive symptoms, parental depression, and parent-adolescent conflict. Effect sizes were in the medium-to-high range for these same contrasts. Exploratory analyses suggested that providing audio with the Web site may enhance some outcomes. This study provided preliminary evidence for the feasibility and efficacy of family-centered online intervention for improving adolescent and family adaptation following pediatric TBI.

The purpose of this study was to examine the efficacy of teen online problems solving (TOPS) in improving executive Function (EF) deficits following traumatic brain injury (TBI) in adolescence (Wade, Walz, Carey, Williams, et al. (2010). Families of adolescents (aged 11-18 years) with moderate to severe TBI were recruited from the trauma registry of 2 tertiary-care children's hospitals and then randomly assigned to receive TOPS (n = 20), a cognitive-behavioral, skill-building intervention, or access to online resources regarding TBI (Internet resource comparison; n = 21). Parent and teen reports of EF were assessed at baseline and a post-treatment follow-up (mean = 7.88 months later). Improvements in self-reported EF skills were moderated by TBI severity, with teens with severe TBI in the TOPS treatment reporting significantly greater improvements than did those with severe TBI in the Internet resource comparison. The treatment groups did not differ on parent ratings of EF at the follow up. This finding suggested that TOPS may be effective in improving EF skills among teens with severe TBI.

BULIMIA NERVOSA

The evidence base for the treatment of adolescents with bulimia nervosa (BN) is limited (Pretorius, Arcelus, Beecham, Dawson, et al. 2009). The aim of this study was to assess the feasibility, acceptability, and clinical outcomes of a web-based cognitive-behavioural (CBT) intervention for adolescents with bulimic symptomatology. Hundred and one participants were recruited from eating disorders clinics or from beat, a UK-wide eating disorders charity. The program consisted of online CBT sessions ('Overcoming Bulimia Online'), peer support via message boards, and email support from a clinician. Participants' bulimic symptomatology and service utilization were assessed by interview at baseline and at three and six months. Participants' views of the treatment package were also determined. There were significant improvements in eating disorder symptoms and service contacts from baseline to three months, which were maintained at six months. Participants' views of the intervention were positive. The intervention has the potential for use as a first step in the treatment of adolescents with bulimic symptomatology.

Cognitive Behavioral Therapy for Anxiety and Depression

The aim in this study was to investigate the effectiveness of an online, self-directed cognitive–behavioral therapy program (MoodGYM) in preventing and reducing symptoms of anxiety and depression in an adolescent school-based population (Calear, Christensen, Mackinnon, Griffiths, & O'Kearney, 2009). A cluster randomized controlled trial was conducted with 30 schools (N = 1,477) from across Australia, with each school randomly allocated to the intervention or wait list control condition. At post-intervention and 6-month follow-up, participants in the intervention condition had significantly lower levels of anxiety than did participants in the wait list control condition (Cohen's d = 0.15–0.25). The effects of the MoodGYM program on depressive symptoms were less strong, with only male participants in the intervention condition exhibiting significant reductions in depressive symptoms at post-intervention and 6-month follow-up (Cohen's d = 0.27–0.43). Although small to moderate, the effects obtained in the current study provide support for the utility of universal prevention programs in schools. The effectiveness of booster sessions should be explored in future research.

Counseling

Kids Help Line (KHL) is a national Australian youth counseling service that provides free online and telephone counseling (Bambling, King, Reid, & Wegner, 2008). This qualitative study examined the experience of 26 online KHL counselors. Using a focus group methodology, counselor responses were organized into categories: privacy and an emotionally safe environment; communication through text; and time. Counselors reported the main benefit of the online environment to be emotional safety, due to reduced client emotional proximity to the counselor, and the main disadvantage to be that reduced emotional proximity and the absence of non-verbal cues could result in communication problems and difficulty in accurately assessing young people's concerns. Time proved a significant issue for counselors, as the slow speed of text exchange could limit their ability to complete interventions. Methods that enhance both the process and effectiveness of online counseling are needed. Potential solutions to the challenges faced by online counselors are discussed.

This study focused upon the development of online counseling services for young people in the UK (Hanley, 2006) using online forums to host an asynchronous focus group with the intention of bringing together the views of a small sample of counselors and counselors in training regarding the subject matter. The focus group lasted a one-month period and initiated 10 threads of discussion and received 41 message postings. These dialogues were analyzed using a Grounded Theory approach. Findings suggested that although there is a great potential for offering therapy in this medium, services need to be appropriately regulated and good practice promoted. Issues around where the parameters of regulation should lie are discussed and recommendations for the minimum requirements of training or experience that counselors working in this field should possess are made.

Counseling and Therapeutic Alliance

The aim of this study was to conduct an exploratory investigation into the in-session processes and behaviors that occur between therapists and young people in online counseling (Williams, Bambling, King, & Abbott, 2009). The Consensual Qualitative Research method was employed to identify in-session behaviors and a coding instrument was developed to determine their frequency of use and assess whether nuances carried in the meaning of text messages have an influential effect during sessions. 85 single-session transcripts were examined in total by two independent coders. Sample statistics revealed that, on average, rapport-building processes were used more consistently across cases with both types of processes having a moderately strong positive effect on young people. However, closer examination of these processes revealed weaker positive effects for in-session behaviors that rely more heavily on verbal and non-verbal cues to be accurately interpreted. Implications for practice: These findings imply that therapists may focus more on building rapport than accomplishing tasks with young people during online counseling sessions due to the absence of verbal and non-verbal information when communicating via text messages.

Mood Charting

Mobile phones may provide a useful and engaging platform for supporting therapeutic services working with adolescents. This article examined the potential benefits of the mobile phone for self-charting moods in comparison to existing methods in current practice (Matthews, Doherty, Sharry, & Fitzpatrick, 2008). The article described a mobile phone application designed by the authors which allows adolescents to record moods on their personal mobile phones. The authors proposed that a personal mobile device is more suitable for adolescents than other devices. A pilot study with a non-clinical adolescent group in schools comparing a mobile and a article diary is presented, along with discussion and analysis of the results. The main finding of the study was that compliance was significantly higher on mobile phones than on article, and the task was not found to be any more difficult to complete using mobile phones than with article charts. A number of salient issues requiring further research were also identified.

Psychotherapy

Digital media offer unique challenges to parents in terms of their efforts to shepherd their children through adolescence. Adolescents' ready access to the Internet makes limit setting and appropriate supervision of teens much more challenging and offers teens qualitatively different dangers and opportunities for acting out than previously existed. The case of a sexually acting out adopted teen (with a history of sexual abuse) who used the Internet as a central vehicle for sexual exploration was discussed, with a particular focus on the ambiguity of appropriate limit setting in the digital era (King, 2012). Implications for case planning in similar situations are also discussed.

School Violence

In this study, Yablon (2008) examined possible advantages of the Internet as a medium for help and support for victims of school violence in Israel. Students in sixth, eighth, and tenth grades were asked about their willingness to seek help on the Internet for dealing with various forms of school violence, and the underlying force-driving processes of such approach was examined. Findings revealed that students are most willing to seek help for relational violence, followed by sexual, physical, and verbal forms of violence. The anonymity that the Internet can provide and the availability of help via Internet are the two foremost contributing factors to the willingness of students to seek help. In addition, the common gender differences in help-seeking behavior were mostly dismissed. Other situational variables and individual characteristics are discussed and possible implications are suggested.

Sexual Exploitation & Individual Differences

This article explored conventional (non-Internet-related) mental health issues and DSM-IV diagnoses seen among a sample of 512 youth receiving mental health services for an Internet-related problem, with particular attention to victims of online sexual exploitation (Wells & Mitchell, 2007). Youth victims of online sexual exploitation were more likely to have a post-traumatic stress disorder than youth with other Internet-related problems. Specific attention was given to differences among subgroups of female and male youth victims of online sexual exploitation as compared with same-gender youth with other Internet-related problems. Findings suggest the importance of including Internet use and victimization as part of a standard clinical assessment.

Smoking Cessation

Although group-based programs remain the most common treatment approach for adolescent smoking cessation, success rates for these programs have been relatively modest, and their reach may be limited. Web-based adjuncts may be one way to boost the efficacy and reach of group-based approaches (Mermelstein & Turner, 2006). The purpose of this study was to evaluate the effectiveness of enhancing the American Lung Association' s Not on Tobacco program (NOT) with a Web-based adjunct (NOT Plus). Twenty-nine high schools were randomly assigned to either the NOT program alone or to the NOT Plus condition, which included access to a specially designed Web site for teens, along with proactive phone calls from the group facilitator to the participant. Self-reported smoking behavior was obtained at end-of-program and at a 3-month follow-up. Using hierarchical linear modeling, accounting for the clustering of students in schools, and controlling for student gender, grade, race, and baseline smoking rate, there was a marginally significant ($p=.06$) condition effect at end-of-treatment and a significant effect at 3-month follow-up ($p<.05$) favoring the NOT Plus condition. Approximately 57% of adolescents reported visiting the Web site, and among the NOT Plus condition, use of the Web site was associated with cessation significantly at end-of-program ($p<.05$), but not at 3 months. Adolescents in urban schools were more likely to access the Web site than those in rural schools. Participants who visited the Web site rated it positively on several dimensions. Reasons for not using the Web site were discussed, as well as its value as an adjunct.

Social Anxiety

Internet-based cognitive behavior therapy (CBT) has been shown effective for university students with social anxiety disorder (SAD) and public speaking fears. The aim of this study was to investigate whether the promising results can be transferred to high school students suffering from this condition (Tillfors, Andersson, Ekselius, Furmark, et al., 2011). A total of 19 speech-anxious high school students with SAD were randomized either into 9 weeks of Internet-delivered CBT or to a wait list control group. Significant improvements were found on measures of social anxiety, general anxiety, and depression. Effects were maintained at 1-year follow-up. The average within- and between-group effect sizes (Cohen's d) for the primary social anxiety scales at posttest were 0.98 and 1.38, respectively. However, the average number of completed modules in the CBT program was low. Although compliance can be improved, the results suggested that Internet-based guided self-help is effective in the treatment of high school students with SAD.

Lohr, Rosenvinge, and Wynn (2011) described a psych educational program, integrated in a basic computer skills course for participants suffering from social anxiety. Computer skills were taught by a qualified teacher. Psych educational and cognitive therapy skills, including topics such as anxiety coping, self-acceptance, and self-regulation were taught by a clinical psychologist. Thirteen of 16 participants completed the course, which lasted 11 weeks. A qualitative analysis was performed, drawing on observations during the course and on interviews with participants, who were positive about the integration of psych educational sessions in the computer course. They described positive outcomes for both elements, including improved computer skills, improved self-esteem, and reduced social anxiety. Most participants were motivated to undertake further occupational rehabilitation after terminating the course.

Substance Abuse

Adolescent substance use disorders (SUDs) encompass a broad spectrum of phenomena involving distinct substances used, a range in quantity and frequency of use, an array of associated problem behaviors, and multiple ecological influences (Waldron & Brody, 2010). SUDs are often viewed as just another manifestation of adolescent disruptive behavior. However, the pharmacological effects and physiologically addictive properties of alcohol and illicit drugs have important and unique implications for treatment relative to those for other adolescent disorders. In addition, unlike other clinical problems, the development and maintenance of SUDs may be influenced by the immediate social environment, including the extent of peer or parent substance abuse, the availability of substances, and the prevailing societal influences (e.g., tobacco and alcohol taxes, stringent law enforcement, bans on nonprescription medications). Another unique feature of adolescent SUDs is that substance use is a covert behavior not always readily apparent to parents, teachers, and health professionals. The majority of teens with SUDs are characterized by lack of motivation to change and resistance to treatment, entering treatment only under a court mandate or in lieu of school suspension.

Consequences associated with SUDs can be severe. Potential adverse consequences include school failure and dropout, substance-related injuries, and increased risk for sexually transmitted infections, HIV/AIDS, teen pregnancy, violent exchanges, overdoes, and death. Substance use can also interfere with crucial developmental tasks, such as prosocial identity formation, interpersonal and educational skill acquisition, and meeting family and work responsibilities (Bentler, 1992). Youths with SUDs often have co-occurring conduct, depressive, bipolar, posttraumatic stress, and anxiety disorders, bulimia, and other problem behaviors. Evidence indicates that dual diagnosis increases the likelihood of continued problem behaviors and is associated with poorer treatment outcomes. The negative consequences associated with SUDs, the co-occurrence of other psychiatric disorders, and the associated problems facing these youths and their families underscore the need for evidence-based practice.

The influence of the family on the development and maintenance of substance use problems is widely recognized. Parental and sibling use, family members' attitudes towards use, poor family management practices, disturbed marital and family relationship functioning, and a host of other family factors have been linked to adolescent substance abuse and have been conceptualized as interdependent and bidirectional influences.

Moreover, treatment-outcome research has shown that family-based interventions are associated with higher rates of treatment engagement and retention, significant reductions in substance use, and improved functioning in other behavioral domains.

Synchronous, Single Session Counseling

Kids Help Line (KHL) is a national Australian youth counseling service that provides free online and telephone counseling (Bambling, King, Reid, & Wegner, 2008). This qualitative study examines the experience of 26 online KHL counselors. Using a focus group methodology, counselor responses were organized into categories: privacy and an emotionally safe environment; communication through text; and time. Counselors reported the main benefit of the online environment to be emotional safety, due to reduced client emotional proximity to the counselor, and the main disadvantage to be that reduced emotional proximity and the absence of non-verbal cues could result in communication problems and difficulty in accurately assessing young people's concerns. Time proved a significant issue for counselors, as the slow speed of text exchange could limit their ability to complete interventions. Methods that enhance both the process and effectiveness of online counseling are needed. Potential solutions to the challenges faced by online counselors are discussed.

CONCLUSION

From all the studies reviewed in this chapter, one can draw a positive conclusion on how the Internet is going to be the treatment of choice with adolescents who are growing up communicating and texting online.

Chapter 9

COUPLES AND FAMILIES[*]

This will be the shortest chapter in this volume because Hertlein and Blumer (2014) have already reviewed thoroughly online and offline interventions with couples and families. Their excellent and highly-recommended work made it unnecessary to bring up-to-date and, therefore, duplicate research relevant to couples and families, even though L'Abate and McMahan (2001) did study the effects of programmed writing with seminarian couples with some positive short-term results, a study in sour need of updating and replication. Nonetheless, among others, online/offline couples and family interventions, in their many forms, still remain an important topic to consider.

HOME NURSING CARE

Home care for technology-dependent children is one of the fastest growing segments of the U.S. health care industry, but nursing literature lacks clear directions to guide home care nurses in planning a family-centered practice. The purpose of this study was to address this gap in the literature by eliciting descriptions of ideal home nursing care for technology-dependent children from the perspective of their parents (Mendes, 2013). A qualitative, descriptive design with formal, semi-structured interviews was used. Seven participants (three couples and one mother) were interviewed. Data analysis revealed four components of ideal home nursing care: 1) competence in technical, assessment, clinical decision-making, and problem-solving skills; 2) a caring manner; 3) relinquishing control of the child's care to the parents; and 4) fitting in with the family and their routines. These findings have implications for both home care nurses and the care managers who supervise the care of children who are technology dependent and their families.

COUPLE QUESTIONNAIRES

This study examined the psychometric equivalence of paper-and-pencil and Internet formats of key questionnaires used in couple research (Brock, Barry, Lawrence, Dey, et al.,

[*] I am grateful to Dr. Katherine Hertlein for her contribution to this chapter.

2012). Self-report questionnaires assessing interpersonal constructs (relationship satisfaction, communication/conflict management, partner support, emotional intimacy) and intrapersonal constructs (individual traits, psychological symptoms, contextual influences) were administered to young adults in committed dating relationships. The same measures were administered twice via paper-and-pencil and/or Internet over a 2-week period. Method order was counterbalanced among participants and temporal stability was controlled. Intrapersonal and interpersonal measures generally remained reliable when administered online and demonstrated qualitative and quantitative equivalence across methods. Implications of online administration of questionnaires were discussed and specific recommendations were made for researchers who wish to transition to online data collection.

Internet Addiction

Although the Internet is used effectively in many areas of life, some users experience problems because of over-use due to a lack of control. The diagnostic criteria for Internet addiction include disruptions in family relationships, but adequate data on the attachment styles and family functioning associated with this condition are limited. This study aimed to investigate the attachment styles and family functioning of patients with Internet addiction (Senormanci, Senormnci, Güclü, & Konkan, 2014). The sample included 30 male patients consecutively admitted to the Bakırköy Mental Health and Research Hospital Internet Addiction Outpatient Clinic, who were diagnosed in clinical interviews as having Internet addiction according to Young's (1998) criteria. Thirty healthy males who were matched with the experimental group in terms of socio-demographic characteristics were included as control subjects. Both groups provided socio-demographic data and completed the Beck Depression Inventory (BDI), the Experiences in Close Relationships Questionnaire-r (ECR-r) and the Family Assessment Device (FAD). Patients with Internet addiction had higher BDI scores ($P<.001$) and higher attachment anxiety sub-scores on ECR-r ($P<.001$) compared with those in the control group. Patients with Internet addiction evaluated their family functioning as more negative and reported problems in every aspect addressed by the FAD. Scores on the FAD behavior control, affective responsiveness, and problem-solving subscales ($P<.05$) and on the FAD communication, roles, and general functioning subscales ($P<.001$) were significantly higher in the patient compared with the control group. Conclusion: Patients with Internet addiction have more anxious attachment styles as well as prominent disruptions in family functioning. Thus, it may be important to evaluate the attachment styles and family functioning of patients with Internet addiction. Indeed, comprehensive treatment approaches including other family members may make important contributions to treatment success. This conclusion is supported by the work of Hooper et al., 2014; note of author).

Online Dating

This article explores gendered patterns of online dating and their implications for heterosexual union formation (Kreager, Cavanagh, Yen, & Yu, 2014). Using 6 months of online dating data from a midsized Southwestern city (N = 8,259 men, 6,274 women), the authors found that men and women tend to send messages to the most socially desirable alters in the dating market regardless of their own desirability levels. They also found that male initiators connect with more desirable partners than men who wait to be contacted, but female initiators connect with equally desirable partners as women who wait to be contacted. Female-initiated contacts are also more than twice as likely as male-initiated contacts to result in a connection, but women send 4 times fewer messages than men. Finally, the authors compared partner desirability levels over repeated exchanges and concluded that couple similarities are more likely to result from relationship termination (i.e., nonreciprocity) than initial homophilous preferences.

Online Infidelity

Internet chat rooms have introduced unprecedented dynamics into marital relationships: never in history has it been so easy to enjoy both the stability of marriage and the thrills of the dating scene at the same time (Mileham, 2007). This study examined the phenomenon of online infidelity in chat rooms, a process whereby individuals involved in a long-term committed relationship seek computer synchronous, interactive contact with opposite-sex members. The following factors were investigated: (a) what elements and dynamics online infidelity involves and how it happens; (b) what leads individuals specifically to the computer to search for a relationship "on the side"; (c) whether individuals consider online contacts as infidelity and why or why not; and (e) what dynamics chat room users experience in their marriages. The results revealed three theoretical constructs that represent married individuals' chat room experiences. The first construct, Anonymous Sexual Interactionism, refers to these individuals' predilection for anonymous interactions of a sexual nature in chat rooms. The allure of anonymity gains extra importance for married individuals, who can enjoy relative safety to express fantasies and desires without being known or exposed. The second, Behavioral Rationalization, denotes the reasoning that chat room users present for conceiving their online behaviors' as innocent and harmless (despite the secrecy and highly sexual nature). The third, Effortless Avoidance, involves chat room users' avoidance of psychological discomfort by exchanging sexual messages with strangers. Happily married individuals also join such rooms, a trend that is also discussed. Together, these constructs symbolize chat room dynamics and serve as a foundation upon which further studies can build.

Parents of Preterm Infants

The objective of this study was to study the experiences of parents of preterm infants who use social networking sites and the potential of such sites for gathering information and facilitating personal exchange (Gabbert, Metze, Bührer, & Garten, 2013). An anonymous self-reporting questionnaire was administered to parents of infants below 1,500 g birth weight born between January 1, 2009 and December 31, 2010 in two tertiary neonatal intensive care units. Of the 278 families who were sent a questionnaire, 141 responded; 53.6 % of respondents claimed to be presently members of online social networking sites. However, only 10.7 and 18.6 % used the Internet to exchange information about their infants during the NICU stay and after discharge, respectively.

Most (64.0 %) responding parents considered that currently available commercial Internet sites inadequately met their need to exchange information as parents of preterm infants. Overall, 79.1 % of respondents reported that they would be interested in joining a native-language online networking site providing (1) general information on prematurity, (2) explanations of abbreviations commonly used in a hospital setting, and (3) details of common medical problems and the treatment thereof, including the availability of local therapists and follow-up services. Also, parents wanted to engage in personal exchange online not only with other parents but also with medical staff. Conclusion: The support of parents of hospitalized preterm infants by neonatal nurses and doctors could be extended by developing an expert-controlled, online networking site providing reliable and updated information and facilitating personal exchange among parents.

Parents of Premature Infants

Using a qualitative framework to capture the voices and stories of parents of premature infants, this study explored the role of online social support through the use of the March of Dimes, Share Your Story site (Morris & Bertram, 2013). Given the growing trend of computer mediated communication usage in the lives of individuals and family members experiencing medical challenges, this study adds to the broad array of research on online social support, while specifically contributing to the limited literature on the parental experience of premature birth and online social support. The research also connects marriage and family therapists and other family practitioners to the role of online social support opportunities for families.

Parenting Infants and Toddlers

This study was conducted to explore childrearing concerns through an analysis of online parenting message boards managed by popular parenting magazines (Porter & Isoa, 2013). Increasingly, mothers appear to be turning to the Web for childrearing advice and support. However, no previous studies have examined the childrearing concerns of mothers of infants and toddlers through the analysis of online message board postings. Ethnographic content analysis methods were used to analyze the online postings. Methods. A total of 120 messages posted in 2007 by mothers of 0-2 year olds on the websites of two best-selling parenting magazines in the United States were submitted to ethnographic content analysis. Each message pertained to one or more of six childrearing domains: Feeding/Eating, Sleep, Development, Discipline, Toilet-Training and Mother-Child Relationships. Results. Questions and pleas for support were most prominently centred on feeding/eating and sleep issues. Mothers expressed concerns about when and how their children should begin to sleep and eat independently. In addition to the themes specific to particular domains, across-domain themes were identified involving mothers' parenting stress, questioning of advice from families/pediatricians and worries that children were not developing normally. Online forums have become a space where mothers can openly describe their own negative emotions towards parenting and ask questions or gain reassurance to resolve mixed messages about how one should rear infants and toddlers. Pediatric nurses should be aware that mothers are confused about conflicting messages, especially in the domains of sleeping and eating. Reviewing parenting message boards occasionally would give nurses continuing insight into common parenting concerns.

Parents' Concerns about Youth Internet Use

Many parents feel uncertain about the actions and experiences their teenage children have on the Internet, thus causing worry and concern. The aim of the study was to examine parents' worries and concerns in relation to their teenagers' use of the Internet (Sorbring, 2014). The participants were 798 Swedish parents (307 fathers, 491 mothers) and their teenage children (aged between 13 and 15 years). The results indicate that parents' worries and concerns vary, in certain aspects, according to age and gender of the child. Furthermore, parents' own Internet skills, experience of using the Internet, and attitudes toward the Internet are related to the type and nature of their worries and concerns. Parents' beliefs about their teenager's skills in using the Internet and the teenagers' Internet use and experiences are related to the parents' concerns. Parents with an accurate understanding of their children's negative Internet experiences are those who are the most worried.

Risky Behaviors

Parents and children use the Internet differently with the majority of parents reporting that they have rules at home for Internet use and routinely check the computer histories so they can know where online their child has been., Both parents and children were reporting that they are participating in risky online behaviours such as talking to strangers and using the Internet to harass someone intentionally. Parents are concerned about the child's exposure to sexually explicit materials and online strangers, but the majority of parents do not know where to report negative or unsafe Internet experiences., Abstract Using the Internet is a daily occurrence for parents and children in today's world. Although they use the Internet differently, many individuals may face online hazards that they may be ill equipped to deal with. To better understand Internet use and online behaviors, a study (Dowdell, 2013) was conducted with 227 parents of early adolescent (ages 11 to 14 years) middle school students (grades 6, 7 and 8). Four important findings emerged: (1) parents were using the Internet like their children but have different online behaviors; (2) parents have Internet use rules at home; (3) parents were participating in risky Internet behaviors (electronic aggression, intentional online harassment and communication with online strangers); and (4) parents were concerned about their child's online safety, specifically about the exposure to sexually explicit materials and online strangers, but the majority of parents do not know where to report negative or unsafe Internet experiences. Nurses, clinicians, healthcare providers and other professionals can and do provide comprehensive care to families by identifying needs and areas of knowledge deficit. By asking Internet use questions, nurses and other professionals should be able to develop plans of care for all family members that will promote Internet safety and healthy lifestyle choices.

SEXTING AND RELATIONSHIP SATISFACTION

The effects of sexting on relationship satisfaction and the conditions under which sexting occurs in adult romantic relationships was the focus of the study (Parker, Blackburn, Perry, & Hawks, 2013). Participants were recruited through social networking websites to participate in an online survey. The sample (n = 86) included 44 participants who were married or living together and 42 participants who were in a dating relationship. Results indicated that couples who scored higher on the consensus scale were more likely to have sexted. Hedonism and was found to be motivators of sexing behaviors. Clinical implications were discussed.

SUCCESS IN ONLINE PARENTING

The present study involved an examination of the extent to which a wide range of child, parent, family, and program-related factors predicted child behavior and parenting outcomes after participation in an 8-session online version of the Triple P-Positive Parenting Program (Dittman, Sanders, Farruggia, Palmer, et al., 2014). Participants were mothers and fathers of 97 children aged between 3 and 8 years displaying elevated levels of disruptive behavior problems. For both mothers and fathers, poorer child behavior outcomes at post-intervention were predicted by the number of sessions of the intervention completed by the family. For mothers, post-intervention child behavior was also predicted by the quality of the mother-child relationship at baseline; for fathers, baseline child behavior severity was an additional predictor. Mothers' post-intervention ineffective parenting was predicted by session completion and pre-intervention levels of ineffective parenting, whereas the only predictor of fathers' ineffective parenting at post-intervention was pre-intervention levels of ineffective parenting. Socioeconomic risk, parental adjustment, and father participation in the intervention were not significant predictors of mother- or father-reported treatment outcomes. The implications of the findings for the provision of online parenting support are discussed.

CONCLUSION

The major issue with this research lies in its long-term outcome. For instance, given the questionable results of couple therapy after a 5 years follow up (Marin, Christensen, & Atkins 2014), where forgiveness seems the "only significant predictor of posttraumatic growth" (Heintselman, Murdock, Krycak, & Seay, 2014, 13), it would seem that programmed distance writing should be the first step in dealing with forgive-ness. Programmed interactive practice exercises, administered as homework before moving to most expensive and perhaps more prolonged F2F TB interventions, would appear perhaps as irrelevant issues in the long term. This would be the case, especially if forgiveness in couples and families is not considered from the very outset of any couple and family intervention (L'Abate, 1986, 2011c).

SECTION IV. DYSFUNCTIONALITIES

Chapter 10

PHYSICAL ILLNESSES AND OLD AGE

Marks et al., (2007):

"...sourced 19 studies, including 15 RCTs, of nine computer psychotherapy (CP) systems for a range of adult problems not otherwise included in their review. Physical problems included pain (headache, back pain, pain during burn-would dressing), tinnitus, insomnia, jetlag, sexual problems, and schizophrenia. A Swedish netCP system improved users' headaches in two RCTsl attrition rates were not cut by adding small support and therapist-initiated phone calls. A USA RCT improved headache modestly in the third of users who rated at the two-month follow-up. Back pain improved similarly with Swedish netCP and a waitlist, though netCP reduced catastrophizing more. A USA virtual reality system to reduce pain during burn-wound dressings needs more research. For tinnitus distress,

Swedish net CP plus email support was more effective than a waitlist and as effective as a group CBT to one-year follow-up after having required less therapist time per patient. Compare to a waitlist, Swedish netCP plus email therapist support improved insomnia more on only one of nine sleep measures. A USA CP system reduced self-rated jet lag in beta study. Couples reported positive engagement and improved sexual knowledge and behavior one to two weeks after using the Canadian Sexpert CP prototype for a single session in four RCTs. In schizophrenia sufferers in USA-based (p. 169) CP system to improve cognitive skills found more gains in three RCTs but did not control for placebo effects, while a Scottish psycho-education system had no effect. The waitlist design used in many of the CP studies could not rule out attention-placebo effects. The Swedish netCP systems netbiblioCBT whose efficacy needs to be tested in less educated subjects "(p. 172).

More recently, Gallego and Emmelkamp (2012) concluded that: "Cognitive-Behavioral Interventions have shown to have positive effects on health conditions such as pain, sleep problems, headache, cancer and many others (p. 410). They closed their review with this statement: "In general, Internet CBT programs for health problems may have some promise, but the promise is as yet unfulfilled given that the effect sizes are generally lower than Internet-based CBT for anxiety and depression" (p. 411). Hence, research included in this chapter will need to support or question the validity of such a conclusion a few years later.

The purpose of this chapter, therefore, is to include Internet evaluations and interventions with physical illnesses. For instance, in 2004, the International Society for Research on

Internet Interventions (ISRII) was formed to encourage eHealth researchers to collaborate in their efforts to further the science behind developing, testing, and disseminating Web-based treatment programs (Ritterband, Andersson, Christensen, Carlbring, & Cuijpers, 2006). This group held its second meeting (April 2006) to clarify the Society's direction and identify key issues that need addressing in the field. These issues are identified and examined in the current paper. Given the success of using the Internet to treat a range of medical and mental health problems, and the growing need for better dissemination of health care, Internet interventions will almost certainly play a prominent role in global health. ISRII plans to provide the necessary venue to ensure the science driving this field is strong, enabling researchers to conduct the highest quality research and permitting meaningful conclusions from completed studies.

This review provided an updated summary of recent controlled trials of Internet interventions for health conditions and how the Internet is used to promote health. Ritterband, Andersson, Christensen, Carlbring, and Cuijpers (2006) identified 18 published trials including studies on diabetes, cancer, pain conditions, obesity, irritable bowel syndrome, stress management, hypertension, metabolic syndrome, cerebral palsy, infertility, HIV infection, and fruit/vegetable consumption. Of the 18 trials, one-third targeted children and adolescents. Two cancer studies investigated the role of peer support in an online environment that failed to result in any major improvements. Overall, several trials did not result in any substantial significant improvements, but there are exceptions, such as treatment of irritable bowel syndrome, headache, and chronic pain. Although a few of the reviewed studies had sufficient sample sizes, the majority were small and underpowered. In particular, this was the case for the studies on children and adolescents. This review suggested that Internet interventions hold some promise as a complement to other treatments such as cognitive behavior therapy. The benefits from participating in online peer support groups are not clear. Although studies on children and adolescents have emerged, there is a lack of studies on older adults with health problems (this conclusion about senior citizens will be corrected by studies about senior citizens reported later on in this chapter, note of author).

Chronic illness accounts for the majority of healthcare expenditures in the United States. Innovative telemedicine programs have been developed to help lessen the chronic illness burden, yet few have been developed to address comorbidity (Turvey, Willyard, Hickman, Klein, et al., 2007). Programs accommodating comorbidity are needed because most older adults suffer from two or more chronic illnesses. One of the most common and serious comorbidities in chronic illness is major depression, which has been shown to exacerbate morbidity, mortality, and cost. This study presents data on a telephone-based interactive voice recording (IVR) home monitoring program that was expanded to include quarterly screens for depression using the Patient Health Questionnaire (PHQ). Patients in an ongoing telehealth heart failure program were administered the PHQ-2 and PHQ-9 in November 2005 (Round 1) and February 2006 (Round 2). Patients were informed about the screen beforehand and an emergency protocol was established. At both screens, more than 90% of the patients completed the screen. Approximately 30% of the patients endorsed one of the PHQ-2 items in both rounds. Patients endorsing either of the PHQ-2 items then completed the full PHQ-9. Nurse care-managers contacted those scoring above the threshold of 10 on the PHQ-9 indicating possible depression. One patient expressed suicidality and was appropriately assessed for safety. There was no indication that patients were less likely to complete the screen in Round 2, although their average depression scores were slightly lower when compared with Round 1. A regular telephonic IVR screen for depression can be integrated into a standard illness management protocol. Following a pre-established emergency plan for the assessment of suicidality was successful. This serves as a model for using technology to manage comorbid depression and chronic illness.

Since medication nonadherence is considered to be an important health risk, numerous interventions to improve adherence have been developed. During the past decade, the use of Internet-based interventions to improve medication adherence has increased rapidly. Internet interventions have the potential advantage of tailoring the interventions to the needs and situation of the patient (Linn, Vervloet, van Dijk, Smith, et al., 2011). The main aim of this systematic review was to investigate which tailored Internet interventions are effective in improving medication adherence. The authors undertook comprehensive literature searches in PubMed, PsycINFO, EMBASE, CINAHL, and Communication Abstracts, following the guidelines of the Cochrane Collaboration. The methodological quality of the randomized controlled trials and clinical controlled trials and methods for measuring adherence were independently reviewed by two researchers.

A total of 13 studies met the inclusion criteria. All included Internet interventions clearly used moderately or highly sophisticated computer-tailored methods. Data synthesis revealed that there is evidence for the effectiveness of Internet interventions in improving medication adherence: 5 studies (3 high-quality studies and 2 low-quality studies) showed a significant effect on adherence; 6 other studies (4 high-quality studies and 2 low-quality studies) reported a moderate effect on adherence; and 2 studies (1 high-quality study and 1 low-quality study) showed no effect on patients' adherence. However, most studies used self-reported measurements to assess adherence, which is generally perceived as a low-quality measurement. In addition, we did not find a clear relationship between the quality of the studies or the level of sophistication of message tailoring and the effectiveness of the intervention. This might be explained by the great difference in study designs and the way of measuring adherence, which makes results difficult to compare. There was also large variation in the measured interval between baseline and follow-up measurements.

This review showed promising results on the effectiveness of Internet interventions to enhance patients' adherence to prescribed long-term medications. Although there is evidence according to the data synthesis, the results must be interpreted with caution due to low-quality adherence measurements. Future studies using high-quality measurements to assess medication adherence were recommended to establish more robust evidence for the effectiveness of eHealth interventions on medication adherence.

The Internet has become a major component to health care and has important implications for the future of the health care system. One of the most notable aspects of the Web is its ability to provide efficient, interactive, and tailored content to the user. Given the wide reach and extensive capabilities of the Internet, researchers in behavioral medicine have been using it to develop and deliver interactive and comprehensive treatment programs with the ultimate goal of impacting patient behavior and reducing unwanted symptoms. To date, however, many of these interventions have not been grounded in theory or developed from behavior change models, and no overarching model to explain behavior change in Internet interventions has yet been published. The purpose of this article was to propose a model to help guide future Internet intervention development and predict and explain behavior changes and symptom improvement produced by Internet interventions (Ritterband, Thorndike, Cox, Kovatchev, & Gonder-Frederick, 2009).

The model purports that effective Internet interventions produce (and maintain) behavior change and symptom improvement via nine nonlinear steps: the user, influenced by environmental factors, affects website use and adherence, which is influenced by support and website characteristics. Website use leads to behavior change and symptom improvement through various mechanisms of change. Improvements are sustained via treatment maintenance. By grounding Internet intervention research within a scientific framework, developers can plan feasible, informed, and testable Internet interventions, and this form of treatment will become more firmly established (Ritterband, Thorndike, Cox, Kovatchev, & Gonder-Frederick. 2009).

Persons with severe functional disabilities are the highest users of health care services. Caring for the needs of this population represents a significant percentage of our national health care costs (Forducey, Glueckauf, Berquist, Maheu, & Yutsis, 2012). A growing body of research has demonstrated the efficacy of self-management strategies and caregiver engagement for effective long-term care for individuals with chronic medical conditions. Economic forces over the past decade have led to new challenges and resulted in major changes in health care delivery resulting in shortened length of inpatient stays and greater limits on the length of outpatient treatment. Telehealth is an innovative method for health care delivery and a means of meeting this new challenge.

This article highlights the findings of 3 pilot studies on the use of telecommunications technologies in promoting self-care management and enhancing health care outcomes in persons with severe disabilities and their family caregivers. The importance of matching technology to the needs of this population, lessons learned from these investigations, and future directions for research were addressed.

BEREAVEMENT

Research so far has shown little evidence that written disclosure facilitates recovery from bereavement (Van der Houwen, Schut, van den Bout, Stroebe, et al., 2010). There are good reasons to assume that written disclosure may only benefit those bereaved who are at risk for developing problems or who are experiencing significant psychological problems as a result of their loss, and only when appropriate writing instructions are used. Drawing on previous work in the area of post-traumatic stress, a writing intervention was designed to test these assumptions. Bereaved individuals, who were still significantly distressed by their loss, were randomly assigned to the intervention condition (N = 460) or a waiting list control condition (N = 297). Both groups filled in questionnaires online at baseline, and 3 and 6 months later. The intervention was administered via e-mail immediately after baseline measurement. Results showed that writing decreased feelings of emotional loneliness and increased positive mood, in part through its effect on rumination. However, writing did not affect grief or depressive symptoms. Contrary to expectations, effects did not depend on participants' risk profile or baseline distress level. Implications of these findings are discussed.

Cancer Tribal Clinics in Northwest

This project is aimed at determining the feasibility and effect of using Videoconferencing to deliver cancer-related pain management education and case consultation to health care providers in rural AI/AN communities (Haozous, Doorenbos, Demiris, Eaton, et al., 2012). The project provided four educational sessions and nine case conferences to health care providers at tribal clinics in Washington State and Alaska using Videoconferencing with pain experts at the University of Washington. A cross-sectional, descriptive study design was used to survey the participating providers. Measures included satisfaction with the telehealth system and self-perceived competence in pain management. Results: Fifty-two providers from 11 sites attended the educational sessions. Ninety-three providers from 16 sites participated in the case conferences. Case conference participants scored significantly higher on perceived competence in treating pain compared with clinic providers who did not attend. Educational session participants and case conference participants both reported a high level of satisfaction with videoconferencing. Conclusions: Telehealth is a feasible and effective way to deliver cancer-related pain management education and increase competence among rural health care providers.

Cancer Genetic Counseling

Meropol, Daly, Vig, Manion et al., (2011) examined the feasibility of home videoconferencing for providing cancer genetic education and risk information to people at risk. Adults with possible hereditary colon or breast and ovarian cancer syndromes were offered Internet-based counseling. Participants were sent web cameras and software to install on their home PCs. They watched a prerecorded educational video and then took part in a live counseling session with a genetic counselor. A total of 31 participants took part in Internet counseling sessions. Satisfaction with counseling was high in all domains studied, including technical (mean 4.3 on a 1–5 scale), education (mean 4.7), communication (mean 4.8), psychosocial (mean 4.1) and overall (mean 4.2). Qualitative data identified technical aspects that could be improved. All participants reported that they would recommend Internet-based counseling to others. Internet-based genetic counseling is feasible and associated with a high level of satisfaction among participants.

Cancer and Insomnia

Insomnia is highly prevalent among cancer survivors. Previous research suggested that cancer survivors may prefer non-pharmacological insomnia treatments and are especially amenable to alternative treatments such as hypnosis. Yet, little is known about the applicability of hypnosis to treat insomnia among cancer survivors. This study (Farrell-Carnahan, Ritterband, Bailey, Thorndike, Lord, & Baum, 2010) investigated feasibility and preliminary efficacy of self-hypnosis recordings available on the Web to improve sleep, fatigue, mood, and quality of life in cancer survivors. Twenty-eight cancer survivors with insomnia were randomly assigned to a self-hypnosis group that immediately received a

4-week self-hypnosis intervention for insomnia (n =14) or to a waitlist control group (n = 14). The main outcomes of sleep, fatigue, mood, and quality of life were assessed via online pre- and post-treatment questionnaires and sleep diaries. Intervention usage, perceived impact, and feedback were also obtained. Overall adjusted effect sizes show small self-hypnosis treatment effects in sleep, fatigue, mood, and quality of life; however, with this small sample size, improvements were not found to be statistically significant. Most participants utilized the intervention and all perceived it as at least somewhat helpful. This simple, easy to disseminate, Web available self-hypnosis intervention may be a promising self-treatment option for cancer survivors with insomnia.

Cancer Oncology

This clinical study examined the barriers to using telehealth for oncologic visits and was performed by the British Columbia Cancer Agency's Vancouver Island Centre (BCCAVIC) and the Vancouver Island Health Authority in 2006–2007 (Weinerman, et al. (2012). One of the major barriers encountered was physician engagement. The current observational study was to determine whether patients' enthusiasm and the introduction of telehealth in a study resulted in telehealth becoming integrated within BCCAVIC. Telehealth appointment statistics continued to be kept after the original study was completed.

Data were kept on the number of visits, the type of visit (follow-up or new patient), the oncologist seeing the patient, the location of the patient, and the type of cancer. During the study, 106 patients were seen via telehealth. In the years following the trial, the number of telehealth follow-up patients seen markedly increased, so that in 2010–2011, close to 1,200 patients were seen. Medical oncology saw 91.4% of these. The introduction of oncology telehealth in BCCSVIC/Vancouver Island Health Authority was in an ethics-approved study.

Following the completion of the trial, there was a 10-fold increase in follow-up patients seen using this modality. Reluctance to see new patients through telehealth probably relates to the necessity to change the patient encounter paradigm. There is a need to develop a model where patients who are a distance from specialists concentrated in larger centers have reasonable access to the same standard of care, without incurring the time and financial burdens. Telehealth would be a part of that model.

Caregivers

The aim of this study was to examine the impact on dementia caregivers' experienced stress and health status of 2 Internet-based intervention programs (Marziali & Garcia, 2011). Design and methods: Ninety-one dementia caregivers were given the choice of being involved in either an Internet based chat support group or an Internet-based video conferencing support group. Pre-post outcome measures focused on distress, health status, social support, and service utilization. Results: In contrast to the Chat Group, the Video Group showed significantly greater improvement in mental health status. Also, for the Video

Group, improvements in self-efficacy, neuroticism, and social support were associated with lower stress response to coping with the care recipient's cognitive impairment and decline in function. Implications: The results show that, of 2 Internet-based intervention programs for dementia caregivers, the video conferencing intervention program was more effective in improving mental health status and improvement in personal characteristics were associated with lower caregiver stress response.

A large randomized trial evaluated the benefits of online education, support, and self-care promotion for caregivers of persons with dementia (Hayden, Glenn, Hahn, Randall, & Randolph, 2012), Anecdotal reports from participants indicated enjoyment of the materials, convenient access from home, and support from professionals and other caregivers. A substantial number of screened caregivers experienced obstacles of access, cost, and time regarding use of technology. Telephone options are being explored, and future caregiving generations are expected to have increased exposure and willingness to use computer technology, such as the program described here.

Carers Telehealth Monitoring

The aim of this study was to investigate acceptance and usage issues in relation to Telehealth products as used by frail older clients of the Transition Care Program and their carers (Wade, Shaw, & Cartwright, 2012). The study design was a quasi-randomised controlled clinical trial. A stratified random sample of participants was allocated to one of five groups using a random number table. Study participants who were already in possession of a pendant alarm provided by the study service provider at study commencement, or were assessed as needing a pendant alarm, were allocated to the first number out of 1 (control group), 4 or 5 (home Telehealth monitoring with a pedant alarm up to 12 or 24 weeks) on the random number table list. If they were in possession of a pendant alarm that was not from the study service provider they were automatically allocated to the control group. If they were assessed as not needing a pendant alarm they were allocated to the first number on the list out of 2 or 3 (home Telehealth monitoring up to 12 or 24 weeks). In all instances, when a participant was allocated to the first applicable number on the list, that number was crossed off the list. A total of 43 participants who commenced the study used Teleheath equipment. There was a 13% Telehealth reading failure rate. There was no significant difference between clients with and clients without carers for the reading failure rate. This non-significant difference was consistent across all of the identified reasons for why readings failed including staff not following up, participant non-compliance (with and without carer), equipment failure, participants not returning a call from the staff investigating non-reading and user error. If the health of the client requires high reading rate reliability, the fact that the client has a carer to assist them cannot be assumed to increase the safe usage of the Telehealth equipment for reading rate reliability. As such staff should ensure that they are diligent in monitoring in-home Telehealth regardless of the presence or absence of a carer.

Coronary Artery Bypass Graft: Telephone-Delivered Care for Depression

Depressive symptoms commonly follow coronary artery bypass graft (CABG) surgery and are associated with less positive clinical outcomes. The objective of this study was to test the effectiveness of telephone-delivered collaborative care for post-CABG depression vs. usual physician care (Rollman, Belnap, & LeMenager, 2009). Single-blind effectiveness trial at 7 university-based and community hospitals in or near Pittsburgh, Pennsylvania. Participants were 302 post-CABG patients with depression (150, intervention; 152, usual care) and a comparison group of 151 randomly sampled post-CABG patients without depression recruited between March 2004 and September 2007 and observed as outpatients until June 2008. Eight months of telephone-delivered collaborative care provided by nurses working with patients' primary care physicians and supervised by a psychiatrist and primary care physician from this study. Mental health-related quality of life (HRQL) was measured by the Short Form-36 Mental Component Summary (SF-36 MCS) at 8-month follow-up; secondary outcome measures included assessment of mood symptoms (Hamilton Rating Scale for Depression [HRS-D]), physical HRQL (SF-36 PCS), and functional status (Duke Activity Status Index [DASI]); and hospital readmissions.

After the intervention, patients reported greater improvements in mental HRQL (all $P <$ or $= .02$) (SF-36 MCS: Delta, 3.2 points; 95% confidence interval [CI], 0.5-6.0), physical functioning (DASI: Delta, 4.6 points; 95% CI, 1.9-7.3), and mood symptoms (HRS-D: Delta, 3.1 points; 95% CI, 1.3-4.9); and were more likely to report a 50% or greater decline in HRS-D score from baseline (50.0% vs. 29.6%; number needed to treat, 4.9 [95% CI, 3.2-10.4]) than usual care patients ($P < .001$). Men with depression were particularly likely to benefit from the intervention (SF-36 MCS: Delta, 5.7 points; 95% CI, 2.2-9.2; $P = .001$). However, the mean HRQL and physical functioning of intervention patients did not reach that of the non-depressed comparison group. Compared with usual care, telephone-delivered collaborative care for treatment of post-CABG depression resulted in improved HRQL, physical functioning, and mood symptoms at 8-month follow-up.

Cystic Fibrosis

Cox, Alison, Rasekaba, & Holland (2012) conducted a systematic review of the use of telehealth in people with Cystic Fibrosis (CF). The studies reviewed were of adults and children with CF, and incorporated telehealth for monitoring symptoms, assessing adherence to prescribed therapies or providing a therapeutic intervention. Searches of four electronic databases returned 293 references. Eight studies met the inclusion criteria. Variability in study design and outcome measures precluded meta-analysis. Seven studies assessed telemonitoring feasibility for patient usability and acceptance, or for physiological monitoring. Two studies were randomised controlled trials, although only one showed differences in outcome between the intervention and usual care with improved spirometry stability and significantly increased antibiotic use in the intervention group. In four studies participants were asked to transmit data on spirometry (FEV_1) or symptoms. Participant non-compliance with data reporting ranged from 43–63%. Generally, participants reported being able to use the required technology. There is insufficient evidence to reach a firm conclusion about the benefits of telehealth in people with CF, but it remains a promising area for future investigation.

DIABETES

Management of type 1 diabetes mellitus (T1DM) requires a continual balancing of insulin, fuel intake, and metabolic demand (e.g., exercise). This can only be accomplished with knowledge of where one's blood glucose (BG) is and where it is going, and knowledge of how to manipulate insulin, fuel, and exercise to manage BG. Blood Glucose Awareness Training® (BGAT®) is a psycho-educational intervention that in part addresses these needs. Fifteen research studies from the U.S and Europe, involving single site and multicenter projects, are reviewed. BGAT® has been consistently demonstrated to improve the ability to detect and diminish both hypoglycemia and hyperglycemia, while reducing the sequeli of extreme BGs (e.g., episodes of severe hypoglycemia and driving mishaps). BGAT® has recently been transformed for Internet delivery, making it available both for clinicians to use with their patients and for individuals with T1DM to pursue as a self-directed tutorial.

Thirteen U.S. and European studies have documented the benefits of blood glucose awareness training (BGAT) (Cox, Ritterband, Magee, Clarke, & Gonder-Frederick, 2008). These benefits include improvements in detecting and reducing the occurrences of extreme blood glucose levels and their sequelae, e.g., reducing occurrence of ketoacidosis, severe hypoglycemia, hypoglycemia-related driving mishaps, and fear of hypoglycemia. The authors hypothesized that an internet version of BGAT would be perceived as useful, be completed efficiently, and produce greater clinical benefits compared with a wait list control group.

Mobile technology enhances the potential to assess, prompt, educate, and engage individuals with diabetes. The near-ubiquitous presence of mobile phones allows real-time contextually relevant support for diabetes self-care. Mulvaney, Ritterband, and Bosslet (2011) reviewed the design of mobile interventions included in a recent meta-analysis. Although mobile programs can lead to improvements in glycemic control, many aspects, such as the role of the diabetes clinician, real-time features, and patient engagement have not been documented. Studies with the greatest impact on hemoglobinA1c integrated patient feedback and a role for clinicians. Research is needed regarding feasible and efficacious roles for clinical support in mobile interventions. Recommendations for design and research include the following: consideration of patient and clinician burden; identification of patterns and metrics for patient treatment adherence and engagement; integration of goal setting and problem solving; enhancing patient education; a greater focus on patient-centered motivational strategies; and utilization of study designs that relate intervention design elements to outcomes.

The objectives of this study were to demonstrate the feasibility of telehealth technology to provide a team approach to diabetes care for rural patients and determine its effect on patient outcomes when compared with F2F diabetes visits (Ciemins, Coon, Peck, Holloway, Min, 2011). Materials and Methods: An evaluation of a patient-centered interdisciplinary team approach to diabetes management compared telehealth with face-to-face visits on receipt of recommended preventive guidelines, vascular risk factor control, patient satisfaction, and diabetes self-management at baseline and 1, 2, and 3 years post-intervention.

Results: One-year post-intervention the receipt of recommended dilated eye exams increased 31% and 43% among telehealth and F2F patients, respectively (p = 0.28). Control of two or more risk factors increased 37% and 69% (p = 0.21). Patient diabetes care satisfaction rates increased 191% and 131% among telehealth and F2F patients, respectively (p = 0.51). A comparison of telehealth with F2F patients resulted in increased self-reported blood glucose monitoring as instructed (97% vs. 89%; p = 0.63) and increased dietary adherence (244% vs. 159%; p = 0.86), respectively. Receipt of a monofilament foot test showed a significantly greater improvement among F2F patients (17% vs. 35%; p = 0.01) at 1 year post-intervention, but this difference disappeared in years 2 and 3. Telehealth proved to be an effective mode for the provision of diabetes care to rural patients. Few differences were detected in the delivery of a team approach to diabetes management via telehealth compared with face-to-face visits on receipt of preventive care services, vascular risk factor control, patient satisfaction, and patient self-management. A team approach using telehealth may be a viable strategy for addressing the unique challenges faced by patients living in rural communities.

Diabetes in Youth

The objective of this study was to report results from YourWay, an Internet-based self-management intervention for adolescents with Type 1 diabetes (Mulvaney, Rothman, Wallston, Lybarger, et al., 2010). A total of 72 adolescents with type 1 diabetes, ages 13–17 years, were randomized to a usual-care-plus-Internet support or a usual-care group. The intervention was designed to enhance problem-solving barriers to self-management. A1C was obtained from medical records, and problem-solving and self-management were obtained via adolescent report. Group differences were not statistically significant using intent-to-treat analyses. Using as-treated analyses, adolescents in the treatment condition showed statistically significant improvement in self-management (d = 0.64; P = 0.02) and important improvements in problem-solving (d = 0.30; P = 0.23) and A1C (d = −0.28; P = 0.27). Mean A1C for the intervention group remained constant (−0.01%), while the control group increased (0.33%). This brief trial suggested that self-management support delivered through a secure website may improve self-management and offset typical decreases in adolescent glycemic control.

Epilepsy

The study was conducted to test the feasibility of a telephone-based self-management program for adults with epilepsy (DiIorio, Reisinger, Yeager, & McCarty, 2009). This program was based on social cognitive theory and principles of motivational interviewing (MI). Twenty-two adults with epilepsy were recruited from hospital-based epilepsy clinics. The mean age of participants was 43 years, and 68% were men. Participants were randomly assigned to the intervention or control group. Those in the intervention group received a five-session intervention with a nurse trained in MI counseling. Following an in-person introductory session, the remaining four sessions were conducted by phone. Ninety-five percent of the 55 planned MI sessions and the 44 planned courtesy calls for those in the control group were completed, demonstrating high acceptance of the program. Participants were very satisfied with the program and noted the benefits of the telephone delivery method. Analysis of outcomes provided support for continued development and testing of the program.

FEMALE SEXUAL DYSFUNCTION

There has been limited evaluation of the effectiveness of psychological interventions for female sexual dysfunction (FSD). Furthermore, none of these studies have evaluated the effectiveness of these programs delivered over the Internet (Jones & McCabe, 2011). The current study evaluated an Internet-based psychological treatment program for FSD. Revive consisted of three well-established and validated treatment components: communication skills training, sensate focus exercises, and regular contact with a therapist. Outcome measures included: the Female Sexual Function Index; the Depression, Anxiety, Stress Scale; the Sexual Function Scale; and the Personal Assessment of Intimacy in Relationships. In total, 39 women (17 in treatment group and 22 in control group) completed the program. The mean age for the treatment group was 34.91 (standard deviation [SD] = 10.27) and 33.30 years (SD = 9.34) for the control group. The results demonstrated that women who completed treatment reported improved sexual and relationship functioning in comparison with those who received no treatment. These findings highlight the suitability of the Internet for providing psychological treatment for FSD and for targeting the individual and relationship factors often associated with these disorders.

HEPATITIS C VIRUS

The standard treatment for chronic hepatitis C (pegylated interferon and ribavirin) causes challenging physical and psychological side effects. The current pilot study evaluated the efficacy of a brief, telephone-based, cognitive-behavioral self-management intervention designed to address mood and quality of life within a sample of veterans on antiviral treatment for hepatitis C (Silberbogen, et al. (2012), Results from this pilot study support the feasibility of this telehealth intervention, showing that veterans were highly satisfied with the content of the intervention and compliant with the telephone calls. Findings further indicate that symptoms of depression and anxiety and mental health quality of life either remained stable or improved in those participants who received the brief telephone intervention, while those receiving usual care showed significant declines in mood and mental health quality of life. The findings from this study provide evidence that a brief, clinician-administered phone intervention may help individuals on antiviral therapy for hepatitis C to cope more effectively with the negative treatment side effects.

HIV/STD

In recent years, Internet-based or online counseling has emerged as an effective way to assess psychological disorders and discuss destructive behaviors with individuals or groups of individuals (Moskowitz, Melton, & Owczarzak, 2009). This study explored the application of online counseling to HIV/STD risk-taking behavior among men who have sex with men (MSM). PowerON, an organization that provides sexual health information to MSM exclusively online, used instant message technology to counsel MSM in real time through computer-mediated means. A sample of 279 transcripts of instant message exchanges between PowerON counselors and Gay.com users were recorded and qualitatively analyzed. Approximately 43% of the instant message sessions discussed information about HIV/STD testing. Risk-taking behaviors were addressed in 39% of the sessions. Information about HIV/STDs and general counseling were given in 23% and 18% of the counseling sessions, respectively. The data showed that these instant message sessions to be a potentially feasible forum for HIV/STD counseling. One practice implication relates to information ordinarily disseminated at health clinics could be successfully distributed through the Internet to MSM.

Hypertension

Older adults residing in rural areas often lack convenient, patient-centered, community-based approaches to facilitate receipt of routine care to manage common chronic conditions (Hovey, Kaylor, Alwan, & Resnick, 2011). Without adequate access to appropriate disease management resources, the risk of seniors' experiencing acute events related to these common conditions increases substantially. Further, poorly managed chronic conditions are costly and place seniors at increased risk of institutionalization and permanent loss of independence. Novel, telehealth-based approaches to management of common chronic conditions like hypertension may not only improve the health of older adults, but may also lead to substantial cost savings associated with acute care episodes and institutionalization. The aim of this report is to summarize practical considerations related to operations and logistics of a unique community-based telemonitoring pilot study targeting rural seniors who utilize community-based senior centers. This article reviews the technological challenges encountered during the study and proposes solutions relevant to future research and implementation of telehealth in community-based, congregate settings.

Insomnia

An Internet-based program for CBT improved sleep in adults with chronic insomnia (Ritterband, 2010). Insomnia is a major health problem, with significant psychological, health, and economic consequences. Studies have demonstrated that cognitive-behavioural therapy can effectively treat insomnia; however, treatment availability is limited by many factors, including a lack of trained clinicians. One potential way to overcome these barriers is to use the Internet to deliver treatment. Toward this aim, Thorndike, Saylor, Bailey, Gonder-Frederick, Morin, and Ritterband (2008) developed a self-guided, interactive, tailored Internet intervention for adults with insomnia (SHUTi: Sleep Healthy Using The Internet). The current paper provides a detailed description of SHUTi and examines users' perceptions of the intervention's usefulness and effectiveness. The study was part of a larger randomised controlled trial (RCT) to test the efficacy of SHUTi, but findings in this paper are based only on the 21 participants who completed the post-assessment after using SHUTi. The overwhelming majority rated SHUTi as convenient, understandable, and useful. Nearly all (95%) indicated that the program had at least somewhat improved their sleep, sleep efficiency, and overall quality of life. Ninety percent perceived the intervention as effective and predicted it would be effective in producing a long-term cure. Although these results were based on a small sample, they provide encouraging evidence of the potential for Internet interventions to be accepted by patients.

Insomnia is a major health problem with significant psychological, health, and economic consequences. However, availability of one of the most effective insomnia treatments, cognitive behavioral therapy, is significantly limited. The Internet may be a key conduit for delivering this intervention. The purpose of this study was to evaluate the efficacy of a structured behavioral Internet intervention for adults with insomnia (Ritterband, Thorndike, Gonder-Frederick, Magee, Bailey, Saylor, & Morin, 2009).

Forty-five adults were randomly assigned to an Internet intervention (n = 22) or wait list control group (n = 23). Forty-four eligible participants (mean [SD] age, 44.86 [11.03] years; 34 women) who had a history of sleep difficulties longer than 10 years on average (mean [SD], 10.59 [8.89] years) were included in the analyses. The Internet intervention is based on well-established face-to-face cognitive behavioral therapy incorporating the primary components of sleep restriction, stimulus control, sleep hygiene, cognitive restructuring, and relapse prevention.

The Insomnia Severity Index and daily sleep diary data were used to determine changes in insomnia severity and the main sleep variables, including wake after sleep onset and sleep efficiency. Intention-to-treat analyses showed that scores on the Insomnia Severity Index significantly improved from 15.73 (95% confidence interval [CI], 14.07 to 17.39) to 6.59 (95% CI, 4.73 to 8.45) for the Internet group but did not change for the control group (16.27 [95% CI, 14.61 to 17.94] to 15.50 [95% CI, 13.64 to 17.36]) ($F_{1,42} = 29.64$; $P < .001$). The Internet group maintained their gains at the 6-month follow-up. Internet participants also achieved significant decreases in wake after sleep onset (55% [95% CI, 34% to 76%]) and increases in sleep efficiency (16% [95% CI, 9% to 22%]) compared with the non-significant control group changes of wake after sleep onset (8% [95% CI, −17% to 33%) and sleep efficiency (3%; 95% CI, −4% to 9%). In conclusion, participants who received the Internet intervention for insomnia significantly improved their sleep, whereas the control group did not have a significant change. The Internet appears to have considerable potential in delivering a structured behavioral program for insomnia.

Although the Insomnia Severity Index (ISI) is already administered online, this frequently used instrument has not been validated for Web delivery. This study compares online and paper-and-pencil ISI versions completed by participants in a randomized controlled trial testing an Internet-delivered intervention for insomnia (Thorndike, Ritterband, Saylor, Magee, Gonder-Frederick, & Morin, 2011). Forty-three adults with insomnia completed both ISI versions during pre- (Assessment 1) and post-intervention (Assessment 2). Correlations between total scores of both versions were significant ($rs \geq .98$, $ps < .001$). For both ISI versions, internal consistency was acceptable (Assessment 1, $\alpha = .61$;

Assessment 2, α ≥ .88). Among participants not receiving the parent study intervention, correlations between 1 format at Assessment 1 and the alternative format at Assessment 2 were generally significant (rs = .26–.82). Together, findings suggest the ISI can be delivered online.

Internet-delivered treatment is effective for insomnia, but little is known about the beneficial effects of support. The aim of the current study was to investigate the additional effects of low-intensity support to an internet-delivered treatment for insomnia (Lancee, van den Bout, Sorbi, & van Straten, 2013). Two hundred and sixty-two participants were randomized to an internet-delivered intervention for insomnia with (n = 129) or without support (n = 133). All participants received an internet-delivered cognitive behavioral treatment for insomnia. In addition, the participants in the support condition received weekly emails. Assessments were at baseline, post treatment , and 6-month follow-up. Both groups effectively ameliorated insomnia complaints. Adding support led to significantly higher effects on most sleep measures ($d = 0.3-0.5$; $p < 0.05$), self-reported insomnia severity ($d = 0.4$; $p < 0.001$), anxiety, and depressive symptoms ($d = 0.4$; $p < 0.01$). At the 6- month follow-up, these effects remained significant for sleep efficiency, sleep onset latency, insomnia symptoms, and depressive symptoms ($d = 0.3-0.5$; $p < 0.05$). Providing support significantly enhances the benefits of internet-delivered treatment for insomnia on several variables. It appears that motivational feedback increases the effect of the intervention and encourages more participants to complete the intervention, which in turn improves its effectiveness.

Insomnia is frequently comorbid with other medical and psychological disorders. This secondary data analysis investigated whether an Internet-delivered cognitive behavioral therapy for insomnia (CBT-I) intervention could also reduce comorbid psychological and fatigue symptoms (Thorndike, Ritterband, Gonder-Frederick, Lord, Ingersoll, & Morin, 2013). Data from a pilot randomized controlled trial (RCT) testing the efficacy of Internet-delivered CBT-I relative to a waitlist control was used to examine changes in symptoms of depression, anxiety, mental health quality of life (QOL), and fatigue. Group by time interactions from repeated measures analyses revealed significant post intervention improvements in Internet participants (n = 22) relative to control participants (n = 22) on all psychological symptoms, mental health QOL, and fatigue. A small post hoc subsample of Internet participants with mild or moderate depression also showed large effect size changes in these constructs (depression, anxiety, mental health QOL, and fatigue). Internet-delivered CBT-I appears to not only improve sleep but also reduce comorbid psychological and fatigue symptoms.

CBT is effective in reducing insomnia complaints, but the effects of self-help CBT have been inconsistent (Lancee, van den Bout, van Straten, & Spoormaker, 2012). The aim of this study was to determine the effectiveness of self-help for insomnia delivered in either electronic or paper-and-pencil format compared to a waiting-list. Participants kept a diary and filled out questionnaires before they were randomized into electronic (n = 216), paper-and-pencil (n = 205), or waiting-list (n = 202) groups. The intervention consisted of 6 weeks of unsupported self-help CBT, and post-tests were 4, 18, and 48 weeks after intervention. At 4-week follow-up, electronic and paper-and-pencil conditions were superior ($p < .01$) compared to the waiting-list condition on most daily sleep measures ($\Delta d = 0.29–0.64$), global insomnia symptoms ($\Delta d = 0.90–1.00$), depression ($\Delta d = 0.36–0.41$), and anxiety symptoms ($\Delta d = 0.33–0.40$). The electronic and paper-and-pencil groups demonstrated equal effectiveness 4 weeks after treatment (Δd = 0.00–0.22; p > .05). Effects were sustained at 48-week follow-up. This large-scale unsupported self-help study shows moderate to large effects on sleep measures that were still present after 48 weeks. Unsupported self-help CBT for insomnia therefore appears to be a promising first option in a stepped care approach.

IRRITABLE BOWEL SYNDROME

The aim of this study was to investigate if cognitive behavior therapy (CBT) based on exposure and mindfulness exercises delivered via the Internet would be effective in treating participants with irritable bowel syndrome (IBS). (Ljótsson, Falk, Vesterlund, Hedman, et al., 2010). Participants were recruited through self-referral. Eighty-six participants were included in the study and randomized to treatment or control condition (an online discussion forum). One participant was excluded after randomization. The main outcome measure was IBS-symptom severity and secondary measures included IBS-related quality of life, GI-specific anxiety, depression and general functioning. Participants were assessed at pre-treatment, post-treatment and 3 month follow-up (treatment condition only). Four participants (5% of total sample) in the treatment condition did not participate in post-treatment assessment. Participants in the treatment condition reported a 42% decrease and participants in the control group reported a 12% increase in primary IBS-symptoms. Compared to the control condition, participants in the treatment group improved on all secondary outcome measures with a large between group effect size on quality of life (Cohen's d = 1.21). The authors concluded that CBT-based on exposure and mindfulness delivered via the Internet can be effective in treating IBS-patients, alleviating the total burden of symptoms and increasing quality of life.

Ljótsson, Hedman, Lindfors, Hursti, T., et al., (2011) conducted a follow-up of a previously reported study of internet-delivered cognitive behavior therapy (CBT) for IBS, based on exposure and mindfulness exercises (Ljótsson et al. (2010, a randomized controlled trial. Seventy-five participants from the original sample of 85 (88%) reported follow-up data at 15–18 months (mean 16.4 months) after completing treatment. The follow-up sample included participants from both the original study's treatment group and waiting list after it had been crossed over to treatment. Intention-to-treat analysis showed that treatment gains were maintained on all outcome measures, including IBS symptoms, quality of life, and anxiety related to gastrointestinal symptoms, with mainly large effect sizes (within-group Cohen's d = 0.78–1.11). A total of fifty participants (59% of the total original sample; 52% of the original treatment group participants and 65% of the original waiting list participants) reported adequate relief of symptoms. Improvements at follow-up were more pronounced for the participants that had completed the full treatment and maintenance of improvement did not seem to be dependent on further treatment seeking. This study suggests that internet-delivered CBT based on exposure and mindfulness has long-term beneficial effects for IBS-patients.

OBESITY

The objective of this systematic review is to update a previous systematic review on the effectiveness of internet-based interventions for weight loss and weight loss maintenance in overweight and obese people with new or additional studies (Manzoni, Pagnini, Corti, Molinari, et al., 2011). A literature search from 2008 to March 2010 was conducted. Studies were eligible for inclusion if: participants were adults with a body mass index ≤ 25, at least one study arm involved an internet-based intervention and the primary aims were weight loss or maintenance. Eight additional studies over the eighteen included in the previous review met the inclusion criteria. Data were extracted on sample characteristics, attrition, weight loss, duration of treatment and maintenance of weight loss. Effect sizes (Hedges g) and relative 95% confidence intervals were calculated for all two-way comparisons within each study. No attempt was made to pool the data in a meta-analysis because of the great heterogeneity of designs among studies. An examination of effect sizes show that the higher significant effects pertain studies that found a superiority of behavioral internet-based programs enhanced by features such as tailored feedback on self-monitoring of weight, eating and activity over education only internet-based interventions. However, control groups are very different among studies and this heterogeneity probably accounts for much of the variance in effect sizes. Hence, questions still remain as to the effectiveness of web-based interventions in achieving weight loss or maintenance. Implications for further research include using a "real" control group in order to make meta-analysis possible and developing multi-factorial design in order to separate components of interventions and identify which of them or patterns of them are keys to success.

The feasibility and efficacy of Internet treatment programs for overweight and obese people have been demonstrated in a series of randomized trials. Initial studies examined various approaches to Internet behavioral treatment. Other studies have examined delivery of group behavioral counseling using Internet chat rooms, using the Internet for long-term maintenance of weight loss, and enhancing motivation in Internet programs. These interventions have produced weight losses of 4–7 kg over 6 months to 1 year when support via e-mail, automated messages, or chat rooms is provided. Outcomes and lessons learned with application to the treatment of substance use and misuse are provided (Tate, 2011).

PHYSICAL PAIN

Given the increasing penetration and health care related use of the Internet, Bender et al., (2011) examined the evidence on the impact of Internet-based interventions on pain. A search of Medline, CINAHL, PsycINFO, and the Cochrane Library was conducted for literature published from 1990 to 2010 describing randomized controlled trials that assessed the effects of Internet-based interventions on patients with pain of any kind. Of 6724 citations, 17 articles were included. The studies evaluated the effects of interventions that provided cognitive and behavioral therapy, moderated peer support programs, or clinical visit preparation or follow-up support on 2503 people in pain. Six studies (35.3%) received scores associated with high quality. Most cognitive and behavioral therapy studies showed an improvement in pain (n=7, 77.8%), activity limitation (n=4, 57.1%) and costs associated with treatment (n=3, 100%), whereas effects on depression (n=2, 28.6%) and anxiety (n=2, 50%) were less consistent. There was limited (n=2 from same research group) but promising evidence that Internet-based peer support programs can lead to improvements in pain intensity, activity limitation, health distress and self-efficacy; limited (n=4 from same research group) but promising evidence that social networking programs can reduce pain in children and adolescents; and insufficient evidence on Internet-based clinical support interventions. Internet-based interventions seem promising for people in pain, but it is still unknown what types of patients benefit most. More well-designed studies with diverse patient groups, active control conditions, and a better description of withdrawals are needed to strengthen the evidence concerning the impact of Internet-based interventions on people in pain.

Pain Management

Pain is generally undertreated in the United States, owing to a number of barriers including geographic distance from specialty treatment providers; functional disability that limits mobility; treatment-related stigma; economic limitations; and educational barriers. Pain under-treatment exacerbates pain chronicity and emotional disruption that can significantly erode a pain patient's quality of life, and there is widespread agreement that pain care must evolve to address this significant problem (McGeary, McGeary, & Gatchel, 2012). The growing field of telehealth (defined for the purposes of this paper as technology that allows for distance interaction between providers and/or patients) offers a novel opportunity to expand pain assessment, consultation, and treatment services beyond the walls of the specialty pain clinic, but there is limited availability of resources describing how to best use this technology to improve access to care. A recent literature review (September 2011) using universally endorsed MeSH search criteria revealed only 32 MEDLINE references focusing on telehealth for pain. This is surprising in light of the very large number of references covering telehealth (14,164 references) and pain (104,564 references), respectively. Of the studies available, there were very few randomized trials of telehealth pain care and only one general overview of e-health and chronic pain, which dedicates just a few paragraphs to telehealth. This manuscript represented one of the first comprehensive reviews of the current state of telehealth and pain management research and practice. The goals were to provide a rationale for the potential benefit of telehealth-based pain management services; describe the various applications of telehealth technology for pain management; orient the reader to cost models for telehealth; present examples of services in place; and offer recommendations for future research based on the current state of knowledge.

Chronic Pain in Children & Youth

Cognitive–behavioral therapy (CBT) interventions show promise for decreasing chronic pain in youth (Palermo, Wilson, Peters, Lewandowski, et al., 2009). However, the availability of CBT is limited by many factors including distance to major treatment centers and expense. This study evaluated a more accessible treatment approach for chronic pediatric pain using an

Internet-delivered family CBT intervention. Participants included 48 children, aged 11–17 years, with chronic headache, abdominal, or musculoskeletal pain and associated functional disability, and their parents. Children were randomly assigned to a wait list control group or an Internet treatment group. Primary treatment outcomes were pain intensity ratings (0–10 NRS) and activity limitations on the Child Activity Limitations Interview, both completed via an online daily diary. In addition to their medical care, the Internet treatment group completed 8 weeks of online modules including relaxation training, cognitive strategies, parent operant techniques, communication strategies, and sleep and activity interventions. Youth randomized to the wait list control group continued with the current medical care only. Findings demonstrated significantly greater reduction in activity limitations and pain intensity at post-treatment for the Internet treatment group and these effects were maintained at the three-month follow-up. Rate of clinically significant improvement in pain was also greater for the Internet treatment group than for the wait list control group. There were no significant group differences in parental protectiveness or child depressive symptoms post-treatment. Internet treatment was rated as acceptable by all children and parents. Findings support the efficacy and acceptability of Internet delivery of family CBT for reducing pain and improving function among children and adolescents with chronic pain.

Phantom Limb Pain-Virtual Reality

Treatment for phantom limb pain could consist of the movement of the intact limb shown through Virtual Reality (Murray, Pettifer, Howard, Patchick, et al., 2007) or the use of the full-body virtual feedback (Schmalzi, Thomke, Ragno, Nilseryd, et al., 2011).

Postnatal Help

The internet offers an accessible and cost-effective way to help women suffering with various types of postnatal mental illness and also can provide resources for healthcare professionals. (Moore & Ayers, 2011). Many websites on postnatal mental illness are available, but there is little information on the range or quality of information and resources offered. The current study therefore aimed to review postnatal health websites and evaluate their quality on a variety of dimensions. A systematic review of postnatal health websites was conducted. Searches were carried out on four search engines (Google, Yahoo, Ask Jeeves and Bing) which are used by 98% of web users. The first 25 websites found for each key word and their hyperlinks were assessed for inclusion in the review. Websites had to be exclusively dedicated to postnatal mental health or have substantial information on postnatal mental illness. Eligible websites (n = 114) were evaluated for accuracy of information, available resources and quality. Results showed that information was largely incomplete and difficult to read; available help was limited and website quality was variable. The top five postnatal mental illness websites were identified for (1) postnatal mental illness sufferers and (2) healthcare professionals. It is hoped these top websites can be used by healthcare professionals both for their own information and to advise patients on quality online resources.

Pregnancy

The loss of a child during pregnancy results in significant psychological stress for many women, and may lead to long-lasting grief and psychological illnesses. However, only a small percentage of those affected seek or receive traditional forms of psychological treatment, and therefore novel treatment approaches and methods are required. This article introduced an Internet-based psychotherapy program or patients after pregnancy loss (Kersting, Kroker, Schlicht, & Wagner, 2011). The five-week intervention comprises two components: structured writing disclosure and cognitive-behavioural therapy. Communication between the therapist and patient is text-based and asynchronous. The writing protocol consists of three treatment phases: self-confrontation, cognitive reappraisal and social sharing. A case report is presented to illustrate the course of the treatment and clinical considerations associated with delivering Internet-based interventions to patients after pregnancy loss.

The loss of a child during pregnancy can be a traumatic event associated with long-lasting grief and psychological distress. This study examined the efficacy of an internet-based cognitive behavioral therapy program for mothers after pregnancy loss (Kersting, Kroker, Schlicht, Baust, et al., 2011). In a randomized controlled trial with a waiting list control group, 83 participants who had lost a child during pregnancy were randomly allocated either to 5 weeks of internet therapy or to a 5-week waiting condition. Within a manualized cognitive behavioral treatment program, participants wrote ten essays on loss-specific topics. Posttraumatic stress, grief, and general psychopathology, especially depression, were assessed pretreatment, post treatment , and at 3-month follow-up. Intention-to-treat analyses and completer analyses were performed. Relative to controls, participants in the treatment group showed significant improvements in posttraumatic stress, grief, depression, and overall mental health, but not in anxiety or somatization. Medium to large effect sizes were observed, and the improvement was maintained at 3-month follow-up. This internet-based cognitive behavioral therapy program represents an effective treatment approach with stable effects for women after pregnancy loss. Implementation of the program can thus help to improve the health care provision for mothers in this traumatic loss situation.

Senior Citizens: Cardiovascular Disease and Depression

Depression, cardiovascular disease (CVD) risk factors and cognitive impairment are important causes of disability and poor health outcomes (Cockayne, Glozier, Naismith, Christensen, Neal, & Hickie, 2011). In combination they lead to an even worse prognosis. Internet or web-based interventions have been shown to deliver efficacious psychological intervention programs for depression on a large scale, yet no published studies have evaluated their impact among patients with co-existing physical conditions. The aims of this randomized controlled trial are to determine the effects of an evidence-based internet intervention program for depression on depressive mood symptoms, cognitive function and treatment adherence in patients at risk of CVD. This study is an internet-based, double-blind, parallel group randomized controlled trial. The trial will compare the effectiveness of online cognitive behavioral therapy with an online attention control placebo. The trial will consist of a 12-week intervention phase with a 40-week follow-up. It will be conducted in urban and rural New South Wales, Australia and will recruit a community-based sample of adults aged 45 to 75 years. Recruitment, intervention, cognitive testing and follow-up data collection will all be internet-based and automated. The primary outcome would be a change in severity of depressive symptoms from baseline to three-months. Secondary outcomes were changes in cognitive function and adherence to treatment for CVD from baseline to three, six and 12-months.

Prior studies of depression amongst patients with CVD have targeted those with previous vascular events and major depression. The potential for intervening earlier in these disease states appears to have significant potential and has yet to be tested. Scalable psychological programs using web-based interventions could deliver care to large numbers in a cost effective way if efficacy were proved. This study will determine the effects of a web-based intervention on depressive symptoms and adherence to treatment among patients at risk of CVD. In addition it will also precisely and reliably define the effects of the intervention upon aspects of cognitive function that are likely to be affected early in at risk individuals, using sensitive and responsive measures.

INDEPENDENT LIVING ARRANGEMENTS

Senior Citizens: Multiple Health Issues

Rapid advances in technology combined with increasing demand for interventions that can "bend the cost curve" have stoked widespread interest in telehealth technologies (Wilson, & Cram, 2012). Telehealth has been broadly defined as "the use of electronic information and telecommunications technologies to support long-distance clinical health care, patient and professional health-related education, public health, and health administration."[1] In this issue of the Archives, Takahashi et al., [2] reported on the results of a rigorous randomized controlled trial of telemonitoring in older adults at high risk for hospitalization. They found that in-home monitoring of biometrics (e.g., blood pressure and weight) and symptoms failed to reduce hospital readmissions or the need for emergency department (ED) visits compared with usual care.

Cognitive control is defined by a set of neural processes that allow us to interact with our complex environment in a goal-directed manner. Humans regularly challenge these control processes when attempting to simultaneously accomplish multiple goals (multitasking), generating interference as the result of fundamental information processing limitations. It is clear that multitasking behavior has become ubiquitous in today's technologically dense world, and substantial evidence has accrued regarding multitasking difficulties and cognitive control deficits in our ageing population. Here Anguera, Boccanfuso, Rintoul, Al-Hashimi, et al. (2013) showed that multitasking performance, as assessed with a custom-designed three-dimensional video game (NeuroRacer), exhibited a linear age-related decline from 20 to 79 years of age. By playing an adaptive version of NeuroRacer in multitasking training mode, older adults (60 to 85 years old) reduced multitasking costs compared to both an active control group and a no-contact control group, attaining levels beyond those achieved by untrained 20-year-old participants, with gains persisting for 6 months. Furthermore, age-related deficits in neural signatures of cognitive control, as measured with electroencephalography, were remediated by multitasking training (enhanced midline frontal theta power and frontal-posterior theta coherence). Critically, this training resulted in performance benefits that extended to untrained cognitive control abilities (enhanced sustained attention and working memory), with an increase in midline frontal theta power predicting the training-induced boost in sustained attention and preservation of multitasking improvement 6 months later. These findings highlight the robust plasticity of the prefrontal cognitive control system in the ageing brain, and provide the first evidence, to our knowledge, of how a custom-designed video game can be used to assess cognitive abilities across the lifespan, evaluate underlying neural mechanisms, and serve as a powerful tool for cognitive enhancement.

Senior Citizens: Telehealth Service

Finkelstein, Speedie, Zhou, Potthoff, Ratner (2011) conducted a randomized controlled trial to evaluate the perception, satisfaction and utilization of a home telehealth service for frail elderly people living independently in their home communities. Control group subjects continued with their usual care and intervention group subjects were able to supplement their usual care with the use of a web portal. The web portal allowed videoconferencing and electronic messaging between home care nurses and clients, ordering health-related and home care services, access to health-related information and general access to the Internet. A total of 99 eligible people (59 female, 40 male) from one urban and one rural study site agreed to participate in the study. Eighty-four subjects were active participants for nine months. There were no significant differences in perception of technology between the two groups at baseline. At 60-day follow-up, the intervention group was significantly more positive towards technology compared to their own baseline ($P < 0.001$) and compared to the 60-day scores for the controls ($P < 0.001$). The intervention group indicated that overall the telehealth service met their expectations (mean score 9 out of 10) and they would recommend it to others (mean score 9.5 out of 10). All subjects were able to use the portal without difficulty after brief instructions from the nurses. A total of 1054 videoconferences were conducted with the intervention subjects. Fifty-six of these (5%) had to be discontinued after successful connection because of technical problems. Intervention subjects made fewer emergency department visits than control subjects, more visits to the eye doctor, fewer visits in all categories of home care utilization, and lower use of transportation services. Frail elderly people are able to adopt home telehealth technologies which may enable them to maintain.

Sleep Apnea

Obstructive sleep apnea is common, but access to diagnosis remains limited (Parikh, TouVelle, Wang, Zallak, 2011). Telemedicine may allow greater access to care; however, its effect on patient satisfaction and treatment adherence is unknown. This study compares patient satisfaction and continuous positive airway pressure (CPAP) adherence of patients seen by videoconference with those seen in person. Materials and Methods: New patients seen via video or in person at a sleep center completed a survey, with three questions pertaining to satisfaction with the provider. Questions were scored 1–5; the sum was the patient satisfaction score. CPAP adherence was retrospectively analyzed in patients who met the physician via video or in person. Percentage of nights CPAP was used for ≥4 h and average minutes of CPAP use per night over 2 consecutive weeks were compared. Results: A Mann–Whitney test compared patient satisfaction of the 90 subjects (of whom, 56 met physician in person and 34 via video). Mean scores (in person, 14.82; video, 14.91; p=0.851) did not differ between groups. Mann–Whitney tests compared CPAP adherence in the 172 subjects (of whom, 111 met physician in person and 61 via video). Mean percentage of nights CPAP was used ≥4 h (in person, 71%; video, 65%; p=0.198) and the average minutes per night of CPAP use (in person, 340.55; video, 305.31; p=0.153) did not differ between groups. Conclusions: The findings indicate that patients were equally satisfied with their provider and adherent to CPAP treatment whether they were seen in person or via video. Videoconferencing may improve access to patient care without reducing patient satisfaction or treatment adherence.

SLEEP MONITORING

In 2009, Spaulding, Stevens, and Velasquez, S. E. (2011) established a pilot telehealth service to a sleep laboratory in Garden City, Kansas, approximately 600 km from the Kansas University Medical Center. Videoconferencing was used for polysomnography (PSG) study follow-up, patient monitoring and sleep laboratory medical management. It allowed the sleep specialist to treat patients and collaborate with sleep laboratory personnel from a distance without extensive travel. In the first six months the telemedicine clinic was held on six occasions. There were 18 new patient evaluations and four follow up visits. The most common diagnosis was obstructive sleep apnoea. The videoconferencing equipment and the intraoral camera worked well. Interviewing and examining patients via telemedicine was very similar to doing it in-person. Telemedicine was effective for the physician-patient interaction and for visualizing airway structures. Although more research is needed, the use of videoconferencing for sleep study follow-up and laboratory oversight appears very promising.

STUTTERING

This paper seeks to demonstrate the possibility of manipulating the frequency of stuttering using virtual reality environments (VREs; Brundage, Graap, Gibbons, Ferrer, & Brooks, 2006). If stuttering manifests itself in VREs similarly to the way it manifests itself in real world interactions, then VREs can provide a controlled, safe, and confidential method for treatment practice and generalization. Though many researchers and clinicians recognize the need for generalization activities in the treatment of stuttering, achieving generalization in a clinical setting poses challenges to client confidentiality, safety, and the efficient use of a professionals' time. Virtual reality (VR) technology may allow professionals the opportunity to enhance and assess treatment generalization while protecting the safety and confidentiality of their clients. In this study, we developed a VR job interview environment which allowed experimental control over communication style and gender of interviewers. In this first trial, persons who stutter (PWS) experienced both challenging and supportive VR job interview conditions. The percentage of stuttered syllables was calculated for both interviews for each participant. Self-reported ratings of communication apprehension and confidence were also obtained, and were not significantly correlated with stuttering severity. Results indicated that interviewer communication style affected the amount of stuttering produced by participants, with more stuttering observed during challenging virtual interviews. Additionally, the amount of stuttering observed during the VR job interviews was significantly, positively correlated with the amount of stuttering observed during an interview with the investigator prior to VR exposure. Participants' subjective reports of the VR experience indicate reactions similar to those they report experiencing in the real world. Possible implications for the use of VR in the assessment and treatment of stuttering are discussed.

TINNITUS

The aim of this randomized controlled trial was to investigate the effects on global tinnitus severity of 2 Internet-delivered psychological treatments, acceptance and commitment therapy (ACT) and cognitive behavior therapy (CBT), in guided self-help format (Hesser, Gustafsson, Lundén, Henrikson, et al., 2012). Ninety-nine participants (mean age = 48.5 years; 43% female) who were significantly distressed by tinnitus were recruited from the community. Participants were randomly assigned to CBT ($n = 32$), ACT ($n = 35$), or a control condition (monitored Internet discussion forum; $n = 32$), and they were assessed with standardized self-report measures (Tinnitus Handicap Inventory; Hospital Anxiety and Depression Scale; Quality of Life Inventory; Perceived Stress Scale; Tinnitus Acceptance Questionnaire) at pre-, post- treatment (8 weeks), and 1-year follow-up. Results: Mixed-effects linear regression analysis of all randomized participants showed significant effects on the primary outcome (Tinnitus Handicap Inventory) for CBT and for ACT compared with control at post treatment (95% CI [−17.03, −2.94], $d = 0.70$, and 95% CI [−16.29, −2.53], $d = 0.68$, respectively). Within-group effects were substantial from pretreatment through 1-year-follow-up for both treatments (95% CI [−44.65, −20.45], $d = 1.34$), with no significant difference between treatments (95% CI [−14.87, 11.21], $d = 0.16$). Acceptance-based procedures may be a viable alternative to traditional CBT techniques in the management of tinnitus. The Internet can improve access to psychological interventions for tinnitus.

WEIGHT LOSS

Nondirective support (NS; collaborative, flexible) is positively associated with successful disease management, healthy lifestyles, quality of life and support satisfaction, whereas directive support (DS; prescriptive, protocol driven) has negative or no associations with these outcomes (Gabriele, 2009). However, DS is advantageous in acute, stressful situations and when an individual lacks skills to handle a challenge. This study manipulated these support types through e-mail exchanges and evaluated their effects on weight loss, physical activity, dietary behavior, engagement, alliance, and satisfaction in a 12-week e-counseling program. Overweight individuals ($N = 104$) were randomly assigned to one of three conditions: NS, DS, or minimal support (MS). All participants received two e-mails each week: (1) weight loss lesson and web link to report weight, daily calories, and exercise; (2) feedback graphs. Participants in the NS and DS conditions also received individualized weight loss support following protocols reflecting each type of support. Participants in the NS condition reported greater NS and a greater ratio of NS to DS than participants in the DS condition indicating participants were sensitive to the support manipulation. There was no effect for weight loss based on treatment condition. Secondary analyses revealed a gender-by-condition interaction. Females lost more weight in the DS condition (10.61 pounds) than in the NS (5.51 pounds) or MS (5.98 pounds) conditions (number of males insufficient for between-group analyses). Participants in the DS condition had greater changes in physical activity than participants in the NS and MS conditions. There were no group differences for dietary behavior and engagement. Those in NS reported greater goal collaboration than those in DS and greater goal collaboration, task orientation, and bond than those in MS. Support satisfaction was greater in NS than DS or MS conditions. General program satisfaction in NS was equivalent to satisfaction in DS and higher than in MS. These findings indicate that DS is advantageous to females during the beginning of a weight loss program, underscore the value of individualized weight loss support to alliance and program acceptability, and point to the importance of analysis of specific aspects of social support and its relationships with behavior and satisfaction.

WOMEN BODY IMAGE

A group dissonance-based eating disorder prevention program, in which young women critique the thin ideal, reduces eating disorder risk factors and symptoms, but it can be difficult to identify school clinicians with the time and expertise to deliver the intervention (Stice, Rohde, Durant, & Shaw, 2012). Thus, we developed a prototype Internet version of this program and evaluated it in a preliminary trial. Method: Female college students with body dissatisfaction ($N = 107$; M age = 21.6 years, $SD = 6.6$) were randomized to the Internet intervention, group intervention, educational video condition, or educational brochure condition. Results: Internet and group participants showed greater pre-post reductions in eating disorder risk factors and symptoms than video controls (M ds = 0.47 and 0.54, respectively) and brochure controls (M ds = 0.75 and 0.72, respectively), with many effects reaching significance. Effects did not differ significantly for Internet versus group participants (M ds = –0.13) or for video versus brochure controls (M d = 0.25). Effect sizes for the Internet intervention were similar to those previously observed for group versions of this intervention. Conclusions: Results suggest that this prototype Internet intervention is as efficacious as the group intervention, implying that there would be merit in completing this intervention and evaluating it in a fully powered trial.

YOUTH CHRONIC FATIQUE SYNDROME

Chronic fatigue syndrome is characterized by persistent fatigue and severe disability. Cognitive behavioural therapy seems to be a promising treatment, but its availability is restricted. Nijhof, Bleijenberg, Uiterwaal, Kimpen, et al. (2012) developed a program entitled

Fatigue In Teen-agers on the interNET (FITNET), the first dedicated internet-based therapeutic program for adolescents with this disorder, and compared its effectiveness with that of usual care. Adolescents aged 12–18 years with chronic fatigue syndrome were assigned to FITNET or usual care in a 1:1 ratio at one tertiary treatment centre in the Netherlands by use of a computer-generated blocked randomization allocation schedule. The study was open label. Primary outcomes were school attendance, fatigue severity, and physical functioning, and were assessed at 6 months with computerized questionnaires. Analysis was by intention to treat. Thereafter, all patients were offered FITNET if needed. This trial is registered, number ISRCTN59878666. Sixtyeight of 135 adolescents were assigned to FITNET and 67 to usual care, and 67 and 64, respectively, were analyzed. FITNET was significantly more effective than was usual care for all dichotomized primary outcomes at 6 months—full school attendance (50 [75%] versus 10 [16%], relative risk 4·8, 95% CI 2·7–8·9; $p<0{\cdot}0001$), absence of severe fatigue (57 [85%] versus 17 [27%], 3·2, 2·1–4·9; $p<0{\cdot}0001$), and normal physical functioning (52 [78%] versus 13 [20%], 3·8, 2·3–6·3; $p<0{\cdot}0001$). No serious adverse events were reported. FITNET seemed to offer a readily accessible and highly effective treatment for adolescents with chronic fatigue syndrome. The results of this study justify implementation on a broader scale.

CONCLUSION

There is no question that Internet-derived interventions have achieved an important if not crucial status in the treatment of physical illness to the point that they could be considered Standard Operating Procedures before moving on to more expensive, unstructured, and prolonged F2F interventions.

Chapter 11

SERIOUS MENTAL ILLNESSES AND OBSESSIVE COMPULSIVE DISORDER

A technical expert panel convened by the Agency for Healthcare Research and Quality and the National Institute of Mental Health was charged with reviewing the state of research on behavioral intervention technologies (BITs) in mental health and identifying the top research priorities. BITs refers to behavioral and psychological interventions that use information and communication technology features to address behavioral and mental health outcomes (Mohr, Burns, Schueller, Clarke, et al. 2013). Videoconferencing and standard telephone technologies to deliver psychotherapy have been well validated. Web-based interventions have shown efficacy across a broad range of mental health outcomes. Social media such as online support groups have produced disappointing outcomes when used alone. Mobile technologies have received limited attention for mental health outcomes. Virtual reality has shown good efficacy for anxiety and pediatric disorders. Serious gaming has received little work in mental health. Research focused on understanding reach, adherence, barriers and cost is recommended. Improvements in the collection, storage, analysis and visualization of big data will be required. New theoretical models and evaluation strategies will be required. Finally, for BITs to have a public health impact, research on implementation and application to prevention is required.

Intervening early in the course of psychotic illness may improve the long-term outcome. Early intervention requires early recognition, and one factor that influences early recognition is the level of mental health literacy (MHL) in the population (Lawlor, Breslin, Renwick, Foley, et al., 2008). To investigate the level of MHL regarding depression and psychosis in an Irish population. The researchers invited the registered users of Ireland‘s most popular community website (http://www.boards.ie) to participate in an online survey. Two standardized vignettes depicting depression and psychosis were presented, and respondents were asked about what they thought the conditions were and who might be best placed to help the person. Participants were asked a series of knowledge-based questions about psychosis. Nine hundred and ninety-eight (770 males, 228 females) people participated. Using a case vignette model, 78% and 93% of respondents correctly identified depression and psychosis/schizophrenia, respectively. However, half of the participants described schizophrenia as a ‘split personality disorder‘. Neither age nor urbanicity influenced the probability of correctly identifying the diagnosis, but females and university students were more likely to correctly identify the diagnosis. More than 90% believed intervening early in psychosis is likely to improve outcome. Conclusion: The Internet users in this survey have high levels of MHL, identify appropriate pathways to care, and their views on management are consistent with evidence-based treatments.

This study examined psychologists' knowledge of their legal and ethical responsibilities with imminently dangerous clients. Pabian, Welfel, and Beebe (2009) randomly surveyed 1,000 psychologists from four states and received 300 useable responses (30%). Most psychologists (76.4%) were misinformed about their state laws, believing that they had a legal duty to warn when they did not, or assuming that warning was their only legal option when other protective actions less harmful to client privacy were allowed. Moreover, in spite of the inaccuracy of their knowledge, many respondents were confident that they understood the duty to protect in their own state. Contrary to expectation, we found no significant association between legal knowledge and continuing education in legal and ethical issues, graduate training in ethics, or clinical experience with dangerous clients. These findings suggest that educational experiences during and after graduate school may not be meeting the needs of professionals to understand the complicated array of state laws and ethical duties regarding dangerous clients. We recommend several changes in the provisions of these experiences to better protect psychologists and clients from unintentional risks.

Do people with serious mental illness (SMI) and substance use disorder (SUD) use the Internet to receive health information (Clayton, Borzekowski, Himelhoch, Dixon, Potts, Medoff, Hackman, & Balis, 2009)? One hundred people with SMI were surveyed in community mental health clinics. Participants with SUD were significantly less likely to use the Internet compared to those who without SUD (.34 [.12–.95] $p = .04$). Internet users with SUD were significantly more likely to report accessing sites topically related to substance abuse ($p = .01$). Few participants with SMI and SUD used the Internet. Attention to educating patients about quality health information on the Internet may be warranted.

TEMPERMENT AND PSYCHOPATHOLOGY

The internet provides a research opportunity for psychiatry and psychology. This article presented the development and preliminary data of a large web-survey created to study how temperament relates to other psychological measures, behavior and psychiatric disorders (Lara, Ottoni, Brunstein, Frozi, et al., 2012). The authors used the Affective and Emotional Composite Temperament Scale (AFECTS) to evaluate temperament and we selected several self-report instruments to evaluate behavior, psychological constructs and mental disorders. The system provided anonymous psychological (phase 1) and psychiatric (phase 2) feedback and included questions to assess the validity of the answers. Each phase had around 450 questions. This system was broadcasted utilizing Brazilian media. After the exclusion of 21.5% of the volunteers (those who failed the validation questions), 41,427 participants concluded the first part of the system (mean age = 31.2 ± 10.5 yrs, 26.9% males), and 21,836 (mean age = 32.5 ± 10.9 yrs, 25.1% males) completed phase 2. Around 25% had received a psychiatric diagnosis from a mental health professional. Demographic and temperament profiles of those who completed either only 80 questions, only phase 1, or the whole system were similar. The rate of non-serious answers (e.g., on bizarre behaviors) was very low and congruency of answers was very high. The internal consistency of classical trait scales (TCI-R and PANAS) was high (Cronbach's alpha > 0.80) for all dimensions. A limitation of this study was a relatively high dropout rate due to the length of the process and an overrepresentation of female, young and well-educated participants. The BRAINSTEP provides valid and abundant data on psychological and psychiatric measures (note of author: the 25% of the population receiving a psychiatric diagnosis is well within the theoretical predictions made by RCT (Colesso, Cusinato, & L'Abate, 2013; Cusinato & L'Abate, 2012; L'Abate et al., 2010).

Bipolar Disorder

Psycho-educational approaches are promising interventions for the long-term management of bipolar disorder (Smith, Griffiths, Poole, di Florio, Barnes, et al., 2011). In consultation with professionals, patients, and their families, the authors developed a novel web-based psycho-educational intervention for bipolar disorder called Beating Bipolar. They undertook a preliminary exploratory randomized trial to examine efficacy, feasibility and acceptability. This was an exploratory randomized controlled trial of Beating Bipolar (current controlled trials registration number: ISRCTN81375447). The control arm was treatment-as-usual and the a priori primary outcome measure was quality of life [measured by the brief World Health Organization Quality of Life (WHOQOL-BREF) scale]. Secondary outcomes included psychosocial functioning, insight, depressive and manic symptoms and relapse, and use of healthcare resources. Fifty participants were randomized to either the Beating Bipolar intervention plus treatment-as-usual or just treatment-as-usual. The intervention was delivered over a four-month period and outcomes were assessed six months later.

There was no significant difference between the intervention and control groups on the primary outcome measure (total WHOQOL-BREF score) but there was a modest improvement within the psychological subsection of the WHOQOL-BREF for the intervention group relative to the control group. There were no significant differences between the groups on any of the secondary outcome measures. Beating Bipolar is potentially a safe and engaging intervention which can be delivered remotely to large numbers of patients with bipolar disorder at relatively low cost. It may have a modest effect on psychological quality of life. Further work is required to establish the impact of this intervention on insight, knowledge, treatment adherence, self-efficacy and self-management skills.

There is growing evidence that patients with bipolar affective disorder (BAD), who use medication, respond well to further psychotherapeutic interventions. Internet-based psycho-education is typically centered on the interaction between a client and therapist via the Internet. Multiple methods were required to investigate existing psych educational and psychotherapeutic strategies used on patients suffering from BAD (Latalova, Prasko, Kamaradova, Jelenova, et al., 2013). Systematic reviews and original reports of all trials of psycho-education in BAD patients were retrieved. Patients with BAD, who were hospitalized in a psychiatric department or attended a day hospital program, were exposed to the first version of the program during the treatment, and then questioned about understandability, comprehensibility, and usefulness of each lecture. Twelve modules of the Internet E-Program for BAD were developed and the intervention was a pilot tested with twelve patients. Internet psycho-education program for BAD is an intervention designed for universal implementation that addresses heightened learning needs of patients suffering from BAD. It is designed to promote confidence and reduce the number of episodes of the disorder by providing skills in monitoring warning signs, planning daily activities and practicing communication skills.

PHYSICAL ACTIVITY

The prevalence of mental health disorders among college students is rising and the increasing rates of anxiety and depression have important societal implications. Physical activity has been proposed as an adjuvant to traditional treatment approaches (i.e., psychotherapy or pharmacotherapy), and the internet is a potentially useful means of delivering physical activity information to the college-aged population (L'Abate, 2013c). This randomized pilot trial examined the effects of an internet-based physical activity intervention on physical activity, self-efficacy, depression, and anxiety in college students ($n = 47$) receiving mental health counseling (Mailey, Wójcicki, Motl, Hu, et al., 2010). Physical activity, depression, anxiety, exercise self-efficacy, and barriers self-efficacy were assessed at baseline and post-intervention. There was a significant time effect for physical activity, with both groups increasing their physical activity levels across the 10-week intervention but with a larger increase in the intervention condition ($d = 0.68$) than the control condition ($d = 0.05$). Exercise and barriers self-efficacy declined across the intervention, but more so in the control than intervention condition. Effects on depression and anxiety were non-significant. Finally, correlation analyses showed increases in physical activity were associated with increases in exercise self-efficacy ($r = 0.62$) and barriers self-efficacy ($r = 0.63$) and decreases in depression ($r = -0.44$) in the intervention condition, but not in the control condition. These results suggested that an internet-delivered physical activity intervention may be a promising approach to promoting physical activity among college students undergoing mental health counseling.

PSYCHOTIC DISORDERS

The aim of this review was to investigate to what extent information technology may support self-management among service users with psychotic disorders (van der Krieke, Wunderink, L., Emerencia, de Jonge, et al. (2014). The investigation aimed to answer the following questions: What types of e-mental health self-management interventions have been developed and evaluated? What is the current evidence on clinical outcome and cost-effectiveness of the identified interventions? To what extent are e-mental health self-management interventions oriented toward the service user? Methods: A systematic review of references through July 2012 derived from MEDLINE, PsycINFO, AMED, CINAHL, and the Library, Information Science and Technology database was performed. Studies of e-mental health self-management interventions for persons with psychotic disorders were selected independently by three reviewers. Results: Twenty-eight studies met the inclusion criteria. E-mental health self-management interventions included psycho-education, medication management, communication and shared decision making, management of daily functioning, lifestyle management, peer support, and real-time self-monitoring by daily measurements (experience sampling monitoring). Summary effect sizes were large for medication management (.92) and small for psychoeducation (.37) and communication and shared decision making (.21). For all other studies, individual effect sizes were calculated. The only economic analysis conducted reported more short-term costs for the e-mental health intervention. People with psychotic disorders were able and willing to use e-mental health services. Results suggest that e-mental health services are at least as effective as usual care or nontechnological approaches. Larger effects were found for medication management e-mental health services. No studies reported a negative effect. Results must be interpreted cautiously, because they are based on a small number of studies.

Suicide Prevention

Luxton, June, and Kinn (2010) reported on current and emerging technologies for suicide prevention. Technology-based programs discussed included interactive educational and social networking websites, email-based outreach, and programs that use mobile devices and texting. The authors described innovative applications, such as virtual worlds, gaming, and text analysis that are currently being developed and applied to suicide prevention and outreach programs. Luxton, June, and Kinn also discussed the benefits and limitations of technology-based applications and discuss future directions for their use.

Mental Health Care-givers or Carers

Around six million adults in the United Kingdom take on the role of an informal caregiver to friends or relatives who have mental health issues (Darcy, Brunsden, & Hill, 2011). Accessing support can be difficult because of both the demands of the caring role and the social stigma attached to mental ill health. However, the Internet offers opportunities to access peer support in a more immediate and protective way. This study explored the use of an online mental health discussion board by informal caregivers. An interpretative phenomenological analysis was conducted using 487 postings from 82 users. A superordinate theme of "gaining a different perspective" emerged which consisted of three subordinate themes, specifically, "insights into mental ill health," "an insider viewpoint" and "rediscovering hope." Findings suggested that use of the board brought positive benefits not only from the sharing of experiences with other caregivers but more importantly from those who experienced mental ill health themselves.

This paper investigated the acceptance of in-home telehealth by frail older adults and carers of the Transition Care Program (TCP), and evaluates telehealth acceptance as a predictor for usage compliance (Wade, Cartwright, & Shaw, 2012). A stratified random sample of participants was allocated to one of five groups: either a control group or to receive telehealth monitoring of their vital signs for a period of 12 or 24 weeks; with or without a medical alarm pendant. Before being trained in and using telehealth, the majority of participants and carers demonstrated acceptance of the technology by reporting that they perceived it would be "useful" and "easy to use." This acceptance was also reported post-TCP (up to 12 weeks of usage). The "perceived ease of use" of the telehealth equipment increased significantly from pre-telehealth training and usage to post-TCP (up to 12 weeks of usage) (P = 0.001). There was no change, (pre-training and usage to post-TCP) in the "perceived usefulness" of the telehealth equipment. The telehealth acceptance constructs of "ease of use" and "usefulness," at pre-telehealth training and usage, approached statistical significance as a predictor of future compliance (P = 0.06). "Perceived ease of use," at pre-training and usage, had a positive relationship with future compliance (P = 0.02). There is currently limited knowledge about the influences and determinants of home telehealth compliance in frail older people and their carers, potentially a significant user group for the technology into the future. This study's finding that frail older people and their carers perceive that home telehealth is useful and easy to use demonstrates their acceptance of home telehealth as a therapeutic tool. Further, perceived ease of use of home telehealth is a significant predictor of compliance with frail older people and their carers' use of home telehealth. Additional research is required in order to identify other influences and determinants of home telehealth compliance with this group. Knowledge about the influences and determinants of home telehealth compliance may assist the development of targeted interventions aimed at encouraging high compliance with users who are recording lower reading rates.

Online Support Groups

Online support groups have been used extensively, in numerous areas of distress, for 15 years. Researchers have presented conflicting findings and ideas about their effectiveness in helping people cope with respective problems. Barak, Boniel-Nissim, and Suler (2008) reviewed quantitative studies and their own qualitative exploration of the nature of the experiences that occur in such groups. This review showed that several factors operate to potentially affect participants. Personal and interpersonal dynamics, which are central in producing effects in these groups, are induced and accelerated by the powerful online disinhibition effect. These factors, including the very impact of writing, expressions of emotions, collecting information and thereby improving understanding and knowledge, developing social relationships, and enhancing decision-making skills and consequent behavioral actions all serve as possible generators of a sense of personal empowerment for people in distress. This view may explain why empirical research has frequently found little or no specific outcomes from participating in online support groups; however, it has found much support for nonspecific personal impacts of this means of intervention. Thus, we contend that online support groups are designed to foster, and many of them actually do, well-being, a sense of control, self-confidence, feelings of more independence, social interactions, and improved feelings – all nonspecific but highly important psychological factors. As such, participating in an online support group could foster personal empowerment, which is much needed in handling specific conditions of distress. Nonetheless, this participation has potential costs, too, especially developing dependence, distancing from in person contacts, and exposure to unpleasant experiences typical of social engagement in cyberspace.

Health Promotion-Self-Guided Interventions

Positive psychology is paving the way for interventions that enduringly enhance well-being and the internet offers the potential to disseminate these interventions to a broad audience in an accessible and sustainable manner (Mitchell, Stanimirovic, Klein, & Vella-Brodrick, 2009). There is now sufficient evidence demonstrating the efficacy of internet interventions for mental illness treatment and prevention, but little is known about enhancing well-being. The current study examined the efficacy of a positive psychology internet-based intervention by adopting a randomised controlled trial design to compare a strengths intervention, a problem solving intervention, and a placebo control. Participants (n = 160) completed measures of well-being (PWI-A, SWLS, PANAS, OTH) and mental illness (DASS-21) at pre-assessment, post-assessment and 3-month follow-up. Well-being increased for the strengths group at post- and follow-up assessment on the PWI-A, but not the SWLS or PANAS. Significant changes were detected on the OTH subscales of engagement and pleasure. No changes in mental illness were detected by group or time. Attrition from the study was 83% at 3-month follow-up, with significant group differences in adherence to the intervention: strengths (34%), problem solving (15.5%) and placebo control (42.6%). Although the results are mixed, it appears possible to enhance the cognitive component of well-being via a self-guided internet intervention.

Positive Psychology

This paper reviewed two relatively young fields of research - positive psychology and internet interventions - and discusses the potential of online positive psychology interventions (OPPIs) as an effective and sustainable health promotion tool within a comprehensive approach to mental health care (Mitchell, Vella-Brodrick, & Klein, 2010). The paper started with a review of positive psychology, in particular well-being theory and contemporary research, and then followed by an overview of the advantages (e.g., accessibility and sustainability) and disadvantages (e.g., digital divide) of delivering mental health interventions via the internet. Finally, the results of a literature review combining the two fields of research are presented. Five randomised controlled trials were identified testing the efficacy of OPPIs as a means of enhancing well-being, with three studies demonstrating increased well-being compared to a control group. In the three studies that had populations with mild to moderate depression symptoms at baseline, there was significant symptom reduction, suggesting that well-being interventions, while primarily targeted at improving wellness, may also have an illness treatment and prevention function. While this review is limited by the small number of studies currently available, researchers, practitioners and consumers are asked to consider the opportunities and benefits of delivering well-being interventions online.

Obsessive Compulsive Disorder

Here is a summary of Marks et al., (2007) findings about OCD:

"Computer therapy (CP) for OCD has only been studied in three systems. The USA UK IVR BTSteps system was studied with 314 patients. Home use of BTSteps plus its workbook improved OCD in two open studies and two RCTs is clinically efficacious as (National Institute for Clinical Excellence of England and Wales (NICE) recognized, and was cost-effective on several criteria. Scheduled brief support by phone enhanced improvement for BTSteps, which saves over 80% of clinician time. In its new Internet form BTSeps is called OCFighter. An Australian CAVE System improved OCD in an open study in 13 volunteers (p. 61)

Recently, a major new category classification of disorders, the obsessive-compulsive related disorders (OCRDs), has been proposed (Hollander, Braun, & Simeon, 2008). The proposed disorders that would fall in this category are associated with efficacious treatments, but have not been widely disseminated. Recent developments in telehealth have made treatment available to a wider range of clients with putative OCRDs. This paper evaluated the efficacy of these treatments when delivered using telehealth methodologies (Brand, & McKay, 2012). While the evidence is preliminary, the early results are encouraging for the delivery of cognitive-behavior therapy for a wide range of OCRDs. Additional research directions are suggested in light of these emerging technologies for treatment delivery.

OCD is a prevalent, chronic and disabling anxiety disorder. Despite the efficacy and strength of pharmacologic interventions for OCD, medications are not always well accepted or effective, making an efficacious psychosocial alternative especially attractive (Himle, Fischer, Muroff, Van Etten, et al., 2006). Cognitive-behavioral therapy (CBT) has been established as an effective treatment for adult OCD, yet access to such treatment is limited, especially in rural areas. Technological advances allow for therapy to be provided in a real-time format over a videoconferencing network. This method allows therapists to provide state-of-the-art treatment to patients who would not otherwise have access to it. This paper presents three cases of OCD successfully treated via videoconferencing CBT. The presence of OCD was established via structured clinical interview and clinician-rated outcome measures were completed by evaluators blinded to the method of treatment. A multiple baseline across individuals design was used to support the internal validity of the CBT outcome data. Patient ratings of therapeutic alliance were high across all three cases. Information gathered from qualitative interviews post-treatment confirmed quantitative measures finding high levels of patient satisfaction. This pilot study suggested that videoconferencing-based CBT is a promising method to bring appropriate treatment to thousands who live far distances from well-trained therapists.

Cognitive behavior therapy (CBT) is widely regarded as an effective treatment for obsessive compulsive disorder (OCD), but access to CBT therapists is limited. Internet-based CBT (ICBT) with therapist support is a way to increase access to CBT but has not been developed or tested for OCD. The aim of this study was to evaluate ICBT for OCD (Andersson, et al. (2011). Method: An open trial where patients (N = 23) received a 15-week ICBT program with therapist support consisting of psychoeducation, cognitive restructuring and exposure with response prevention. The primary outcome was the Yale-Brown Obsessive

Compulsive Scale (Y-BOCS), which was assessed by a psychiatrist before and immediately after treatment. Secondary outcomes were self-rated measures of OCD symptoms, depressive symptoms, general functioning, anxiety and quality of life. All assessments were made at baseline and post-treatment.

All participants completed the primary outcome measure at all assessment points. There were reductions in OCD symptoms with a large within-group effect size (Cohen's d = 1.56). At post-treatment, 61% of participants showed a clinically significant improvement and 43% no longer fulfilled the diagnostic criteria of OCD. The treatment also resulted in statistically significant improvements in self-rated OCD symptoms, general functioning and depression. In conclusion, ICBT with therapist support reduces OCD symptoms, depressive symptoms and improves general functioning. Randomized trials are needed to confirm the effectiveness of this new treatment format.

For most patients with obsessive-compulsive disorder (OCD) the availability of exposure-based therapy is limited. In our study six outpatients with obsessive-compulsive disorder (OCD) received 15 sessions of therapy delivered only over teleconference (six sessions) and cell phones (nine sessions) over a 3-month period of time (Vogel, Launes, Moen, Solem, et al., 2012). Five of the patients were women and the average age of the participants was 31.5 (SD = 8.1). Patients presented a variety of OCD symptoms which were treated with standard exposure and response prevention exercises both during treatment sessions and as a part of homework exercises. All patients rated the treatment format as acceptable and rated the quality of the working alliance as high. At the end of therapy four of the six patients were highly improved and no longer met diagnostic criteria for OCD according to the Anxiety Disorders Interview Schedule for DSM-IV and the Yale-Brown Obsessive Compulsive Scale. The same was true at 3-month follow-up although some small increases in OCD symptoms had occurred. The innovative treatment format shows promise as a method of delivery that may make treatment accessible for patients with poor access to specialty clinics.

The present study evaluates efficacy of a new Internet-administered cognitive behavioral therapy (CBT) protocol, The OCD Program, designed to treat obsessive–compulsive disorder (OCD) remotely (Wootton, Titov, Dear, Spence, et al., 2011). This protocol comprised 8 online lessons delivered over 8 weeks and incorporates cognitive and behavioral techniques. Twenty-two individuals with a principal diagnosis of OCD received CBT-based online lessons, homework assignments, twice weekly contact from a clinical psychologist, and automated emails. Eighty-one percent of participants completed the lessons within the 8-week program. Post-treatment and 3-month follow-up data were collected from 21/21 (100%) and 19/21 (91%) participants, respectively. Participants improved significantly on the primary outcome measures, the Yale-Brown Obsessive Compulsive Scale and Obsessive Compulsive Inventory-Revised, with within-groups effect sizes (Cohen's d) at follow-up of 1.28 and 0.60, respectively. Participants rated the procedure as highly acceptable despite receiving an average of only 86 min (SD = 54.4 min) telephone contact with the therapist over the 8 weeks. These results provided preliminary support for efficacy of Internet-administered treatment for OCD.

Obsessive-compulsive disorder (OCD) is a disabling anxiety disorder, but most individuals delay seeking treatment (Wootton, Titov, Dear, Spence, et al., 2011). Internet-based cognitive behavioural therapy (iCBT) is an innovative service delivery method that may help to improve access to care, but the acceptability to consumers of such programs has not yet been established. People with symptoms of OCD were invited to complete an online survey enquiring about demographic characteristics, symptom severity, and acceptability of Internet-based treatment. Demographic and symptom severity data were compared with people with OCD identified in a national epidemiological survey and with a sample of patients with OCD from a specialist outpatient anxiety clinic. Participants were 129 volunteers to an online Internet survey, 135 patients at a specialist anxiety disorders outpatient clinic, and 297 cases identified in a national epidemiological survey. Demographic characteristics, and severity of symptoms as measured by the Kessler 10-Item scale, the 12-item World Health Organization Disability Assessment Schedule-Second Edition and the Yale Brown Obsessive Compulsive Scale-Self Report Version. The Internet sample was similar demographically but reported more severe symptoms than the comparison groups, although had similar severity of symptoms of OCD compared with other clinical samples reported in the literature. Participants reported Internet-based treatment for OCD would be highly acceptable. Internet-based treatment may reduce barriers to accessing treatment to people with OCD. Individuals in this study were similar demographically to other samples and had similar severity of symptoms as those identified in other clinical samples, suggesting that Internet-based treatment using techniques employed in face-to-face treatment may be effective in this group. Internet-based treatments for OCD need to be developed and evaluated.

Given the burdens of early-onset obsessive-compulsive disorder (OCD), limitations in the broad availability and accessibility of evidence-based care for affected youth present serious public health concerns (Comer, Furr, Cooper-Vince, Kerns, et al., 2014). The growing potential for technological innovations to transform care for the most traditionally remote and underserved families holds enormous promise. This article presents the rationale, key considerations, and a preliminary case series for a promising behavioral telehealth innovation in the evidence-based treatment of early-onset OCD. We developed an Internet-based format for the delivery of family-based treatment for early-onset OCD directly to families in their homes, regardless of their geographic proximity to a mental health facility. Video teleconferencing (VTC) methods were used to deliver real-time cognitive-behavioral therapy centering on exposure and response prevention to affected families. Participants in the preliminary case series included 5 children between the ages of 4 and 8 (M[sub]Age[/sub] = 6.5) who received the Internet-delivered treatment format. All youth completed a full treatment course, all showed OCD symptom improvements and global severity improvements from pre- to post- treatment, all showed at least partial diagnostic response, and 60% no longer met diagnostic criteria for OCD at post-treatment. No participants got worse, and all mothers characterized the quality of services received as "excellent." The present work adds to a growing literature supporting the potential of VTC and related computer technology for meaningfully expanding the reach of supported treatments for OCD and lays the foundation for subsequent controlled evaluations to evaluate matters of efficacy and engagement relative to standard in-office evidence-based care.

HOARDING AS OBSESSIVE COMPULSIVE BEHAVIOR

This study tested the effectiveness of an existing private online CBT-based group intervention designed to help people with hoarding (Muroff, Steketee, Himle, & Frost, R. 2010. Web-group participants were hypothesized to show more improvement in hoarding symptoms over time compared to those placed on a naturalistic waitlist. This web-based self-help group (N = 106 members, N = 155 waitlisted) includes a formal application process and requires that participants post action steps and progress at least once monthly. Members have access to educational resources on hoarding, cognitive strategies, and a chat group. Potential research participants were invited to complete an anonymous web-based survey about their hoarding behaviors and clinical improvement on five occasions (3 months apart). The sample was mainly middle-aged, female and White. Regression analyses show that Recent members reported greater improvement and less clutter at 6 months (than Waitlist). Long-term members reported milder hoarding symptoms than Recent ones, suggesting benefits from group participation over time. All members showed reductions in clutter and hoarding symptoms over 15 months. Less posting activity was associated with greater hoarding severity. Online CBT-based self-help for hoarding appears to be a promising intervention strategy that may extend access to treatment. Evaluating the benefits of internet self-help groups is critical given growing popularity of and demand for web-based interventions.

CONCLUSION

While one could argue that Internet-derived interventions may be ancillary to F2F therapy, from the evidence introduced here, one could also conclude that especially with OCD Internet-derived interventions may well be the primary treatment of choice, within an stepped-care framework. Nonetheless, for other mental disorders one cannot conclude that only Internet-derived treatments should be considered as the only treatment of choice. Such treatments will need to be administered together with medication and many other psycho-educational activities already available to the public and to mental and physical health professionals (L'Abate, 2013c).

Chapter 12

POST-TRAUMATIC STRESS-RELATED DISORDERS

There are so many studies about these disorders (PTSD) that they deserve and need a chapter of their own. This phenomenal growth about treating these disorders is due in part to veterans from Afghanistan and Iraq who come back with what was originally called during World War I "Shell-shocked." In WWII some stressed soldiers were given medication and sent back to the frontlines where they came from to avoid the development of guilt feelings for having "abandoned" their comrades. Furthermore, one characteristic of PTSD is mass violence—whether intentional attacks or the result of natural disasters—adversely affects survivors and often causes widespread disruption, displacement, and disability (Jain, 2011). Epidemiological studies have reported PTSD or symptoms of PTSD in almost one-third of communities affected by mass violence. Evidence-based psychological therapies used to treat PTSD are available, but obstacles such as a shortage of mental health care professionals and patient stigma toward treatment often limit accessibility to these therapies. PTSD is associated with significant socio-occupational dysfunction; therefore, an imperative need exists for approaches that enhance access to treatment while preserving effectiveness of important factors such as the therapeutic relationship between patients and mental health care professionals.

Although medical service delivery via home-based telehealth technology (HBT) is gaining wider acceptance in managing chronic illnesses such as diabetes or chronic obstructive pulmonary disease, few studies have tested HBT applications of psycho-therapy. Clinicians, administrators, and researchers question whether delivering psycho-therapeutic services to patients in their homes via video-conferencing technology compromises patient safety, potency of treatment, or data security. Despite these concerns, HBT service delivery may increase access to evidence-based psychotherapies for veterans with PTSD, who may be less willing or less able to receive weekly treatment at a VA medical center or outpatient clinic due to symptom severity or other similar barriers to care. Indeed, although combat-exposed service members endorse high rates of psychiatric disorders, few appear to initiate mental health services or receive an adequate dose of treatment. Thus, using HBT technologies to administer evidence-based therapies remains uncharted territory in both the clinical and research arenas. This manuscript described an ongoing four year randomized controlled trial comparing in-person Prolonged Exposure (PE) – a specialized evidence-based psychotherapy for PTSD – and PE delivered via HBT, with a particular focus on the selection, application, and strengths/weaknesses of HBT procedures (Strachan, Gros, Yuen, Ruggiero, et al., 2012).

A meta-analysis summarized the findings of outcome research on the degree to which telehealth treatments reduce PTSD-related symptoms (Sloan, Gallagher, Feinstein, Lee, et al., 2011). In a search of the literature, 13 studies were identified for inclusion in the meta-analysis and were coded for relevant variables. A total of 725 participants were included. Results indicated that telehealth treatments were associated with significant pre- to post-reduction in PTSD symptoms ($d = 0.99$, 95% confidence interval [CI]: 0.87-1.11, $p < .001$), and result in superior treatment effects relative to a wait list comparison condition ($d = 1.01$, 95% CI: 0.76-1.26, $p < .001$). However, no significant findings were obtained for telehealth intervention relative to a supportive counseling telehealth comparison condition ($d = 0.11$, 95% CI: - 0.38 to 0.60, $p = .67$), and telehealth intervention produced an inferior outcome relative to a face-to-face intervention ($d = - 0.68$, 95% CI: - 0.39 to - 0.98, $p < .001$). Findings for depression symptom severity outcome were generally consistent with those for PTSD outcome. Telehealth interventions produced a significant within-group effect size ($d = 0.98$, 95% CI: 0.86 to 1.10, $p < .001$) and superior effect relative to wait list comparison condition ($d = 0.80$, 95% CI: 0.56-1.05, $p < .001$). Relative to F2F interventions, telehealth treatments produced comparable depression outcome effects ($d = 0.13$, 95% CI: - 0.55 to 0.28, $p = .53$). Taken together, these findings support the use of telehealth treatments for individuals with PTSD-related symptoms. However, the major issue is to evaluate this disorder before and after intervention of whatever kind.

PTSD Scales

Several interviews are available for assessing PTSD (Blake, Weathers, Nagy, & et al., 1995). These interviews vary in merit when compared on stringent psychometric and utility standards. Of all the interviews, the Clinician-Administered PTSD Scale (CAPS-1) appears to satisfy these standards most uniformly. The CAPS-1 is a structured interview for assessing core and associated symptoms of PTSD. It assesses the frequency and intensity of each symptom using standard prompt questions and explicit, behaviorally-anchored rating scales. The CAPS-1 yields both continuous and dichotomous scores for current and lifetime PTSD symptoms. Intended for use by experienced clinicians, it also can be administered by appropriately trained para-professionals. Data from a large scale psychometric study of the CAPS-1 have provided impressive evidence of its reliability and validity as a PTSD interview.

The psychometric properties of the PTSD Checklist (PCL), a new, brief, self-report instrument, were determined on a population of 40 motor vehicle accident victims and sexual assault victims using diagnoses and scores from the CAPS (Clinician Administered PTSD Scale) as the criteria (Blanchard, Jones-Alexander, Buckley, & Forneris, 1996). For the PCL as a whole, the correlation with the CAPS was 0.929 and diagnostic efficiency was 0.900 versus CAPS. Examination of the individual items showed wide ranging values of individual item correlations ranging from 0.386 to 0.788, and with diagnostic efficiencies of 0.700 or better for symptoms. The authors supported the value of the PCL as a brief screening instrument for PTSD.

Online therapy offers many advantages over F2F therapy. Interapy includes psycho-education, screening, effect measures, and protocol-driven treatments via the Internet for people suffering from posttraumatic stress and grief in a group of people who manifested mild to relatively severe trauma symptoms (Lange, Rietdijk, Hudcovicova, van de Ven, et al., (2003). Participants in the treatment condition (n-69) improved significantly more than participants in the waiting list control condition (n=32) on trauma-related symptoms and general psychopathology. The effect sizes were large. On most subscales, more than 50%of the treated participants showed reliable change and clinically significant improvement, with the highest percentages being found for depression and avoidance.

This paper was reviewed by Marks et al., (2007) with the following comments:

"With regard to computer psychotherapy for PTSD, too few details are available to properly gauge the value of a Dutch Interplay system...It is unclear if it saves therapist time given apparently extensive time used for email support. A US system improved PTSD in a small waitlist-control RCT. VR systems are not detailed for reasons noted earlier" (p. 61).

COGNITIVE BEHAVIORAL THERAPY

Litz, Engel, Bryant, and Papa (2007) reported on an 8-week randomized, controlled proof-of-concept trial of a new therapist-assisted, Internet-based, self-management CBT versus Internet-based supportive counseling for PTSD. Service members with PTSD from the attack on the Pentagon on September 11th or the Iraq War were randomly assigned to self-management cognitive behavior therapy (N=24) or supportive counseling (N=21). The dropout rate was similar to regular cognitive behavior therapy (30%) and unrelated to treatment arm. In the intent-to-treat group, self-management cognitive behavior therapy led to sharper declines in daily log-on ratings of PTSD symptoms and global depression. In the completer group, self-management cognitive behavior therapy led to greater reductions in PTSD, depression, and anxiety scores at 6 months. One-third of those who completed self-management cognitive behavior therapy achieved high-end state functioning at 6 months. Self-management cognitive behavior therapy may be a way of delivering effective treatment to large numbers with unmet needs and barriers to care.

This study was an open trial evaluation of a 10-week therapist-assisted CBT internet intervention (PTSD Online) undertaken with people with a primary clinical diagnosis of PTSD (n=22) at pre-assessment (Klein, Mitchell, Abbott, Shandley, et al., 2010). Participants were reassessed at post-assessment and 3-month follow-up. Significant improvements on PTSD severity ratings and related PTSD symptomatology were observed at post-assessment and maintained at 3-month follow-up. At post-assessment, 69.2% of the sample showed clinically significant improvement and 77% of the sample at follow-up assessment. Non-significant, yet improved, change was observed on all other general psychological measures. Overall, treatment satisfaction was good (69%), participant therapeutic alliance ratings were high (87.5%), and the average total therapist time required was 194.5 min. PTSD Online appears to be an efficacious treatment option for people with PTSD that can be provided entirely remotely, with far less therapist time than traditional F2f treatment, and without compromising the therapeutic alliance.

The present study was designed to evaluate the efficacy of an internet-based therapy (Interapy) for PTSD in a German speaking population (Knaevelsrud & Maercker, 2007). Also, the quality of the online therapeutic relationship, its development and its relevance as potential moderator of the treatment effects was investigated. Ninety-six patients with posttraumatic stress reactions were allocated at random to ten sessions of Internet-based cognitive CBT) conducted over a 5-week period or a waiting list control group. Severity of PTSD was the primary outcome. Secondary outcome variables were depression, anxiety, dissociation and physical health. Follow-up assessments were conducted at the end of treatment and 3 months after treatment. From baseline to post-treatment assessment, PTSD severity and other psychopathological symptoms were significantly improved for the treatment group (intent-to-treat group × time interaction effect size d = 1.40).

Additionally, patients of the treatment condition showed significantly greater reduction of co-morbid depression and anxiety as compared to the waiting list condition. These effects were sustained during the 3-months follow-up period. High ratings of the therapeutic alliance and low drop-out rates indicated that a positive and stable therapeutic relationship could be established online. Significant improvement of the online working alliance in the course of treatment and a substantial correlation between the quality of the online relationship at the end of treatment and treatment outcome emerged. Interapy proved to be a viable treatment alternative for PTSD with large effect sizes and sustained treatment effects. A stable and positive online therapeutic relationship can be established through the Internet which improved during the treatment process. (italics mine, n/e), so much for therapists who insist that the therapeutic alliance can be established only in F2F TB therapy. See additional evidence about the online therapeutic alliance in Chapter 16 of this volume, authors' note).

PTSD is a severe and disabling condition and few receive appropriate care. Internet-based treatment of PTSD shows promise in reducing barriers to care and preliminary evidence suggests it is efficacious in treating symptoms of PTSD (Spence, Titov, Dear, Johnston, Solley, et al., (2011). Forty-two individuals with a diagnosis of PTSD confirmed by clinician interview completed a randomized controlled comparison of Internet-based CBT with a waitlist control condition. Large pre- to post-treatment effect sizes (ESs) were found for the Treatment group on measures of PTSD symptoms, depression, anxiety, and disability. A small between-group ES was found for PTSD symptoms and moderate between-group ESs were found for depression, anxiety, and disability. Results provided preliminary support for Internet-based CBT as an efficacious treatment for individuals with a confirmed primary diagnosis of PTSD.

Exposure Therapy

Exposure to potentially traumatic events is a common occurrence. Most individuals exposed to such an event are resilient or recover rapidly, although some individuals develop psychological problems that warrant treatment. However, a small percentage of individuals seek traditional treatment, thereby calling for novel approaches or methodologies of treatment. Amstadter, Broman-Fulks, Zinzow, Ruggiero, and Cercone, (2009) provided a comprehensive and critical review of the extant literature on computerized and internet-based interventions (IBIs) for traumatic stress-related conditions (i.e., panic disorder, posttraumatic stress disorder/complicated grief, depression, comorbid anxiety and depression, alcohol abuse, smoking cessation). Generally, computerized or IBIs for depression and anxiety are yielding effect sizes that are comparable to traditional psychosocial treatment. Interventions aimed at alcohol and smoking cessation generally have lower effect sizes than do IBIs for anxiety and depression. Most interventions reviewed in this paper included common components (e.g., were developed through a cognitive behavioral framework and included psycho-education, cognitive restructuring, goal setting, exposure). Therefore, it is possible that these shared features may in part account for symptom reduction. Little is known regarding mechanisms of change. Future directions for novel web-based approaches to treatment are provided.

Service personnel involved in Operation Enduring Freedom/Operation Iraqi Freedom are at high risk for trauma-related physical injury and emotional problems, including PTSD and major depression (Gros, Strachan, Ruggiero, Knapp, et al., 2011). Although evidence-based psychotherapies are increasingly available and effective in treating symptoms of PTSD, a large number of service personnel are reluctant to seek mental health treatments due to both perceived stigma associated with these treatments and geographically-based barriers to care at specialized treatment facilities. The present investigation evaluated an innovation in service delivery designed to address these concerns. Specifically, the authors are compared exposure-based therapy for PTSD delivered via traditional, in-person settings to the same exposure-based treatment delivered via telehealth technology. The proposed project is a prospective, randomized repeated measures design with two treatment groups (telehealth and in-person) assessed at pre-treatment, mid-treatment, post-treatment and 3- and 12-month follow-up points. Outcome measures ascertain longer-term effects of the treatments on three domains: clinical, process, and economic. Non-inferiority and superiority analyses will be conducted to determine symptom changes between pre-treatment, post-treatment, and follow-up time points between the two treatment conditions. The study will determine whether an exposure therapy for PTSD delivered via telehealth is at least as successful as the same exposure-based therapy delivered in-person in treating the symptoms of PTSD in both sub-threshold and fully diagnosed cases.

Recent research has focused on the effectiveness of evidence-based psychotherapy delivered via telehealth services. Unfortunately to date, the majority of studies employ very small samples and limited predictor and moderator variables. To address these concerns and further replicate and extend the literature on telehealth, the present study investigated the effectiveness of 12-session exposure therapy delivered either via telehealth (n = 62) or in person (n = 27) in veterans with PTSD (Gros, Yoder, Tuerk, Lozano, & Acierno, 2011). Findings demonstrated that although older veterans and Vietnam veterans were more likely to complete the telehealth treatment, telehealth findings were not influenced by patient age, sex, race, combat theater, or disability status. Exposure therapy delivered via telehealth was effective in reducing the symptoms of PTSD, anxiety, depression, stress, and general impairment with large effect sizes. Interestingly, exposure therapy via telehealth was less effective than exposure therapy delivered in person; however, lack of random assignment to condition limits conclusions of differential effectiveness. Overall, these findings supported the utility of telehealth services to provide effective, evidence-based psychotherapies.

Tuerk, Yoder, Ruggiero, Gros, et al., (2010) presented a pilot study of 12 veterans diagnosed with combat-related PTSD and treated with prolonged exposure therapy (PE) via telehealth technology. A reference sample of 35 combat veterans treated with in-person PE in the same clinic is also included for a comparison. Feasibility and clinical outcomes of interest include technical performance and practicality of the telehealth equipment, patient safety, treatment completion rates, number of sessions required for termination, and clinical outcomes. Results indicated large statistically significant decreases in self-reported pathology for veterans treated with PE via telehealth technology. Preliminary results supported the feasibility and safety of the modality. Suggestions for the implementation of PE via telehealth technology were discussed.

Medication

Recent innovations in PTSD research have identified new treatments with significant potential, as well as novel enhancements to empirically-validated treatments (Cukor, Spitalnick, Difede, Rizzo, & Rothbaum, 2009). This paper reviewed emerging psychotherapeutic and pharmacologic interventions for the treatment of PTSD. It examines the evidence for a range of interventions, from social and family-based treatments to technological-based treatments. It described recent findings regarding novel pharmacologic approaches including propranolol, ketamine, prazosin, and methylene-dioxymethamphetamine. Special emphasis was given to the description of virtual reality and D-cycloserine as enhancements to prolonged exposure therapy.

Mindfulness

This pilot study examined two telehealth interventions to address symptoms of combat-related PTSD in veterans (Niles, Klunk-Gillis, Ryngala, Silberbogen, et al., 2011). Thirty-three male combat veterans were randomly assigned to one of two telehealth treatment conditions: mindfulness or psychoeducation. In both conditions, participants completed 8 weeks of telehealth treatment (two sessions in person followed by six sessions over the telephone) and three assessments (pretreatment, post treatment , and 6-week follow-up). The mindfulness treatment was based on the tenets of mindfulness-based stress reduction and the psychoeducation manual was based on commonly used psychoeducation materials for PTSD. Results for the 24 participants who completed all assessments indicate that: (1) Telehealth appeared to be a feasible mode for delivery of PTSD treatment for veterans; (2) Veterans with PTSD were able to tolerate and report high satisfaction with a brief mindfulness intervention; (3) Participation in the mindfulness intervention was associated with a temporary reduction in PTSD symptoms; and (4) A brief mindfulness treatment may not be of adequate intensity to sustain effects on PTSD symptoms.

Multiple Treatments

In the prevention of PTSD after severe traumatic injury, easily applicable, accessible, cost-efficient early interventions are needed that use well-established techniques for decreasing acute psychological stress reactions (Mouthaan, et al., 2011). Whereas most studies delivered cognitive behavioral techniques F2F or as a curative treatment, we incorporated them into a brief internet-based early intervention program to reduce acute psychological distress and prevent long-term symptoms of PTSD in trauma victims. By means of interactive elements, visual and auditory materials, the intervention contains psycho-education, modeling, in vivo exposure, stress management and social support. In this article, we describe the design of the program and the outcomes of an initial feasibility study among trauma patients (n = 5) and healthy controls (n = 5). Participants reviewed the program as useful and clear. neither patients nor controls experienced adverse psychological reactions after completing the intervention. The results showed that the intervention is well-received and feasible for implementation in severely injured trauma survivors.

VIDEOCONFERENCING

Telehealth, or health care via videoconferencing, constitutes a clinical option that makes it possible to treat patients remotely (Germain, Marchand, Bouchard, Drouin, & Guay, 2009). A growing number of studies have demonstrated that telehealth is a feasible and effective method for diagnostic interviews and psychiatric consultations. However, few studies have assessed the effectiveness of psychotherapy given by videoconference. This study examines the effectiveness of cognitive behavioural therapy (CBT) administered by videoconference for PTSD. Forty-eight participants with PTSD were recruited for the study: 16 in the videoconferencing condition and 32 in a control face-to-face condition. Each participant received CBT for 16 to 25 weeks and completed various questionnaires before and after treatment. The results show a significant decline in the frequency and severity of posttraumatic symptoms after treatment in both conditions. A clinical improvement in overall functioning was also observed. No significant difference was observed in the effectiveness of the two therapeutic conditions. The examination of effect sizes supports these results. A number of clinical implications and certain avenues for future research are discussed.

Tele-psychotherapy is a cutting-edge intervention that shows great promise in the mental health care field (Germain, Marchand, Bouchard, Guay, & Drouin, 2010). However, the possibility of developing a high-quality therapeutic alliance is often doubted when psychotherapy is provided remotely. This study assessed the development of a therapeutic alliance in individuals with PTSD who were treated either by Videoconference therapy or a F2F therapy. Forty-six participants with PTSD received cognitive behavioral therapy, 17 of them by videoconference and 29 in person. A variety of questionnaires evaluating the quality of the therapeutic relation-ship were administered at five different times during treatment. Each session was also assessed by the therapist and the participant immediately afterwards. The results indicated that a therapeutic alliance can develop very well in both treatment conditions and that there is no significant difference between the two. Certain clinical and practical implications were discussed.

This article summarized two ongoing randomized controlled trials that compare individual in-person psychotherapy with psychotherapy provided using video teleconferencing for military veterans with posttraumatic stress disorder. Thorp, Fidler, Moreno, Floto, et al., (2012) described training methods, populations, technology, challenges, successes, and lessons learned so far during the trials.

Although evidence-based treatments for PTSD have been available for some time, many treatment-seeking trauma survivors are unable to access such services. This is especially the case in remote and rural areas where access to specialists is an exception rather than a rule. Advances in videoconferencing-based technologies are improving rural residents' access to specialized psychological services. However, at present, little is known about the viability and efficacy of providing psychological interventions via distal technologies to individuals who present at rural domestic violence and rape crisis centers. The present study attempted to partially address this void by evaluating, in the context of an uncontrolled trial, the effectiveness and feasibility of providing evidence-based, trauma-focused treatment via videoconferencing to rural survivors of domestic violence and sexual assault (Hassija & Gray, 2011). Participants in the present study were clients referred to the Wyoming Trauma Telehealth Treatment Clinic (WTTTC) for psychological services via videoconferencing from distal domestic violence and rape crisis centers located in the state of Wyoming. Fifteen female victims of assaultive violence who received at least four sessions of trauma-focused treatment via videoconferencing-based technology at distal rape and domestic violence crisis centers were included in the present study. Participants completed measures of PTSD and depression symptom severity and client satisfaction. Participants evidenced large reductions on measures of PTSD ($d = 1.17$) and depression ($d = 1.24$) symptom severity following treatment via video-conferencing. Additionally, participants reported a high degree of satisfaction with videoconferencing-administered services. Results provided evidence in support of Videoconferencing as an effective means to provide psychological services to rural domestic violence and sexual assault populations. Clinical implications and avenues for future research were discussed.

Until recently, only one study was published on CBT of PTSD in individual therapy via videoconference (Germain, Marchand, Bouchard, Drouin, & Guay, 2009); however, it only assessed the post treatment effect. This study presented the follow-up of Germain et al.'s (2009) study (Marchand, Beaulieu-Prevost, Guay, Bouchard, et al., 2011). The main goal was to compare the effectiveness after six months of CBT for PTSD either F2F ($n = 24$) or by videoconference ($n = 12$). Each participant received CBT for 16 to 25 weeks and completed various questionnaires before and after treatment and at a six-month follow-up. The two treatments had equivalent levels of symptom reduction (Modified PTSD Symptom Scale: $\eta^2 < 0.01$, $p > .05$) and proportion of patients with a clinically significant change in symptoms (42% for face-to-face vs. 38% for videoconferencing, $p > .05$). Thus, CBT for PTSD via videoconference seems to be a viable alternative when adequate face-to-face treatments are less available.

Virtual Reality

Virtual reality exposure (VRE) therapy is a promising treatment for a variety of anxiety disorders and has recently been extended to the treatment of PTSD. In this article, Reger and Gahm (2008) briefly reviewed the rationale for VRE and its key processes. They illustrate the treatment with an active-duty Army soldier diagnosed with combat-related PTSD. Six sessions of VRE were provided using an immersive simulation of a military convoy in Iraq. Self-reported PTSD symptoms and psychological distress were reduced at post treatment relative to pretreatment reports, as assessed by the PTSD Checklist–Military Version and the Behavior and Symptom Identification Scale–24. The case outcomes paralleled those reported in the research with other disorders and suggest the applicability of VRE in treating active duty soldiers with combat-related PTSD.

Exposure therapy, therefore, is an evidence-based treatment for (PTSD, but research evaluating its effectiveness with active duty service members is limited. This report examined the effectiveness of virtual reality exposure therapy (VRE) for active duty soldiers (N = 24) seeking treatment following a deployment to Iraq or Afghanistan (Reger, Holloway, Candy, Rothbaum, et al., 2011). Relative to their pretreatment self-reported symptoms on the PTSD Checklist, Military Version (M = 60.92; SD = 11.03), patients reported a significant reduction at post-treatment (M = 47.08; SD = 12.70; $p < .001$). Sixty-two percent of patients (n = 15) reported a reliable change of 11 points or more. This study supported the effectiveness of exposure therapy for active duty soldiers and extends previous research on VRE to this population.

Repeated combat deployments to Iraq and Afghanistan are resulting in increased rates of PTSD among military personnel (Reger, Gahm, Rizzo, Swanson, et al., 2008). Although exposure therapy is an effective treatment for this disorder, some personnel do not significantly respond to treatment, possibly due to poor activation of the trauma memory or a lack of emotional engagement during therapy. In addition, some service members do not seek mental healthcare due to treatment stigma. Researchers recently developed a virtual reality (VR) Iraq to attempt to improve activation of the traumatic memory during exposure therapy and to provide a treatment approach that may be more appealing to some service members, relative to traditional face-to-face talk therapy. Initial validation of the application requires an assessment of how well it represents the experiences of previously deployed service members. This study evaluated the realism of the VR Iraq application according to the subjective evaluation of 93 U.S. Army soldiers who returned from Iraq in the last year. Those screening negative for PTSD used and evaluated a VR tactical convoy and a VR dismounted patrol in a simulated Middle Eastern city. Results indicated that 86% of soldiers rated the overall realism of the VR convoy as ranging from adequate to excellent. Eighty-two percent of soldiers reported adequate-to-excellent overall realism of the city environment. Results provided evidence that the VR Iraq presents a realistic context in which VR exposure therapy can be conducted. However, clinical trials are needed to assess the efficacy of VR exposure therapy for Iraq veterans with PTSD.

Numerous reports indicated that the growing incidence of PTSD in returning Operation Enduring Freedom (OEF), Operation Iraqi Freedom (OIF) military personnel is creating a significant health care and economic challenge (Rizzo, Difede, Rothbaum, Reger, et al., 2010). These findings have served to motivate research on how to better develop and disseminate evidence-based treatments for PTSD. Virtual reality-delivered exposure therapy for PTSD has been previously used with reports of positive outcomes. The current paper will detail the development and early results from use of the Virtual Iraq/Afghanistan exposure therapy system. The system consists of a series of customizable virtual scenarios designed to represent relevant Middle Eastern contexts for exposure therapy, including a city and desert road convoy environment. The process for gathering user-centered design feedback from returning OEF/OIF military personnel and from a system deployed in Iraq (as was needed to iteratively evolve the system) will be discussed, along with a brief summary of results from an open clinical trial using Virtual Iraq with 20 treatment completers, which indicated that 16 no longer met PTSD checklist-military criteria for PTSD after treatment.

This preliminary study endeavored to evaluate the use of virtual reality (VR) enhanced exposure therapy for the treatment of PTSD consequent to the World Trade Center attacks of September 11,2001 (Difede, Cukor, Jayasinghe, Patt, Jedel, Spielman, Giosan, & Hoffman, 2007). Participants were assigned to a VR treatment (N = 13) or a waitlist control (N = 8) group and were mostly middle-aged, male disaster workers. All participants were diagnosed with PTSD according to DSM-IV-TR criteria using the Clinician-Administered PTSD Scale (CAPS). The study was conducted between February 2002 and August 2005 in offices located in outpatient buildings of a hospital campus. Results: Analysis of variance showed a significant interaction of time by group ($p < .01$) on CAPS scores, with a between-groups post treatment effect size of 1.54. The VR group showed a significant decline in CAPS scores compared with the waitlist group ($p < .01$). Conclusions: Our preliminary data suggest that VR is an effective treatment tool for enhancing exposure therapy for both civilians and disaster workers with PTSD and may be especially useful for those patients who cannot engage in imaginal exposure therapy.

PTSD has been estimated to affect up to 18% of returning Operation Iraqi Freedom (OIF) veterans (Gerardi, Rothbaum, Ressler, Heekin, & Rizzo, 2008). Soldiers need to maintain constant vigilance to deal with unpredictable threats, and an unprecedented number of soldiers are surviving serious wounds. These risk factors are significant for development of PTSD; therefore, early and efficient intervention options must be identified and presented in a form acceptable to military personnel. This case report presents the results of treatment utilizing virtual reality exposure (VRE) therapy (virtual Iraq) to treat an OIF veteran with PTSD. Following brief VRE treatment, the veteran demonstrated improvement in PTSD symptoms as indicated by clinically and statistically significant changes in scores on the Clinician Administered PTSD Scale (CAPS; Blake et al., 1990) and the PTSD Symptom Scale Self-Report (PSS-SR; Foa, Riggs, Dancu, & Rothbaum, 1993). These results indicate preliminary promise for this treatment.

Most of the virtual environments currently available in the field of psychological treatments were designed to solve a specific problem (Banos, Botella, Guillen, Garcia-Palacios, et al., 2009). This research group developed a versatile virtual reality system (an adaptive display) called 'EMMA's world', which can address a wide range of problems. It was designed to assist in clinical situations where a person has suffered a stressful experience, for example PTSD, adjustment disorder, and pathological grief. To accomplish therapeutic goals, a series of emotional virtual elements were used and personalized so that they would be meaningful to the user and contained the fundamental emotional elements that a person must confront. Effectiveness data relating to the system for stress-related disorders were presented (However, one needs to see the effects sizes achieved before reaching a definitive conclusion about the effectiveness of this approach, note of Author.

Writing Therapy

To engage more US combat veterans in PTSD treatment, Possemato, Ouimette, and Knowlton (2011) offered a psychological intervention that could be initiated in primary care and completed using the Internet. Participants (n = 31) were randomized to complete either Written Emotional Disclosure (WED) or time management narratives on a secure Internet website. In the WED group, participants wrote about their thoughts and emotions regarding one traumatic combat experience in three 20-min sessions. Writing instructions encouraged exposure to traumatic memories and cognitive processing of trauma. The intervention was found to be feasible and safe to implement. Although follow-up assessments did not reveal significant group differences in PTSD symptoms, half of the WED participants reported symptom reductions. Content analyses revealed that participants who expressed more emotion and cognitions were significantly more likely to experience decreased PTSD symptoms. WED may have promise as a brief intervention for veterans with PTSD. These results support the use of interactive practice exercises or workbooks specifically programmed for PTSD (L'Abate, 2011c, 2013b).

CONCLUSION

Evidence to support Internet-based CBT treatments for PTSD seems overwhelming. Nonetheless, there is a great deal of overlap among seemingly different treatments. For instance, Exposure Therapy overlaps with Virtual Reality and both approaches overlap with Videoconferencing. One treatment cannot occur without the other. In spite of these possible shortcoming, there is no doubt that PTSD can be treated successfully at a distance through remote means of presentation and involvement. Consequently, do-nothing or waiting-list, or F2F treatment-as-usual control groups may become irrelevant if research will inevitably compare one modality of treatment, e. g., Virtual Reality versus Videoconferencing.

SECTION V. INTERVENTIONS

Chapter 13

COUNSELING

Counseling and psychotherapy has been influenced by technology for over 50 years (Goss & Anthony, 2009). During this time, the rate at which ways that technology of one kind or another can assist therapists and counselors has seemed to increase exponentially. Contributions to the subject of technological enhancements or extensions of routine counseling practice will be introduced and summarized in this chapter. While the variety of technologies referred to is far from exhaustive, the chapter offers a representative sampling of the range available to practitioners from the now relatively familiar email, internet chat and video conferencing through to the cutting edge of developments in virtual reality, mood influencing packages and services that, like Web 2.0, can be based upon the needs and designs of the users themselves. For instance, cyber- or computer-mediated communication is transforming school counselor education in curriculum delivery, supervision, and professional development, as well as changing the nature of interactions among counselors, school personnel, parents, counselor educators, students, and field supervisors (Wilczenski & Coomey, 2006). New techno-logies are influencing school counseling practice and helping counselor educators to train the next generation of school counselors. This chapter is encouraging a critical dialogue about the issues, ethics, and unanswered questions pertaining to the use of computer technology in school counselor practice and education.

The emergence of online counseling services for addressing problems ranging from poor self-esteem, stressful relationships and addictions raises serious ethical concerns in this new electronic Certified Counselors' Standards for the Ethical Practice of Web-Counseling was described (Bloom, 1998). Shaw and Shaw (2006) used a 16-item Ethical Intent Checklist, developed from the American Counseling Association's (1999) Ethical Standards for Internet Online Counseling, to assess the current practices of 88 online counseling Web sites. Results showed fewer than half of online counselors were following the accepted practice on 8 of the 16 items. Online counselors who identified themselves as licensed or as association members had significantly higher mean checklist scores. As technology is increasingly integrated into the field of counseling, email stands out as having immeasurable promise for improving and enhancing the counseling process.

Yet, email also has immense potential for ethical problems (Vanderslice, 2009). TechnoEthics (TE) pertains to the ethics and standards that govern the use of technology. The purpose of this quantitative study was to examine counselors' usage of TE precautions in professional email and the factors associated with the use/nonuse of TE precautions. This study was both descriptive and exploratory in nature. Ninety Texas counselors comprised the convenience sample. An online survey was designed specifically to deal with the technical nature of TE. Chi-Square and descriptive statistics were used in the data analyses, which were performed using Microsoft Excel and SPSS. Analysis of the survey results revealed that overall the majority of counselors in Texas are not using TE precautions with their professional email. Findings from the knowledge section of this study demonstrated that higher levels of TE capabilities and TE awareness are associated with higher levels of TE precautions usage. Results from the attitudes section of the study indicated that higher levels of perceived usefulness and ease of use were associated with greater rates of TE precautions usage. These results were used to form the Knowledge to Usage theory stating that knowledge influences attitudes and attitudes impact usage. Finally, demographic variables were not associated with the overall use/nonuse of TE precautions.

These conclusions together provide the counseling field with a detailed look at the status of TE precautions usage/non-usage and factors associated with usage/non-usage. With this initial description of the problem, leaders in the field can now proceed to the next phase in the problem solving process of creating, planning, and implementing interventions to increase the ethical use of email. The Process of Planned TE Interventions gives step by step guidelines for implementing TE precautions for email and other technologies. The counseling field needs to act quickly and decisively to deal with the TE threat just as individual counselors must take action to safeguard their own e-mail usage.

E-mail is a cost effective and convenient way of connecting clients and professionals. The emerging research into online psychotherapy, counseling and advice work suggests that e-mail does enable effective therapeutic work. The present article discussed client contact styles used to engage with an online advice service, which is part of an action research project into the development and running of an online sexual health and relationship skills website called Sex-and-Relationships1 (Stummer, 2009). The methodology used for this study was action research, a cyclical process of enquiry, which uses both qualitative and quantitative data. It has been used to explore and develop practice-based and situational knowledge of how to best deliver an online advice or counseling service via Sex-and-Relationships. This article presented figures for overall usage of the e-mail advice service over two years to contextualize data on how service users have engaged with the service. Two client contact styles are identifiable in the data, namely single question-response pairs and in-depth, therapeutic dialogues, which will be illustrated by two case vignettes. Both contact styles are appropriate with respect to individual clients' needs and can be supported via e-mail. Practitioners working online need to have considerable experience of offline long-term work to engage in therapeutic dialogue online, but also need to be able to tolerate the abruptness of the majority of short online exchanges.

COUNSELING EFFECTIVENESS AND LIMITATIONS

This study investigated the effects of differing amounts of informed consent information (potential limitations, risks, and benefits associated with online counseling), on consumers' opinions regarding those counseling services (Barthelmeus, 2000). Ninety three voluntary male and female Internet consumers were asked to view one of three different simulated online counseling websites, each containing a different amount of information about the potential limitations, risks and benefits of online counseling. After viewing a site, participants completed a questionnaire designed to obtain their opinions regarding the desirability of the online counseling service they had just viewed, and also their preference of counseling environment (online versus face to face), based on information provided at the counseling website. It was found that greater disclosure of informed consent information at online counseling websites resulted in a significant decrease in desirability of those services to participants. Further, it was revealed that the amount of information provided at an online counseling website significantly affected participants' preference of counseling environment (online versus face to face).

Those exposed to a counseling website in which there was no disclosure of informed consent information, indicated a preference toward online counseling nearly twice as often as participants viewing partial or full disclosure sites. However, of the total sample, 70 participants (75.3%) indicated a preference for face to face counseling services, regardless of the amount of informed consent information provided. Results also suggest that participants' perceptions of the informativeness of an online counseling service are, to a great extent, accurate appraisals of the amount of information provided at a counseling website. Additional comparisons found that gender, age, and educational background are not significant factors in participants' decisions regarding the desirability of an online counseling service, or whether enough information was provided to make a decision to use or not use a service. The absence of standards and regulatory measures for Internet counseling may account for the greatly differing levels of disclosure presently provided by online counseling services. Consumers entering into an online therapeutic relationship without receiving sufficient information from which to make an informed choice may be subject to misleading advertising and potentially harmful experiences.

This study investigated the emerging practice of online counseling (Chester & Glass, 2006). Although the traditional practice of counseling involves F2F interaction between counselor and client, a growing number of practitioners are providing counseling or therapy services via the Internet. In the present study, a total of 67 online counselors completed a questionnaire exploring the backgrounds, services, fees, and communication technologies of practitioners offering online counseling to the public. Results suggest that online counseling is conducted by relatively experienced, primarily Western-based practitioners and is characterized by the use of email. Online clients are mainly female and receive relatively short-term interventions. Although the field appears to be evolving as its popularity increases, some ethical concerns raised by early research remained inadequately addressed.

Schultze (2006) described a number of special effectiveness factors of internet counseling which represent advantages over F2F counseling. These factors were explored in a large-scale internet counseling project that ran for several years. Caffery and Smith (2006). investigated the relation between the response time of an email-based counseling system and the re-utilization of the service. Activity data from the Kids Help Line (KHL) for a 22 month period were examined. The median response time for participants who re-used the KHL service (n = 2822) was 140 h (interquartile range, IQR 37-257 h) which was significantly less than for participants who did not re-use the service (n = 2781, median 183 h, IQR 45–289 h). The re-use rate was highest for a 4 h response time, and decreased as the response time lengthened. Response times less than 32 h did not have a significant difference between the observed and expected re-use rates, whereas response times of 32 h and greater did. The results showed that a greater delay in counselor response time was associated with a lower re-use rate. Response time is a performance indicator which may be important in the ultimate success or failure of an email based counseling service.

Online counseling services are rapidly becoming a common means of therapy. Despite the rapid emergence of this modality of treatment, however, many counseling psychologists are not involved in the provision of these services or the empirical investigation of the viability of these services. Accordingly, the purpose of the present study was to empirically investigate one aspect of online counseling: whether disclosure rates of participants differ when they are online versus face-to-face (Camillus, 2008). Specifically, the study sought to examine any differences in participants' disclosure patterns between online and face-to-face conditions to explore how the internet may play a role in willingness to disclose. In addition, to the extent possible, the study attempted to determine whether gender or ethnic differences in response rates would emerge. A battery consisting of six demographic questions, a social desirability measure, and a set of personal questions was administered to 121 undergraduate students enrolled in an introductory psychology course at a large, Midwestern university.

A preliminary study was conducted to determine the "intimacy categories" of the personal questions (Camillus, 2008). Participants had the option of enrolling in either a F2F modality or an online modality. The primary hypotheses were as follows: (1) participants in the online modality will disclose at higher rates than participants in the face-to-face modality, and (2) the gap in disclosure rates between modalities will increase as intimacy ratings of the personal questions increase. As expected, participants in the online modality disclosed at a higher rate than participants in the face-to-face modality. With regard to the second hypothesis, there was no significant difference between response rates in the online versus the face-to-face setting for low intimacy questions, nor was there a significant difference between response rates for high intimacy questions. The only subset of questions that produced a statistically significant difference in disclosure rates was the set of moderate intimacy questions. Thus, while the trend from low to moderate supported the author's hypothesis that differences in response rates between the two modalities would increase as the questions became more intimate, this trend appeared to reverse itself when the high intimacy questions were considered.

As the availability of new communication technologies increases, mental health professionals have incorporated these innovations into their practice and research (Preziosa, Grassi, Gaggioli, & Riva, 2009). Up to now several studies have presented promising results in using the power and convenience of the Internet for clinical care. While multiple contributions focus on the potential and the advantages of therapies delivered through the Internet, mental health practitioners may take into account new technological opportunities to improve their practice. Mobile phone diffusion is expanding worldwide at breath-taking speed. In fewer than 20 years, mobile phones have gone from being rare and expensive pieces of equipment used primarily by the business elite, to a pervasive low-cost personal item. In many countries, mobile phones now outnumber land-line telephones, with most adults and many children now owning mobile phones. With high levels of mobile telephone penetration, a mobile culture has evolved, where the phone becomes a key social and cultural tool. The purpose of this paper was to explore the potentialities that mobile phones may offer in clinical care. The paper investigated in which areas of clinical interventions mobile phones have already been successfully applied. Moreover, the paper discussed these opportunities by presenting the results of two different studies based on the use of the mobile phone for anxiety management.

This paper examined the empirical research concerning counseling psychologists who utilize the internet in their practice (Hanley & Reynolds, 2009). More specifically, the authors summarized the quantitative research of online therapeutic outcomes and alliances reported in text-based therapeutic encounters. Online therapy creates much debate within the therapeutic world. Many question the validity of entering into these relatively uncharted waters, while others have begun working productively in this territory. To date, a small pool of research examining the efficacy of such work has emerged and provides the focus for this paper. A review of the literature was conducted with a two-fold strategy. Initially a review of 16 quantitative outcome studies investigating this area are presented and discussed - these have been selected from Barak, Hen, Boniel-Nissim and Shapira's (2008) comprehensive review of the effectiveness of internet-based psychotherapeutic interventions. Following this, the focus was moved to the concept of the online therapeutic alliance. A systematic review of the existing literature outlined five pertinent quantitative studies and these are discussed in relation to key qualitative work in this area. Conclusions highlighted work in this medium that shows great promise, with both successful outcomes and strong alliances being reported online. Such findings, although limited due to the dearth of the research available, challenge the views of those skeptical of counseling psychologists entering into virtual arenas.

The Internet has become a new force within the mental health delivery system, resulting in a need for examination of its social impact (McLeod, 2008). Minimal information is available concerning the long-term effects or the ethical integrity of online counseling as an intervention strategy. This non-experimental descriptive study, grounded in social systems theory, investigated the attitudes and knowledge of professional counselors in order to determine whether significant relationships existed among variables. The sample was drawn from a database of professional counselors who were sent surveys exploring issues related to their attitudes, opinions, and level of knowledge regarding the practice of online counseling. The issues addressed included confidentiality, informed consent, ability to provide specific interventions to online clients, necessary computer skills, nonverbal communication, online counseling training, and licensure. T-tests, correlation, and analysis of variance were used to analyze the data.

Results indicated some significant relationships between counselors' professional degree and opinions regarding online counseling and between counselors' computer skill level and opinions regarding online counseling (McLeod, 2008). No significant relationships were found among the counselors' demographic traits and their knowledge level. However, the results also indicated an overall below average opinion and knowledge of online counseling. The social change implication of this study is that it uncovers the need for several changes: conducting additional research from a broader, multicultural perspective, developing a multidisciplinary regulatory body, requiring accredited courses on Internet counseling for membership renewal, and requiring courses on this topic for degree attainment in mental health professions.

Barnett (2005) commented on previous articles that explored the developing field of online counseling from the unique perspective of counseling psychology. The authors of those articles examined the body of available research and relevant clinical, ethical, legal, and practical issues and make recommendations for counseling psychologists who desire to participate in online counseling. This article provided a critique of their contributions, finds support for much of what they present, offers additional suggestions for counseling psychologists, and makes recommendations for counseling psychology to resolve challenges that at present, limit online counseling's value, effectiveness, and impact. The author makes recommendations for practical research that studies the actual online-counseling process, establishing additional standards, more effectively disseminating information, enhancing training, expanding access through innovative programs, and increasing advocacy efforts.

Counseling licensure boards report emerging needs to regulate technology-assisted distance counseling and supervision. An analysis of published regulations and telephone interviews with board administrators nationwide suggests that boards agree generally on 7 aspects of technology-assisted distance practice that need to be regulated. Nevertheless, boards are disparate and often polarized in their views regarding the extent and type of regulation needed for each aspect. Current trends may have important implications for counselor education, supervision, and practice (McAdams & Wyatt, 2010).

TELEPHONE INTERVENTIONS

The main reason for including phone counseling in this chapter is to indicate how this medium may be another important addition to online counseling. For instance, in a study of the telephone counseling process (Bobevski, Holgate, & McLennan, 1997), 40 experienced telephone counselors each responded to a standardized crisis call from the same scripted role-playing client. All the interviews were audio-recorded. At the conclusion of each call the subjectively-perceived helpfulness of the counselor was assessed by the caller. Seven of the counselors were rated as being extremely helpful, while nine counselors were rated as being notably less helpful. Analysis of the calls showed that what distinguished the more helpful counselors was that they were more verbally active, took the initiative to structure the interview and systematically explore all aspects of the problem situation, and addressed practical as well as emotional concerns of the caller. Overall, the more effective counselors altered the caller's perspective on her circumstances.

To assess the effectiveness of telephone-based interventions for mental illness, a systematic search of the literature was conducted using the databases PsycINFO and PubMed, and the search engine Google Scholar (Leach & Christensen, 2006). The search identified 14 studies evaluating telephone-based interventions in the areas of depression (n = 6), anxiety (n = 3), eating disorders (n = 3), substance use (n = 1) and schizophrenia (n = 1). Although these studies provide evidence that telephone interventions can be effective, the few studies conducted, small sample sizes and lack of randomized controlled trial methodology prevent firm conclusions from being drawn. The articles reviewed suggest that an effective telephone intervention includes clearly structured therapy sessions and homework tasks. However, further evidence using large-scale, randomized controlled trials must be obtained in order to inform government and telephone counseling agencies about the efficacy of telephone interventions.

Telephone counseling clients reported that convenience, accessibility, control, and inhibition were the most attractive attributes of receiving counseling (not crisis intervention) via telephone (Reese, Conoley, & Brossart, 2006). The results mirror many opinions in the literature. Of the 186 counseling clients who responded to the survey, 96% would be willing to seek telephone counseling again compared with 63.1% who reported being willing to seek face-to-face counseling. More than half (58%) of the respondents who had experienced both telephone and face-to-face counseling preferred telephone counseling.

Burgess, Christensen, Leach, Farrer, and Griffiths (2008) studied the mental health profile of callers to a generalist helpline. A survey was conducted in a large telephone counseling centre over a four-week period in 2006. Telephone counselors administered the survey at the completion of a user's call. The centre answered a total of 1404 calls in the study period. Of these, 439 calls met the inclusion criteria and 270 callers agreed to participate. The survey collected data from callers on demographic variables, anxiety, depression, panic and social phobia, alcohol use, frequency of help seeking from the service, sources of professional help, attitudes to help services and access to the Internet. Callers experienced high levels of anxiety and depression. More frequent callers were older, with very frequent callers more likely to be never married. More frequent callers were more likely to report concerns with loneliness, physical illness and anxiety. There was a significant difference on the Goldberg Anxiety Scale ($P < 0.05$), with more frequent callers having higher anxiety scores. However, there was no significant difference on the Goldberg depression scores as a function of call frequency ($P > 0.05$). Panic attacks were more common among more frequent callers. These results will be useful in developing new telephone-administered anxiety and depression treatment programs.

Telephone counseling with adolescents is well known in many countries all over the world, due to its special characteristics, which seem to suit to adolescents. Some of these characteristics are the low cost, the easy access, the anonymity, as well as the possibility for the callers to have the control over the call regarding its duration as they can hang up the phone whenever they feel like it. Based on the experience gained from the operation of the telephone counseling helpline in Greece for children and adolescents, counter-transference phenomena that appear during telephone counseling are presented in the present article (Christogiorgos, Vassilopoulo, Florou, Xydou, Douvou, Vgenopoulou, & Tsiantis (2010). More specifically, the link between those counter-transference phenomena and the special characteristics of telephone counseling, with the characteristics of the period of adolescence, with the existence of psychopathology in the callers and, moreover, with factors regarding the counselors themselves was presented. Experiences with telephone counseling were used to illustrate potential problems for e-therapy: therapy becoming conversational, problems of transference and counter-transference, and the effects of client's control and immediacy of contact (Lester, 2006).

Kids Help Line is a national service providing free telephone counseling and online counseling to young people in Australia (King, Bambling, Reid, & Thomas, 2006). This study used a naturalistic design and standardized measures to compare outcomes, session impact and therapeutic alliance for samples of 100 young people receiving a single session of telephone counseling and 86 young people receiving a single session of online counseling, provided by Kids Help Line. Results suggested that telephone counseling is associated with better counseling outcomes, higher session impact and stronger counseling alliance when compared with online counseling. The limitations imposed by a naturalistic design require caution in interpretation of the results. However, the pattern of results suggested that there are differences in effectiveness between telephone and online counseling. The most likely explanation is the greater communication efficiency of telephone counseling, which enables more counseling work to be undertaken in the time available. Implications for further development of online counseling are discussed.

STUDENTS' ATTITUDES TOWARD CYBER COUNSELING

The present study explored college students' attitudes toward and needs related to Cyber Counseling, describing and comparing its current and future use in the U.S.A. and South Korea (Han, 2008). To achieve this goal, the following two groups of participants were recruited for this study: (1) Millennial Generation in the U.S.A and (2) the Net Generation in South Korea, both of whom were born after 1980. Research question one was how attitudes toward Cyber Counseling differ between the Millennial Generation and the Net Generation as assessed by the Student Survey: College Students' Attitudes toward and Needs related to Cyber Counseling (CSANCC). Research question two was how needs related to Cyber Counseling differ between the Millennial Generation and the Net Generation by the CSANCC. An analysis of variance (ANOVA) test was performed on the data to examine attitudes toward technology and Cyber Counseling between the Millennial Generation and the Net Generation (at the .05 probability level). The Chi Square (X2) test was also performed on the data to examine the needs related to Cyber Counseling between the Millennial and the Net Generation (at the .05 probability level). The results of this study suggested that the Millennial Generation has more positive attitudes toward technology than the Net Generation, and the Net Generation has more positive attitudes toward Cyber Counseling than the Millennial Generation. The findings of this study also indicated some valuable insight for what counselors may include in their counseling website. Further implications for multicultural counseling are discussed. Limitations of the study and recommendations for future research were also discussed.

This study used a Consensual Qualitative Research methodology to explore the motivations and experiences of young people who utilize the Internet for counseling over other counseling media. Semi-structured online group interviews (focus groups) were conducted with 39 participants from the Kids Help Line, a 24-hour national telephone and counseling service located in Australia. Analysis revealed five domains relevant to the adolescents' motives and experiences and the frequency of categories within and across cases were analyzed to generate and understand themes and patterns. Specific motivators and barriers are identified and discussed, as are implications for practice and continued research (King, Bambling, Lloyd, Gomurra, et al., 2006).

COUNSELING SATISFACTION

This article compared Global Assessment of Function (GAF) and Client Satisfaction Survey scores for clients receiving either F2F or online counseling (Murphy, Parnass, Mitchell, Hallett, et al., 2009). Clients were assessed by phone and then assigned to one of the two modalities. Analyses of variance were conducted with $\alpha = 0.05$, to examine differences between counseling modalities. No significant differences were found for degree of change in GAF between assessment and closing between the two modalities. Some differences were found in Client Satisfaction Scores. Implications for screening and social work practice were discussed. This is a very incomplete study since it did not control for other variables, such a level of education, income, age, or gender. Hence, we cannot take these results at their face value. Furthermore, no cost-comparison was made. Give the same results in outcome, one must chose the less expensive treatment (Note of author).

School Counseling

Existing literature in the field of school counseling discussed how technology may be used for service delivery; however, the translation of this knowledge to practice among school counselors has been minimally examined (Carlson, Portman, & Bartlett, 2006). Three hundred eighty-one school counselors in Colorado, Iowa, and New York completed a survey regarding their comfort with and use of technology. Findings indicated that the majority of those surveyed were very comfortable with technology. Implications for school counselors were presented .

The purpose of this study was to determine levels of perceived importance of technological competencies among school counselors, school counseling students, supervisors, and counselor educators as the competencies relate to their work (Sabella, Poynton, & Isaacs, 2010). Results indicated that technology competencies relating to Ethical Standards and Data Management practices were rated as most important. Technological competencies rated lowest for level of importance related to Multimedia and Web Development. Four of the other subscales were very similar in overall average ratings and included Word Processing, World Wide Web, Communication and Collaboration, and Operating Systems. In addition, findings indicated that neither the participant's age, level of practice, or position (e.g., graduate student vs. practitioner) affects the perceived importance of technological competencies included in this survey. Implications for practice, training, and future research were included.

This paper proposed that the provision of online counseling services for young people accessed through their local school website has the potential to assist students with mental health issues as well as increasing their help seeking behaviors (Glasheen & Campbell, 2009). It stems from the work of the authors who trialed an online counseling service within one Australian secondary school. In Australia, online counseling with the adult population is now an accepted part of the provision of mental health services. Online provision of mental health information for young people is also well accepted. However, online counseling for young people is provided by only a few community organizations such as Kids Help Line within Australia. School based counseling services which are integral to most secondary schools in Australia, seem slow to provide this service in spite of initial interest and enthusiasm by individual school counselors. This discussion is the product of reflection on the potential benefits of this trial with a consideration of relevant research of the issues raised. It highlights the need for further research into the use of computer mediated communication in the provision of counseling within a school setting.

Boundary Considerations

As psychologists and clients increasingly use the Internet for personal and professional activities, they run the risk of having more incidental contacts online. This survey examined the experiences of 227 mental health professionals of various disciplines and training levels about both accidental and intentional experiences of encountering client information on the Internet (Kolmes & Taube, 2014). One hundred and nine participants (48%) intentionally sought information about current clients in non-crisis situations, and 63 participants (28%) accidentally discovered client information on the Internet. This paper explored how clinicians responded to these encounters and clinicians' beliefs about how they influenced treatment. Recommendations were made for how mental health professionals may begin to address such issues in the clinical relationship. One major issue that needs further conceptual and critical evaluation is to define boundaries between what is called "counseling" and what is called "psychotherapy (note of author).

Conclusion

From the research included in this chapter, it is clear that online counseling is here to stay and to thrive to the point of becoming the first step in any stepped care approach in mental health services delivery.

A crucial point that needs further research is cost effectiveness, an important topic that will be covered in greater detail in Chapter 16 of this volume.

Chapter 14

CRISIS INTERVENTION AND PSYCHOTHERAPY

The purpose of this chapter is to include research about psychotherapy and crisis interventions Online and Offline, beginning with early proposals and testimonials included in Chapter 1 of this volume, and then reviewing evidence to support such proposals. The use of technology to provide remote psychological assessment and intervention services is growing rapidly (Yuen, Goetter, Herbert, & Forman, 2012). Remote assessment, treatment, training, and consultation options, particularly those provided via the Internet (e.g., Videoconferencing, self-help Web sites, handheld devices), have the potential to increase access to high-quality psychological services. Despite the promise of these technologies, a variety of clinical, ethical, and logistical challenges accompany the remote delivery of such services. Among these challenges are issues involving security, competence, the therapeutic alliance, usability, and technical difficulties. The authors elucidated some of the challenges posed by these technologies and suggest preliminary recommendations for psychologists considering their use.

Alleman (2002) asserted that the MH profession is unprepared for the likely growth and related implications of MH therapy delivered over the Internet. Clinical, ethical, and economic issues were addressed. Conclusions are that therapy can be done online, that it can be done ethically, and that online services might not be a serious threat to F2F therapy. Regulatory and professional organizations are strongly advised to cooperate with each other. Suggestions included how practitioners and educators might develop skills, how ethics and legislation might be coordinated, how research might be facilitated, and how certain support systems might be established.

In line with Alleman's (2002) thinking, concerns and considerations have emerged as MH professionals contemplate the provision of MH treatment over the Internet. This paper identified perceptions of online mental health treatment among a national sample of 2,098 social workers, psychologists, and other professionals (Wells, Mitchell, Finkelhor, & Becker-Blease, 2007). These professionals were unlikely to provide online mental health treatment, although some used the Internet as an adjunct to clinical practice. They noted specific concerns related to the provision of mental health treatment online, including confidentiality of client information and liability issues. The authors explored these issues and discussed implications for professionals who provide mental health treatment. Since publication of this article and its concerns, attitudes toward remote online treatment have changed drastically among MH professionals, as shown by more recent articles and research (note of author).

Here is an example of what was the thinking over a decade ago. In an early testimonial about psychiatry and the Internet, Bailey, Yager, and Jenson (2002) discussed the use of computer technology in the practice of good psychiatry, with reference to other historical technological innovations that have been incorporated by clinicians and patients. Two clinical vignettes were presented to illustrate the Internet both as a feature of the psychiatric landscape and as a tool for psychiatric intervention. The 1st case described the computer-facilitated enhancement of social life for a 15-yr-old male patient with social phobia. The 2nd case described email as an adjunctive treatment tool in the outpatient management of a 17-yr-old female with anorexia nervosa. These cases illustrate the point that new technologies can yield examples of classic psychotherapeutic phenomena and dilemmas. Suggestions for future usage, clinical issues, ethical matters, and the limitations of computer technology in delivering psychiatric care were discussed.

The provision of health care over the Internet is a rapidly evolving and potentially beneficial means of delivering treatment otherwise unsought or unobtainable. Internet interventions are typically behavioral treatments operationalized and transformed for Web delivery with the goal of symptom improvement. The literature on the feasibility and utility of Internet interventions is limited, and there are even fewer outcome study findings. This article reviews empirically tested Internet interventions and provides an overview of the issues in developing and/or using them in clinical practice. Future directions and implications are also addressed. Although Internet interventions will not likely replace face-to-face care, there is little doubt that they will grow in importance as a powerful component of successful psycho-behavioral treatment (Ritterband, Gonder-Frederick. Cox, Clifton, West, & Borwitz, 2003). This paper raised a basic issue about online/offline MH interventions on whether: "....... Internet will not likely replace face-to-face care"... depends on how either approach is less expensive than the other, all other variables being equal.

The pervasive use of Internet technologies has created new ethical dilemmas for psychology trainees and professionals (Lehavot, Barnett, & Powers, 2010). In particular, Web sites that allow users to post personal information have sparked controversy regarding the amount of freedom psychologists should have in placing personal information online and how discovering such information may impact professional relationships, including the therapeutic relationship. Results from a graduate student survey (N = 302) address the prevalence of the use of online social networking sites, security measure efforts that limit public access, incidents of client access to psychotherapists' personal Web sites and Internet use by psychotherapists to obtain client information, and their subsequent effect on the therapeutic relationship. Using applicable ethical principles and standards, we provide recommendations for the field in an effort to decrease potential harm and maximize areas of opportunity for psychologists and constructive professional relationships.

Over the last decade, integrated care models have increased in both public and private sectors (Kelly & Coons, 2012). This trend is especially apparent in primary care settings. Integrated care is designed to offer comprehensive and coordinated health services while addressing the economic realities and failures of the current health care system. Proposed integrated care models such as Accountable Care Organizations and Patient Centered Medical Homes include marked changes in health care delivery, financing, and reimbursement, which are designed to create a more cost-effective health system. This article provides an overview of integrated care to help practicing psychologists develop a better understanding of interprofessional health care and evaluate their interest in and readiness to provide professional services in health care. The advantages and challenges associated with integrated care will be provided.

A mailed survey was used to evaluate psychologists' endorsements of four Internet-based treatment modalities (e-mail, individual chat, group chat, and video conferencing) as either adjunctive or alternative forms of treatment (Mora, Nevid, & Chaplin, 2008). Participants were 138 psychologists recruited from a state psychological organization's membership directory. Participants provided endorsements for each Internet-based intervention based on a hypothetical case in which past treatment history was manipulated in a randomized design. Overall, psychologists provided low levels of endorsement of Internet-based services; however, significantly higher levels of endorsement were found for a case vignette that lacked any mention of past treatment history as compared to an otherwise identical case that mentioned previous treatment for major depression. Additionally, participants provided higher endorsements for e-mail applications than other modalities and cognitive-behaviorally-oriented practitioners more strongly endorsed the use of Internet-based interventions than psychoanalytically-oriented practitioners.

Baur (2000) analyzed doctor–patient use of e-mail within the context of the evolving doctor–patient relationship and ongoing changes in the US health care system in terms of market-driven health care delivery. Evidence from the published literature on doctor–patient relationships and doctor–patient communication, empirical studies of uses of the Internet by doctors and patients, and commentaries about the Internet's role in health care were examined and discussed to reveal common, unsupported assumptions about the likely impact of e-mail on the doctor–patient relationship and also the value structure associated with current e-mail practices between doctors and patients. Existing research did not yet adequately account for the technical, professional, and economic forces that are shaping doctor–patient use of e-mail. It is concluded that physicians‘ preferences for technical, instrumental exchanges with patients will likely mitigate the positive influence that e-mail could have on the doctor–patient relationship, and doctor–patient communication is unlikely to improve as a result of their use of e-mail.

Internet interventions, clearly, promise an efficacious, scalable, and cost-effective prevention and treatment option, with significant potential for public health impact. These interventions lower many of the barriers that patients face when accessing traditional forms of care, including the difficulties in finding a skilled clinician for a specific disorder, inconvenience of scheduling face-to-face appointments, missing work/school, travel to and from a clinician's office, expense, and many others. They also offer many advantages from an intervention delivery perspective including the ability to provide treatments in a standardized manner with fidelity across a variety of settings. They may also enhance the ability of health care providers to better utilize their time and possibly reallocate valuable face-to-face time to those who require a more intensive intervention by allowing the clinical needs of some patients to be addressed through the use of Internet interventions. There is an unprecedented opportunity for comprehensive evidence-based treatments to be more widely disseminated via the Internet, reaching patients at doctors‘ offices, school, work, and home (Ritterband & Tate, 2009).

While the ultimate goal for many Internet intervention researchers is to provide prevention and treatment programs to anyone with Internet access at low cost with proven outcome results similar to face-to-face care, this standard of success may be unnecessarily stringent, as it is often better to receive some helpful treatment as opposed to none at all.

Internet interventions can provide an option to those who cannot or choose not to seek face-to-face treatment. Many of these treatments can be used as additive or adjunctive components of traditional treatment, supplementing material, skills, or time that clinicians may not have. They can be used as part of a stepped-care model. In addition, the potential for wide scale dissemination is significant. Individuals, who would otherwise be unable or unwilling to receive care, might have access to Internet prevention or treatment options, particularly those in rural areas. If designed and used correctly, Internet interventions can become a powerful tool in helping reduce health disparities, particularly among the geographically isolated (Ritterband & Tate, 2009).

The feasibility of Internet interventions is now well established. However, without a scientific underpinning, the field may flounder. It might be easy to dismiss eHealth generally, and Internet interventions specifically, as a fad or as something more of a niche area only for technologically sophisticated and willing individuals. This, however, would be inaccurate and would be dismissing a prolific decade of research. And now, with the field both solidifying and expanding its base, Internet interventions are to be regarded as a critical evidence based intervention option. The articles in this special series provide a solid foundation from which this field can and will continue to grow and expand (Ritterband & Tate, 2009).

One of the main drawbacks of computer-assisted psychology tools developed up to now is related to the real time customization and adaptation of the content to each patient depending on his/her activity. In this paper, Alcaniz, Botella, Banos, Zaragoza, and Guixeres (2009) proposed a new approach for mental e-health treatments named Intelligent e-Therapy (eIT) with capabilities for ambient intelligence and ubiquitous computing. From a technical point of view, an eIT system is based on four fundamental axes: ambient intelligence for capturing physiological, psychological and contextual information of the patient; persuasive computing for changing/reinforcing behaviors; ubiquitous computing for using the system at any place, and at any time; and multiple technological platforms support.

Nonetheless, the field of Internet-supported therapeutic interventions has suffered from a lack of clarity and consistency. The absence of professional leadership and of accepted governing approaches, terminology, professional standards, and methodologies has caused this field to be diffused and unstructured. Numerous terms have been used to label and describe the activities conducted over the Internet for mental and physical health purposes: web-based therapy, e-therapy, cyber-therapy, eHealth, e-Interventions, computer-mediated interventions, and online therapy (or counseling), among others.

As technology advances, psychologists increasingly have the opportunity to engage with patients or other users of psychological services via less traditional methods (Baker & Bufka, 2011). However, little guidance exists to prepare psychologists to navigate the legal, regulatory, reimbursement, and ethical issues that can arise when providing psychological services via technology. A review of relevant state and federal laws reveals inconsistencies even in the terminology used to describe provision of services via technology with some referring to "telehealth," others to "telemedicine," and others using additional terms. The following overview of laws, regulations, and existing guidelines in the area of telehealth and telemental health provided some preliminary guidance for psychologists as they attempt to meet the needs of their patients using available and emerging technologies. Specific issues addressed included the applicability of the HIPAA Privacy and Security Rules, informed consent and reimbursement by third party payers.

In between impressionistic testimonial and thoughtful proposals, Internet-based psychotherapeutic interventions have been used for more than a decade, but no comprehensive review and no extensive meta-analysis of their effectiveness have been conducted. A number of ethical issues involved in F2F therapy are examined in relation to online therapy (etherapy). (Midkiff & Wyatt, 2008). E-therapy is defined and its strengths and weaknesses discussed. Specific ethical issues addressed include boundaries of competence, basis in science, avoidance of harm, confidentiality, avoidance of false or deceptive statements, forums, testimonials, solicitation of clients, fees, and informed consent. A concluding section briefly addressed legal issues, particularly interstate e-therapy. It was recommended that federal licensing legislation be enacted, informed by the NASW, the APA, and similar groups.

BEHAVIORAL COGNITIVE THERAPY

A new treatment form has emerged that merges cognitive behavior therapy with the Internet (Andersson, 2009). By delivering treatment components, mainly in the form of texts presented via web pages, and provide ongoing support using e-mail promising outcomes can be achieved. The literature on this novel form of treatment has grown rapidly over recent years with several controlled trials in the field of anxiety disorders, mood disorders and behavioural medicine. For some of the conditions for which Internet-delivered CBT has been tested, independent replications have shown large effect sizes, for example in the treatment of social anxiety disorder. In some studies, Internet-delivered treatment can achieve similar outcomes as in face-to-face CBT, but the literature thus far is restricted mainly to efficacy trials. This article provides a brief summary of the evidence, comments on the role of the therapist and for which patient and therapist this is suitable. Areas of future research and exploration are identified.

Cognitive-behavioral therapy (CBT) has demonstrated efficacy and effectiveness for treating mood and anxiety disorders. Dissemination of CBT via videoconference may help improve access to treatment (Stubbings, Rees, Roberts, & Kane, 2013). The present study aimed to compare the effectiveness of CBT administered via videoconference to in-person therapy for a mixed diagnostic cohort. A total of 26 primarily Caucasian clients (mean age 30 years, SD 11) who had a primary Diagnostic and Statistical Manual of Mental Disorders, 4th edition text revision (DSM-IV-TR) diagnosis of a mood or anxiety disorder were randomly assigned to receive 12 sessions of CBT either in-person or via videoconference. Treatment involved individualized CBT formulations specific to the presenting diagnosis; all sessions were provided by the same therapist. Participants were recruited through a university clinic. Symptoms of depression, anxiety, stress, and quality of life were assessed using questionnaires before, after, and 6 weeks following treatment. Secondary outcomes at post treatment included working alliance and client satisfaction.

Retention was similar across treatment conditions; there was one more client in the videoconferencing condition at post-treatment and at follow-up. Statistical analysis using multilevel mixed effects linear regression indicated a significant reduction in client symptoms across time for symptoms of depression ($P<.001$, $d=1.41$), anxiety ($P<.001$, $d=1.14$), stress ($P<.001$, $d=1.81$), and quality of life ($P<.001$, $d=1.17$). There were no significant differences between treatment conditions regarding symptoms of depression (P=.165, d=0.37), anxiety (P=.41, d=0.22), stress (P=.15, d=0.38), or quality of life (P=.62, d=0.13). There were no significant differences in client rating of the working alliance (P=.53, one-tailed, d=–0.26), therapist ratings of the working alliance (P=.60, one-tailed, d=0.23), or client ratings of satisfaction (P=.77, one-tailed, d=–0.12). Fisher's Exact P was not significant regarding differences in reliable change from pre- to post-treatment or from pretreatment to follow-up for symptoms of depression (P=.41, P=.26), anxiety (P=.60, P=.99), or quality of life (P=.65, P=.99) but was significant for symptoms of stress in favor of the videoconferencing condition (P=.03, P=.035). Difference between conditions regarding clinically significant change was also not observed from pre- to post-treatment or from pretreatment to follow-up for symptoms of depression (P=.67, P=.30), anxiety (P=.99, P=.99), stress (P=.19, P=.13), or quality of life (P=.99, P=.62). The findings of this controlled trial indicate that CBT was effective in significantly reducing symptoms of depression, anxiety, and stress and increasing quality of life in both in-person and videoconferencing conditions, with no significant differences being observed between the two.

A growing body of literature suggests that computerized cognitive-behavioral therapies (CCBT) are effective in community settings in terms of symptom reduction, favorable client satisfaction, attrition comparable to standard cognitive-behavioral therapy, reduced clinician time, high cost-effectiveness, and ease of integration into community clinics (Green & Iverson, 2009). Clinicians report lack of knowledge about computerized programs as the main reason that they have not used CCBT in their practice. To mitigate this disconnect between empirical evidence and dissemination, this article first reviews empirical studies focusing on the efficacy of CCBT for specific psycho-logical disorders, followed by a review of research on the effectiveness of CCBT in community settings. Next, issues related to dissemination and barriers to CCBT adoption by clinicians were discussed. Finally, the implications of CCBT for research and practice and the possible role of CCBT in a stepped care model of treatment is discussed in terms of cost-effectiveness, standards of care, and implications for public policy.

There is mounting evidence in clinical trials that therapist-assisted Internet cognitive behavior therapy (TAICBT) is efficacious in the treatment of depression and anxiety. Nevertheless, many clinical service providers (both individuals and organizations) question whether offering this form of treatment in clinical practice is feasible. As such, having information on the factors involved in the development of this service is essential. In this article, Hadjistavropoulos, Thompson, Ivanov, Drost, et al., 2011) described the steps taken to develop a TAICBT service that registered professionals and students (under supervision) can use with clients suffering from symptoms of depression, generalized anxiety, and panic disorder. The authors shared salient decisions made in developing this web application and the necessary unit policies and procedures. We also offer lessons learned and practical recommendations to providers who may want to translate this promising TAICBT research into practice.

Emergency Management

Telepsychiatry, in the form of live interactive videoconferencing, is an emerging application for emergency psychiatric assessment and treatment and can improve the quality and quantity of mental health services, particularly for rural, remote and isolated populations (Shore, Hilty, & Yellowlees, 2007). Despite the potential of emergency tele-psychiatry, the literature has been fairly limited in this area. Drawing on the combined clinical and administrative experiences of its authors, this article reviews the common administrative, legal/ethical and clinical issues that arise in emergency tele-psychiatry. An initial set of guidelines for emergency tele-psychiatry is presented to generate further discussion to assist those who are considering establishing general tele-psychiatry and/or emergency tele-psychiatry services. In conclusion, the practices and techniques of emergency tele-psychiatry are relatively new and require further examination, modification and refinement so that they may be fully utilized within comprehensive mental health service systems.

Game Therapy

There has been research on the use of offline video games for therapeutic purposes but online video game therapy is still fairly under-researched (L'Abate, 2009: Wilkinson, Ang, & Goh, 2008). Online therapeutic interventions have only recently included a gaming component. Hence, this review represented a timely first step toward taking advantage of these recent technological and cultural innovations, particularly for the treatment of special-needs groups such as the young, the elderly and people with various conditions such as ADHD, anxiety and autism spectrum disorders. A review integrating research findings on two technological advances was conducted: the home computer boom of the 1980s, which triggered a flood of research on therapeutic video games for the treatment of various mental health conditions; and the rise of the internet in the 1990s, which caused computers to be seen as conduits for therapeutic interaction rather than replacements for the therapist. The authors discussed how video games and the internet can now be combined in therapeutic interventions, as attested by a consideration of pioneering studies. Future research into online video game therapy for MH concerns might focus on two broad types of game: simple society games, which are accessible and enjoyable to players of all ages, and online worlds, which offer a unique opportunity for narrative content and immersive remote interaction with therapists and fellow patients. Both genres might be used for assessment and training purposes, and provide an unlimited platform for social interaction. The MH community can benefit from more collaborative efforts between therapists and engineers, making such innovations a reality.

Group Therapy

Morland, Hynes, Mackintosh, Resnick, et al. 2011) reported clinical findings from the pilot cohort of the first prospective, non-inferiority-designed randomized clinical trial evaluating the clinical outcomes of delivering a cognitive–behavioral group intervention for posttraumatic stress disorder (PTSD), cognitive processing therapy (CPT), via video teleconferencing (VT) compared to the in-person modality. The treatment was delivered to 13 veterans with PTSD residing on the Hawaiian Islands. Results supported the general feasibility and safety of using VT. Both groups showed clinically meaningful reductions in PTSD symptoms and no significant between-group differences on clinical or process outcome variables. In keeping with treatment manual recommendations, a few changes were made to the CPT protocol to accommodate this population. Novel aspects of this trial and lessons learned were discussed.

INDIVIDUAL DIFFERENCES

Extraversion, neuroticism, and gender as predictors of online counseling help-seeking behavior were investigated (Tsan & Day, 2007). A total of 176 college student participants, 30 men and 146 women, were given the NEO-PIR and ATSPPH-S that assessed, respectively, their personalities and attitudes toward seeking professional psychological help through different modes: traditional F2F counseling, video-conferencing, e-mail, instant text message, and microphone. Results were analyzed using MANOVA and MANCOVA. Subjects were grouped by scores on personality variables: low, medium, and high. Findings suggested that attitudes toward different modes of seeking counseling were associated primarily with gender and extraversion but not with neuroticism.

MINDFULNESS

Mindfulness has been shown to be effective in treating various medical and mental problems (Glück & Maercker, 2011; L'Abate, 2013c). Especially its incorporation in cognitive-behavioural interventions has improved long-term outcomes of those treatments. It has also been shown, that brief mindfulness-based trainings are effective in reducing distress. There have been few web-based interventions incorporating mindfulness techniques in their manual and it remains unclear whether a brief web-based mindfulness intervention is feasible. Methods: Out of 50 adults (different distress levels; exclusion criteria: < 18 years, indication of psychotic or suicidal ideation in screening) who were recruited via e-mail and screened online, 49 were randomized into an immediate 2-weeks-treatment group (N = 28) or a waitlist-control group (N = 21), starting with a 2-week delay. Distress (BSI), perceived stress (PSQ), mindfulness (FMI), as well as mood and emotion regulation (PANAS/SEK-27) were measured at pre-, post- and 3-month follow-up (3MFU). Intention-to-treat analyses using MI for missing data and per-protocol analyses (≥ 50% attendance) were performed. Results: 26 participants of the treatment group completed post-measures. Most measures under ITT-analysis revealed no significant improvement for the treatment group, but trends with medium effect sizes for PSQ (d = 0.46) and PANASneg (d = 0.50) and a small, non-significant effect for FMI (d = 0.29). Per-protocol analyses for persons who participated over 50% of the time revealed significant treatment effects for PSQ (d = 0.72) and PANASneg (d = 0.77). Comparing higher distressed participants with lower distressed participants, highly distressed participants seemed to profit more of the training in terms of distress reduction (GSI, d =

0.85). Real change (RCI) occurred for PSQ in the treatment condition (OR = 9). Results also suggested that participants continued to benefit from the training at 3MFU. This study of a brief web-based mindfulness training indicated that mindfulness can be taught online and may improve distress, perceived stress and negative affect for regular users. Although there were no significant improvements, but trends, for most measures under ITT, feasibility of such a program was demonstrated and also that persons continued to use techniques of the training in daily life.

Online and Offline Treatments Combined

As evidenced by several trials, cognitive behavior therapy (CBT) is a highly effective treatment for many conditions including panic disorder with or without agoraphobia. However, therapists are short in supply, and patients with conditions like agoraphobia may not seek therapy due to fear of leaving their homes or traveling certain distances. A major challenge, therefore, is to increase the accessibility and affordability of empirically supported psychological treatments. The results of randomized controlled trails testing Internet delivered self-help programs generally provided evidence to support the continued use and development for a range of conditions. However, there are special treatment aspects that need to be taken into consideration such as internet access and the idiosyncrasies provided in traditional F2F therapies (Carlbring & Andersson, 2006).

Palliative Care

There is a lack of evidence-based research in the use of Telehealth within palliative care in the UK, particularly in Scotland (Johnston, Kidd, Wengstrom, & Kearney, 2012). The aim of this project was to evaluate the current use of Telehealth applications within palliative care across Scotland, and how these and future applications are perceived by patients, carers and professionals. This paper reports on the qualitative findings from focus groups with patients and carers in three geographical areas in Scotland, and individual interviews with key stakeholders from across Scotland, who currently work within areas of high and low Telehealth activity. The key findings indicated that Telehealth initiatives are welcomed by patients and carers but that these should be an adjunct to clinical care rather than an alternative. The stakeholder interviews revealed several notable differences between those working within areas of high and low Telehealth activity. Principally, areas of high Telehealth activity appear to be driven by national and local policy and seem to benefit from a greater level of investment in Telehealth equipment and facilities than in the more central, and hence accessible, parts of Scotland.

Pastoral Care

Computer-based information and communication technologies (ICT) have become a part of many people's working lives (Mills, 2006). Such technology is used in the form of e-mails and video-conferencing across many sectors of society and these are sometimes claimed to have replaced the need for face-to-face meetings. However, certain areas of work still seem to need face-to-face meetings; this paper focuses on one such area of work, that of Christian pastoral care. The article discusses the needs of clients and carers involved in crisis care within a Christian ethos and assesses why ICT tools seem to be mainly superfluous in situations where crisis caring has to take place at a distance. Caplan's model of crisis is used to indicate typical characteristics of people in crisis. Evidence from the Foot and Mouth epidemic of 2001 in the UK is used to investigate the usage of ICT in a real situation where distance pastoral care was essential. The findings show that the telephone was by far the best ICT tool although e-mail and the Internet were used in more formal business situations.

Personal Goals

The Assessment of Personal Goals (APG) was reviewed along with case examples that demonstrate how the APG can be used in personal counseling, career coaching, and business consulting. The APG is an online tool for helping people identify the sources of their discontent and possible pathways for satisfying core personal goals (Henderson, 2009).

Health Promotion-Self-Guided Interventions

This paper reviewed two relatively young fields of research - positive psychology and internet interventions - and discusses the potential of online positive psychology interventions (OPPIs) as an effective and sustainable health promotion tool within a comprehensive approach to mental health care (Mitchell, Vella-Brodrick, & Klein, 2010). The paper started with a review of positive psychology, in particular well-being theory and contemporary research, and then followed by an overview of the advantages (e.g., accessibility and sustainability) and disadvantages (e.g., digital divide) of delivering mental health interventions via the internet. Finally, the results of a literature review combining the two fields of research are presented. Five randomised controlled trials were identified testing the efficacy of OPPIs as a means of enhancing well-being, with three studies demonstrating increased well-being compared to a control group. In the three studies that had populations with mild to moderate depression symptoms at baseline, there was significant symptom reduction, suggesting that well-being interventions, while primarily targeted at improving wellness, may also have an illness treatment and prevention function. While this review is limited by the small number of studies currently available, researchers, practitioners and consumers are asked to consider the opportunities and benefits of delivering well-being interventions online.

Positive psychology is paving the way for interventions that enduringly enhance well-being and the internet offers the potential to disseminate these interventions to a broad audience in an accessible and sustainable manner (Mitchell, Stanimirovic, Klein, & Vella-Brodrick, 2009). There is now sufficient evidence demonstrating the efficacy of internet interventions for mental illness treatment and prevention, but little is known about enhancing well-being. The current study examined the efficacy of a positive psychology internet-based intervention by adopting a randomised controlled trial design to compare a strengths intervention, a problem solving intervention, and a placebo control. Participants (n = 160) completed measures of well-being (PWI-A, SWLS, PANAS, OTH) and mental illness (DASS-21) at pre-assessment, post-assessment and 3-month follow-up. Well-being increased for the strengths group at post- and follow-up assessment on the PWI-A, but not the SWLS or PANAS. Significant changes were detected on the OTH subscales of engagement and pleasure. No changes in mental illness were detected by group or time. Attrition from the study was 83% at 3-month follow-up, with significant group differences in adherence to the intervention: strengths (34%), problem solving (15.5%) and placebo control (42.6%). Although the results are mixed, it appears possible to enhance the cognitive component of well-being via a self-guided internet intervention.

Private Practice

The aim of this study was to evaluate the use of the internet to access mental health-related information in a private practice sample, and to understand how this influenced health behaviors in this group (Lam-Po-Tang & Mckay, 2010). The authors undertook a cross-sectional survey of adult outpatients attending two group psychiatric practices. The content included internet usage, types of information located, disclosure with treating psychiatrist, and perceived influence on decision-making. We collected both quantitative and qualitative data. The internet was often used to access mental health-related information. Respondents most commonly looked for information about symptoms, treatment, side effects and diagnoses. Approximately one-third of those who sought mental health information on the internet discussed this with their psychiatrist, and those who did so were more likely to report an influence of this information on their decision-making. Respondents' comments suggested an appreciation of the utility of the internet, combined with an understanding of its limitations. Private practice patients frequently access mental health information from the internet. When discussed within the therapeutic setting, it appears more likely to influence health-related decision-making. As part of ongoing therapy, clinicians should actively discuss what patients have read on the internet.

Professional Concerns

There are many ways in which our digital era is influencing development. There is greater difficulty in delaying gratification, interference in the growth of the capacity for empathy, more trouble in developing the ability to relate face-to-face, and overuse of two-dimensional communication. All of these have implications for clinical work. This article presented one case in point, and some suggestions for ways to attempt to address these difficulties. It is suggested that the clinical situation itself is uniquely valuable as an antidote to the problems posed by the technological world of today (Levy-Warren, 2012).

Consulting psychologists have recognized the importance of providing comprehensive consultation and clinical services for consumers with special needs (Miller, 2006). Often because of distance and access to consultation services, remote and underserved populations may not have the necessary access to consultant specialists in psychology and other disciplines. Such services are now available through an innovative model of telehealth. Telehealth technology and services have gained the attention of scientists, clinicians, consultants, and health educators in a variety of settings. Examined are consultation case scenarios using telehealth qualitative observations of consultants who have used telehealth and liability issues consultants may face using this technology. A model release of liability is provided for consulting psychologists who may consider its use in their consultation practice. Case examples using telehealth applications are discussed, as are special applications for health care delivery to undeserved rural populations using telehealth technology.

In the face of the ever-growing popularity of social media, psychologists continually encounter new dilemmas regarding ethical and professional principles. Negotiating the balance between the intrinsically public nature of social media participation and the highly private nature of the therapeutic relationship can be a challenge (Tunick, Mednick, & Conroy, 2011). Psychologists working with children and adolescents are of particular interest, given both the popularity of social media among children and teens and the specific treatment concerns on which clinical work often focuses. The authors surveyed 246 psychologists and psychologists-in-training regarding their own blogging and social networking practices, as well as their behavior around their clients' online presence. A majority of respondents indicated that they participate in some form of social media and a lesser, though sizable, percentage reported viewing information about their clients online. Many respondents indicated that they have encountered concerning material on their clients' social media pages, and there does not appear to be a clear consensus about how psychologists handle matters of Internet safety and privacy with their underage clients. Based on the responses to this survey, a series of considerations and guidelines for our professional practice are proposed, and psychologists are encouraged to engage in thoughtful self-reflection as they establish their own policies regarding these matters.

Van Allen and Roberts (2011) identified critical incidents in psychologists' use of technology in their service provision with clients. Study coordinators sent messages out to various listservs requesting that practicing psychologists respond to an online survey for their reports of how the integration of certain technology advances (e.g., e-mail, electronic health records, social-networking websites, etc.) may have compromised client privacy or confidentiality. Twenty-eight participants responded to the survey and noted a variety of concerns, including themes of (a) unauthorized access to electronic client records, (b) inappropriate dissemination of client information via technology, and (c) unique client concerns associated with social-networking websites (e.g., Twitter, Facebook, etc.). We discuss ramifications and strategies related to these ethical concerns in education, practice, and ethical standards and principles.

This article reviewed legal issues related to providing mental health services via the Internet. It provides a general overview of the field and discusses jurisdiction, licensure, legal duties (competence, consent, confidentiality), and other legal concerns related to the business of online counseling (Zack, 2008). It surveyed potential criminal and civil liability issues, noting procedural and substantive aspects of the relevant law. The author concluded that, although providers face a variety of challenges, their efforts in providing a service needed and desired by an important segment of the help-seeking population are worthwhile.

Self-Disclosure & Transparency

All psychotherapists engage in self-disclosure with their clients (Zur, Williams, Lehavot, & Knapp, 2009). At times it may be deliberate or non-deliberate, verbal or nonverbal, avoidable or unavoidable. Yet, modern-day Internet technologies have redefined the meaning and applications of self-disclosure and transparency in psycho-therapy. Consumers of mental health services can easily access large amounts of information about their psychologists. Clients' online searches about their psychotherapists may range from normal curiosity to criminal stalking. Following an examination of these issues, three invited experts share their commentaries on the issues raised. A historical review of self-disclosure in the mental health professions and the opposition of many theorists and practitioners to its use are provided. Further, the roles of Internet social networking and online communities for psychotherapists and their clients and prospective clients are explored, along with the clinical meaning of the ever-increasing digital transparencies of psychologists, trainees, and clients. Advice is provided for how to view, understand, and consider web postings by psychotherapists, clients, and others. Implications for clinical practice and training are provided along with recommendations for how to effectively address issues of digital transparency.

Self-Help

This article described the development and empirical status of guided Internet-delivered self-help (Andersson, Bergstrom, Buhrman, Carlbring, Hollandare, Kaldo, et al., 2008). This treatment approach combines the benefits of bibliotherapy with book-length text materials and the support given online via web pages and e-mail. Interactive features such as online registrations, tests, and online discussion forums are also included. Cognitive behavior therapy (CBT) guided the research and clinical implementations of this approach, as it lends itself more easily to the self-help format compared with other presently available psychotherapy approaches. The authors included an overview of the research, current issues and research in service delivery, lessons learned through a program of research, and directions for future investigations. Some of these issues were reviewed by Harwood and L'Abate, 2010, note of author).

Social Media by Health Care Professionals

Many health care professionals are considering or have begun using social media such as Facebook and Twitter in their professional practices. These relatively new forms of technologies come with benefits and risks to both professionals and their clients. This article overviewed some of these costs, benefits and resources that are provided for developing professional social media practices to minimize ethical and legal risks (Drude, 2012).

Social Work Online Practitioners

In the last decade the helping professions have seen a growing interest in the provision of online counseling and therapeutic services for individuals (Menon & Rubin, 2011). Like most fields of work, social work also has experienced a growth in the creative use of technology in various areas of professional work. Based on this growing interest and the need for such services and research on its efficacy, a study was conducted to learn from e-therapists across the United States on their experiences with this mode of service delivery. This paper elicited results from the online survey and provides recommendations to better serve our clients in the tech savvy world and future research endeavors. The main findings of this preliminary study included: (a) Many theoretical perspectives and models are being used to ground online practice (italics ours, no overarching theory is able to integrate various models and theories) (b) e-therapists are beginning to use videoconferencing for online practice supplementing their face-to-face sessions, and (c) e-therapists believe that online interventions benefit their clients.

Support Groups

Online support groups have been used extensively, in numerous areas of distress, for 15 years. Researchers have presented conflicting findings and ideas about their effectiveness in helping people cope with respective problems. This review (Barak, Boniel-Nissim, & Suler, 2008) of quantitative studies and our qualitative exploration of the nature of the experiences that occur in such groups show that several factors operate to potentially affect participants. Personal and interpersonal dynamics, which are central in producing effects in these groups, are induced and accelerated by the powerful online disinhibition effect. These factors, including the very impact of writing, expressions of emotions, collecting information and thereby improving understanding and knowledge, developing social relationships, and enhancing decision-making skills and consequent behavioral actions all serve as possible generators of a sense of personal empowerment for people in distress. This view may explain why empirical research has frequently found little or no specific outcomes from participating in online support groups; however, it has found much support for nonspecific personal impacts of this means of intervention. Thus, we contend that online support groups are designed to foster, and many of them actually do, well-being, a sense of control, self-confidence, feelings of more independence, social interactions, and improved feelings--all nonspecific but highly important psychological factors. As such, participating in an online support group could foster personal empowerment, which is much needed in handling specific conditions of distress. Nonetheless, this participation has potential costs, too, especially developing dependence, distancing from in-person contacts, and exposure to unpleasant experiences typical of social engagement in cyberspace.

Early socialization experiences have a long-term impact on newcomers' satisfaction, performance, and intention to stay in a group. We know that newcomers proactively shape their own socialization, but we know little about the behavioral tactics they employ, or how the words they choose affect their acceptance by the group (Burke, Kraut, & Joyce, 2010). The present article highlights three common conversational strategies of newcomers to online groups: (a) group-based membership claims, in which newcomers describe initial participation in the group; (b) identity-based membership claims, in which they describe their similarity to the group's focal social category; and (c) information requests, in which they ask for help. Using machine learning to identify these conversational strategies automatically in 12,000 newcomers' messages to approximately 100 online groups, we find that they are correlated with increased group responsiveness. We follow this analysis with two controlled field experiments to demonstrate that when individuals attest to previous group participation and make specific requests for information, community responsiveness increases, but claims of shared identity with the group have no impact.

E-therapy has emerged as an apparently popular alternative to F2F therapy, with some evidence of effectiveness and of the ability of therapist and client to develop a good therapeutic relationship. As yet, however, little is known about those choosing this form of therapy. The present study investigated self-disclosure style and attitudes towards e-therapy in three groups: current e-therapy clients, current users of Internet mental health support groups, and current f2f counseling clients (Skinner & Latchford, 2006). Participants completed a measure of self disclosure (the SD-40) and answered questions asking about the influence of factors thought to be potentially important in influencing a decision to undertake e-therapy, adapted by the authors. Two versions were used, pencil and paper and web-based. Unfortunately, too few e-therapy clients were recruited for the data to be analyzed. There was no significant difference in self-disclosure style between Internet support group users and f2f therapy users, though the latter had a higher tendency to self-disclose. Attitudes were generally not extreme, but Internet support group users were significantly more positive about the influence of using computers to communicate with a therapist. In summary, the study found that Internet support group users had broadly positive views of the advantages of e-therapy, particularly if they had had some personal experience of therapy. Experience of both using the Internet and therapy appear to be important in determining attitudes towards e-therapy. Self-disclosure was also found to be related to some attitudes to e-therapy. The difficulties recruiting e-therapy participants was a surprise given the efforts to do this, and may reflect the fact that e-therapy is not widely used. This raises the question of why those who appear to have positive attitudes to e-therapy are not, in fact, engaging in it.

Online support groups have been used extensively, in numerous areas of distress, for 15 years. Researchers have presented conflicting findings and ideas about their effectiveness in helping people cope with respective problems. Barak, Boniel-Nissim, and Suler (2008) reviewed quantitative studies and their own qualitative exploration of the nature of the experiences that occur in such groups. This review showed that several factors operate to potentially affect participants. Personal and interpersonal dynamics, which are central in producing effects in these groups, are induced and accelerated by the powerful online disinhibition effect. These factors, including the very impact of writing, expressions of emotions, collecting information and thereby improving understanding and knowledge, developing social relationships, and enhancing decision-making skills and consequent behavioral actions all serve as possible generators of a sense of personal empowerment for people in distress. This view may explain why empirical research has frequently found little or no specific outcomes from participating in online support groups; however, it has found much support for nonspecific personal impacts of this means of intervention. Thus, we contend that online support groups are designed to foster, and many of them actually do, well-being, a sense of control, self-confidence, feelings of more independence, social interactions, and improved feelings--all nonspecific but highly important psychological factors. As such, participating in an online support group could foster personal empowerment, which is much needed in handling specific conditions of distress. Nonetheless, this participation has potential costs, too, especially developing dependence, distancing from in-person contacts, and exposure to unpleasant experiences typical of social engagement in cyberspace.

TAPE RECORDING

A tape-recorded session of an early moment in an 8-year-old girl's psychotherapy experience is presented. The use of the recording device is immediately taken up by the child as a means of creating a "witness" for her depiction of both intensely distorted experiences of her therapist and poignant portrayals of her life as miserable and despairing. A discussion of both the process and the content generated from the use of the tape recorder is described, with implications drawn as to its effectiveness in the therapeutic process (Tuber & Seckin, 2012).

TELEPHONE-DELIVERED PSYCHOTHERAPY

Telephone-delivered psychotherapy has increased utility as a method of service delivery in the current world, where a number of barriers, including economic hardships and limited access to care, may prevent people from receiving the treatment they need (Brenes, Ingram, & Danhauer, 2011). This method of service provision is practical and has the potential to reach large numbers of underserved people in a cost-effective manner. The aim of this article is to review the state-of-the-art of telephone-delivered psychotherapy and to identify improvements and possible solutions to challenges. Results of randomized, controlled trials indicate high client acceptance and positive outcomes with this method of delivering psychotherapy. Nonetheless, psychotherapists wishing to deliver psychotherapy by telephone face a number of challenges, including a lack of control over the environment, potential compromises of privacy and confidentiality, developing therapeutic alliance without face-to-face contact, ethical and legal issues in providing psychotherapy by telephone, handling crisis situations at a distance, and psychotherapist adjustment to conducting psychotherapy in an alternative manner. There remains a need for further research, including direct comparisons of face to face psychotherapy with telephone-delivered psychotherapy and feasibility of telephone delivery of psychotherapies other than cognitive–behavioral therapy.

This report described the implementation of a six-session telephone-based Reminiscence Group Therapy (RGT) intervention for veterans enrolled in a Home Based Primary Care Program (HBPC).(Davis, Guyker, & Persky, 2012). HBPC psychologists face challenges not routinely encountered in the traditional office setting, and the intervention demonstrated the feasibility of conducting semi structured group treatment by telephone. Post group feedback indicated that the veterans found meaning in shared experiences and connection with themselves and others. The RGT intervention allowed for efficiency in service delivery while also providing an opportunity for veterans to socialize and gain a sense of meaningfulness and identity through facilitated recall of past experiences.

The use of the telephone for providing health care is growing. A significant amount of social meaning is derived from visual information, and the absence of visual stimuli provides unique barriers to communication and increases the risks for misunderstandings and distractions (Rothwell, Ellington, Planalp, & Crouch, 2012). Understanding challenges to telephone communication can provide insight into training opportunities for overcoming these difficulties and improving patient care. The purpose of this research was to explore through focus groups the challenges of phone communication perceived by specialists in poison information. General types of challenges to effective phone communication included developing new communication skills to compensate for lack of visual information, difficulty assessing caller understanding, difficulty managing caller misunderstandings, maintaining distinctive assessments for routine calls, and managing the multifaceted aspects of job stress. The desire for training to enhance telehealth and cultural competency skills was also mentioned, and these findings might provide guidance for the development of training opportunities for telehealth professionals.

Telephone support groups are an important modality for meeting the growing needs of family caregivers and frail older adults (Toseland, Naccarato, & Wray, 2007). Studies suggested that these groups can provide information, support, coping skills, and other benefits. This paper described the knowledge and skills that clinicians need to develop, implement, and lead telephone groups. Particular attention was paid to the clinical adaptations that are needed when leading telephone as compared with in-person groups. Technical and ethical issues were also described.

Treatment Dropouts

The purpose of this review was to present an in-depth analysis of literature identifying the extent of dropout from Internet-based treatment programs for psychological disorders, and literature exploring the variables associated with dropout from such programs (Melville, Casey, & Kavanagh, 2010). A comprehensive literature search was conducted on PSYCHINFO and PUBMED with the keywords: dropouts, drop out, dropout, dropping out, attrition, premature termination, termination, non-compliance, treatment, intervention, and program, each in combination with the key words Internet and web. A total of 19 studies published between 1990 and April 2009 and focusing on dropout from Internet-based treatment programs involving minimal therapist contact were identified and included in the review. Results. Dropout ranged from 2 to 83% and a weighted average of 31% of the participants dropped out of treatment. A range of variables have been examined for their association with dropout from Internet-based treatment programs for psychological disorders. Despite the numerous variables explored, evidence on any specific variables that may make an individual more likely to drop out of Internet-based treatment is currently limited. This review highlighted the need for more rigorous and theoretically guided research exploring the variables associated with dropping out of Internet-based treatment for psychological disorders (italics author's to highlight the importance of theory-derived interventions, as discussed in the last Chapter 16 of this volume).

VIDEOCONFERENCE PSYCHOTHERAPY

Individuals with mental health problems may face barriers to accessing effective psychotherapies. Videoconferencing technology, which allows audio and video information to be shared concurrently across geographical distances, offers an alternative that may improve access. Backhaus, Agha, Maglione, Repp, et al., (2012) conducted a systematic literature review of the use of videoconferencing psychotherapy (VCP), designed to address 10 specific questions, including therapeutic types/formats that have been implemented, the populations with which VCP is being used, the number and types of publications related to VCP, and available satisfaction, feasibility, and outcome data related to VCP. After electronic searches and reviews of reference lists, 821 potential articles were identified, and 65 were selected for inclusion. The results indicate that VCP is feasible, has been used in a variety of therapeutic formats and with diverse populations, is generally associated with good user satisfaction, and is found to have similar clinical outcomes to traditional face-to-face psychotherapy. Although the number of articles being published on VCP has increased in recent years, there remains a need for additional large-scale clinical trials to further assess the efficacy and effectiveness of VCP.

Alternative videoconferencing technologies for providing telemedicine via the Internet were described by Liu, Zhang, Locatis, and Ackerman (2011). Background information about how digital video applications were instantiated using Internet protocols is presented. Specific methods for encoding and decoding video were discussed and video applications tested at the National Library of Medicine were reviewed. This article suggested that no one technology is best and that the appropriateness of a method depends on specific applications. Some technologies, however, have lower, more flexible bandwidth requirements and are more standardized, making them more practical. Still, emerging, yet-to-be-standardized applications offer new capabilities warranting further investigation.

Martin-Khan, Wootton, Whited, and Gray (2011) conducted a systematic review of studies of observer agreement for medical specialist diagnosis via videoconferencing. The review was based on searches of electronic databases and a hand search of relevant journals and reference lists between 1966 and June 2010. There were 20 studies comparing videoconferencing diagnosis with a non-telemedicine alternative by reporting a measure of agreement. Half of the studies were in the field of dermatology; these studies provided solid support for the reliability of videoconferencing. The other 10 studies were in psychiatry, geriatrics, minor injuries, neurology and rheumatology. Reliability of diagnosis via videoconferencing was confirmed in all studies. In the studies where physical examination was an element of the diagnostic process, results were reliable but authors recommended greater care during the diagnostic process (e.g., good equipment, onsite support, additional camera angles). Four studies incorporated a second group to measure agreement in paired face-to-face assessments. Although useful evidence for the reliability of diagnosis via videoconferencing was provided by the studies in the review, the range of medical specialties was small. The variation in research methodology and statistical analysis suggested a lack of clarity about which research design is appropriate for measuring observer agreement in relation to diagnostic reliability.

Richardson, Frueh, Grubaugh, Egede, et al. (2009) reviewed recent literature on providing mental health care via videoconferencing (Mohr, 2009). Videoconferencing is one of a growing number of telecommunications technologies used to provide telemental health care. This commentary places videoconferencing in the broader field of telemental health care and discusses some of the areas that are crucial to the advancement of the field. To this end, the assumption that telemental health intervention improves access to care is explored. The notion that different telemental health telecommunications media, including the telephone and Internet, may have different benefits and disadvantages with respect to both efficacy and access is discussed. Existing and emerging telecommunications technologies not only allow us to extend access to mental health care, but they also provide opportunities to develop fundamentally new treatment paradigms. To support this development, we are in need of new theories and conceptual frameworks that can promote the development and evaluation of new telemental health interventions.

Using data from a sample of 169 patients, this study evaluates the acceptability and feasibility of telehealth videoconferencing for preclinic assessment and follow-up in an inter-professional memory clinic for rural and remote seniors (Morgan, Crossley, Kirk, McBain, et al., 2011). Patients and caregivers were seen via telehealth prior to the in-person clinic and followed up at 6 weeks, 12 weeks, 6 months, 1 year, and yearly. Patients were randomly assigned to in-person (standard care) or telehealth for the first follow-up, then alternating between the two modes of treatment, prior to 1-year follow-up. On average, telehealth appointments reduce participants' travel by 426 km per round trip. Findings showed that telehealth coordinators rated 85% of patients and 92% of caregivers as comfortable or very comfortable during telehealth. Satisfaction scales completed by patient–caregiver dyads show high satisfaction with telehealth. Follow-up questionnaires reveal similar satisfaction with telehealth and in-person appointments, but telehealth is rated as significantly more convenient. Predictors of discontinuing follow-up are greater distance to telehealth, old-age patient, lower telehealth satisfaction, and lower caregiver burden.

Real-time videoconferencing, therefore, is an innovative service delivery method to address the striking access gaps to psychological services, particularly in rural communities (Nelson & Velasquez, 2011). The authors drew upon decades of programmatic experience and national guidelines to address key areas in televideo implementation. They described the initial needs assessment as well as long-term outreach components, including training and sustainability. They summarized protocol-driven service that addresses technology, personnel, sessions, and follow-up. The authors emphasized creative strategies to translate psychology's best ethical practices to the televideo setting.

Chronic pain has been recognized as a highly prevalent problem, and interdisciplinary treatments have been shown to be effective in the treatment of chronic pain (Palyo, Schopmeyer, & McQuaid, 2012). An integrated cognitive–behavioral and physical therapy group protocol has been developed and then implemented at remote sites using videoconferencing technology to provide pain management for veterans. The treatment model was summarized and recommendations are made for addressing challenges in implementing this type of treatment via video-conferencing.

How can psychologists aid in addressing current disparities in accessibility to meet the mental health needs of rural areas? In this paper, McCord, Elliott, Wendel, Brossart, et al., (2011) discussed an innovative partnership created between community leaders in a rural county and an APA-accredited doctoral training program and its mental health clinic at a regional Federally Qualified Health Center (FQHC) to provide mental health services. We describe the efforts to build community capacity to develop the partnership and provide sustainable mental health services via teleconferencing to a remote site in a rural county. Also, to present initial evidence of the services' effectiveness in alleviating client distress, as well as meeting the expectations of referral sources and community stakeholders, the authors used the Patient Health Questionnaire (PHQ), the SF-12v.2, and using a qualitative community survey they examined data from a maximum of 68 clients (M age = 40.5, SD = 14.1; 48 females and 20 males); the number of available client data varied by analysis. We found that clients showed significant decreases in depressive symptoms (M decrease = 5.88, SD = 7.16, $p < .001$) and significant increases Mental Health Composite Scores (MCS; M increase = 11.39, SD = 7.94, $p < .005$). Results from the community survey revealed encouraging results as well as areas for improvement. Implications of developing community capacity for sustainable psychological services in rural areas were discussed.

The objective of this study was to examine professional medical interpreters' perspectives of in-person and remote interpreting modalities. A survey of interpreters at three medical centers assessed satisfaction with aspects of communication using each modality, and adequacy of videoconferencing medical interpretation (VMI) and telephonic interpretation for 21 common clinical scenarios in the hospital and ambulatory care settings. Fifty two interpreters completed the survey (73% response). All modalities were equally satisfactory for conveying information. Respondents favored in-person to telephonic interpretation for establishing rapport (95% versus 71%, p=.002) and for facilitating clinician understanding of patients' social and cultural backgrounds (92% versus 69%, p=.002). Scenarios with substantial educational or psychosocial dimensions had no more than 70% of respondents rating telephonic interpretation as adequate (25-70%); for all of these scenarios, VMI represented an improvement (52-87). From the interpreter perspective, telephonic interpretation is satisfactory for information exchange, but less so for interpersonal aspects of communication. In scenarios where telephonic interpretation does not suffice, particularly those with substantial educational or psychosocial components, VMI offers improved communication. Differences in interpreters' perspectives of modalities based on communication needs and clinical scenario suggested that a mixed use of multiple modalities may be the best language access strategy.

The provision of mental health services via videoconferencing tele-mental health has become an increasingly routine component of mental health service delivery throughout the world. Emphasizing the research literature since 2003, Richardson, Frueh, Grubaugh, Egede, et al., (2009) examined (a) the extent to which the field of tele-mental health has advanced the research agenda previously suggested and (b) implications for tele-mental healthcare delivery for special clinical populations. Previous findings have demonstrated that tele-mental health services are satisfactory to patients, improve outcomes, and are probably cost effective. In the very small number of randomized controlled studies conducted to date, tele-mental health has demonstrated equivalent efficacy compared to face-to-face care in a variety of clinical settings and with specific patient populations. However, methodologically flawed or limited research studies are the norm, and thus the research agenda for tele-mental health has not been fully maximized. Implications for future research and practice were discussed.

Research into the use of videoconferencing for clinical purposes, in particular psychotherapy, is gradually expanding. A number of case studies and case series have suggested that videoconferencing can be clinically effective and acceptable to patients. Nevertheless, there is a lack of methodologically rigorous studies with adequate sample sizes from which we can draw any generalizable conclusions and a dearth of randomised controlled studies. Many of the preliminary projects in this area have been feasibility studies with minimal focus on outcome and even less on process issues in psychotherapy. Few studies have explored the cost-effectiveness of this compared with other modes of therapy delivery. This paper aims to review the work that has been done to date within this field, and to explore the issues which need to be addressed if videoconferencing is to be taken seriously in the future as a legitimate and reliable means of delivering psychotherapy services (Simpson, 2009).

Videoconferencing has become an increasingly viable tool in psychiatry, with a growing body of literature on its use with a range of patient populations. A number of factors make it particularly well suited for patients with psychosis. For example, patients living in remote or underserved areas can be seen by a specialist without need for travel (Sharp, Kobak, & Osman, 2011). However, the hallmark symptoms of psychotic disorders might lead one to question the feasibility of videoconferencing with these patients. For example, does videoconferencing exacerbate delusions, such as paranoia or delusions of reference? Are acutely psychotic patients willing to be interviewed remotely by videoconferencing? To address these and other issues, the authors conducted an extensive review of Medline, PsychINFO, and the Telemedicine Information Exchange databases for literature on videoconferencing and psychosis. Findings generally indicated that assessment and treatment via videoconferencing is equivalent to in person and is tolerated and well accepted. There is little evidence that patients with psychosis have difficulty with videoconferencing or experience any exacerbation of symptoms; in fact, there is some evidence to suggest that the distance afforded can be a positive factor. The results of two large clinical trials support the reliability and effectiveness of centralized remote assessment of patients with schizophrenia.

The VA Maryland Health Care System introduced videoconferencing technology to provide psychiatry, evidenced-based psychotherapy, case management, and patient education at rural clinics where it was difficult to recruit providers (Koch, 2012). Telemental health services enable rural clinics to offer additional services, such as case management and patient education. Services have been expanded to urban outpatient clinics where a limited number of mental health clinic hours are available. This technology expands the availability of mental health providers and services, allowing patients to receive services from providers located at distant medical centers.

A media space provides the communications channels to support the interactions between people at different locations using video and audio links and shared access to data. This paper looked at a telehealth implementation of outpatient consultations for tertiary-level pediatric surgical patients, consultations which exercise a high degree of interpersonal and data-sharing communication between the participants (Stevenson, 2011). Framing the telehealth situation as a media space invites the designer of the telehealth system to access a large body of prior work which identifies and discusses many of the issues that will arise in this complex multi-participant telehealth context. This paper presents, as a case study, a two-year project that developed and deployed a whole-of-room telehealth system in partnership with surgeons from The Royal Children's Hospital (RCH), Melbourne, Australia. Based on observations at the hospital and discussions with the surgeons, a descriptive model of the proposed telehealth consultation (and of its deployment in a clinical trial) was developed. This descriptive model became the vehicle for gathering requirements and for design and evaluation of the telehealth system. The evaluation contained four major components: two human factors studies, an observational study of training and process change for the clinicians and a clinical trial of the resulting system. The case study demonstrates the flow of design decisions from concept to deployment. It highlights the gaps that appeared in the descriptive model when the transition was made from the laboratory to deployment in the hospital. The conclusion is that, at this relatively unexplored level of telehealth, there are likely to be gaps in such a descriptive model that are not uncovered by laboratory experiments or by analytic evaluation but emerge only during a clinical trial with actual patients, clinicians and patient data.

Virtual Reality

Virtual reality as a medium for exposure therapy in the treatment of social anxiety was utilized in a private-practice setting for two different courses of individual treatment: weekly psychotherapy and a 3-day intensive course of therapy (Anderson, Rothbaum, & Hodges, 2003). Participants met diagnostic criteria for social phobia with prominent public speaking fears, and completed self-report questionnaires at pre-treatment and post-treatment. During exposure therapy, participants were presented with a virtual audience, consisting of video of actual people embedded within a virtual classroom environment. Results indicated that treatment was successful as measured by completion of a behavioral avoidance test at the end of treatment, decreases in self-reported measures of public speaking anxiety comparable to controlled clinical outcome trials for social phobia, and qualitative feedback. Follow-up data, obtained from 1 participant, showed continued improvement after therapy was completed. These preliminary findings suggest that virtual reality may be a useful tool for exposure therapy within a comprehensive treatment of social anxiety.

For many clinicians, the use of VR in psychiatric practice better resembles a movie scene than their everyday experience (Luo, 2007). However, today's computer hardware and software has sufficiently improved enough to create a virtual world in the typical office. In particular, with computer central processing units following Moore's Law—transistor density of circuits doubles every 18 months for the same cost—computers today have the capability of processing large amounts of information quickly enough to produce sufficient visual stimulation in simulations. Computer games are an example of how visual effects have become a vital component of game play as well as evoking the imagination with various storylines and engaging the player with a breadth of activity. High resolution liquid crystal display and plasma monitors have become more commonplace at home and in the office. These technologies help convey a sense of participation in the virtual world, which may be sufficient in lieu of expensive traditional headsets. These headsets have also matured becoming lighter and better at integrating movement information into the virtual environment at lower costs. This article reviews the history of VR treatment and explores future developments in the field.

Several VR applications for the understanding, assessment and treatment of mental health problems have been developed in the last 15 years (Riva, 2009).Typically, in VR the patient learns to manipulate problematic situations related to his/her problem. In fact, VR can be described as an advanced form of human–computer interface that is able to induce a feeling of 'presence' in the computer-generated world experienced by the user. This feature transforms VR in an 'empowering environment', a sheltered setting where patients can start to explore and act without feeling threatened. With such assurance, they can freely explore, experiment, feel, live out and experience feelings and/or thoughts. The paper presents the current state of clinical research in this area. Furthermore, the open source 'NeuroVR' system and its potential clinical applications are presented and discussed.

Conclusion

On the basis of this review, the winners in the field of online psychotherapy seem to be therapeutically, CBT and practically, videoconferencing. A close practical approach seem VR. There is a logical sequence in CBT, however, such a structure. If not following CBT, one runs in the danger of offering unstructured videoconferencing unless a structure is provided as well (L'Abate, in press).

Chapter 15

TRAINING

The rise in popularity and use of computer-mediated modes of communication such as email and synchronous chat have resulted in the potential for new delivery methods of mental health services. The present study investigated the dynamics of an initial counseling session held in a synchronous chat environment between therapists-in-training at various graduate programs across the country and a trained confederate posing as a client (Mallen, 2006). Transcripts from online sessions were analyzed to investigate therapist responses and interventions in the online environment. Therapists-in-training were also asked to respond to questions concerning their satisfaction with the experience, the relationship they were able to form with the client, and previous online experience. Participants gave an assessment of the client and responded to statements about online counseling. Results demonstrated that therapists-in-training expressed more positive views about online counseling after they had conducted the session in terms of the potential for a therapeutic alliance and desire for future training; however, participants expressed more negative views about the amount of work that could be accomplished during online counseling sessions. Therapists-in-training were also able to accurately diagnose their client's presenting concerns at the conclusion of the session. The implications for the future directions of online counseling research and practice were addressed.

For more than 60 years, the Centers for Disease Control and Prevention (CDC) have responded to a broad spectrum of natural and human-caused disasters, including food- and waterborne illnesses, disease outbreaks, chronic health challenges, terrorism incidents, hurricanes, and earthquakes. Until recently, the highly educated professionals who deploy to hot spots around the world received little training on how to deal with the potential mental and emotional effects of the stressors to which they might be exposed. In the aftermath of the 2004 tsunami, because of widespread injuries and the potential for disease outbreak, CDC deployed a few dozen people to Thailand and Indonesia. While these individuals were experts in their respective fields, they ran into challenges. Direct exposure to this level of destruction is an experience that most U.S. citizens never face. Realizing that more needed to be done to better prepare these emergency responders, behavioral science experts at CDC reviewed stressors that CDC emergency responders could encounter. A team member was introduced to the use of virtual reality for clinical treatment of PTSD after attending a national conference. It made sense to see if this kind of immersive training tool could help prepare someone to cope with the disturbing sights, sounds, and smells they might experience once deployed, sustain resiliency, and increase their ability to perform their jobs effectively (Klomp, Spitalnick, & Reissman, 2011).

School-based mental health initiatives designed to address mental health difficult-ties in young people face a number of challenges that can limit their effectiveness and sustainability. These include challenges to participation, challenges to knowledge uptake and challenges to timely and ongoing evaluation. Santor and Bagnell (2008) reviewed how each of these challenges affects the effectiveness of school-based mental health programs and how they can be addressed, in part, through interactive, internet-based resources and tools, while maximizing the sustainability of those programs. Never before has a single delivery system such as the internet had the capacity to reach such a large number of young people simultaneously.

BIBLIOTHERAPY

Technology proficiency expectations have proliferated in counselor education; how-ever, limited information in the counseling literature details how to effectively evaluate or refine online resources from a design/utility standpoint (McMillen & Pehrsson, 2009). This description of a small-scale usability study demonstrates a cost-effective strategy for improving counselor education Web sites. Counselor education students completed specific tasks related to the target Web site's purpose and functionality. Error and completion rates were tracked and process comments were recorded. Combined qualitative and quantitative results clearly indicated what worked and what did not, allowing the Web site designers to prioritize needed changes in content organization, format/graphics, and workflow.

CAREERS

Assessment

The growing use of the Internet by professionals and laypeople alike, together with rapidly improving technology, has resulted in dramatic growth of assessment Web sites (Barak, 2003). Although these tests are being used for a number of purposes, their employment for career-related assessment and decisions seems to be prevailing. This development stems from the search for easy-to-obtain, free (or inexpensive) aids to assist in decision making; a general awareness and acceptance of the Internet as a legitimate informative; and professional and nonprofessional site owners' exploitation of the provision of remote testing services. Although empirical research generally supports the psychometric properties and utility of Internet-based assessment, there are numerous ethical and professional issues involved. A large listing of concerns is presented, followed by a recommendation to take action in three concomitant directions: focused legislation (including international conventions), Internet-specific training for professionals, and public education aimed at increasing awareness and understanding.

Counseling

The article focused on the online career practices and trends. Career services available online were presented including career counseling/coaching, resume/cover letter development and distribution, and mock online interviews. Some of the trends in career services are Web 2.0 platforms, digital portfolio, live online career sessions. Resource sites for online career counselors from the Center for Credentializing and Education, and the Online Therapy Institute were also included (Jencius & Rainey, 2009).

Development

Career HOPES is an Internet-delivered group counseling intervention designed to facilitate occupational exploration and career decision making (Herman, 2010). This intervention included automated interactive lessons and self-assessments, homework assignments, and group discussions in private online forums. A randomized, controlled experiment (N = 64) was conducted to evaluate (a) the efficacy of Career HOPES and (b) the contribution of professional moderation of the online group discussions to outcomes. Participants in two treatment conditions showed greater gains than control condition participants in career decidedness as measured by the Occupational Alternatives Questionnaire (d = .54), occupationally relevant self-knowledge (d = .58), and emission of career exploration behaviors (d = .50). In one of the treatment conditions, the online group discussions were moderated by a psychologist with career counseling experience; in the other treatment condition, the discussions were un-moderated. Professional moderation resulted in better outcomes on several variables and greater overall satisfaction with the intervention.

Explorations

Using a Web-based program he developed, one educator is helping students understand how their career and lifestyle choices are linked (Beutler, 2008). MyLife, a Web-based life-planning program for young people, offers comprehensive budget activity in which participants develop simulations of their fantasy futures and calculate their future monthly bills--including rent or house payments, car payments, car maintenance, gasoline, insurance, utilities, groceries, clothing, and entertainment. MyLife also motivates students to explore careers to determine which occupations are good fits for them, as well as those that will support their lifestyle choices. The author, career counselor at Minot High School in Minot, North Dakota, created MyLife as an introduction to career exploration and planning. A life simulation activity like MyLife engages students by getting them interested in their futures and helping them to understand the importance of education--encouraging them to work harder in school.

College Students Counseling

The National Board for Certified Counselors described cyber-counseling as the provision of some aspects of counseling through technology, via such applications as e-mail, Web-based information access, course registration, academic advising, and career guidance (Maples & Han, 2008). The authors explored the characteristics of cyber-counseling, describe its current use in the United States and South Korea, explored its advantages and disadvantages, and considered issues and concerns for college counselors.

The development of a university-based cyber-counseling certificate program through the continuing education department of a graduate faculty of social work was described (Murphy, MacFadden, & Mitchell, 2008). This web-based program consisted of two levels: introductory and advanced, and offers experienced F2F counselors training in an asynchronous, e-mail form of cyber-counseling. Ethical issues such as cross-jurisdictional concerns, client appropriateness, and counselor insurance are discussed. A system developed to provide online e-mail security through web-based access and encryption is highlighted. Several techniques for e-mail counseling such as presence, and spacing and pacing are discussed and illustrated. Demographics of learners and feedback from graduates are presented and lessons learned are discussed.

COUNSELORS

Education

The Internet is the latest arena in which counseling services are available for a variety of issues. This study surveyed counselor education professionals about their perceptions regarding the use of online counseling to address various mental health issues including career counseling (Lewis & Coursol, 2007). It also examined their perceptions about 3 formats of online counseling: e-mail, text-based chat, and videoconferencing. Results indicated that counselor education professionals were open to the use of online counseling to address career issues. The implications for the practice of online career counseling and for the training of counselors are discussed.

Experiences

Online counseling has been an emerging and much debated phenomenon. The number of web sites is constantly growing; yet compared to this growth there is still scarce qualitative research on communication dynamics of online counseling. This study aims\ed to demystify the online counseling experience of the counselors and the online counseling process (Akmehmet-Sekerler, 2009). Three chat and three email counseling examples conducted by six pioneers of online counseling are demonstrated for this purpose. The methodology is informed by phenomenology and symbolic interactionism and employs a constant-comparative design. Interviews were conducted with the six online counselors. Actual transcripts of 34 emails and 18 chat sessions were analyzed. The results provide in-depth understanding of online counselors' practices. Four major themes emerge to be important in describing the online counseling experience of the counselors: finance, convenience, trust, and assessment. Participants view online counseling as an expansion of their face-to-face counseling practices. Findings also suggest that online counseling should not be described as a one-dimensional modality. Email and chat counseling are identified as having considerable differences. Online counseling skills observed in the sessions can be categorized as transferred, modified, and newly devised skills. This study suggests that the boundaries of the counseling profession are both challenged and expanded by the emergence of computer-mediated counseling.

Research Training

To address the need for research regarding online counseling, the authors explored the experiences of 4 female and 2 male Caucasian counseling students who facilitated 5 chat-based online counseling sessions (Haberstroh, Parr, Bradley, Morgan-Fleming, & Gee, 2008). Conducting semi-structured interviews based in grounded theory methods, the authors discussed technological barriers, counseling without visual and verbal cues, online counseling techniques, counseling from home, and factors related to the pace of the sessions. They suggested that online counseling requires specific technical, ethical, and clinical considerations.

Email Social Services

A survey of 384 Central Pennsylvania social workers explored email use, attitudes, and difficulties (Finn, 2006). Results showed that approximately three-fourths of social workers use email at work, primarily with co-workers. Almost one-third has used email with clients, although the majority of social workers believe that email for therapeutic purposes is both unethical and ineffective. A small minority of social workers has experienced difficulties that include violating a client's confidentiality through email, sending email to the wrong person, and receiving harassing email. There is considerable variation in agency policy and training related to email. Implications for agency policy and continuing education are discussed.

Internet Training

For several years, the China American Psychoanalytic Alliance (CAPA) has provided treatment, training, and supervision to Chinese mental health professionals over the Internet (Fishkin, Fishkin, Leli, Katz, & Snyder, 2011). The lack of Chinese analysts and mentors has created an intense demand for psychodynamic psychotherapy training and treatment that CAPA is addressing using Skype™ and other distance communication technologies. This article describes the project, its history, scope, and activities, and the experiences of CAPA teachers and clinicians in exploring and developing the usefulness and power of this very new teaching method. Some particular characteristics of Chinese culture have become apparent as a result of the teaching experience. Aspects of the transference and countertransference that are shaped by the virtual nature of the technology are discussed, using case material. Our hope is that, in helping to train our Chinese students in psychodynamic psychotherapy, they will go on to train future generations of clinicians. This model of teaching and training could also be applied in other underserved areas.

Online Counseling

Seventy-six Counselor Education doctoral students rated the degree to which text-based computer mediated communication (CMC) counseling exchanges had therapeutic relationship qualities (Atanasoff, 2006). The participants read either a treatment or alternate treatment counseling scenario posted on the World Wide Web and then rated the scenarios on the strength of a working alliance and relational communications of intimacy. There was a significant difference found between the groups indicating that it was not the medium itself that defined the quality of the counseling relationship, but rather the counseling scenario that study participants read. Participants' perceptions about e-mail technology were a significant covariate. Implications of this study for counseling online and counselor education along with future research directions were discussed.

Patient Education/Psychiatric Hospitals

Internet-based patient support systems are widely assumed to predict a future trend in patient education (Anttila, Välimäki, Koivunen, Luukkaala, Kaila, Pitkänen, & Kontio, 2011). .Coherent information is still lacking on how patient education is adopted in psychiatric hospitals and how information technology is used in it. Our aim was to describe nurses‘ adoption of an Internet-based patient education program and the variables explaining it. The study was based on Rogers' model of the diffusion of innovation. The Internet-based patient education sessions were carried out by nurses on nine acute psychiatric inpatient wards in two Finnish hospitals. They were evaluated with reports and analysed statistically. Out of 100 nurses, 83 adopted the program during the study period. The nurses fell into Rogers' groups, late majority (72%), laggards (17%), early majority (7%), early adopters (3%) and innovators (1%). Three groups were formed according to their activity: laggards, late majority, adopters (including early majority, early adopters, innovators). There was a statistical difference between the nurses' programmed adoption between the two hospitals ($P = 0.045$): more laggards (65% vs. 35%) and adopters (73% vs. 27%) in the same hospital. The findings help to provide insight into the contexts and settings when adopting information technology programs in the area of MH care.

Peer-Mentoring

The present study compared the relative impact of peer-mentoring that took place either F2F or through electronic chat (Smith-Jentsch, Scielzo, Yarbrough, & Rosopa, 2008). Protégés were 106 college freshmen randomly assigned to a senior college student mentor and to one of the two communication modes. Fifty-one mentors interacted with one of these proteges F2F and one solely through electronic chat. Electronic chat resulted in less psychosocial support, career support, and post-mentoring protege self-efficacy for those with male but not female mentors. Analyses of coded transcripts revealed that males condensed their language to a greater extent than did females in the electronic chat condition relative to the face-to-face condition. Dyads in the electronic chat condition had more interactive dialogue than did those in the face-to-face condition. Finally, dialogue interactivity predicted post-mentoring self-efficacy but only for those who communicated through electronic chat.

Problematic Internet Experiences

This study utilized data from clinical reports of 1441 youth and adults in the USA to examine the types of problematic Internet experiences mental health professionals report as clients‘ primary or secondary presenting problems (Mitchell & Wells, 2007). Overall, clients who presented in treatment with an Internet problem are more likely to have problems related to overuse of the Internet; use of adult pornography; use of child pornography; sexual exploitation perpetration; and gaming, gambling, or role-playing. Other Internet-related problems, such as isolative-avoidant use, sexual exploitation victimization, harassment perpetration, and online infidelity were equally likely to present in treatment as a primary problem or secondary to other mental health concerns. Some differences between youth and adult clients were also identified. Findings suggest some initial support for the importance of including Internet use, experiences, and behavior as part of an initial clinical assessment.

Psychologists Training

Psychology licensing laws have a short history and were created to regulate the professional interactions between a psychologist and a client within a single jurisdiction (DeMers, Van Horne, & Rodolfa, 2008). Societal and technological changes in the way psychologists are trained and practice challenge licensing boards to provide new mechanisms to regulate professional behavior that recognize these changes yet still offer adequate protection of the public. This article describes the problems psychologists encounter related to professional mobility, temporary practice across jurisdictional boundaries, distance learning, and consistency in the handling and reporting of disciplinary actions. The article also describes the efforts of the Association of State and Provincial Psychology Boards to help its licensing board members to address these challenges. Finally, the article raises some potentially dramatic changes being considered in the way psychologists are admitted to professional practice using a competency assessment approach to complement the traditional use of course credits, supervised experience hours, and performance on a knowledge-based exam.

This pilot study explored the outcomes of clinical psychology trainees delivering treatments via videoconferencing (Dunstan & Tooth, 2012). A noncurrent, multiple baseline across subjects and settings. Setting: University outpatient psychology clinic. Participants: Six clients (two men and four women) with an anxiety or depressive disorder were randomly assigned to received six sessions of individual therapy (either via videoconferencing or face to face) from a male or female clinical psychology trainee. Main outcome measures:

Participants provided daily ratings (0–10) of subjective distress/well-being via text messaging, and at pre-, post-, and 1 month follow-up of treatment, completed the Depression Anxiety Stress Scales and the Outcome Questionnaire-45. Along with the trainees, participants also provided feedback on the therapy experience.

The subjective well-being of all participants improved, and all videoconferencing participants showed a statistically and clinically significant reduction in symptomatology and gains in general life functioning. Feedback comments were positive. This study suggested that there is value in clinical psychology trainees gaining experience in the delivery of treatments via videoconferencing. Further study is needed to demonstrate the potential for university clinics to deliver mental health services, via this modality, to rural and remote areas.

Information and communication technologies are increasingly being used to remotely deliver psychological services. This delivery method confers clear advantages to both client and therapist, including the accessibility of services by otherwise unserved populations and cost-effective treatment (Shandley, Klein, Kyrios, Austin, et al., 2011). Remote services can be delivered in a real-time or delayed manner, providing clients with a wealth of therapy options not previously available. The proliferation of these services has outstripped the development and implementation of all but the most rudimentary of services. Integrating mandatory training on the delivery of online psychological services into accredited postgraduate psychology courses would aid in addressing this issue. The purpose of this article was to outline issues of consideration in the development and implementation of such a training program. An online e-therapy training program developed by Swinburne University's National eTherapy Centre was used as an example throughout.

School Counselors Trainees

This study investigated the efficacy of a 12-week, Web-based peer supervision group in increasing school counselor trainees' collective self-esteem (i.e., positive feelings in identifying as a school counselor) and written case conceptualization ability (Butler & Constantine, 2006). Results suggested that school counselor trainees who participated in a Web-based peer supervision group reported significantly higher collective self-esteem and case conceptualization skills than did their counterparts who did not participate in Web-based peer supervision. Implications of the findings for e-counselors in training and practicing school counselors were presented.

Teaching

As technology advances and the use of online counseling becomes more routine, attention must be paid to instruction regarding online counseling skills. The authors presented considerations for teaching basic online counseling skills to master's-level counseling students. Recommendations are made for helping students to establish and maintain therapeutic relationships online. Suggestions specific to counselor preparation and future research were provided (Trepal, Haberstroh, Duffey, & Evans, 2007).

Therapist Preferences

One barrier to the dissemination of evidence-based psychological treatments is the fact that few clinicians have received training in how to implement them (Helgadottir & Fairburn, 2014). A potential solution is "web-centred training." For any training program to be successful it must match the perceived needs of the trainee as otherwise there is likely to be poor compliance. As part of the groundwork for developing a web-centred training program, a questionnaire on training preferences was sent to 373 therapists who had expressed interest in the website, of whom 183 responded. The top

Priorities were a clinically relevant website that demonstrated in detail how to implement the treatment. The overall characteristics and functioning of the website were also a major concern. There was little interest in being in touch with others learning the treatment. These findings demonstrated the importance of surveying users' views in advance and during the website development process.

Training: Clients with Problematic Internet Experiences

This paper examined clients' exposure to problematic Internet experiences among a national sample of 2,098 social workers, psychologists, marriage and family therapists, and other mental health professionals (Wells, Mitchell, Finkelhor, & Blease, 2006). This analysis found that mental health professionals are working with clients experiencing a range of problems related to Internet use. However, these professionals have generally not been exposed to training or information in the professional literature on the topic of working with clients with problematic Internet experiences. The authors identified several areas in which additional training is needed and review practical implications for mental health professionals.

Virtual Psychiatric Emergency

Bhandari, Tiessen, and Snowdon (2011) discussed a telehealth project aimed at delivering mental health crisis interventions to patients in two rural hospitals in Southern Ontario, Canada, by creating a virtual psychiatric emergency department (ED) using telehealth technology. A participatory action research approach was followed as a design framework for this project. A formal process based on Kouzes and Posner's five practices of exemplary leadership was crafted and closely followed, given the critical role of leadership necessary for the success of this project. The programme achieved its goal and was well received by patients and staff. ED physicians felt supported by the available psychiatric and mental health nursing expertise. Staff satisfaction with the protocols and processes were high, and ED physicians felt confident in the support they received during the decision-making process for appropriate disposition of the patient.

Web Consulting

This paper referred to a brief interaction with a mental health professional via written electronic communication (Efstathiou, 2009). Web consulting services have proved popular, but there is controversy regarding the efficacy of such brief interventions to address problems and enable service users to access other forms of counseling. University students are accustomed to new technologies and often present difficulties suitable for simple intervention. Additionally, interventions of this type lead to the creation of a 'database' of students' issues that can be used by future service users, alleviating the heavy workload of most services. Data from prior investigations are presented and ways to further investigate, validate and evaluate the function and outcome of web consulting in the context of students' psychological counseling are discussed.

CONCLUSION

This chapter contains only the tip of the iceberg. Online training to convey information has only began to show how online training is bound to proliferate to the point that new degree programs will eventually supplant traditional educational programs (L'Abate, 2009). These developments raise the question on whether universities and institutions of higher learning will need additional physical structures and classrooms to teach. It is now feasible and possible for teachers to never meet and see their students.

SECTION VI. CONCLUSION

Chapter 16

PRESENT STATUS AND FUTURE PERSPECTIVES FOR ONLINE INTERVENTIONS

The purpose of this conclusive chapter is to touch on critical issues that will determine the future of psychological interventions in mental health, both online and offline. Are online interventions as effective as offline ones and are they less expensive to administer than offline interventions? Let the results speak for themselves. However, perhaps the answer lies on: "It depends on which intervention is used." Nonetheless, in the past several years, the practice and profession of psychology have been greatly influenced by digital culture and social media (Kolmes, 2012). We are changing from a ears-mouth (auditory-oral) to an eyes-hands (visual-digital) culture (L'Abate, in press).

The prevalence of psychologists using websites and technology to engage, socialize, market, and interact has created new opportunities and challenges for practitioners, particularly in regard to potential therapeutic and extra-therapeutic interactions with clients on the web (L'Abate, 2013c). Given the speed with which these media are permeating the mental health world, one can expect to see a proliferation of new issues, challenges, and opportunities for clinical practice and the delivery of services. Kolmes (2012) provided an overview of the relevant issues, ongoing trends, and what the future holds for psychology, psychologists, and populations mental health professionals serve. Current and future technological and policy shifts will influence clinical practice, clinical training, and professional responsibilities as providers of clinical care will need to consider and to prepare for by updating their skills for a new age (Anthony, Nagel, & Goss, 2010; Gallego & Emmelkamp, 2012; L'Abate, 2011c).

COST EFFECTIVENESS OF INTERNET

One of the basic issues pervading all the contributions in this volume is cost-effectiveness. For instance, the objective of this study was to explore expectations and experiences of online cognitive behavioral therapy (CBT) among primary-care patients with depression, focusing on how this mode of delivery impacts upon the therapeutic experience (Beattie, Shaw, Kaur, & Kessler, 2009). The design of this study was qualitative, using repeat semi-structured interviews with patients before and after therapy. The study was conducted in parallel with a randomized controlled trial examining the *effectiveness and cost-effectiveness of online CBT for patients with depression.* Twenty-four patients with depression recruited from five general practices in southwest England, who were offered up to 10 sessions of CBT, delivered via the internet by a psychologist.

Most participants accessed the therapy from their home computer and found this to be a major advantage, in terms of convenience and fitting therapy into their daily routine, with any technical problems quickly resolved. Two key themes regarding expectations and experiences of online CBT were: developing a virtual relationship with a therapist, and the process of communicating thoughts and emotions via an online medium. Online CBT seems to be acceptable to, and experienced as helpful by, certain subgroups of patients with depression, particularly those who are familiar with computers, feel comfortable with writing their feelings down, enjoy the opportunities to review and reflect that written (or typed) communication offers are attracted to the 'anonymity' of an online therapeutic relationship and are open to the proactive requirements of CBT itself. However, online CBT may feed into the vulnerability of depressed people to negative thoughts, given the absence of visual cues and the immediate response of face-to-face interaction. Online CBT has the potential to enhance care for patients with depression who are open to engaging in 'talking' (or typing) therapies as part of their treatment. If online CBT is to be provided via the NHS, it is important to establish patient preferences regarding this mode of delivery and ensure that referral practices are appropriately targeted. The results of our main trial will provide evidence regarding the effectiveness and cost-effectiveness of receiving therapy via this modality.

Social Anxiety Disorder (SAD) is highly prevalent and associated with a substantial societal economic burden, primarily due to high costs of productivity loss (Hedman, Andersson, Ljotsson, Andersson, et al., 2011). Cognitive behavior group therapy (CBGT) is an effective treatment for SAD and the most established in clinical practice. Internet-based cognitive behavior therapy (ICBT) has demonstrated efficacy in several trials in recent years. No study has however investigated the cost-effectiveness of ICBT compared to CBGT from a societal perspective, i.e., an analysis where both direct and indirect costs are included. The aim of the present study was to investigate the cost-effectiveness of ICBT compared to CBGT from a societal perspective using a prospective design. Hedman, Andersson, Ljotsson, Andersson, et al., 2011) conducted a randomized controlled trial where participants with SAD were randomized to ICBT (n=64) or CBGT (n=62). Economic data were assessed at pretreatment, immediately following treatment and six months after treatment. Results showed that the gross total costs were significantly reduced at six month follow-up, compared to pretreatment in both treatment conditions. As both treatments were equivalent in reducing social anxiety and gross total costs, ICBT was more cost-effective due to lower intervention costs. We conclude that ICBT can be more cost-effective than CBGT in the treatment of SAD and that both treatments reduce societal costs for SAD.

Telehealth has been touted as one solution to the shortage of mental health providers within the military. Despite developing evidence for the equivalence of telehealth mental health care, there is no research that covers the use of telehealth for population mental health screening, a standard component of post deployment medical screening (Jones, Etherage, Harmon, & Okiishi, 2012). This paper summarized soldier perceptions of three separate screening events in which telehealth was used and the cost-effectiveness of telehealth versus in-person implementations of the same screening. Soldiers who have not been through telehealth screening reported a strong preference for in-person screening. Soldiers who have been through telehealth screening still reported preference for in-person screening, but they expressed more ambivalence about the screening method. Using telehealth only mental health screening for large numbers of soldiers within a compressed time frame seems more expensive than in-person screening. Telehealth resulted in higher referral rates than in-person screening. Government and military leaders should use care when making decisions about telehealth implementation. Although telehealth for small numbers may be sufficiently equivalent and economical, there is no evidence of cost savings or improved acceptability for telehealth mental health post-deployment screening.

This study assessed the costs associated with a group behavioral weight loss intervention and compare cost-effectiveness based on treatment delivery modality (in-person vs. Internet). (Krukowski, Tilfor, Harvey-Berino, & West, 2011). A randomized controlled trial examined efficacy of a group behavioral obesity intervention across in-person and Internet treatment modalities. Participants (N = 323, 93% women, mean BMI = 35.8) from two centers were randomized to treatment modality, and contact time was matched between conditions. Primary outcome was weight loss. Cost-effectiveness measures calculated life years gained (LYG) from changes in weight at 6 months, based on excess years of life lost (YLL) algorithm and the cost of the two modalities. In-person participants had significantly greater weight losses (−8.0 ± 6.1 kg) than Internet participants (−5.5 ± 5.6 kg), whereas differences in LYG were insignificant. Estimated LYG was 0.58 (95% confidence interval: 0.45, 0.71) and 0.47 (95% confidence interval: 0.34, 0.60) for the in-person and Internet condition, respectively. Total cost of conducting the in-person condition was $706 per person and the Internet condition was $372 per person with the difference mainly due to increased travel cost of $158 per person. The incremental cost-effectiveness ratio was $2,160 per (discounted) LYG for the Internet modality relative to no intervention/no weight loss and $7,177 per (discounted) LYG for the in-person modality relative to the Internet modality. Participant time costs were recognized as an important cost of medical and behavioral interventions. When participant time costs were included in an economic evaluation of a behavioral weight loss intervention, Internet-based weight loss delivery may be a more cost-effective approach to obesity treatment.

Longevity in senior citizens and cost effectiveness need to be related in some way or another. Therefore, the objective of this research was to evaluate whether providing healthcare for the elderly is one of the expectations of a telemedicine system to reduce the isolation of the aging and enhance the quality of long-term care for the elderly (Wang, 2011). Based on the experiences in Taiwan, this research aimed at investigating the influences of longevity on the demand for health services through telecommunications and conventional F2F methods and to note the relationship between telemedicine and conventional health services. Multiple regression analysis was undertaken on a sample that covered the period from 1995 to 2004. Results indicated that a 1% increase in the proportion of elderly relative to the population significantly increases the quantity demanded of telehealth by 305.73 and the quantity demanded of F2F health services by 1.99×10^7. On the relationship between longevity and telemedicine, the society begins to request telehealth when the elderly proportion is >2.06%. With current 9.5% elderly proportion, there is a potential to provide 2,274.86 telemedicine health services that are currently provided at only 954.9 and underprovided by 1.38 times. On the relationship between longevity and conventional health services, when the elderly proportion is >0.56%, the needs for F2F health services increase in the elderly percentage. With 9.5% elderly proportion, the estimated volume of health services via conventional medical care system is 1.54×10^8. The current quantity of such services is 1.11×10^8 and underprovided by 38%. Estimation results revealed that online and conventional health services are complementary for enhancing health status in an aging society.

EXTENT OF THERAPIST'S INVOLVEMENT AND THERAPEUTIC ALLIANCE

Cost-effectiveness is linked to how much professional time is necessary to obtain optimal results: The longer professional is required the higher the cost of the intervention will be. Therefore, we need to distinguish among: (1) full-time assistance with or without professional feedback, either after one single homework assignment completed or after two or more assignments; (2) assistance at the end of a series of homework assignments; or (3) no professional assistance, participants are on their own, with or without pre-post-interventions evaluation and follow-up.

Part of this forgoing process about the extent of professional involvement is related to the nature of the therapeutic working alliance set online. One of the major issues raised by offline practitioners lied on the importance of the F2F TB therapeutic working alliance. It would be impossible to replicate this process online according to this view. In spite of this view, online counseling is a growing area of clinical work with relatively little empirical evidence about the kind of clients that use the medium, advantages and disadvantages of online counseling, and satisfaction with relationships and treatment service (Leibert, Archer, Munson, & York, 2006). Sociodemographics were collected on 81 self-selected clients using online counseling, and self-reported therapeutic alliance and satisfaction with online counseling were assessed for comparison to past studies of clients using traditional face-to-face counseling. Online clients were predominantly female, were already regular Internet users, and enjoyed the convenience and anonymity of the service. They were satisfied with their relationships and treatment online but not as satisfied as clients who have undergone traditional F2F counseling. The main disadvantage, the loss of nonverbal information, was offset by the advantage of anonymity when sharing shameful personal information. Research limitations and clinical implications of the study were discussed and covered by the next source.

Furthermore, the provision of online counseling and online therapy is steadily increasing (Knaevelsrud & Maercker, 2006). Results of a number of controlled trials investigating the efficacy of online approaches indicated that some of these new treatment alternatives might indeed be effective. Yet, little is known about how the therapeutic relationship (or working alliance) evolves over the Internet and whether it influences treatment outcome as it does in traditional face-to-face therapy. The working alliance has been defined as the extent to which a patient and a therapist work collaboratively and purposefully and connect emotionally. The aim of the study was to investigate the quality and predictive relevance of the therapeutic alliance for patients receiving a short-term, Internet-based, cognitive-behavioral therapy program for posttraumatic stress reactions. After rigorous screening for exclusion criteria of high dissociative tendencies, risk of psychosis, and suicidal tendencies, 48 patients, who had experienced a traumatic event in the past, were included in the online treatment study. The short form of the Working Alliance Inventory (WAI-S) was administered at the fourth treatment session. The relevance of the therapeutic relationship for treatment outcome was assessed in terms of residual gain from pretreatment assessment to the end of treatment. The revised Impact of Event Scale (IES-R) and the depression and anxiety subscales of the Brief Symptom Inventory (BSI) were used to assess treatment outcome.

The total of 48 participants was included in the analysis. Overall, high alliance scores were found. In contrast to previous studies of conventional F2F therapy, there was only a low to modest association (.13 to .33) between the quality of the therapeutic relationship and treatment outcome. *High alliance scores indicated that it was possible to establish a stable and positive therapeutic relationship online* (italics mine). However, the therapeutic relationship was found to be a less relevant predictor of the therapy outcome than in F2F approaches. The authors discussed whether this finding can be attributed to methodological reasons, such as the restricted range of alliance ratings obtained or the time of administration of the WAI-S, or whether the therapeutic relationship might be less relevant to the treatment outcome of online therapy approaches.

This article described e-mail therapy with a teenager whom professionals found difficult to communicate with and understand (Roy & Gillett, 2008). Anne had a 4-year history of low mood and unpredictable self-harming behavior that in the past had led to admission to a secure unit. Therapy involved weekly e-mails over a 3-month period and ended when she was transferred to adult services. The article focused on how e-mail enabled engagement to occur. The therapeutic relationship allowed Anne to explore and understand past experiences, and start resolving present problems. Diagnosis also became clearer. Another study examined counselor-client concurrence and variation on working alliance and session impact in cyber-counseling and F2F counseling conditions (Li, Chen, & Wang, 2008). Counselors were three second-year graduate students in a counseling practicum who provided 50-minute sessions to clients through cyber-counseling and face-to-face counseling. After each session, counselors and clients independently completed the Working Alliance Inventory (WAI) and Session Impact Questionnaire (SEQ) to assess the strength of working alliance and impact of counseling session. Transcripts from both cyber-counseling and face-to-face counseling sessions were analyzed using the helping skill system developed by Hill and O'Brien (1999). Results indicated the following: In cyber-counseling condition, counselors used open-ended and close-ended questions the most, and challenging the least. In F2F counseling condition, counselors used close-ended questions and restatement the most. Working alliance had an increasing trend in both cyber-counseling and F2F counseling conditions, while session impact (coherence, depth, & positivity) varied according to the number of sessions.

Hanley (2009) examined the quality of the working alliance in online counseling relationships with young people. A mixed method approach has been adopted which combines the completion of a self-report quantitative measure (the 'Therapeutic Alliance Quality Scale') and qualitative interviews with service users of a UK-based service (Kooth.com). Findings were generally positive, with approximately three quarters of respondents reporting the working alliance to have been of a medium or high quality. To give a more detailed sense of what users found helpful or unhelpful in developing good quality online working alliances, key themes from the interviews were also presented. Finally, the implications and limitations of the study were discussed before outlining some thoughts for future development.

Although numerous efficacy studies in recent years have found internet-based interventions for depression to be effective, there has been scant consideration of therapeutic process factors in the online setting (Preschl, Maercker, & Wagner, 2011). In F2F therapy, the quality of the working alliance explains variance in treatment outcome. However, little is yet known about the impact of the working alliance in internet-based interventions, particularly as compared with F2F therapy. This study explored the working alliance between client and therapist in the middle and at the end of a cognitive-behavioral intervention for depression. Participants were randomized to an internet-based treatment group (n = 25) or F2F group (n = 28). Both groups received the same cognitive behavioral therapy over an 8-week timeframe. Participants completed the Beck Depression Inventory (BDI) post-treatment and the Working Alliance Inventory at mid- and post- treatment. Therapists completed the therapist version of the Working Alliance Inventory at post-treatment.

With the exception of therapists' ratings of the tasks subscale, which were significantly higher in the online group, the two groups' ratings of the working alliance did not differ significantly (Preschl, Maercker, Andreas, & Wagner, 2011). Further, significant correlations were found between clients' ratings of the working alliance and therapy outcome at post-treatment in the online group and at both mid- and post-treatment in the face-to-face group. Correlation analysis revealed that the working alliance ratings did not significantly predict the BDI residual gain score in either group. *Contrary to what might have been expected, the working alliance in the online group was comparable to that in the F2F group. However, the results showed no significant relations between the BDI residual gain score and the working alliance ratings in either group* (italics mine).

Many parents who would benefit from parenting skills training via live coaching do not receive it due to barriers such as time, distance, and the unavailability of skilled providers (Wade, Oberjohn, Conaway, Osinska, et al. (2011). This report described an innovative web-based parenting skills program for families of young children with traumatic brain injury (TBI)—Internet-Based Interacting Together Everyday, Recovery After Childhood TBI (I-InTERACT). I-InTERACT is a web-based parenting skills program of 10–14 sessions that combines self-guided web modules with live coaching via videoconferencing. The authors described the feasibility and utility of this approach, as well as the unique nature of the therapeutic process, detailing the perspectives of 13 parents of children with TBI who participated in the program and 6 therapists who delivered the program. Nine of 13 parents preferred the web-based coaching to traditional treatment; they cited its ease of use and the comfort of doing it at home. Therapists uniformly liked coaching over the web despite the need to address boundaries and troubleshoot technological difficulties. Therapeutic alliance was comparable to traditional therapy with nearly all families expressing a strong connection to the therapist. Individuals with less computer experience particularly liked the program because it gave them access to the web and a sense of empowerment. These preliminary findings support the utility of web-based parenting skills training for families from diverse backgrounds, while underscoring the potential for clinical use with other underserved populations.

Adherence to Online Treatment

Gallego and Emmelkamp (2012) considered various challenges facing online treatments, either predictable or unforeseeable. Among those reviewed by those authors and in this chapter, the major challenge remains drop-out rates and adherence to online treatment. Two variables seem related to such a rate, one is extent of contact with a therapist, as discussed above, and the other is length of a program. Predictably, the shorter the program the lower the drop-out will be. Indeed, most programmed distance writing workbooks (L'Abate, 2011c) suggest that no more than six sessions be administered before a re-evaluation of outcome.

FUTURE TRENDS IN INTERNET-SUPPORTED MH INTERVENTIONS

Despite growing research in the past two decades involving Internet-supported or online mental health interventions, there has been only a few attempts to provide a synthesis of the research findings and future trends (Barak & Grohol (2011). The Internet has grown exponentially during this time, providing greater access to a wider population than ever before. Consequently, online mental health interventions have the potential to be cost-effective, convenient, and reach a more diverse population than traditional, face-to-face interventions. Barak & Grohol (2011) also reviewed and summarized the current research for online mental health interventions and discussed future trends. These interventions range from psycho-educational static web-pages and complex, personalized, interactive cognitive-behavioral-based self-help programs, to videoconferencing, self-help support groups, blogging, and professional-led online therapy (L'Abate, 2013c).

Future trends in online interventions include the greater prevalence of online therapy and the use of video chat and videoconferencing technologies to enhance and extend the therapeutic relationship. The use of texting or short message service (SMS), mobile communications, smart phone applications, gaming, and virtual worlds extends the intervention paradigm into new environments not always previously considered as intervention opportunities. Barak & Grohol (2011) found that there is strong evidence to support the effective use and future development of a variety of online mental health applications.

It is increasingly urgent for psychologists to confront the difficult questions raised by the way that information and communication technologies are altering not only health care, but also the human experience worldwide (Maheu, Pulier, McMenamin, & Posen, 2012). Whether psychologists embrace or resist aspects of technology, they should recognize how advanced technologies are changing the way we communicate and process information, anticipate needed growth, and prepare to meet ensuing challenges to professional psychology. Exponential growth of technology is enabling new mental health services, extending existing ones, and augmenting options available to individuals for self-monitoring and decision making, both with and without professional involvement. Professional organizations can help retain psychology's leadership position by promulgating more specific guidelines and policy for science, practice, and education. Protection of clients already requires new legal and regulatory initiatives for licensure, referrals, client education, privacy, screening, assessment, record keeping, reimbursement, and self-help product development. Protections for psychologists require new risk management procedures and adaptations by malpractice carriers as multidisciplinary teams evolve within and beyond health care into new public and private sector arenas. Key technologies that presage future trends include video teleconferencing, "smart" mobile devices, cloud computing, virtual worlds, virtual reality, and electronic games. Predicting change and adapting psychology accordingly will enable psychologists to future-proof their workplaces. Equipping future generations of psychologists and patients to collaborate more successfully in all potential growth areas requires educators and trainers to increase their focus on technology in graduate education, training, and supervision.

Mental illness imposes a staggering public health burden in USA (Comer & Barlow, 2014; L'Abate, 2001, 2002, 2007, 2013c, 2014), Although the past 40 years have witnessed tremendous advances in the identification of evidence-based practices (EBP) in psychological treatments, gaps persist between treatment in experimental settings and services available in the community. In response, considerable attention and large financial commitments have focused in recent years on broad dissemination and implementation efforts designed to improve the quality of psychological services delivered by a variety of generalist practitioners across practice settings. These advances hold enormous potential, and yet, given the tremendous diversity of mental health problems and human suffering, broad dissemination and implementation efforts to generalists alone may not be sufficient to adequately address the burden of mental illness. Some EBPs may prove too complex for universal implementation, and the time and expense required for quality dissemination and implementation preclude large scale training in the treatment of low base rate disorders. As dissemination and implementation efforts work to insure a quality generalist mental health workforce, herein Comer and Barlow highlight the vital need for available specialty care in the delivery of psychological treatments. Given traditional barriers that interfere with the accessibility of specialty care, Comer and Barlow *proposed the transformative potential of a specialty behavioral telehealth care workforce, transacting with the generalist practitioner workforce to collectively insure the highest quality and timely delivery of needed treatments to affected individuals* (italics mine). I proposed such a curriculum years ago (L'Abate, 2008a).

Emphasis on specialty telehealth care combined with a generalist workforce, as suggested by Comer and Barlow (2014), will inevitably lead to a hierarchy of different levels of board diplomats and doctorates overlooking, directing, and supporting a wide range of para-professionals specialized in the technical aspects of concrete and specific evaluations and mental health interventions online and offline (L'Abate, 2001, 2013b, 2013c). The more an organization grows in complexity the greater will be the need to differentiate various functions and matching roles necessary to complete the stated mission of that organization. This means that with growing specializations, MH professionals will need to start differentiating between technical versus para-professional roles, and para-professional roles from professional ones (L'Abate, 2001, 2008a, 2008b, 2013c). This differentiation will occur according to the degree of structure and, therefore, to the replicability of evaluations and interventions. For instance, SOPs in evaluation and re-evaluation can be administered and scored by clerical or technical personnel, while interpretation and reporting of test results could be left in the hands (and minds) of professionals, unless such an interpretation and results are obtained mechanically. The issue of structure in clinical interventions will be examined below.

Structured versus Unstructured Interventions

The basic issue in future Internet applications and interventions will lie on whether they are structured or unstructured, as discussed at length elsewhere (L'Abate, in press). Even though there are varying degrees of structure and, therefore replicability, the majority of these interventions will remain unfortunately unstructured and, therefore, as artistic practices, they will not be replicable, just as is the case of traditional F2F talk (L'Abate, 2013b, in press). Such a trend will continue to produce online -- as was the case offline—confusing and confused professional Towers of Babel unless professional organizations will make replicability of SOPs a major *sine-qua-non* requirement for responsible professional practices.

Identifying Who will Profit by which Online Treatment and Who will not

As the meta-analysis by Mewton, Smith, Rossouw, and Andrews (2014) as well as all the evidence cited in this volume indicate, we are still far away from identifying who will profit by which treatment, online and offline. The reason for such a failure can be explained in terms of an incorrect and misguided search for individuals rather than for concrete and specific concerns, reasons for referral, and symptomatic behaviors. No matter what holistic rhetoric may say, we cannot treat individuals, couples, of families but we can treat only the concrete and specific concerns, reasons for referral, and symptoms, that emanate from their personalities, relationships, and interactions. Of course, it is acknowledged that concerns, reasons for referral, and symptoms develop and grow within an interpersonal context (Cusinato & L'Abate, 2012; Hooper et al., 2014; L'Abate, 2005, 2013a, 2013b; L'Abate et al., 2010). However, by creating a new context based on concreteness and specificity in evaluation and interventions, MH professionals can address most concerns, reasons for referrals, and symptomatic behavior head-on, without distracting ourselves with abstractions and generalities that continue to plague psychology in general and clinical psychology practices in particular (L'Abate, in press).

Technology-based self-help and minimal contact therapies have been proposed as effective and low-cost interventions for anxiety and mood disorders. The present article reviewed the literature published before 2010 on these treatments for anxiety and depression using self-help and decreased therapist-contact interventions (Newman, Szkodny, Llera, & Przeworski, 2011). Treatment studies were examined by disorder as well as amount of therapist contact, ranging from self-administered therapy and predominantly self-help interventions to minimal contact therapy where the therapist is actively involved in treatment but to a lesser degree than traditional therapy and predominantly therapist-administered treatments involving regular contact with a therapist for a typical number of sessions. In the treatment of anxiety disorders, it was concluded that self-administered and predominantly self-help interventions are most effective for motivated clients. Conversely, minimal-contact therapies have demonstrated efficacy for the greatest variety of anxiety diagnoses when accounting for both attrition and compliance. Additionally, predominantly self-help computer-based cognitive and behavioral interventions are efficacious in the treatment of sub-threshold mood disorders. However, therapist-assisted treatments remain optimal in the treatment of clinical levels of depression. *Although the most efficacious amount of therapist contact varies by disorder, computerized treatments have been shown to be a less-intensive, cost-effective way to deliver empirically validated treatments for a variety of psychological problems* (italics author's).

Technology-based self-help and minimal contact therapies have been proposed as effective and low-cost interventions for addictive disorders, such as nicotine, alcohol, and drug abuse and addiction (Newman, Szkodny, Llera, & Przeworski, 2011). The present article reviewed the literature published before 2010 on computerized treatments for drug and alcohol abuse and dependence and smoking addiction. Treatment studies were examined by disorder as well as amount of therapist contact, ranging from self-administered therapy and predominantly self-help interventions to minimal contact therapy where the therapist is actively involved in treatment but to a lesser degree than traditional therapy and predominantly therapist-administered treatments involving regular contact with a therapist for a typical number of sessions. In the treatment of substance use and abuse it is concluded that *self-administered and predominantly self-help computer-based cognitive and behavioral interventions are efficacious, but some therapist contact is important for greater and more sustained reductions in addictive behavior* (italics ours).

Guided by the Uses and Gratifications (U&G) perspective, this study examined the influence of unwillingness to communicate, loneliness, Internet-use motives, and Internet (CMC) use and interaction (amount and types of use and self-disclosure) in online communication satisfaction and online relationship closeness. There were 261 participants in this study. Overall, participants who perceived their F2F communication to be rewarding, used CMC for self-fulfillment, and disclosed their personal feelings to others tended to feel close to their online partners. Moreover, those who used the Internet for purposes of self-fulfillment and affection and intended to disclose their feelings to others felt satisfied with their online communication. The associations among the constructs extend our knowledge of the U&G theoretical model, how and why people communicate interpersonally in CMC settings, and the influence of individual differences on CMC for relational communication (Pornsakulvanich, Haridakis, & Rubin, 2008).

This is one reason for creating dozens of concretely and specifically written, completely replicable interactive homework assignments, i. e., workbooks, that can be administered remotely at a distance between needy participants and helpful mental health professionals (Hooper et al., 2014; L'Abate, 1986, 1990, 1992, 2002, 2011c, in press; L'Abate, L'Abate, & Maino, 2005; Smyth & L'Abate, 2001). Many rationales given in previous writings just cited indicated that it is indeed possible to match a concern, a reason for referral, and symptomatic behavior with a concrete workbook that addresses the specific nature and context of that concern, reason for referral, and symptomatic behavior (L'Abate, 2013a, 2013b, 2013c). Evaluation and treatment can be indeed matched provided interactive practice exercises and homework assignments are part and parcel of every day responsible clinical practices.

THE ROLE OF THEORY IN ONLINE INTERVENTIONS

With the advancements of technology and its increasing use in all spheres of life, clinicians too are faced with the decision of whether to adopt or refrain from adopting certain innovations in their practice, as discussed in the Preface to this volume. For instance, Lovejoy, Demireva, Grayson, and McNamara (2009) discussed the process of adopting clinical innovations within a theoretical framework, namely diffusion of innovations theory (DIT; Rogers, 2003). DIT constructs were applied to the example of online therapy adoption into clinical practice. Nine adoption barriers were identified, including issues of dehumanizing the therapeutic environment, start-up cost and reimbursement, infrastructure and training, licensure and jurisdiction concerns, ethical guidelines, both client and clinician suitability factors, and professional reputation and acceptance within the field. The authors concluded with a theory-based discussion of activities that may help to accelerate the adoption of online therapy among professional psychologists. This model (and not a theory) and its applications will need further replication to be disseminated outside a narrow circle of followers. Nonetheless, I share its emphasis on the need for a theoretical background to guide clinical practice (Author's note).

As Hertlein and Blumer (2014) have argued: "The identification of a distinct field and framework allows for practicing therapists to organize their existing treatment approaches under an umbrella that takes into account the unique aspects of technology into their clients' lives (p. 200). Therefore, in addition to organizing knowledge and hopefully link theory with practice online as well as offline, the functions of a theory are many. First, one must differentiate among paradigms as a way to see reality from theories as inventions dependent on models that are in turn evaluated and validated through measurable dimensions (Colesso et al., 2014; L'Abate, 2009, 2010, 2013a, in press). Second, a theory's function is to integrate previous knowledge in a meaningful whole. Third, another function of a theory is to account for behaviors not heretofore visible to most viewers, develop new and original methods of evaluation, and then link concrete and specific interventions to specific parts of the theory. An example of such a theory is Relational Competence Theory (RCT), already cited above in a variety of sources (Cusinato & L'Abate, 2012; L'Abate et al., 2010). In competing with Attachment Theory (AT), however, RCT assumes the role of David versus Goliad, an upstart with minimal verification and validation outside of Italy and nowhere else versus AT that has been verified repeatedly around the world (L'Abate, 2013a).

Attachment Theory versus Relational Competence Theory

The purpose of this section is to compare Attachment Theory (AT) with Relational Competence Theory (RCT) according to at least five different comparisons. A previous critique of AT has been published already giving as many references as possible (L'Abate, 2013a). To avoid unnecessary duplication, no specific references to AT will be given here.

Reliance on Paper-and-Pencil Self-Report Questionnaires versus Observable Bases

Anxiety and Avoidance, as the major two basic dimensions of AT, are evaluated by paper-and-pencil self-reports. Nothing wrong with self-report except that these two dimensions are not shared by the psychological community in terms of two concretely and specifically visible dimensions of *space*-as evaluated by a distance among individuals, who approaches or avoids whom and what, and by *time*-evaluated by how fast or slow one approaches or avoid someone, something, or somewhat (Hooper et al., 2014; L'Abate, 2005, 2009). Unless, relying on self-report, both Anxiety and Avoidance are not directly visible but *inferred* constructs, or, at least no suggestions or recommendations are given on how to observe them directly in real life. The whole theory, therefore, hinges completely on self-report rather than on directly visible behaviors. As Lewis (2014, p. 209) noted: "The use of questionnaires may be helpful in generating hypotheses or in devising models of effect. However, they may well serve poorly as sources of data on parental behaviors as causes of children's outcomes." Furthermore, as Hooper et al. (2014) have shown, there are tremendous gaps in self-awareness, and consequently, in self-reporting in many apparently "normal" or at least functioning individuals. Self-report scales may be statistically valid, as those developed by AT researchers are, yet they could miss aspects of relationships that are outside the realm of awareness.

Description and Explanation of Functional and Dysfunctional Behavior

Another function of a theory is to describe and hopefully explain functional and dysfunctional behavior according to a variety of different but redundant and connected models and dimensions. Being presented linearly and non-hierarchically like RCT, AT fails to indicate how its components correlate with other components, as done by hierarchically presented RCT that mirrors dimensionally concrete psychiatric categories (Colesso, Cusinato, & L'Abate, 2013; Cusinato & L'Abate, 2012; L'Abate, 2005, 2006; L'Abate et al., 2010). Even though an attempt was made to link part of AT to certain selected psychiatric categories, such connections were at best speculative and at worst lacking empirical evidence.

Failure to Integrate Different Models into a Relational Whole

While RCT has attempted to expand and even explain 16 different theoretical models, such as resilience (L'Abate, 2009), bullism, parentification, parent alienation syndrome, and the Stockholm syndrome among others (Hooper et al., 2014). AT seemingly has not been able integrate diverse models available in the research literature-identity and intimacy- as present also in communication and relationship sciences (L'Abate, 2013a). If that is the case, what is the good of a theory?

Attachment as the Catch-All Concept to Describe and Explain All Relationships

Lewis (2014) has been especially critical of the attachment construct related specifically to the child-mother dyad and not considering a social network view (pp. 200-2008). There are many other direct and indirect influences that relate to an infant's socialization, including the father, other siblings, and accidental friends, and neighbors, as proposed and evaluated by

RCT. An egregious example of overusing the "attachment" construct is found in the research by Woolgar and Scott (2014), who found negative consequences of over-diagnosing attachment disorders in adopted children.

Failure to Connect Constructs to Specific Interventions

Thus far, AT has failed to link specific and concrete predictions from its components to specific therapeutic interventions. For instance, most of the interventions claiming to derive from AT were performed verbally, making practically impossible to link theory with practice, since words are not replicable, while programmed writing is replicable *ad infinitum* with definite interactive practice exercises derived directly from models of RCT (L'Abate, 2013a). Furthermore, AT includes a surplus of emotionally-related terms that do not show any clear and direct links to components of the theory. For instance, one of DCT's models (No. 15), about intimacy, defined is a the sharing of joys and hurt feelings as well as fears of hurt feelings (L'Abate, 2011a), including forgiveness of one's transgressions. From this definition derive quite a few concrete and specific interactive practice exercises or workbooks (L'Abate, 2011c).

CONCLUSION

The major important outcome of this review about research on online-offline interventions lies on finding a meager number of research studies about externalizing behaviors as seen most often in Cluster B personality disorders (see Chapter 6 of this volume). One could almost conclude that the population in most need of online interventions is found in jails and penitentiaries. In spite of early efforts to connect with representative members of that population (L'Abate, 1992, 2011c; L'Abate, Reed, & McMahan, 2001) through case studies, the field of distance and remote writing online with criminals and inmates using programmed and non-programmed writing remains widely open. Nonetheless, Gallego and Emmelkamp's (2012) early conclusion can be considered still valid:

Clearly, tele-therapy is not suited for all patients (e.g., patients who dissociate, psychotic and suicidal patients) and adequate measures have to be taken that such patients are not enrolled in tele-therapy programs. Further, the system must allow appropriate actions to be take in case of emergencies (see Kleespies, 2014 for an introduction to deal with emergencies, author's note).

There is a clear and urgent need of guidelines and formal regulation by professional associations of assessment through the Internet and tele- therapy" (p. 413).

APPENDICES

APPENDIX A. TELEMENTAL HEALTH OUTSIDE THE USA

The purpose of this Appendix is to include illustratively representative summaries about the status of telemental health outside USA. This inclusion excludes specific research performed in any of these countries whose origin is unknown or irrelevant.

Arabia

The internet is becoming a widely used source of accessing medical research through various on-line databases (Takriti, El-Sayeh, & Adams, 2005). This instant access to information is of benefit to busy clinicians and service users around the world. The population of the Arab World is comparable to that of the United States, yet it is widely believed to have a greatly contrasting output of randomized controlled trials related to mental health. This study was designed to investigate the existence of such research in the Arab World and also to investigate the availability of this research on-line. Survey of findings from three internet-based potential sources of randomized trials originating from the Arab world and relevant to mental health care. A manual search of an Arabic online current contents service identified 3 studies, MEDLINE, EMBASE, and PsycINFO searches identified only one study, and a manual search of a specifically indexed, study-based mental health database, PsiTri, revealed 27 trials. There genuinely seem to be few trials from the Arab world and accessing these on-line was problematic. Replication of some studies that guide psychiatric/psychological practice in the Arab world would seem prudent.

Australia

Videoconferencing for clinical genetics services, or telegenetics, is becoming an increasingly utilized method of delivering genetic counseling to rural areas; however, there has been little qualitative exploration of the practitioner's experience, particularly for hereditary breast/ovarian cancer counseling (Zilliacus, Meiser, Lobb, Dudding, 2010). Semi structured interviews were conducted with genetic practitioners (n=15) delivering tele-genetics services in New South Wales, Australia. Interviews explored experiences, perceived aims of the service, satisfaction, and the advantages and disadvantages of the technology. Interviews were audiotaped, transcribed, and thematically analyzed. Results: All practitioners were highly satisfied with telegenetics. They perceived the advantages of videoconferencing as primarily increased efficiency and convenience for genetic clinicians, minimized travel for the patient, reduced costs, and increased access to rural areas. Disadvantages included the inhibition of rapport building between genetic clinician and patient and the difficulty in detecting nonverbal cues. Telegenetics was seen as a structured interaction that allowed less time for emotional exploration than a traditional face-to-face consultation. Technical disadvantages involved visual resolution, connection speed, and interruptions to voice transmission. Conclusion: Practitioners were satisfied with telegenetics and perceived the advantages as outweighing the disadvantages.

Stain, Payne, Thienel, Michie, et al. (2011) conducted a pilot study of the feasibility of videoconferencing as a mode of neuropsychological assessment in young people (14–30 years) from a rural area of New South Wales experiencing early psychosis. All participants ($n = 11$) completed assessments both face-to-face and by videoconference at a bandwidth of 384 kbit/s. Assessments included confirmation of diagnosis, quality of life and neurocognitive functioning. There was a strong correlation between modes of assessment for most instruments. Bland-Altman plots indicated that in general the mean difference between face-to-face and videoconference modes of assessment was close to zero with significant bias only evident for general cognitive functioning (WTAR), where videoconferencing produced higher ratings than face-to-face assessments. Feedback from the participants indicated strong acceptability of assessment by videoconferencing, thus supporting further investigation of use of this mode of assessment for clinical and research purposes.

Wade, Elliott, and Hiller (2012) examined how Australian telehealth service providers perceived and addressed ethical, medico-legal and clinical governance matters arising from service delivery. Thirty-seven telehealth clinicians and managers were interviewed and a qualitative content analysis was conducted. The services covered six Australian jurisdictions and a range of clinical disciplines. There were 11 medical specialties, surgery, mental health, paediatrics, nursing and allied health. Thirty services (83%) used video consulting and 25 (68%) delivered services to rural areas. Telehealth was reported to be beneficial by reducing adverse events, improving health outcomes, offering increased patient choice of service delivery, and improving access to services for rural areas and home care. There were observations of gains or no change in patient-provider rapport compared to face-to-face communication, with some patients reportedly preferring video. Those interviewed reported some problems with privacy and security, and variable informed consent practices. No examples of malpractice were raised, although there was a common misperception that distant providers were not responsible for clinical care. With respect to clinical governance, telehealth was seen as enabling improved quality, integration and implementation of evidence-based care, and to be a major support for the rural health workforce. Although there were potential ethical, medico-legal and governance problems in Australian telehealth services, these had been easily managed in practice.

Canada

Telehealth coordinators practicing in Canada were invited to respond to an online survey and participate in a telephone interview. For the present study, the definition of 'telehealth' was limited to the use of videoconferencing (Lynch & Gay, 2012). The coordinators were recruited with the assistance of the Ontario Telemedicine Network (OTN) and the Canadian Telehealth Forum (CTF). The response rate to the online survey from the OTN cohort was 4% (n = 13) and from the CTF cohort was 36% (n = 34). Of the 47 people who completed the survey, 16 also participated in a telephone interview. Most respondents were female; their mean age was 40 years. Most telehealth coordinators had some form of post-secondary education. Most, 66% (n = 31) coordinated both clinical and educational videoconferences. About half of the telehealth coordinators (55%, n = 26) indicated that their job was dedicated solely to telehealth, although 32% (n = 15) reported that their jobs involved responsibilities outside telehealth. About half of the respondents worked full-time (51%, n = 24). Most respondents either strongly agreed or agreed with the statement that 'If a telehealth coordinator's role involves patient care then that individual should be a member of a regulated health profession'. The need for organizations to more clearly define the role, better recognize and support telehealth coordinators and develop mechanisms for continuing professional education and certification were recurrent themes in the interviews.

China

Internet addiction among college students has become a serious problem in China (Su, Fang, Miller, & Wang, 2011). This pilot study involved the development of an online expert system named Healthy Online Self-helping Center (HOSC) as an intervention tool to help those who wish to reduce online usage. The study also explored the effectiveness of HOSC for college students' Internet addiction behavior. Participants ($N = 65$) were recruited from a university in Beijing, and were randomly assigned to one of four conditions: using HOSC within a laboratory environment, using HOSC within a natural environment, using a non-interactive program, and a control group. All the participants were asked to answer questionnaires at the baseline and at the 1-month follow-up. The questionnaires included the participants' online hours per week, the legitimate ratio of Internet usage, online satisfaction, and the Young's Diagnostic Questionnaire. The results revealed that HOSC under both natural and laboratory environments could effectively reduce the participants' online hours per week as well as their Young's Diagnostic Questionnaire score, and improve online satisfaction at a 1-month follow-up. Participants using a non-interactive program also had similar results. The article concludes with a discussion of the limitations of the study, as well as the implications of the findings and future research directions.

Iraq

In the past 20 years, war and human rights violations have led to high rates of exposure to traumatic events among the Iraqi population (Wagner, Schulz, & Knaevelsrud, 2012). Due to the ongoing violence, many physicians and mental health professionals have left Iraq in recent years. The Internet offers new possibilities for the psychological treatment of PTSD in conflict areas. A therapist-supported cognitive-behavioral treatment manual that has been evaluated in Western countries was translated into Arabic and culturally adapted. The treatment was conducted via the Internet by Arabic-speaking therapists and was evaluated in an uncontrolled pilot study with 15 participants. Main outcome measures were PTSD Scale, depression, anxiety (Hopkins Symptom Check List-25 (HSCL-25)), and quality of life (EUROHIS). The intervention resulted in a highly significant decrease in symptoms of PTSD, depression, and anxiety. Quality of life was higher at post-treatment. All treatment effect sizes were in the large range, indicating a significant improvement in mental health symptoms and quality of life. Preliminary clinical evidence indicated that new technologies can be used to provide humanitarian aid in the form of e-mental health services, even in areas that remain highly unstable.

Ireland

Universities have a responsibility to develop appropriate interventions to respond to the mental health needs of their students (Richards, 2009). Students' use of technology is an integral part of how they communicate and relate to the world; it is reasonable to consider engaging the internet and Information and Communication Technologies (ICT) for mental health service delivery. Internet-delivered counseling brings with it many distinct advantages, but also challenges. Investigating the effectiveness of any internet-delivered counseling intervention is important so as to establish a sound evidence-based practice. A unique feature of online delivery is that the internet can facilitate community and therefore allow counseling interventions to act therapeutically for an online community of users. This paper reported on the use of the online counseling service at Trinity College Dublin, including its uptake and usage, the issues and benefits of online counseling to students and whether clients are satisfied with their experience of online counseling. The paper highlighted the positive effect of disinhibition and the therapeutic benefit of writing. Single session counseling is discussed as a model that fits the experience of users and the service provider. Users have reported satisfaction with online counseling and the service's impact within the community of users is complementary. The benefits of increasing access, flexibility and on-time and on-demand services are given attention as is the use of online counseling as an element of a stepped care approach to service delivery.

Japan

Web 2.0 has improved interactions among peers on the Internet, especially for the many online patient communities that have emerged over the past decades (Setoyama, Yamazaki, & Namayama, 2011). Online communities are said to be particularly beneficial peer support resources for patients with breast cancer. However, most studies of online patient communities have focused on those members who post actively (posters), even though there are many members who participate without posting (lurkers). In addition, little attention has been paid to the usage of online communities among non-English-speaking patients. The present study explored the differences in peer support received by lurkers and posters in online breast cancer communities. It also examined the effects of such support on both groups' mental health. The authors conducted an exploratory, descriptive, cross-sectional, Web-based survey among members of four Japanese online breast cancer communities. In an online questionnaire, they asked questions regarding socio-demographics, disease-related characteristics, mental health, participation in online communities, and peer support received from those communities. Of the 465 people who accessed the questionnaire, 253 completed it. Of the respondents, 113/220 (51.4%) were lurkers. There was no significant difference between lurkers and posters with regard to socio-demographic variables. About half of the posters had been given a diagnosis of breast cancer less than a year previously, which was a significantly shorter period than that of the lurkers (P = .02).

The 5 support functions extracted by factor analysis were the same for both posters and lurkers. These were emotional support/helper therapy, emotional expression, conflict, advice, and insight/universality. When the support scores were calculated, insight/universality scored highest for both posters and lurkers, with scores that were not significantly different between the two groups. Among the 5 support scores, emotional support/helper therapy and emotional expression were significantly higher among posters. For posters, emotional support/helper therapy and advice were negatively correlated with the anxiety subscale of the Hospital Anxiety and Depression Scale. Emotional expression, advice, and insight/universality were negatively correlated with the anxiety subscale for lurkers. The authors found that posters felt they received more benefits from online communities than lurkers did, including emotional support, helping other patients, and expressing their emotions. Yet even lurkers were found to gain a certain amount of peer support through online communities, especially with regard to advice and insight/universality. The results demonstrated that participation in online communities--even as a lurker--may be beneficial to breast cancer patients' mental health.

Although the Internet has been widely used in Japan, the quality of information on mental health-related issues has not been evaluated so far (Nemoto, Tachikawa, Sodeyama, Endo, et al., 2007). The purpose of the present study was to investigate the current status of Japanese websites that deal with mental health, mental disorders, and their associated matters. Using a search engine, Google, 37 websites were identified that exclusively contain information on mental health or mental disorders. The characteristics of the sites were then examined, along with variety of mental disorders mentioned, and quality of contents for each of the 37 websites. More than half of the websites were set up, at least in part, for commercial purposes and only 27% of sites were owned by professionals. Mood disorder, panic disorder, and schizophrenia were the three most commonly referred disorders on websites. Aside from some exceptions, the quality of information was inadequate, especially that regarding treatment. Most of the websites on mental health and mental disorders examined in the present study have scope for improvement. The challenge is to establish a system to evaluate the sites and to motivate each webmaster to improve the sites.

New Zealand

Both congestive heart failure and chronic obstructive pulmonary disease are more common among Māori than non-Māori people, and the cultural acceptability of home-based remote monitoring technology has not been tested. Venter, A., et al. (2012). conducted a 12-month pilot trial of home telemonitoring. Patients were randomly assigned to the control and intervention groups. Patients in the control group showed no clear differences in quality of life at the end of the trial. The telehealth group showed a consistent trend towards improved quality of life on several instruments, including the SF-36, the St George Respiratory Questionnaire and the K10 questionnaire; the improvement in the latter was significant. Hospitalizations were reduced in both the control (−19%) and telehealth group (−25%). Patient interviews indicated that the technology was acceptable to most patients and their families, including the Māori. The results from the pilot trial suggest that wider implementation with a cost benefit evaluation could be worthwhile.

Nigeria

This study has empirically established that Information and Communication Technology {ICT} as one of the new trends in Educational Sciences could be applied in counseling practice in Anambra State of Nigeria (Oraegbunam, 2009). Results of the study revealed that ICT could be highly applied in the counseling practice. No significant difference was observed in the mean scores of urban and rural based counselors. In view of the findings, recommendations were proffered. These include a curricula review of computer science courses, intensification of ICT training and skill acquisition to make both staff and students ICT compliant. It was also recommended among others that all institutions of learning should be provided with facilities to enhance access to the internet.

Norway

Norwegian psychologists' use of and attitudes towards e-media such as email and mobile text messaging in interaction with clients (e-therapy) were explored. A two-dimensional scale for measuring attitudes towards e-therapy was developed. A total of 1040 (23%) members of the psychologist association responded to a questionnaire June 2003. Of these, 45% had used e-media in interaction with clients. The mean reported attitude towards e-therapy was neutral, with only 3% of the psychologists feeling that use of e-media between client and therapist is unacceptable. Having a psychodynamic theoretical stance was related to attitudes towards e-therapy. Positive attitude was related to clinical use of email and Short Messages Service (SMS). It appears likely that e-therapy will become more common, and that therapist's attitudes will be related to such use (Wangberg, Gammon, & Spitznogle, 2007).

Internet-based cognitive behavioral therapy (ICBT) is a promising approach to the prevention and reduction of depressive symptoms among adolescents. This study aimed to evaluate the feasibility and efficacy of disseminating a self-directed internet-based mental health intervention (MoodGYM) in senior high schools (Lillevoll, Vangberg, Griffiths, Waterloo, at al., 2014). It also sought to investigate possible effects of tailored and weekly e-mail reminders on initial uptake and adherence to the intervention. A baseline survey was conducted in four senior high schools in two Norwegian municipalities (n = 1337). 52.8% (707/1337) of the students consented to further participation in the trial and were randomly allocated to one of three MoodGYM intervention groups (tailored weekly e-mail reminder (n = 175), standardized weekly e-mail reminder (n = 176) or no e-mail reminder (n = 175)) or a waitlist control group (n = 180). We tested for effects of the intervention on depression and self-esteem using multivariate analysis of variance, effects of tailored e-mail and self-reported current need of help on initial uptake of the intervention using logistic regression and the effect of weekly e-mails on adherence using ordinal regression.

There was substantial non-participation from the intervention, with only 8.5% (45/527) participants logging on to MoodGYM, and few proceeding beyond the first part of the program. No significant effect on depression or self-esteem was found among the sample as a whole or among participants with elevated depression scores at baseline. Having a higher average grade in senior high school predicted initial uptake of the intervention, but tailored e-mail and self-reported current need of help did not. Weekly e-mail prompts did not predict adherence. The main reasons for non-use reported were lack of time/forgetting about it and doubt about the usefulness of the program. The overall conclusion of this study was that disseminating a self-directed internet-based intervention to a school population proved difficult despite steps taken to reduce barriers in terms of tailoring feedback and dispatching weekly e-mail reminders. Providing mental health interventions within the school environment is likely to ensure better uptake among senior high school students, but there is a need to effectively communicate that such program can be helpful.

United Kingdom

A major use of the of the internet is for health information-seeking. There has been little research into its use in relation to mental health (Powell & Clarke, 2006). The aim of this study was to investigate the prevalence of internet use for mental health information-seeking and its relative importance as a mental health information source the Method General population survey. Questions covered internet use, past psychiatric history and the 12-item General Health Questionnaire. Eighteen per cent of all internet users had used the internet for information related to mental health. The prevalence was higher among those with a past history of mental health problems and those with current psychological distress. Only 12% of respondents selected the internet as one of the three most accurate sources of information, compared with 24% who responded that it was one of the three sources they would use. Apparently, the internet has a significant role in mental health information-seeking. The internet is used more than it is trusted.

Three trends in the evolution of the UK Learndirect advice service are identified: the partial migration from telephone to web-based services; the trend within the telephone service from information/advice-oriented interventions to more guidance-oriented interventions; and the move from a mainly learning-oriented service to a more career-oriented service (Watts & Dent, 2008). The extent to which these trends are due to changing patterns of customer needs and behaviors, or the effects of policy decisions reflected in social marketing campaigns, was reviewed. Comparable information from New Zealand is presented to indicate the impact of investment in such marketing. Implications for the proposed integration of the Learndirect service in England into a new careers service for adults are discussed. A number of more general conclusions were noted.

Taiwan

A 3-month videoconference interaction program with family members has been shown to decrease depression and loneliness in nursing home residents (Tsai & Tsai, 2011). However, little is known about the long-term effects on residents' depressive symptoms, social support, and loneliness. The purpose of this longitudinal quasi-experimental study was to evaluate the long-term effectiveness of a videoconference intervention in improving nursing home residents' social support, loneliness, and depressive status over 1 year. The authors purposively sampled 16 nursing homes in various areas of Taiwan. Elderly residents (N = 90) of these nursing homes meeting our inclusion criteria were divided into an experimental (n = 40) and a comparison (n = 50) group. The experimental group received at least 5 minutes/week for 3 months of videoconference interaction with their family members in addition to usual family visits, and the comparison group received regular family visits only. Data were collected in face-to face interviews on social support, loneliness, and depressive status using the Social Support Behaviors Scale, University of California Los Angeles Loneliness Scale, and Geriatric Depression Scale, respectively, at four times (baseline, 3 months, 6 months, and 12 months after baseline). Data were analyzed using the generalized estimating equation approach. After the videoconferencing program, participants in the experimental group had significantly lower mean change in instrumental social support scores at 6 months (-0.42, P = .03) and 12 months (-0.41, P = .03), and higher mean change in emotional social support at 3 (0.74, P < .001) and 12 months (0.61, P = .02), and in appraisal support at 3 months (0.74, P = .001) after adjusting for confounding variables. Participants in the experimental group also had significantly lower mean loneliness and depressive status scores at 3 months (-5.40, P < .001; -2.64, P < .001, respectively), 6 months (-6.47, P < .001; -4.33, P < .001), and 12 months (-6.27, P = .001; -4.40, P < .001) compared with baseline than those in the comparison group. This videoconference program had a long-term effect in alleviating depressive symptoms and loneliness for elderly residents in nursing homes. This intervention also improved long-term emotional social support and short-term appraisal support, and decreased residents' instrumental social support. However, this intervention had no effect on informational social support.

Turkey

This is a qualitative study which aimed to find out 15 counselors-in-training students' attitudes towards e-counseling (Tanrikulu, 2009). In order to determine their attitudes, an interview schedule which included questions exploring their attitudes towards online counseling as counselors and clients was developed. The data collected through semi-structured individual interviews were subjected to qualitative data analysis. The results showed that none of the counseling trainees has adequate information and education on the field of online counseling. Although they have some concerns, all participants have positive views about online counseling, and they think it is high time online counseling was incorporated into counselor education in Turkey.

From: http://kspope.com/telepsychology.php
Downloaded 6-11-12

APPENDIX B. TELEPSYCHOLOGY, TELEHEALTH, & INTERNET-BASED THERAPY

Kenneth S. Pope, Ph.D., ABPP

The resources below may help therapists, counselors, and other clinicians to keep abreast of the rapidly evolving professional guidelines, research, treatments, innovations, and practices in the areas of telepsychology, telehealth, internet-based therapy.

PLEASE NOTE: This site is designed to be fully accessible for people with disabilities; please follow this link to change text size, color; please follow this link for other accessibility.

Links to 15 Sets of Professional Guidelines Focusing on Telepsychology and Internet-Based Therapy:

NOTE: Please follow this link for a more comprehensive array of professional standards and guidelines than those below.

American Medical Association: Guidelines for Patient-Physician Electronic Mail

American Medical Informatics Association: Guidelines for the Clinical Use of Electronic Mail with Patients

American Telemedicine Association (ATA): Evidence-Based Practice for Telemental Health

American Telemedicine Association (ATA): Telemedicine Standards & Guidelines

Association for Counselling & Therapy Online: Professional Conduct & Code of Ethics

California Board of Psychology: Information on Telepsychology

Canadian Psychological Association: Ethical Guidelines for Psychologists Providing Psychological Services via Electronic Media

Centers for MedicareU.S. Department of Health & Human Services: Final Rule for Telemedicine Credentialing & Privileging

Federation of State Medical Boards of the United

International Society for Mental Health Online: Suggested Principles for the Online Provision of Mental Health Services

National Association of Social Workers & Association of Social Work Boards: Standards for Technology and Social Work Practice

National Board for Certified Counselors & Center for Credentialing and Education, Inc.: The Practice of Internet Counseling

New Zealand

Ohio Psychological Association: Telepsychology Guidelines

Online Therapy Institute: Ethical Framework for the Use of Social Media by Mental Health Professionals

PLEASE NOTE: In 1997, the American Psychological Association issued a policy statement: "APA Statement on Services by Telephone, Teleconferencing, and Internet." However, when the 2003 ethics code was adopted, APA announced that the policy statement was based on the prior (i.e., 1992) ethics code, and that therefore the policy statement "is considered inactive." A new policy statement has not yet been issued.

APPENDIX C. GUIDELINES FOR PREVENTION IN PSYCHOLOGY INTRODUCTION

The effectiveness of prevention to enhance human functioning and reduce psychological distress has been demonstrated (Catalano, Berglund, Ryan, Lonczak, & Hawkins, 2002; Greenberg, Domitrovich, & Bumbarger, 2001; O'Connell, Boat, & Warner, 2009). Successful preventive interventions are typically theory driven, culturally relevant, developmentally appropriate, and delivered across multiple contexts (Nation et al., 2003). Preventive services and interventions help to further the health and well-being of individuals, communities, and nations (Satcher, 2000; World Health Report, 2008). Expanding preventive services reduces the costs of mental health care (Tolan & Dodge, 2005), while emerging technological innovations (e.g., telehealth) offer promise for preventive interventions (Bull, 2011; Chinman, Tremain, Imm, & Wandersman, 2009).

From infancy through adulthood, access to preventive services and interventions is important to improve the quality of life and human functioning and reduce illness and premature death (Grunberg & Klein, 2009; Konnert, Gatz, & Hertzsprung, 1999). Prevention has typically taken a developmental approach, focusing on children and adolescents, in order to facilitate trajectories leading to positive outcomes (O'Connell et al., 2009). Children and adolescents are at significant risk for substance abuse, violence, sexually transmitted infections, and their access to quality health services is limited (CDC, 2007; Weissberg, Walberg, O'Brien, & Kuster, 2003). Thus, normal development may be impeded at large costs to society, and additional strains on families. In any given year, 14-20% of children and adolescents experience a mental, emotional, or behavioral disorder (O'Connell et al., 2009). In addition, national surveys show that the majority of youth who could potentially benefit from mental health services do not receive services (Ringel & Sturm, 2001). Early and focused interventions can limit the length and severity of symptoms and enhance functioning (Cicchetti & Toth, 1992; Durlak, Weissberg, & Pachan, 2010). Prevention also includes the collaborative design and delivery of strengths-based health promotion and environmental improvement strategies (e.g., Cowen, 1985). Health promotion approaches equip people with life skills and coping competencies, such as problem-solving skills, contributing to their capacity to live more fully while being better able to withstand future stressful life events.

Preventive services and interventions also address issues of health, educational, and social inequities that reflect disparities across demographic groups such as those based on race, gender, and socio-economic class. Environmental improvement prevention strategies, such as consultation to improve community-family-school coordination or interventions to help communities create well-paying jobs, aim to inform social policy, which can minimize or eliminate factors contributing to unhealthy functioning.

The importance of prevention is consistent with the 2010 US Patient Protection and Affordable Care Act which calls for expansion of preventive services to maximize positive health outcomes (www.healthcare.gov) as well as the U.S. National Prevention Strategy which "provides unprecedented opportunity to shift the nation from a focus on sickness and disease to one on wellness and prevention" throughout the lifespan (National Prevention, Health Promotion, and Public Health Council, 2011). Several disciplines, other than psychology, have been historically and currently active in prevention (e.g., public health, social work).) However, beginning in the mid-20th century with the field of community psychology, psychology has begun to play an increasingly important role (e.g., Eby, Chin, Rollock, Schwartz, & Worell, 2011). Even with the increased focus on prevention, psychology training programs rarely require specific courses on prevention (O'Neil & Britner, 2009) . In particular, conceptualizations about best practices in prevention, particularly at the environmental level, are lacking (Snyder & Elliott, 2005). In addition, the Ethical Principles of Psychologists and Code of Conduct (APA Ethics Code) (APA, 2002a, 2010) does not fully address unique ethical issues that may arise in prevention (e.g., Schwartz & Hage, 2009). Therefore, psychologists engaged in prevention can benefit from a set of guidelines that address and inform prevention practices.

Purpose

APA (2002a) refers to guidelines as "statements that suggest or recommend specific professional behavior, endeavors, or conduct for psychologists. Guidelines differ from standards in that standards are mandatory and may be accompanied by an enforcement mechanism. . . . guidelines are aspirational . . . intended to facilitate the continued systematic development of the profession and to help assure a high level of professional practice … . Guidelines are not intended to be mandatory or exhaustive and may not be applicable to every professional and clinical situation. They are not definitive and they are not intended to take precedence over the judgment of psychologists" (p. 1050). Accordingly, the Guidelines for Prevention in Psychology(cited as Prevention Guidelines or Guidelines for the remainder of this document) are intended to "inform psychologists, the public, and other interested parties regarding desirable professional practices" (APA, 2002a, p. 1049) in prevention.

The Prevention Guidelines are, in part, practice guidelines and different from treatment guidelines as defined by APA (2002a). The Guidelines are recommended for the practice of psychology across areas that engage psychologists. The Guidelines are consistent with federal and state laws and regulations. In the event of a conflict between the Guidelines and any federal or state law or regulation, the law or regulation in question supersedes these Guidelines. Psychologists are encouraged to use their education and skills to resolve any conflicts in a way that best conforms to both law and to ethical practice. The Guidelines are consistent with principles of the APA Ethics Code (APA, 2002a, 2010) particularly principles D (justice) and E (respect for people's rights and dignity).

Background

APA convention symposia (Romano, 2002; Kenny, 2003; Hage & Romano, 2006) initiated the development of these Guidelines, followed by a paper describing prevention best practices (Hage, Romano, Conyne, Kenny, Matthews, Schwartz, & Waldo, 2007). These Guidelines were later introduced as new business for APA Council of Representatives whereupon they underwent significant review, including APA governance and public comment periods, in accordance with Association policy relevant to Guidelines (APA Association Rule 30-8).

Definitions

Prevention has been conceptualized as including one or more of the following: (a) stopping a problem behavior from ever occurring, (b) delaying the onset of a problem behavior, especially for those at-risk for the problem, (c) reducing the impact of a problem behavior, (d) strengthening knowledge, attitudes, and behaviors that promote emotional and physical well-being, and (e) promoting institutional, community, and government policies that further physical, social, and emotional well-being of the larger community (Romano & Hage, 2000). This conceptualization is consistent with Caplan's (1964) definition that identified prevention interventions as primary, secondary, and tertiary prevention, and the definition by Gordon (1987) that identified prevention interventions as universal, selected, and indicated for those not at-risk, at-risk, and experiencing early signs of problems, respectively. The Gordon (1987) conceptualization was adopted by the Institute of Medicine (IOM; Mrazek & Haggerty, 1994). A follow-up report of the IOM broadened this universal, selective, and indicated framework to include "the promotion of mental health" (O'Connell et al., 2009, p, 65).

Throughout this document, the terms "prevention," "preventive intervention(s)," "preventive program(s)", or "preventive services" are used. Activities subsumed by these rubrics could focus on any of the five aspects of prevention included in the Romano and Hage (2000) conceptualization of prevention. Although space precludes a thorough exegesis of all types of programs, decisions about how and when to intervene might lead to different outcomes, different ancillary effects, and different ways of approaching issues within cultures and settings.

Documentation of Need

The Prevention Guidelines are recommended based on their potential benefits to the public and the professional practice of psychology. The Guidelines support prevention as an important area of practice, research, and training for psychologists. The Guidelines give increased attention to prevention within APA, encouraging psychologists to become involved with preventive activities relevant to their area of practice.

The National Research Council and Institute of Medicine's Committee on the Prevention of Mental Disorders and Substance Abuse among Children, Youth and Young Adults: Research Advances and Promising Interventions states, "Infusing a prevention focus into the public consciousness requires development of a shared public vision and attention at a higher national level than currently exists" (O'Connell et al., 2009, p. 5). The Guidelines provide added visibility to the importance of prevention across professional practice areas and among the public. The Guidelines also support the U.S. Department of Health and Human Services' calls for health promotion and prevention in *Healthy People* publications outlining national health goals. *Healthy People 2020* continues the tradition of earlier publications by setting goals to eliminate preventable disease, achieve health equity, eliminate health disparities, create social and physical environments to promote good health, and promote healthy development and healthy behaviors across the life-span. Other U.S. government bodies have also emphasized the importance of prevention to the overall health and well-being of the population (Mrazek, 2002).

The U.S. 2010 Patient Protection and Affordable Care Act includes preventive services as an important component of overall health care. The legislation strives to make wellness and preventive services affordable and accessible by requiring health plans to cover preventive services without co-payments. These services include counseling to improve habits of lifestyle (e.g., proper nutrition, weight management), counseling to reduce depression, and preventive services to foster healthy birth outcomes (www.healthcare.gov/law/aboutprovisions/services/index.html).

The contributions and leadership of psychologists are critical in implementing a prevention focus in the health care system. Evidence increasingly suggests that mental illness, such as depression, is linked to chronic health issues such as heart disease and diabetes (Volgelzangs et al., 2008). Therefore, the Guidelines identify best practices for psychologists who engage in preventive activities relating to the interface between physical health and emotional well-being.

The Guidelines also respond to policies and legislation that aim to prevent and reduce problems such as chemical addictions, depression, suicide, school bullying, social violence, and obesity (Mrazek & Haggerty, 1994). The Guidelines respond to social disparities, discrimination, and bias against people based on (but not limited to) their race, ethnicity, immigrant status, sexual orientation, age, gender identity, socioeconomic status, religion, HIV serostatus, physical and psychological health status, and gender (APA, 2003; APA, 2007; Kenny, Horne, Orpinas, & Reese, 2009). The Guidelines offer recommendations to psychologists as they respond to public policy and legislative initiatives that promote positive health behaviors in the name of prevention and health promotion (O'Connell et al., 2009). In addition, the Guidelines endeavor to apply "the science and practice of psychology to the fundamental problems of human welfare and social justice and the promotion of equitable and just treatments of all segments of society through education, training, and public policy" (APA 2010 Annual Report, p. 517).

The Guidelines offer guidance to psychologists on several levels including supporting the value of prevention as important work of psychologists and providing recommendations that give greater visibility to prevention among psychologists regardless of specialty area or work setting (Snyder & Elliott, 2005).

Expiration

Given the evolving nature of prevention, the Guidelines are scheduled to expire in the year 2020. After this date, users are encouraged to contact the APA Practice Directorate to determine if the document remains in effect. The year 2020 was selected because it coincides with the decennial *Healthy People* publications, which set national health goals for the U.S. every 10 years. In addition, it is expected that the U.S. Patient Protection and Affordable Care Act will be implemented fully by 2014, providing a reasonable time frame for these Guidelines, given the evolving nature of health care and psychology's place within the spectrum of health care services and research.

Guidelines

Guideline 1. Psychologists Are Encouraged to Select and Implement Preventive Interventions That Are Theory- and Evidence-Based

Rationale

Preventive interventions that demonstrate sustained effectiveness can be considered as meeting the highest standard for efficacy and maximum benefits to the consumer (National Institute of Mental Health, 1998). Consistent with foundational principles in psychology, theory and research should be inseparably tied to prevention practice. Research suggests that programs developed from a sound theoretical framework are more effective than programs that are not theoretically-based (Weissberg, Kumpfer et al., 2003). Also, preventive programs that are based on theory and regularly evaluated are more likely to consider risk and protective factors that operate across multiple contexts (Black & Krishnakumar, 1998), especially for groups who are historically marginalized (e.g., women, people of color). Accountability to client populations, funding agencies, and policy-makers demands that prevention practices be grounded in theory and research (Vera & Reese, 2000).

Application

Psychologists are encouraged to conduct preventive programs that have been rigorously evaluated (Guterman, 2004; Weissberg, Kumpfer, & Seligman, 2003). While no single theoretical perspective is suggested, psychologists are encouraged to select theoretically-based preventive approaches when considering their prevention goals. The theoretical frameworks and intervention strategies of positive psychology, positive youth development, applied developmental science, risk and resilience, health promotion, competence enhancement, and wellness, among others, can be selected and integrated when designing preventive interventions that will simultaneously prevent negative outcomes and enhance positive outcomes (Weissberg, Kumpfer et al., 2003). It is recommended that preventive programs be selected based on a careful review of empirical evidence in order to choose programs that are empirically supported for their specific contexts and specified goals, in addition to identifying how these relate to both multicultural issues and concerns generated by social inequities. Therefore, it is recommended that psychologists stay informed regarding current outcome research in prevention science to help ensure that the preventive programs they implement offer the most promise for the identified goals and population.

Guideline 2. Psychologists Are Encouraged to Use Socially and Culturally Relevant Preventive Practices Adapted to the Specific Context in Which They Are Implemented

Rationale

Given the increasing diversity of the U.S. population, it is crucial that preventive programs be designed, selected, and implemented with consideration of cultural relevance and cultural competence. Historically, many preventive programs were developed by professionals working with urban and suburban middle class communities and reflect heterosexual European-American values and methods; further, many did not address the unique issues faced by persons with disabilities. Preventive programs that lack relevance to the lives of participants will often fail (Lerner, 1995). Even when a preventive program is effective in one setting, it may not be effective in another setting with different populations (e.g., rural vs. urban communities; individuals above and below the federal poverty guidelines). Research suggests that programs perceived as socially and culturally relevant by their constituents have a greater likelihood of being sustained (Vera & Reese, 2000). As Trickett et al. (2011) note: "Culture is not seen as something to which interventions are tailored; rather, culture is a fundamental set of defining qualities of community life out of which interventions flow" (p. 1412).

Because risk and protective factors are found within individuals and in the multiple social contexts in which individuals are situated, prevention programs that attend to both individual and contextual factors are most advantageous. Focusing only on individuals and the more proximal context of the family may place undue responsibility and blame on the individual and the individual's milieu, without recognizing the roles played by social institutions and culture in determining and sustaining positive human outcomes (Kenny & Hage, 2009). Therefore, psychologists strive to understand the cultural worldviews and community contexts of individuals in order to strengthen prevention interventions, especially interventions that were developed for one cultural group and implemented in another (O'Connell et al., 2009).

Application

Psychologists are encouraged to be aware of, and articulate, the evidence that support their selection of specific prevention programs for implementation in different cultural contexts (Reese & Vera, 2007). Along this line, existing programs may need significant adaptation, or new programs may need to be developed, to meet social, cultural, community and developmental norms of program participants, and to ensure access to all members. Technological advances, such as the use of web-based preventive interventions and social media to promote, deliver, and assess prevention interventions can assist with this process. Psychologists are encouraged to recognize the diversity that exists within cultural groups as cultural values may differ by race, ethnicity, social class, family income, gender, gender identity, sexual orientation, geographic region, education, ability, and acculturation level (Kumpfer, Alvarado, Smith, & Bellamy, 2002). Psychologists are encouraged to examine cultural assumptions and biases of specific preventive programs, and consult the APA's (2003) *Guidelines on Multicultural Education, Training, Research, Practice, and Organizational Change for Psychologists* and the *Guidelines for Assessment of and Intervention with Persons with Disabilities* (APA, 2012) in integrating considerations of culture in the design, implementation, and evaluation of prevention interventions. It is important for psychologists to acquire and demonstrate cultural competence across prevention activities, and to strive to work sensitively with diverse populations. This typically means that the psychologist must immerse him/herself in the community and culture in order to be a sensitive partner with the community.

Psychologists endeavor to include relevant stakeholders in all aspects of prevention planning and implementation to ensure program fit with the local culture and to build community investment in the program. In order to ensure that preventive programs meet local norms, it is recommended that psychologists engage in careful planning and ongoing monitoring and evaluation of programs (Nation et al., 2003). Dynamic trial designs have been proposed that avoid problems associated with randomized clinical trials and focus on whether significant information is lost as the intervention proceeds (Jason & Glenwick, 2012), whether there are unintended consequences (positive and negative) that result from the intervention, and how to consider issues of diversity when statistical power may be low (Rapkin & Trickett, 2005).

Guideline 3. Psychologists Are Encouraged to Develop and Implement Interventions That Reduce Risks and Promote Human Strengths

Rationale

Early prevention interventions focused on reducing risks or causes of psychological dysfunction (Conyne, 2004). However, psychological research has identified personal and environmental protective factors that may also mitigate the probability of negative outcomes in the face of risk and that contribute to optimal health. Research indicates that prevention is most beneficial when attempts to reduce risk are direct and are combined with efforts to build strengths and protective factors (Eccles & Appleton, 2002; Vera & Reese, 2000). Focusing only on building competencies or only on preventing problems may not be as effective as addressing both competencies and problems (Catalano et al., 2002).

Application

Psychologists are encouraged to consider and ameliorate factors that contribute to risk and also to recognize and promote factors that enhance human strengths. Prevention programs can seek to reduce or eliminate factors, such as socioeconomic disparities, negative peer influences, family dysfunction, and school failure, or they can seek to increase social competencies and other protective factors (O'Connell, et al., 2009). Although psychologists may consider only the benefits of either a risk reduction or strength promotion approach, an optimal approach is to address both. Protective factors, such as socio-emotional skills, interpersonal connection, ethical decision-making, graduating from high school, school-to-work transitions, civic engagement, and proper nutrition might be selected as foci of interventions based upon their malleability and their relevance to daily life (Eccles & Appleton, 2002; Nation et al., 2003; Stone et al., 2003). For instance, a focus on expanding the resilience that historically marginalized groups have demonstrated, despite obstacles, might also serve to enhance strengths in other arenas of life (Singh et al., 2011; Singh & McKleroy, 2011).

An emphasis on simultaneously reducing risks and developing competencies is consistent with research on positive youth development, empowerment, advocacy, and participatory community research. Positive youth development posits that (a) protective factors reduce the likelihood of maladaptive outcomes under conditions of risk and (b) freedom from risk is not synonymous with preparation for life (Catalano, Hawkins, Berglund, Pollard, & Arthur, 2002; Pittman et al., 2001). The APA *Task Force on Prevention: Promoting Strength, Resilience, and Health in Young People* recommended that prevention encompass the goals of reducing health problems and promoting health and social competence (Weissberg, Kumpfer, & Seligman, 2003).

Similarly, empowerment interventions focus on helping individuals master and maintain control over life situations. Inherently, empowerment is concerned with competencies and strengths (Zimmerman, 1995; Zimmerman, Israel, Schulz, & Checkoway, 1992). Advocacy interventions also have been implemented with populations such as adjudicated youth (e.g., Smith, Wolf, Cantillon, Thomas, & Davidson, 2004), and women experiencing intimate partner violence (Allen, Bybee, & Sullivan, 2004). And, finally, Participatory Action Research (PAR) interventions, which focus on researcher/participant collaborations, and, thus, utilizing strengths and competencies of the participants, have been successfully implemented with diverse groups of youth (e.g., Foster-Fishman, Law, Lichty, & Aoun, 2010; Jason, Keys, Suarez-Balcazar, Taylor, & Davis, 2003; Smith, Davis & Bhowmik, 2010). It is recommended that PAR be a genuine community/researcher partnership (i.e., the development of shared goals, shared methods, and shared sense of the value of the project and the findings) to successfully implement the methodology (Trickett, 2011).

Guideline 4. Psychologists Are Encouraged to Incorporate Research and Evaluation As Integral to Prevention Program Development and Implementation, Including Consideration of Environmental Contexts That Impact Prevention

Rationale

Prevention research encompasses "theory and practice related to the prevention of social, physical, and mental health problems, including etiology, methodology, epidemiology, and intervention" (O'Connell et al., 2009, p. xxvvii). At its best, prevention research addresses multifaceted contexts (biological, psychological, and socio-cultural levels) and functions (pre-intervention epidemiology, preventive interventions, and preventive service delivery systems) (National Institute of Mental Health, 1998). The contexts and functions of prevention research can inform each other. Problems and their prevention occur at interrelated biological, psychological and socio-cultural levels. Epidemiological research can identify targets for preventive interventions; evaluation of interventions can identify preferred approaches that can be incorporated into service delivery systems; the effectiveness and efficiency of service delivery systems can be assessed by examining their impact on epidemiology. At all stages of the research process, the dynamic interactions between biological, psychological and socio-cultural environments are important to consider (Albee, 1996). Research solely examining intrapersonal factors that affect behaviors might ignore the context in which the individuals' behaviors occur, and could result in incomplete or misleading conclusions (National Institute of Mental Health, 1998). It is important that prevention research examine the etiology of maladaptive behaviors and potential determinants, including biological, intrapersonal, interpersonal, community, and societal risk and protective factors. It is also recommended that evaluations of prevention interventions address how adaptive behavioral changes promoted by a specific program are valued within different environmental contexts.

Application

Psychologists conducting research on prevention are encouraged to take into account the interface between biological, psychological and socio-cultural variables and the best available evidence regarding epidemiology, intervention, and service delivery. Resources are available to identify evidence-based prevention interventions for different demographics, topical areas, and contexts. One such resource is the National Registry of Evidence-Based Programs and Practices (NREPP), published by the U. S. Department of Health and Human Services, Substance Abuse and Mental Health Services Administration (www.nrepp.samhsa.gov).

Psychologists are encouraged to consider the social ecology of the community in which they work (Brofenbrenner, 1979), and to collaborate with community stakeholders on research goals and methods (Caplan & Caplan, 2000; Foster-Fishman, Berkowitz, Lounsbury,

Jacobson, & Allen, 2001; Sullivan et al., 2001). Researchers are encouraged to assess the differential impact of prevention programs on specific communities. Prevention researchers may unknowingly design and evaluate programs using criteria from their own cultural perspectives and worldviews, and may miss important contextual factors that contribute to the success or failure of prevention interventions within specific communities and cultures (e. g., diverse social classes and socioeconomic groups) (Trickett, 1998; Turner, 2000). Community collaboration is important in the interpretation and application of research findings, and on the provision of oversight and monitoring of community-based research. Participatory Action Research is one example of collaborative research that appreciates environmental contexts, and recognizes that knowledge is co-produced through collaborative actions with those who have traditionally been left out of the research process and whose lives are most affected by the research problem (Prilleltensky & Nelson, 2002).

Guideline 5. Psychologists Are Encouraged to Consider Ethical Issues in Prevention Research and Practice

Rationale

Psychologists are required to adhere to ethical standards of the profession and to be mindful of its highest ideals (Ethical Principles of Psychologists and Code of Conduct, APA, 2010). Prevention efforts may raise unique ethical issues (Bond & Albee, 1990; Waldo, Kaczmarek & Romano, 2004). Prevention is typically conducted with numerous participants and has individual, systemic, and societal implications. It is important to evaluate possible negative impacts that preventive interventions may have on individuals, the community, or the larger society (Bloom, 1993; Caplan & Caplan, 1994). For example, conducting preventive interventions that identify higher risk within a historically stigmatized group could be harmful to members of that group. Thus, it is important that confidentiality be adhered to during the prevention intervention process (Bloom, 1993). Additionally, targeted behavior may serve one or more purposes for the individual and community; eliminating the behavior without attention to its possible protective functions may lead to negative consequences for a segment of the community.

Application

Psychologists are encouraged to be knowledgeable regarding methods and designs in prevention research and practice within their boundaries of competence (APA Ethical Standard 2.01). It is important that preventive interventions and research include considerations of the ethical implications of new or promoted behaviors before, during, and after a prevention intervention. Informed consent poses particular challenges with regard to ensuring that individuals and multiple stakeholders comprehend the implications of their participation. Other ethical issues to consider include equitable selection, confidentiality, cultural relevancy, socially and culturally competent research and practice (APA Ethical Standards 8.02 and 2.01b), and researcher bias (Schwartz & Hage, 2009). It is important to evaluate the long-term effects of preventive interventions (Brown & Liao, 1999), especially as they relate to historically marginalized groups.

Guideline 6. Psychologists Are Encouraged to Attend to Contextual Issues of Social Disparity That May Inform Prevention Practice and Research

Rationale

Considerations of social disparities can provide a context for prevention work in which the causes and effects of oppression can be identified and considered. Reducing social disparities is essential for preventing the myriad of problems that they spawn (e. g. Vera, Buhin, & Isacco, 2009). For example, children living in disadvantaged neighborhoods are at risk for childhood behavioral difficulties, including conduct disorders, mental health problems, academic failure, and teen pregnancy (e.g., Goodnight, Lahey, Van Hulle, Rodgers, Rathouz et al., 2012; Harding, 2003; Leventhal & Brooks-Gunn, 2000; Nikulina, Widom, & Czaja, 2011). For adults, those living at or near poverty have a greater incidence of major depressive disorder than those with higher incomes (e.g., Kessler, Berglund, Demler, Jin, Koretz et al., 2003). Further, numerous health problems (e.g., diabetes, obesity, coronary heart disease) have been associated with living in poverty (e.g., Kittleson, Meoni, Wang, Chu, Ford et al., 2006; Ludwig, Sanbonmatsu, Gennetian, Adam, Duncan et al., 2011). Consistent with these considerations, the importance of creating contexts of fairness in order to improve the health and wellness of those served by prevention programs has been emphasized (Lawson, Noblett, & Rodwell, 2009; Prilleltensky, 2001, 2011; Tepper, 2001).

Application

Psychologists strive to be cognizant of the social implications of the preventive services they offer. For example, interventions that fail to consider those structural inequalities and contextual factors (e.g., social class, socioeconomic status) that influence behavior may inadvertently suggest that the problem lies within a particular group instead of acknowledging the influence of being marginalized in society (Walker, 2009). Prevention interventions may have maximum impact if societal inequalities related to social class, economic status, discrimination, and exploitation are considered (Perry & Albee, 1994). Dissemination of prevention findings grounded in the social ecology of the community may aid in acknowledging inequalities that may contribute to or exacerbate a particular behavior that is the target of intervention. For example, lesbian, gay, bisexual, transgender, and queer young people who are bullied in school may not only be experiencing homophobia reactions from peers, but also bullying based on racial/ethnic, gender, and/or class identities (Singh & McKleroy, 2011).

Guideline 7. Psychologists Are Encouraged to Increase Their Awareness, Knowledge, and Skills Essential to Prevention through Continuing Education, Training, Supervision, and Consultation

Rationale

The *Guidelines and Principles for Accreditation of Programs in Professional Psychology* (APA, 2009) stress the importance of education and training that covers the breadth of psychology. Research suggests that prevention helps to reduce the need for remedial interventions (Schwartz & Hage, 2009; Vera, Buhin, & Isacco, 2009). Therefore, remediation and prevention are best viewed as complementary to one another, and not in conflict. However, despite psychology's history with prevention practice and research during the 20th century (Cowen, 1973; Elias, 1987), the education of psychologists continues to emphasize crisis interventions and remedial approaches, giving much less attention to prevention as a core component of training and education (Matthews, 2003; O'Byrne, Brammer, Davidson, & Poston, 2002; Snyder & Elliott, 2005). Although some psychologists learn about the development and implementation of prevention activities in graduate school (e.g., community psychologists), most new prevention interventionists do not have a high level of training in the established content areas of prevention, and more established professionals report low levels of knowledge in newer areas of prevention (e. g. gender and culture issues, economic analysis of prevention) (Eddy, Smith, Brown, & Reid, 2005). This research suggests that much of the education and training in prevention is learned through less formal methods than graduate education. In psychology graduate education there is a need to expand opportunities to learn about prevention by developing prevention-based courses and/or infusing prevention-related content into existing courses (Conyne, Newmeyer, et al., 2008; Matthews & Skowron, 2004).

Application

The training and continuing education of psychologists in awareness, knowledge, and skills related to prevention provides psychologists with resources to be proactive in reducing human suffering and promoting positive aspects of human functioning. Psychologists are encouraged to obtain education and training in preventive approaches through various pathways, including re-specialization programs, postdoctoral fellowships, continuing education programs, self-study, conferences, professional societies that focus on prevention, and combinations of such alternatives. Other avenues include service learning and experiential work in community settings less typical for psychologists (DeLeon, Dubanoski, & Oliveira-Berry, 2005). Pre-doctoral psychology graduate students may also consider taking advantage of coursework, practicum experiences, and pre-doctoral internships that have a prevention focus. Psychology training programs can also encourage enrollment in prevention courses in other disciplines, such as public health, thus encouraging training in interdisciplinary perspectives important to prevention. Those already in practice and unable to participate in concentrated, formal training programs may be able to utilize continuing education programs. Psychologists may also gain supervised experience and consultation working with psychologists, or other professionals, skilled in prevention. Because public health has a strong focus on prevention, increased training and collaboration with professionals in the field of public health is encouraged. Through more formal education, psychology trainees and psychologists may consider earning dual degrees in public health (MPH) and psychology. The collaborative training, which pairs psychologists' understanding of human behavior and public health professionals' knowledge of health and prevention at community- or population-levels, may be particularly effective at creating change at the societal level. Literature relevant to prevention is available through professional journals, including a growing number of applied journals in, for example, psychiatry, public health, and psychology. Prevention research and applications are also disseminated through professional organizations and their respective conferences.

Scholars have noted several knowledge and skill domains important to psychologists engaging in prevention (Conyne, 1997; Hage et al., 2007; O'Neil & Britner, 2009). The domains include: (a) understanding distinctions between preventive and remedial approaches; (b) designing and implementing educational programs; (c) assessing community needs; (d) understanding systemic approaches that incorporate cultural and contextual factors into preventive interventions; (e) using group skills and approaches, when appropriate, in program design and implementation; (f) collaborating with interdisciplinary teams that include professionals and community leaders; (g) grant-writing and marketing skills to address sustainability of preventive efforts; (h) promoting positive development across the lifespan; (i) empowering individuals and communities to work on their own behalf; (j) developing strength-based approaches that reduce risk and enhance resilience in individuals and communities; (k) influencing policy decisions and their impact on preventive efforts; and (l) evaluating preventive interventions. Each of these domains of knowledge and skill in prevention ideally would include attending to the needs and concerns of historically marginalized groups, and consider power differentials as they relate to cultural differences and concerns of social inequalities. In addition, training in newer technologies, such as telepsychology and social media, is important as these technologies are emerging methods for preventive efforts.

Guideline 8. Psychologists Are Encouraged to Engage in Systemic and Institutional Change Interventions That Strengthen the Health of Individuals, Families, and Communities, and Prevent Psychological and Physical Distress and Disability

Rationale

Applications of prevention through systemic interventions are important across many domains. Systemic preventive interventions include those that affect families, schools, communities, and work environments. Individuals may not be able to achieve maximum health or full social participation if systemic barriers, such as classism, racism, sexism and poverty prevail. Preventive programs that focus only on changing individuals are likely to be less effective than those that also address the contexts that support or inhibit development and optimal health. Systemic interventions can be delivered across the lifecycle, but the earlier prevention occurs, the greater the likelihood of reducing risk and strengthening protective factors (Smith, 2006). Systemic preventive programs that focus on developing community norms that promote healthy lifestyle behaviors are effective in reducing societal problems (Orpinas, Horne, et al., 2004).

Application

Psychologists are encouraged to engage in activities that produce positive systemic, institutional, and organizational change. Psychologists can contribute to systemic change that strengthens protective and resiliency factors of individuals, families, schools, workplaces, faith communities, community centers, and health care centers (Johnson & Millstein, 2003; Kumpfer & Alvarado, 2003; Morsillo & Prilleltensky, 2007; Wandersman & Florin, 2003). For example, organizational psychologists can assist in the development of corporate policies to reduce work stress and stress-related illnesses, and increase worker satisfaction and productivity (Murphy, Hurrell, & Quick Campbell, 1992). Other examples include school-based preventive programs that address the multiple needs of students across the school and community. Such programs have yielded positive results and enhanced students' emotional, social, and academic development (e. g., August, Hektner, Egan, Realmuto, & Bloomquist, 2002; Carlson-Newman & Horne, 2004; Greenberg et al., 2003).

School-based interventions that incorporate health promotion, competence enhancement, and youth development as frameworks for prevention can reduce youth risk behaviors and enhance protective factors (e. g., Perry, 1999; Weissberg & Greenberg, 1998). A recent meta-analysis of after school programs indicated that programs that foster personal and social skills of youth provide the greatest benefit (Durlak, Weissberg, & Pachan, 2010).

School-based systemic interventions may also inform policies that address inequities and discrimination among groups of students (Morsillo & Prilleltensky, 2007).

Psychologists can influence the structure, role relationships, premises, rules, and assumptions governing systems to empower communities and to promote justice and equity (Evan, Hanlin, & Prilleltensky, 2007). Psychologists in health care settings can promote employee programs that strengthen employee resiliency in order to inoculate employees against the physical and psychological demands of the work setting (Freeman & Carson, 2007).

Another area of systemic application is advocating for healthy food choices in cafeterias, lunchrooms, and vending machines to promote healthy nutrition, which when coupled with an active lifestyle can reduce obesity and resulting health risks (Hawkes, 2007; Suárez-Balcazar et al., 2007).

Parent- and family-based interventions can help parents and other caregivers learn effective child-rearing skills to strengthen adult and child relationships which, in turn reduce child and adolescent behavior problems and enhance learning (Thornton, Craft, Dahlberg, Lynch, & Baer, 2002). Applications of systemic prevention interventions at later stages of life include community-based programs that support older adults living in their homes. Elders with sufficient physical and emotional capacity will benefit from community preventive programs that involve them in community volunteer opportunities, public policy making, neighborhood networking, and social support groups (Konnert, Gatz, & Hertzsprung, 1999).

Guideline 9. Psychologists Are Encouraged to Inform the Deliberation of Public Policies That Promote Health and Well-Being When Relevant Prevention Science Findings Are Available

Rationale

Psychologists are well positioned to educate and inform policy makers about the importance of prevention to enhance health and well-being (Kiselica, 2001). For example, public policy-based prevention programs such as Project Head Start have been an integral part of preventive initiatives that promote human functioning and reduce negative health outcomes (Ripple & Zigler, 2003). Psychologists are encouraged to apply their expertise by informing policy makers about the value of evidence-based preventive initiatives, and to communicate their research findings clearly and concisely to policy-makers (Coates & Szekeres, 2004; Hage et al., 2007; Ripple & Zigler, 2003).

Application

Psychologists are encouraged to become informed about public policy debates in which prevention research and programs may have relevant information to contribute to the discourse. Psychologists strive to enter such discussion and inform policy makers at local, state and national levels by using their expertise and scholarship in prevention science as appropriate. For example, at the Surgeon General's Conference on Children's Mental Health in 2000, psychologists provided recommendations to help formulate a national policy on children's mental health (Levant, Tolan, & Dodgen, 2002). It is suggested that psychologists become familiar with APA resources that are relevant to health care policy and health promotion. They are also encouraged to consider strengthening their efforts by forming multidisciplinary partnerships that include government, legal, and policy making experts, as well as professionals from the health, social, and educational sciences. For example, Jason (2011) describes a 20 year collaborative effort between psychologists and patient advocacy organizations to effect change in multiple areas regarding the problem of chronic fatigue syndrome, including epidemiological evidence, criteria for diagnosis, and leadership at the Centers for Disease Control and Prevention. As another example of collaboration, in 1965 Head Start, began as a White House initiative that included the collaboration of psychologists, sociologists, and pediatricians focused on the goal of reducing the deleterious effects of poverty on young children (Styfco & Zigler, 2003). Further, it is recommended that graduate programs teach students about the relationship between research and its relevancy to informing policy (Ripple & Zigler, 2003).

Conclusion

The Prevention Guidelines encourage psychologists to strive to engage in prevention practice, research, and education, including those within the policymaking process, to enhance human functioning. Prevention has numerous benefits, including the potential to strengthen the integration of science and practice in psychology (Biglan et al., 2003). Moreover, as discussed throughout the Guidelines, the benefits of prevention have been demonstrated through the reduction of illness and problem behaviors, the enhancement of human functioning, and the potential to reduce health care costs (O'Connell, 2009; Durlak et al., 2010; Mrazek & Haggerty, 1994; Nation et al., 2003). An increased focus on prevention has the potential to mobilize psychologists to respond more effectively and sensitively to conditions that place individuals, communities, and institutions at-risk for various problems, and to promote strengths that contribute to human functioning.

The Guidelines provide a framework for best practices in prevention and the promotion of health and well-being, regardless of an individual psychologist's specialty area, employment setting, or professional interests. Infusing prevention across the profession will help to orient psychologists to a broader application of psychological research and practice, with the goal of more effectively and sensitively responding to major societal needs for all individuals, especially those with the fewest resources and groups historically underserved by the profession.

References

Albee, G. W. (1996). Revolutions and counterrevolutions in prevention. *American Psychologist, 51*, 1130-1133.

Allen, N. E., Bybee, D. I., & Sullivan, C.M. (2004). Battered women's multitude of needs: Evidence supporting the need for comprehensive advocacy. *Violence Against Women, 10,* 1015-1035.

APA (2002a). Criteria for practice guideline development and evaluation. *American Psychologist, 57*, 1048-1051.

APA (2007). *Report of the APA Task Force on Socioeconomic Status.* Washington, DC: American Psychological Association.

APA (2010). American Psychological Association. (2010). Ethical principles of psychologists and code of conduct (APA, 2002, Amended June 1, 2010). Retrieved from http://www.apa.org/ethics/code/index.aspx

APA (2003). Guidelines on multicultural education, training, research, practice, and organizational change for psychologists. *American Psychologist, 58*, 377-402.

APA (2009). *Guidelines and principles for accreditation of programs in professional psychology*. Washington, DC: Author. Retrieved from American Psychological Association website: http://www.apa.org/ed /accreditation/guiding principles. pdf

APA (2011). *APA Guidelines for Psychological Practice with Lesbian, Gay, and Bisexual Clients.* Washington, DC: American Psychological Association.

APA (2012). Guidelines for assessment of and intervention with persons with disabilities. *American Psychologist, 67,* 43-62.

APA Annual Report (2010). *American Psychologist, 66 (suppl),* S1-S48.

August, G. J., Hektner, J.M., Egan, E.A., Realmuto, G. M., & Bloomquist, M. L. (2002). The Early Risers longitudinal prevention trial: Examination of three year outcomes in aggressive children with intent-to-treat and as-intended analysis. *Psychology of Addictive Behaviors, 16,* 27-39.

Biglan, A., Mrazek, P.J., Carnine, D., & Flay, B. R. (2003). The integration of research and practice in the prevention of youth problem behaviors. *American Psychologist, 58*, 433-440.

Black, M. M., & Krishnakumar, A. (1998). Children in low-income, urban settings: Interventions to promote mental health and well-being. *American Psychologist, 53*, 635-646.

Bloom, M. (1993). Toward a code of ethics from primary prevention. *Journal of Primary Prevention, 13*, 173-182.

Bond, L. A., & Albee, G. W. (1990). Training preventionists in ethical implications of their actions. *Prevention in Human Services, 8*, 11-126.

Brofenbrenner, U. (1979). *The ecology of human development.* Cambridge, MA: Harvard University Press.

Brown, C. H., & Liao, J. (1999). Principles for designing randomized preventive trials in mental health: An emerging developmental epidemiology paradigm. *American Journal of Community Psychology, 27*, 673-711.

Bull, S. (2011). *Technology-based health promotion.* Thousand Oaks, CA: Sage.

Caplan, G. (1964). *Principles of preventive psychiatry*. NY: Basic Books.

Caplan, G., & Caplan, R. B. (1994). The need for quality control in primary prevention. *Journal of Primary Prevention, 15*, 15-29.

Caplan, G., & Caplan, R.B. (2000). The future of primary prevention. *Journal of Primary Prevention, 21*, 131-136.

Carlson-Newman, D., & Horne, A. M. (2004). Bully Busters: A psychoeducational intervention for reducing bullying behavior in middle school students. *Journal of Counseling and Development, 82*, 259-267.

Catalano, R. F., Berglund, M. L., Ryan, J. A. M., Lonczak, H. S., & Hawkins, J. D. (2002). Positive youth development in the United States: Research findings on evaluations of positive youth development programs. *Prevention & Treatment, 5*, Article 15. Retrieved August, 1, 2002, from http://journals.apa.org.osiyou.cc.columbia.edu:2048/prevention/volume5/pre0050015a.html

Catalano, R. F., Hawkins, J. D., Berglund, M. L., Pollard, J. A., & Arthur, M. W. (2002). Prevention science and positive youth development: Competitive or cooperative frameworks? *Journal of Adolescent Health, 31*, 230-239.

CDC (2007). Youth Risk Behavior Survey, 2001-2007. Retrieved February 15, 2010 at http://www.cdc.gov/yrbss.

Chinman, M., Tremain, B., Imm, P., & Wandersmann, A. (2009). Strengthening prevention performance using technology: A formative evaluation of Interactive Getting to Outcomes. *American Journal of Orthopsychiatry, 79,* 469-481.

Cicchetti, D., & Toth, S. L. (1992). The role of developmental theory in prevention and intervention. *Development & Psychopathology. Special Developmental Approaches to Prevention and Intervention, 4,* 489-493.

Conyne, R. K. (1997). Educating students in preventive counseling. *Counselor Education and Supervision, 36*, 259-269.

Conyne, R. K., Newmeyer, M. D., Kenny, M., Romano, J. L., & Matthews, C. R. (2008). Two key strategies for teaching prevention: Specialized course and infusion. *Journal of Primary Prevention*, 29, 375-401.

Cowen, E. (1973). Social and community interventions. *Annual Review of psychology, 24,* 423-472.

Cowen, E. (1985). Person-centered approaches to primary prevention in mental health: Situation-focused and competency-enhancement. *American Journal of Community Psychology, 13*, 31-48.

DeLeon, P. H., Dubanoski, R., & Oliveira-Berry, J. M. (2005). An education for the future. *Journal of Clinical Psychology, 61*, 1105-1109.

Durlak, J. A., Weissberg, R. P., & Pachan, M. (2010). A meta-analysis of after-school programs that seek to promote personal and social skills in children and adolescents. *American Journal of Community Psychology, 45,* 294-309.

Eby, M. D., Chin, J. L., Rollock, D., Schwartz, J. P., & Worell, F. C. (2011). Professional psychology training in the Era of a Thousand Flowers: Dilemmas and challenges for the future. *Training and Education in Professional Psychology, 5,* 57-68.

Eccles, J., & Appleton, J. A. (Eds.). (2002). *Community programs to promote youth development.* Washington, DC: National Academies Press.

Eddy, J. M., Smith, P., Brown Hendricks, C., & Reid, J. B. (2005). A survey of prevention science training: Implications for educating the next generation. *Prevention Science, 6,* 59-71.

Elias, M. J. (1987). Establishing enduring prevention programs: Advancing the legacy of Swampscott. *American Journal of Community Psychology, 15,* 539-553.

Evans, S. D., Hanlin, C. E., & Prilleltensky, I. (2007). Blending ameliorative and transformative approaches in human service organizations: A case study. *Journal of Community Psychology, 35*, 329–346.

Foster-Fishman, P.G., Berkowitz, S., Lounsbury, D., Jacobson, S., & Allen, N.A. (2001). Building collaborative capacity in community based coalitions. *American Journal of Community Psychology, 29*, 241-262.

Krysinska, K., & DeLeo, D. (2007). Telecommunication and suicide prevention: Hopes and challenges for the new century. *Omega: Journal of Death and Dying, 55,* 237-253.

Foster-Fishman, P.G., Law, K. M., Lichty, L. F., & Aoun, C. (2010). Youth ReACT for social change: A method for youth participatory action research. *American Journal of Community Psychology, 46,* 67-83.

Freeman, D. G. H., & Carson, M. (2007). Developing workplace resilience: The role of the peer referral agent diffuser. *Journal of Workplace Behavioral Health, 22,* 113-121.

Goodnight, J. A., Lahey, B. B., Van Hulle, C. A., Rodgers, J. L., Rathouz, P. J., Waldman, D., & D'Onofrio, B. M. (2012). A quasi-experimental analysis of the influence of neighborhood disadvantage on child and adolescent conduct problems. *Journal of Abnormal Psychology*, 121, 95–108. *doi: 10.1037/a0025078*

Gordon, R. (1987). An operational classification of disease prevention. In J. A. Sternberg & M. M. Silverman (Eds.), *Preventing mental disorders* (pp. 20-26). Rockville, MD: U. S. Dept of Health and Human Services.

Greenberg, M. T., Domitrovich, C., & Bumbarger, B. (2001). The prevention of mental disorders in school-aged children: Current state of the field. *Prevention & Treatment, 4*, Article 1.

Greenberg, M. T., Weissberg, R. P., O'Brien, M. U., Zins, J. E., Fredericks, L., Resnik, H., & Elias, M. J. (2003). Enhancing school-based prevention and youth development through coordinated social, emotional, and academic learning. *American Psychologist,* 58, 466-474.

Grunberg, N. E., & Klein, L. C. (2009). Biopsychological obstacles to adoption and maintenance of a healthy lifestyle. In S. A. Shumaker, J. K. Ockene, & K. A. Riekert (Eds.), *The Handbook of Health Behavior Change* (3rd ed) (pp. 411-426). NY: Springer.

Guterman, N. B. (2004). Advancing prevention research on child abuse, youth violence, and domestic violence. *Journal of Interpersonal Violence, 19,* 299-321.

Hage, S. M. & Romano, J. L. (Chairs) (August, 2006). *Best practice guidelines: commentary by distinguished scholars in psychology*. Symposium presented at the 114th Annual Convention of the American Psychological Association, New Orleans, LA.

Hage, S. M., Romano, J. L., Conyne, R. K., Kenny, M., Matthews, C., Schwartz, J. P., & Waldo, M. (2007). Best practice guidelines on prevention practice, research, training, and social advocacy for psychologists. *The Counseling Psychologist*, *35*, 493-566.

Harding, D. J. (2003). Counterfactual models of neighborhood effects: The effect of neighborhood poverty on dropping out and teenage pregnancy. *American Journal of Sociology, 109,* 676–719. *doi:10.1086/379217*

Hawkes, C. (2007). Regulating food marketing to young people worldwide: Trends and policy drivers. *American Journal of Public Health, 97*, 1962-1973.

Israel, B., Eng, E., Schultz, A., & Parker, E. (2005). *Methods for conducting community-based participatory research in public health*. San Francisco, CA: Jossey-Bass.

Jason, L. A. (2011). Small wins matter in advocacy movements: giving voice to patients. *American Journal of Community Psychology*. Published online August 2011.

Jason, L. A., & Glenwick, D. S. (Eds). (2012). *Methodological approaches to community-based research.* Washington, DC: American Psychological Association.

Jason, L. A., Keys, C. B., Suarez-Balcazar, Y., Taylor, R. R., & Davis, M. I. Eds. (2003). *Participatory community research: theories and methods in action*. Washington, DC: American Psychological Association.

Johnson, S. B., & Millstein, S. G. (2003). Prevention opportunities in health care settings. *American Psychologist, 58*, 475-481.

Kenny, M. E. (Chair) (August, 2003). *Competencies for prevention training in counseling psychology*. Symposium presented at the 111th Annual Convention of the American Psychological Association, Toronto, Canada.

Kenny, M. E., & Hage, S. M. (2009). The next frontier: Prevention as an instrument of social justice. *The Journal of Primary Prevention, 30*, 1-10.

Kenny, M. E., Horne, A. M., Orpinas, P., & Reese. L. E. (Eds.) (2009). *Realizing social justice: The challenge of prevention interventions*. Washington, DC: American Psychological Association.

Kessler, R. C., Berglund, P., Demler, O., Jin, R., Koretz, D., Merikangas, K. R., Rush, A. J., Walters, E. E., Wang, P. S. (2003). The epidemiology of major depressive disorder. *Journal of the American Medical Association, 289,* 3095-3105. *doi: 10.1001/jama.289.23.3095*

Kiselica, M. S. (2004). When duty calls: The implications of social justice work for policy, education, and practice in the mental health professions. *The Counseling Psychologist,* 32, 838-854.

Kittleson, M. M., Meoni, L. A., Wang, N. Y., Chu, A. Y., Ford, D. E., & Klag, M. J. (2006). Association of childhood socioeconomic status with subsequent coronary heart disease in physicians. *Archives of Internal Medicine, 166,* 2356–2361. *doi:10.1001/ archinte.166.21.2356*

Konnert, C., Gatz, M., & Hertzsprung Myers, E. A. (1999). Preventive interventions for older adults. In M. Duffy (Ed.), *Handbook of counseling and psychotherapy with older adults* (pp. 314-334). NY: John Wiley.

Kumpfer, K. L., & Alvarado, R. (2003). Family-strengthening approaches for the prevention of youth problem behaviors. *American Psychologist, 58*, 457-465.

Kumpfer, K. L., Alvarado, R., Smith, P., & Bellamy, N. (2002). Cultural sensitivity and adaptation in family-based prevention interventions. *Prevention Science, 3,* 241-246.

Kurutz, J. G., Johnson, D. L., & Sugden, B. W. (1996). The United States Postal Service Employee Assistance Program: A multifaceted approach to workplace violence prevention. In G. R. VandenBos & E. Q. Bulatao (Eds.), *Violence on the job: Identifying risks and developing solutions*. American Psychological Association, Washington, DC.

Lawson, K., Noblett, A., & Rodwell, J. (2009). Promoting employee wellbeing: The relevance of work characteristics and organizational justice. *Health Promotion International, 24*, 223-233.

Lerner, R. M. (1995). *America's youth in crisis: Challenges and choices for programs and policies*. Thousand Oaks, CA: Sage.

Levant, R. F., Tolan, P., Dodgen, D. (2002). New directions in children‘s mental health: Psychology's role. *Professional Psychology: Research and Practice, 33*, 115-124.

Leventhal, T., & Brooks-Gunn, J. (2000). The neighborhoods they live in: The effects of neighborhood residence on child and adolescent outcomes. *Psychological Bulletin, 126,* 309 –337. *doi:10.1037/0033-2909.126.2.309*

Ludwig, J., Sanbonmatsu, L., Gennetian, L., Adam, E., Duncan, G. J., Katz, L. F., Kessler, R. C., Kling, J. R., Tessler Lindau, S., Whitaker, R. C., & McDade, T. W. (2011). Neighborhoods, obesity, and diabetes — A randomized social experiment. *New England Journal of Medicine, 365,* 1509-1519. *doi: 10.1056/NEJMsa1103216*

Matthews, C. R. (August, 2003). Training for prevention competency in counseling psychology. In M. Kenny (Chair), *Competencies for prevention training in counseling psychology.* Symposium presented at the 111th Annual Convention of the American Psychological Association, Toronto, Canada.

Matthews, C. R., & Skowron, E. A. (2004). Incorporating prevention into mental health counselor training. *Journal of Mental Health Counseling, 26*, 349-359.

Morsillo, J., & Prilleltensky, I. (2007). Social action with youth: Interventions, evaluation, and psychopolitical validity. *Journal of Community Psychology, 35*, 725-740.

Mrazek, P. J. (2002). *Enhancing the well-being of America's children through the strengthening of natural and community supports: Opportunities for prevention and early mental health intervention.* Paper prepared for the Subcommittee on Children and Families, President's New Freedom Commission on Mental Health.

Mrazek, P. J. & Haggerty, R. J. (Eds.) (1994). *Reducing Risks for mental disorders: Frontiers for preventive intervention research.* Washington, D. C.: National Academy Press.

Murphy, L. R., Hurrell, J. J., & Quick Campbell, J. (1992). Work and well-being: Where do we go from here? In J. Campbell Quick, L. R. Murphy, & J. J. Hurrell, Jr. (Eds.), *Stress and well-being at work: Assessments and interventions for occupational mental health* (pp. 331-347). Washington, DC: American Psychological Association.

Nation, M., Crusto, C., Wandersman, A., Kumpfer, K. L., Seybolt, D., Morrissey-Kane, E. et al. (2003). What works in prevention: Principles of effective prevention programs. *American Psychologist,* 58, 449-456.

National Institute of Mental Health. (1998). *Priorities for prevention research at NIMH: A report by the national advisory mental health council workgroup on mental disorder prevention research* (NIH Publication No. 98-4321). Bethesda, MD: Author.

National Prevention, Health Promotion, and Public Health Council (2011). *National prevention strategy: America's plan for better health and wellness.* Washington, DC: US Department of Health and Human Services, Office of the Surgeon General. Retrieved June 17, 2011 from: http://www. healthcare.gov/center/councils/nphpphc/strategy/report.pdf

Nikulina, V., Widom, C. S., Czaja, S. (2011). The role of childhood neglect and childhood poverty in predicting mental health, academic achievement and crime in adulthood. *American Journal of Community Psychology, 48*, 309-321. doi: 10.1007/s10464-010-9385-y

O'Byrne, K. K., Brammer, S. K., Davidson, M. M., Poston, W. S. C. (2002). Primary prevention in counseling psychology: Back to the future? *The Counseling Psychologist, 30*, 330-344.

O'Connell, M. E., Boat, T., & Warner, K. E. (Eds.) (2009). *Preventing mental, emotional, and behavioral disorders among young people: Progress and possibilities.* Washington, DC: National Academies Press.

O'Neil, J. M., & Britner, P. A. (2009). Training primary preventionists to make a difference in people's lives. In M. E. Kenny, A. M. Horne, P. Orpinas, & L. E. Reese (Eds.),

Realizing social justice: The challenge of primary prevention (pp. 141-162). Washington, DC: American Psychological Association.

Orpinas, P., Horne, A., & Multisite Violence Prevention Project (2004). A teacher-focused approach to prevent and reduce students' aggressive behavior and the GREAT teacher program. *American Journal of Preventive Medicine*, 26, 29-38.

Perry, M., & Albee, G. W. (1994). On "The science of prevention." *American Psychologist, 49*, 1087-1088Perry, C. L. (1999). *Creating health behavior change: How to develop community-wide programs for youth*. Thousand Oaks, CA: Sage.

Pittman, K. J., Irby, M., Tolamn, J., Yohalem, N., & Ferber, T. (2001). *Preventing problems, promoting development, encouraging engagement: Competing priorities or inseparable goals*. Retrieved March 1, 2003, from http://forumforyouthinvestment.org/ preventproblems.pdf

Prilleltensky, I. (2001). Value-based praxis in community psychology: Moving toward social justice and social action. *American Journal of Community Psychology,* 29, 747-778.

Prilleltensky, I., & Nelson, G. (2002). *Doing psychology critically: Making a difference in diverse settings*. Basingstoke, UK: Palgrave.

Prilleltensky, I. (2005). Promoting well-being: Time for a paradigm shift in health and human services. *Scandinavian Journal of Public Health, 33* (suppl 66), 53-60.

Prilleltensky, I. (2011). Wellness as fairness. *American Journal of Community Psychology*. published on-line June 04, 2011.

Rapkin, B.D. & Trickett, E. J. (2005). Comprehensive dynamic trial designs for behavioral prevention research with communities: overcoming inadequacies of the randomized controlled trial paradigm. In E. J. Trickett & W. Pequegnat, Eds. *Community interventions and AIDS*, (pp. 249-277). New York, NY: Oxford University Press.

Reese, L. E. & Vera, E. M. (2007). Culturally relevant prevention: The scientific and practical considerations of community-based programs. *The Counseling Psychology,* 35, 763-778.

Ringel, J., & Sturm, R. (2001). National estimates of mental health utilization and expenditure for children in 1998. *Journal of Behavioral Health Services and Research, 28*, 319-332.

Ripple, C. H., & Zigler, E. (2003). Research, policy, and the federal role in prevention initiatives for children. *American Psychologist, 58,* 482-490.

Romano, J. L. (Chair) (August, 2002). *Teaching prevention in counseling psychology*. Symposium presented at the 110th Annual Convention of the American Psychological Association, Chicago, IL.

Romano, J. L. (Chair) (August, 2011*). Psychologists and Prevention: Conversation about the Proposed APA Prevention Guidelines*. Conversation hour presented at the 119th Annual Convention of the American Psychological Association, Washington, DC.

Romano, J. L. & Hage, S. M. (2000). Prevention and counseling psychology: Revitalizing commitments for the 21st century. *The Counseling Psychologist, 28,* 733-763.

Rutledge, S. E., Roffman, R. A., Mahoney, C., Picciano, J.F., Berghuis, J. P. (2001). Motivational enhancement counseling strategies in delivering a telephone-based brief HIV prevention intervention. *Clinical Social Work Journal, 29,* 291-306.

Satcher, D. (2000). *Foreword in U.S. Public Health Service, Report of the Surgeon General's Conference on Children's Mental Health: A national action agenda*. Washington, DC: U.S. Department of Health and Human Services.

Schwartz, J. P. & Hage, S. M. (2009). Prevention ethics, responsibility, and commitment to public well-being. In M. E. Kenny, A. M. Horne, P. Orpinas, & L. E. Reese. (Eds.), *Realizing social Justice: The challenge of prevention interventions,*(pp. 123-140). Washington, DC: American Psychological Association.

Singh, A. A., Hays, D. G., & Watson, L. (2011). Strength in the face of adversity: Resilience strategies of transgender individuals. *Journal of Counseling and Development, 89*, 1, 20-27.

Singh, A. A., & McKleroy, V. S. (2011). "Just getting out of bed is a revolutionary act": The resilience of transgender people of color who have survived traumatic life events. *Traumatology: An International Journal, 17,* 34-44.

Smith, E. J. (2006). The strength-based counseling model. *The Counseling Psychologist, 34*, 13-79.

Smith, E. P., Wolf, A. M., Cantillon, D. M., Thomas, O., & Davidson, W. S. (2004). The Adolescent Diversion Project: 25 years of research on an ecological model of intervention. *Journal of Prevention & Intervention in the Community, 27,* 29-47.

Smith, L., Davis, K., & Bhowmik, M. (2010). Youth participatory action research groups as school counseling interventions. *Professional School Counseling, 14,* 174-182.

Snyder, C. R., & Elliott, T. R. (2005). Twenty-first century graduate education in clinical psychology: A four level matrix model. *Journal of Clinical Psychology, 61*, 1033-1054.

Stone, E. J., Norman, J. E., Davis, S. M., Stewart, D., Clay, T. E., Caballero, B., Lohman, T. G., & Murray, D. M. (2003). Design, implementation, and quality control in the pathways American-Indian multicenter trial. *Preventive Medicine: An International Journal Devoted to Practice and Theory, 37*, S13-S13-S23.

Styfco, S., & Zigler, E. (2003). Early childhood programs for a new century. In A. Reynolds & M. Wang (Eds.) *The federal commitment to preschool education: Lessons from and for Head Start* (pp. 3-33). Washington, DC: Child Welfare League of America, Inc.

Suárez-Balcazar, Y., Redmond, L., Kouba, J., Hellwig, M., Davis, R., Martinez, L. I., et al. (2007). Introducing systems change in the schools: The case of school luncheons and vending machines. *American Journal of Community Psychology, 39*, 325-345.

Sullivan, M., Kone, A., Senturia, K. D., Chrisman, N. J., Ciske, S. J., & Krieger, J. W. (2001). Researchers and researched community perspectives: Toward bridging the gap. *Health Education & Behavior, 28*, 130-149.

Tepper, B. (2001). Health consequences of organizational injustice: Tests of main and interactive effects. *Organizational Behavior and Human Decision Processes, 20,* 139-158.

Thornton, T. N., Craft, C. A., Dahlberg, L. L., Lynch, B. S., & Baer, K. (2002). *Best practices of youth violence prevention: A sourcebook for community action* (Rev. ed.). Atlanta, GA: CDC, National Center for Injury Prevention and Control.

Tolan, P. H., & Dodge, K. A. (2005). Children's mental health as a primary care and concern: A system for comprehensive support and service. *American Psychologist, 60*, 601-614.

Trickett, E. J. (1998). Toward a framework for defining and resolving ethical issues in the protection of communities involved in primary prevention projects. *Ethics & Behavior, 8,* 321-337.

Trickett, E. J. (2011). Community-based participatory research as worldview or instrumental strategy: Is it lost in translation(al) research? *American Journal of Public Health, 101,* 1353-1355.

Trickett, E. J., Beehler, S., Deutsch, C., Green, L. W., Hawe, P., McLeroy, K., Miller, R. L. Rapkin, B. D., Schensul, J. J., Schultz, A. J., & Trimble, J. E. (2011). Advancing the science of community-level interventions. *American Journal of Public Health, 101,* 1410-1419.

U. S. Department of Health and Human Services (2000). *Healthy people 2010.* Washington, DC: Author.

Vera, E. M. (2000). A recommitment to prevention work in counseling psychology. *The Counseling Psychologist,* 28, 829-837.

Vera, E. M., & Reese, L. E. (2000). Preventive interventions with school-age youth. In S. D. Brown & R. W. Lent (Eds.), *Handbook of counseling psychology* (pp. 411-434). NY: John Wiley.

Vera, E. M., Buhin, L., & Isacco, A. (2009). The role of prevention in psychology's social justice agenda. In M. E. Kenny, A. M. Horne, P. Orpinas, & L. E. Reese. (Eds.), *Realizing social justice: The challenge of prevention interventions* (pp. 79-96). Washington, DC: American Psychological Association.

Vogelzang, S. N., Kritchevsky, S. B., Beekman, A. T., Newman, A. B., Satterfield, S. Simmsick, E.M., Penninx, B. W. (2008). Depressive symptoms and change in abdominal obesity in older persons. *Archives of General Psychiatry, 65,* 1386-1393.

Waldo, M., Kaczmarek, M., & Romano, J. (2004, August). Ethical dilemmas in prevention research and practice. In S. Hage & J. Schwartz (Co-Chairs), *Ethics of prevention: Diverse perspectives within counseling psychology.* Symposium conducted at the meeting of the American Psychological Association, Honolulu, HI.

Walker, L. E. (2009). *The battered woman syndrome* (3rd ed). NY: Springer-Verlag.

Wandersman, A., & Florin, P. (2003). Community interventions and effective prevention. *American Psychologist, 58,* 441-448.

Weissberg, R. P., & Greenberg, M. T. (1998). School and community competence enhancement and prevention programs. In W. Damon (Series Ed.), & I. E. Sigel & K. A. Renninger (Vol. Eds.), *Handbook of child psychology: Vol. 5. Child psychology in practice.* (5th ed., pp. 877-954). NY: John Wiley.

Weissberg, R. P., Kumpfer, K. L., & Seligman, M. E. P. (2003). Prevention that works for children and youth: An introduction. *American Psychologist, 58,* 425-432.

Weissberg, R. P., Walberg, H. J., O'Brien, M. U., & Kuster, C. B. (Eds.) (2003). *Long-term trends in the well-being of children and youth.* Washington, DC: Child Welfare League of America.

World Health Report (2008). Retrieved from http://www.who.int/whr /previous/en/index.html

Zimmerman, M. A. (1995). Psychological empowerment: Issues and illustrations. *American Journal of Community Psychology, 23,* 581-599.

Zimmerman, M. A., Israel, B. A., Schulz, A. J., Checkoway, B. (1992). Further explorations in empowerment theory: An empirical analysis of psychological empowerment. *American Journal of Community Psychology, 20,* 707-727.

Appendix D. Guidelines for Prevention in Psychology

Guideline 1. Psychologists are encouraged to select and implement preventive interventions that are theory- and evidence-based.

Guideline 2. Psychologists are encouraged to use culturally relevant prevention practices adapted to the specific context in which they are implemented.

Guideline 3. Psychologists are encouraged to develop and implement interventions that reduce risks and promote human strengths.

Guideline 4. Psychologists are encouraged to incorporate research and evaluation as integral to prevention program development and implementation, including consideration of environmental contexts that impact prevention.

Guideline 5. Psychologists are encouraged to consider ethical issues in prevention research and practice.

Guideline 6. Psychologists are encouraged to attend to contextual issues of social disparity that may inform prevention practice and research.

Guideline 7. Psychologists are encouraged to increase their awareness, knowledge, and skills essential to prevention through continuing education, training, supervision, and consultation.

Guideline 8. Psychologists are encouraged to engage in systemic and institutional interventions that strengthen the health of individuals, families, and communities, and prevent psychological and physical distress and disability.

Guideline 9. Psychologists are encouraged to inform the deliberation of public policies that promote health and well-being when relevant prevention science findings are available.

Prevention Guidelines Work Group

Work Group members, with current divisional memberships, are listed alphabetically after the Chair. The Work Group wishes to acknowledge and thank many groups, committees, and organizations as well as individuals, too numerous to list here, who contributed to the development of the Prevention Guidelines during the review process and comment periods.

John L. Romano (Chair), (Divisions 17, 52)
G. Anne Bogat (Division 27)
Robert K. Conyne, (Divisions 17, 49)
Sally M. Hage, (Division 17)
Arthur M. Horne, (Divisions17, 49)
Maureen E. Kenny, (Divisions 17, 35)
Connie Matthews, (Divisions 17, 35, 44, 45, 50)
Jonathan P. Schwartz, (Divisions17, 51)
Anneliese Singh, (Divisions 17, 35, 44, 45, 48)
Michael Waldo, (Division 17)
Y. Joel Wong, (Divisions 17, 45, 51), Asian American Psychological Association

Revised: September 10, 2012
Article of Div 17 Newsletter by John L. Romano and Sally M. Hage

Guidelines for Prevention in Psychology Approved by APA Council

The Guidelines for Prevention in Psychology were approved as APA policy during APA Council meetings in February 2013. The Council approved the Guidelines after they received unanimous support from APA's Board of Directors in December 2012. The Guidelines offer guidance to psychologists in supporting the value of prevention as important work of psychologists, and in providing recommendations that give greater visibility to prevention among psychologists regardless of specialty area or work setting.

Members of Division 17's Prevention Section provided early leadership for the Guidelines, dating back to 2002 and 2003 APA convention symposia. Eventually a major contribution "Best Practice Guidelines on Prevention Practice, Research, Training, and Social Advocacy for Psychologists" (Hage, Romano, Conyne, Kenny, Matthews, Schwartz, & Waldo, 2007) was published in *The Counseling Psychologist* (TCP)[†]. The paper was awarded the Outstanding Contribution Award by Division 17 and Sage Publishing at the 2008 APA Convention. After receiving strong support from Division 17's Executive Council, the Guidelines, as published in TCP, were introduced as a new business item to APA Council by Division 17's Council Representatives at the time (Helen Neville, Louise Douce, Sandra Shullman), stating " The purpose of the Guidelines is to address the gap in the psychology practice by: (a) providing both clear standards for the profession of psychology and a vision, moving psychologists toward improving the health and well-being of a greater number of individuals and communities; and (b) assisting psychologists in evaluating their own preparation for engagement in prevention work and in furthering their education and training through increased knowledge, skills, and experience in the area of prevention."

Introduction of the Guidelines to APA Council began a multi-year process of meetings, re-writings, and consultations across APA divisions, boards, and public constituencies. The Guidelines consists of 9 tenets addressing: (1) Prevention interventions, (2) Social and cultural relevancy, (3) Risk and protective factors, (4) Research, (5) Ethics, (6) Social disparities, (7) Education, (8) Systemic and institutional change, and (9) Public policy. The Guidelines will be published in the *American Psychologist*, but they are currently available on the Prevention Section's web site http://www.div17.org/sections/prevention/.

While APA approval of the Guidelines is an historic step, it is only the beginning, as next steps must include broad dissemination, infusing their content into the education and training of psychologists, strengthening prevention goals in the science and practice of psychology, and promoting prevention as critically important to all of society. Members of Division 17 are especially welcome to join in this effort, and may contact John Romano at roman001@umn.edu or Sally Hage at shage@springfieldcollege.edu.

Many people, too numerous to list here, contributed to the Guidelines throughout the development and review process. However, Mary Hardiman (APA Staff: Board of

[†] Hage, S. M., Romano, J. L., Conyne, R. K., Kenny, M., Matthews, C., Schwartz, J. P., & Waldo, M. (2007). Best practice guidelines on prevention practice, research, training, and social advocacy for psychologists. The Counseling Psychologist, 35, 493-566.

Professional Affairs) was especially instrumental in assisting the Prevention Guidelines Work Group throughout the process. Members of the Work Group since 2011 and their APA divisions are:

John L. Romano (Chair), (17, 52)
G. Anne Bogat (27)
Robert K. Conyne, (17, 49)
Sally M. Hage, (17)
Arthur M. Horne, (17, 49)
Maureen E. Kenny, (17, 35)
Connie Matthews, (17, 35, 44, 45, 50)
Jonathan P. Schwartz, (17, 51)
Anneliese Singh, (17, 35, 44, 45, 48)
Michael Waldo, (17)
Y. Joel Wong, (17, 45, 51, Asian American Psychological Association)

Appendix E. Guidelines for Establishing a Telemental Health Program to Provide Evidence-Based Therapy for Trauma-Exposed Children and Families

Jones, Andrea M.; Shealy, Kristen M.; Reid-Quiñones, Kathryn; Moreland, Angela D.; Davidson, Tatiana M.; López, Cristina M.; Barr, Simone C.; de Arellano, Michael A. Psychological Services, Dec 9, 2013, No Pagination Specified. doi: 10.1037/a0034963

Abstract

Although similar rates of traumatic experiences exist in both rural and urban settings, mental health resources available to those living in rural areas are often scarce. Limited resources pose a problem for children and families living in rural areas, and several barriers to service access and utilization exist including reduced anonymity, few "after hours" services, decreased availability of evidence-based treatments, few specialty clinics, and expenses associated with travel, taking time off work, and provision of childcare. As a solution, the authors discussed the utility, use, and set-up of a telemental health program within an existing community outreach program. Suggestions for establishing a telemental health clinic are presented along with guidelines for the delivery of trauma-focused, cognitive–behavioral therapy (TF-CBT) via telemental health videoconferencing technology. Specific guidelines discussed included (1) establishing and using community partnerships, (2) Memoranda of Understanding (MOU), (3) equipment setup and technological resources, (4) videoconferencing software, (5) physical setup, (6) clinic administration, (7) service reimbursement and start-up costs, (8) therapy delivery modifications, and (9) delivering culturally competent services to rural and remote areas. (PsycINFO Database Record (c) 2013 APA, all rights reserved)

APPENDIX F. TELEHEALTH COMPETENCIES*

Introduction

The American Psychological Association (APA) has espoused that the expanding use of telecommunication technology in psychology practice supports the need for the development of guidelines for telepsychology. Over the last decade psychologists have been introduced to rapidly evolving technological media. As a result, psychologists are becoming more dependent on the use of technology in their practices. As the state of Ohio has rules pertinent to telepsychology and the Ohio Psychological Association (OPA) has developed telepsychology guidelines, this document is designed to set forth a fundamental level of core competencies related to telepsychology that all psychologists in the State of Ohio should adhere to in order to demonstrate best practices and assure client welfare. This document is designed to identify basic telepsychology competencies pertinent to the (a) Ohio Board of Psychology Telepsychology Rules (2011); the Ohio Psychological Association Telepsychology Guidelines (2010); The APA Guidelines for Telepsychology (2013); and the Health Insurance Portability and Accountability Act.

I. Psychologist Technical Skills: Foundational technological skills that are needed to establish a therapeutic relationship via technological means for the psychologist and the client.

Knowledge and Skills of Technology Approaches	
Knowledge	Skill
I.a. Knowledge of limits of practice in relation to telepsychology rules and guidelines	Psychologists need to be aware of 2012 State of Ohio Telepsychology Guidelines2011 Ohio Bd. Of Psychology Telepsychology Rule 4732-17-01(1) and 2013 American Psychological Association Telepsychology Guidelines
I.b. Knowledge of telemental health best practice standards and guidelines	Knowledgeable about current telemental health standards and guidelines relevant to telepsychology such as 2013 Practice Guidelines for Video-Based Online Mental Health Services
I.c. Knowledge of evolving technology	Remain abreast of evolving uses of technology in providing psychological services.
I.d. Knowledge of existing technology	Use of current forms of telecommunications such as video teleconferencing, telephone, texting, email, etc.
I.e., Knowledge of how to assess the client's knowledge and skills for receiving services via telecommunications	Evaluating the client's abilities to receive services via telecommunications based upon their knowledge and skills in using the telecommunications that would be used to receive telepsychology services
I.f. Knowledge of how to assess client's needs to determine the most appropriate technological approach for therapeutic services.	Establishing contact with client to conduct an initial assessment to determine their physical capabilities, language requirements, cultural mores, clinical needs and access to devices and services permitting synchronous and/or asynchronous communications.

*These competencies were originally developed by the Ohio Psychological Association. They are published here with the kind permission of Drs. Marc B. Dielman and Michael Ranney (personal communication, November 26, 2013).

(Continued)

Knowledge and Skills of Technology Approaches	
Knowledge	Skill
I.g. Knowledge of current and evolving online assessment tools.	•Conducting a diagnostic interview in order to assess client's psychological needs and issues to align with appropriate online assessments. •Adhere to standardized procedures for conducting online assessments to ensure the integrity of the data. •Awareness of limitations relating to online assessment and interpretation.
I.h. Knowledge of security issues related to telepsychology therapeutic approaches	•Use of encryption •Storage of electronic communications (e.g., time period, location) •Disposal of electronic records of client data

II. Psychologist's Clinical Telepsychology Skills: Set of foundational skills used in the application of telepsychology.

Knowledge and Skills of Clinical Telepsychology	
Knowledge	Skill
II.a. Knowledge of how to conduct therapeutic and/or assessment services online.	Maintain periodic consultation with professional colleagues, attend trainings and professional conferences keep abreast of professional literature as well as meet any future biannual telepsychology requirements of the Ohio State Board of Psychology.
II.b. Knowledge of evolving specialized clinical skills required for online therapeutic services.	Maintain periodic consultation with professional colleagues, attend trainings and professional conferences.
II.c. Knowledge, respect, and awareness of factors pertaining to age, race, ethnicity, language, gender orientation, disability, and culture.	Identify needs and appropriate modifications related to client diversity in regards to therapeutic services and/or online assessments.

III. Psychologist and Client Relationship: Set of foundational skills used in the application of telepsychology to establish a therapeutic online relationship.

Knowledge and Skills for Establishing, Maintaining, and Terminating the Psychologist and Client Relationship	
Knowledge	Skill
III.a. Knowledge pertaining to decision-making regarding client welfare.	Conduct a risk vs. benefit analysis during the three stages (i.e., initial, ongoing, final) of the online therapeutic relationship.
III.b. Knowledge of legal and ethical requirements related to state and federal laws and regulations.	Comply with best practice approaches for the delivery of online therapeutic services via periodic consultation with professional colleagues, attending online trainings and professional conferences.

Initial Stage of Online Therapeutic Relationship	
Knowledge	Skill
III.c. Knowledge of the most appropriate therapeutic approach based on client needs.	Establishing contact with client to conduct an initial assessment to determine their physical capabilities, language requirements, cultural mores, and access to devices and services permitting face-to-face and remote (synchronous and/or asynchronous) communications.
III.d. Knowledge of how to develop and communicate the service or treatment plan and process.	Review the service or treatment plan including therapeutic goals and description of the process and development of therapeutic goals
III.e., Knowledge of HIPAA policies	Review the following with client: • written agreements and informed consent • clarification of fees • financial arrangements • storage of electronic communications (e.g., online session transcripts) • release of information • provisions of disclosures to other professionals
III.f. Knowledge of how to establish an emergency plan	Communicate with client: • 24 hour emergency coverage (i.e., after hour coverage) • Plans for the absence/unavailability of treating psychologist to include a psychologist with telepsychology expertise Securing Client Information • Client's emergency contact information (e.g., alternate emergency contact) Knowledge of Community Resources in Client's Geographic Area • List of emergency contact numbers (e.g., police, crisis agencies, hospital, rescue)
III.g. Knowledge of Limitations of Distance Technology	Awareness of: • Compatibility of electronic equipment and services • Contingency plans for disruption of service • Security risks • Impact of various electronic communication formats on the client-therapist response time
III.h. Knowledge of on-going risk vs. benefit analysis	• Continual assessment of the therapeutic relationship , progress toward client goals, and approach being used online ○ Progress monitoring (e.g., monitoring client's perceptions of satisfaction with telepsychology services) • Modification of treatment plans and/or appropriateness of telepsychology services based on progress monitoring data • Determining whether to continue using telepsychology services versus in-person services, a combination of both, make a referral or discontinue telepsychology services
III.i. Knowledge of When to Terminate Relationship	• Analyze progress monitoring data in relation to the attainment of treatment goals and client benefits and risks.
III.j. Knowledge of How to Terminate Relationship	• Develop follow-up contingency plan • Analyze client's perceptions of satisfaction with telepsychology services

IV. Psychologist's Clinical Supervision Skills Using Telepsychology: Set of foundational skills used in the application of telepsychology to guide a supervisory online relationship.

Supervisor and Supervisee Knowledge and Skills of Technology Approaches	
Knowledge	Skill
IV.a. Knowledge of technology approaches and competency guidelines for client welfare.	• See above I.a – III.j • Establishing compatible telepsychology communications
Knowledge and Skills for Establishing, Maintaining, and Terminating Supervisor and Supervisee Relationship	
IV.b. Knowledge of the most appropriate supervision models based on supervisee's needs.	• Choose a compatible supervisory model based on an analysis of the supervisee's clinical strengths and weaknesses • Determine the appropriateness of the supervisory model for telepsychology supervision.
IV.c. Knowledge of supervisory plan development	• Create a written professional developmental plan of competency attainment for the supervisee that can be implemented via telepsychology and/or face-to-face supervision. • Arrange a systematic schedule for weekly supervision via telepsychology and/or face-to-face meetings. • Clarify supervisor's responsibilities and supervisee's expectations.
IV.d. Knowledge of evaluation and feedback	• Establish a best practices evaluation and feedback approach that encompasses multi-method supervisory techniques (e.g., written, interviews with other professionals working with supervisee, client feedback evaluation on services) • Development of a contingency plan for supervision if telepsychology approaches are not sufficient for adequate developmental professional growth of the supervisee (e.g., requires more intense face-to-face supervision with or without telepsychology supervision).
IV.e. Knowledge of How to Terminate a Supervisory Relationship	• Review written developmental plan of competency attainment identifying areas of growth and areas for continued professional development. • Secure supervisee's feedback and perceptions regarding the use of telepsychology supervisory methods.

V. Ongoing Professional Development Requirements: Continuing education to maintain current knowledge and skill competencies in telepsychology.

Knowledge	Skill
V.a. Knowledge of current telepsychology practices.	Psychologists practicing telepsychology will regularly obtain needed continuing education and training to maintain competence in the area of telepsychology.

Appendix G. Principles/Standards

For purposes of this survey, please assume a situation where there has been success in developing a common set of telepsychology practice principles/standards. Such principles/ standards would recognize that telepsychology occurs within the context of existing ethical standards and principles for practice. Accordingly, in addition to general adherence to ethical principles and best practices, providers of telepsychology also need to be aware of issues particular to the telepsychological service they are offering. The Task Force has proposed the following set of principles/standards specific to telepsychology:

- Psychologists providing telepsychology services will be held to the same standard of care/competence/conduct as they would when providing more traditionally based services.
- Psychologists providing interjurisdictional telepsychology services shall be licensed/registered in good standing in the home jurisdiction from which the services are being provided.
- Psychologists providing telepsychology services shall be aware of the location of the client/patient and ensure the legal entitlement to provide telepsychology services in that jurisdiction.
- At the onset of professional services, psychologists providing telepsychology services shall provide notification to the boards of all jurisdictions into which the telepsychological service will be provided and in which the client/patient resides or is located at the time of service. The psychologist shall identify the home jurisdiction in which they hold a license in good standing.

Please Note: Under Option 4 the psychologist would directly inform the distant jurisdiction(s); under Option 5 and Option 6 the certifying agency would inform the distant jurisdiction(s).

- Psychologists providing telepsychology services shall be aware of applicable laws, rules, regulations, and standards for practice in the jurisdiction into which the service is being delivered, including but not limited to any requirement to have liability insurance in the jurisdiction into which the services are being provided. Where there is a conflict between jurisdictions with regard to laws, regulations, and standards, psychologists shall adhere to the laws, regulations and standards of his/her home jurisdiction in a manner consistent with the distant jurisdiction's laws and regulations as is reasonably possible. The psychologist will inform the patient/client of all significant conflicts that may adversely impact the professional services that the psychologists will provide with a particular emphasis on any limits to confidentiality, privilege, and duties to report.
- Psychologists providing telepsychology services shall be competent in the technology of the service delivery medium and maintain current competency through continuing professional development, consultation or other procedures, in conformance with current regulatory requirements.

- Psychologists providing telepsychology services will ensure the electronic and physical security and integrity of client records, including any electronic data and communications.
- Psychologists providing telepsychology services shall be competent in the maintenance of privacy, confidentiality, and security related to equipment, electronic records and electronic communications or data, including the disposal of such.
- Psychologists providing telepsychology services shall provide the client/patient with the contact information and process for filing a complaint with the regulatory body of the home jurisdiction in which they hold a license in good standing.
- Psychologists providing telepsychology services shall establish and communicate policies with the client/patient regarding technological difficulties or failures.
- Psychologists providing telepsychology services must verify at the onset of each contact the identity of the client/patient, as well as the identity of all individuals privy to any electronically transmitted service, at any time during the contact.
- Psychologists providing telepsychology services must inform the client/patient of any limits to confidentiality, security, and privacy unique to the telepsychology service being provided.

APPENDIX H. INTERDISCIPLINARY PRINCIPLES

From

Reed, G. M., McLaughlin, C. J., & Milholland, K. (in press). Ten interdisciplinary principles for professional practice in telehealth: Implications for psychology.

Professional Psychology: Research and Practice,

Principle 1: The basic standards of professional conduct governing each health care profession are not altered by the use of telehealth technologies to deliver health care, conduct research, or provide education. Developed by each profession, these standards focus in part on the practitioner's responsibility to provide ethical and high quality care.

Principle 2: Confidentiality of client visits, client health records, and the integrity of information in the health care information is essential.

Principle 3: All clients directly involved in a telehealth encounter must be informed about the process, the attendant risks and benefits, and their own rights and responsibilities, and must provide adequate informed consent.

Principle 4: Services provided via telehealth must adhere to the basic assurance of quality and professional health care in accordance with each health care discipline's clinical standards.

Principle 5: Each health care discipline must examine how its patterns of care delivery are affected by telehealth and is responsible for developing its own processes for assuring Competence in the delivery of health care via telehealth technologies.

Principle 6: Documentation requirements for telehealth services must be developed that assure documentation of each client encounter with recommendations and treatments, communication with other health care providers as appropriate, and adequate protection of client confidentiality.

Principle 7: Clinical guidelines in the area of telehealth should be based on empirical evidence, when available, and professional consensus among involved health care disciplines.

Principle 8: The integrity and therapeutic value of the relationship between clients and health care practitioner should be maintained and not diminished by the use of telehealth technology.

Principle 9: Health care professionals do not need additional licensing to provide services via telehealth technologies: At the same time, telehealth technologies cannot be used as a vehicle for providing services that otherwise are not legally or professionally authorized.

Principle 10: The safety of clients and practitioners must be ensured. Safe hardware and software, combined with demonstrated user competence, are essential components of safe telehealth practice.

REFERENCES

Abroms, L. C., Gill, J., Windsor, R., & Simons-Morton, B. (2009). A process evaluation of e-mail counselling for smoking cessation in college students: Feasibility, acceptability and cost. *Journal of Smoking Cessation, 4*(1), 26-33.

Agostinelli, G., Brown, J.M., & Miller, W.R. (1995). Effects of normative feedback on consumption among heavy drinking college students. *Journal of Drug Education, 25*, 31-40.

Aguilera, A., & Muñoz, R. F. (2011). Text messaging as an adjunct to CBT in low-income populations: A usability and feasibility pilot study. *Professional Psychology: Research and Practice, 42*, 472-478.

Akmehmet-Sekerler, S. (2009). A qualitative study of online counselor experiences and online counseling session dynamics. *Dissertation Abstracts International Section A: Humanities and Social Sciences, 69*(11-A), 4252.

Alcaniz, M., Botella, C., Banos, R. M., Zaragoza, I., & Guixeres, J. (2009). The Intelligent e-therapy system: A new paradigm for telepsychology and cybertherapy. *British Journal of Guidance & Counselling, 37*(3), 287-296.

Alemi, F., Haack, M. R., Nemes, S., Aughburns, R., Sinkule, J., & Neuhauser, D. (2007). Therapeutic emails. *Substance Abuse Treatment, Prevention, and Policy,* 2(7).

Alleman, J. R. (2002). Online counseling: The Internet and mental health treatment. *Psychotherapy: Theory, Research, Practice, Training, 39*(2), 199-209.

Alvarez, A. R. G. (2012). "IH8U": Confronting cyberbullying and exploring the use of cybertools in teen dating relationships. *Journal of Clinical Psychology, 68*, 1205–1215.

America Telemedicine Association (2013). *A lexicon of assessment and outcome measures for telemental health*. No address available.

American Psychological Association. (1994). *Diagnostic and statistical manual of mental disorders* (4th ed.). Washington, DC: Author.

Amichai-Hamburger, Y., McKenna, K. Y. A., & Tal, S. (2008). E-empowerment: Empowerment by the internet. *Computers in Human Behavior, 24*, 1776-1789. doi: 10.1016/j.chb.2008.02.002

Amstadter, A. B., Broman-Fulks, J., Zinzow, H., Ruggiero, K. J., & Cercone, J. (2009). Internet-based interventions for traumatic stress-related mental health problems: A review and suggestion for future research. *Clinical Psychology Review, 29*, 410-420. doi:10.1016/j.cpr.2009.04.001

Anderson, P., Rothbaum, B. O., & Hodges, L. F. (2003). Virtual reality exposure in the treatment of social anxiety. *Cognitive & Behavioral Practice, 10*, 240-247.

Anderson, P., Zimand, E., Schmertz, S. K., & Ferrer, M. (2007). Usability and utility of a computerized cognitive-behavioral self-help program for public speaking anxiety. *Cognitive & Behavioral Practice, 14*, 198-207.

Andersson, G. (2009). Using the internet to provide cognitive behaviour therapy. *Behaviour Research and Therapy, 47*, 175-180. doi:10.1016/j.brat.2009.01.010

Andersson, G., Carlbring, P., Holmstrom, A., Sparthan, E., Furmark, T., Nilsson-Ihrfelt, E., & Ekselius, L. (2006). Internet-based self-help with therapist feedback and in vivo group exposure for social phobia: A randomized controlled trial. *Journal of Consulting and Clinical Psychology, 74*, 677-686.

Andersson, G., Estling, F., Jakobsson, E., Cuijpers, P., & Carlbring, P. (2011). Can the patient decide which modules to endorse? An open trial of tailored Internet treatment of anxiety disorders. *Cognitive Behaviour Therapy, 40*, 57-64.

Andersson, G., Hesser, H., Veilord, A., Svedling, L., Andersson, F., Sleman, O., Mauritzson, L., Sarkohi, A., Claesson, E., Zetterqvist, V., Lamminen, M., Eriksson, T. & Carlbring, P. (2013). Randomised controlled non-inferiority trial with 3-year follow-up of internet-delivered versus face-to-face group cognitive behavioural therapy for depression. *Journal of Affective Disorders, 151*(3), 986-994.

Andersson, G., Ljótsson, B., & Weise, C. (2011). Internet-delivered treatment to promote health. *Current Opinion In Psychiatry, 24*(2), 168-172.

Andersson, G., Ritterband, L., & Carlbring, P. (2008). A primer for the assessment, diagnosis and delivery of Internet interventions for (mainly) panic disorder. Lessons learned from our research groups. *Clinical Psychologist, 12,* 1-8.

Andersson, G., Waara, J., Jonsson, U., Malmaeus, F., Carlbring, P., & Öst, L. (2013). Internet-based exposure treatment versus one-session exposure treatment of snake phobia: A randomized controlled trial. *Cognitive Behaviour Therapy, 42*(4), 284-291.

Anguera, J.A., Boccanfuso, J., Rintoul, J.L., Al-Hashimi, O., Faraji, F., Janowich, J., Kong, E., Larraburo, Y., Rolle, C., Johnston, E., & Gazzaley, A. (2013). Video game training enhances cognitive control in older adults. *Nature, 501*(7465), 97-101.

Anthony, K., Nagel, D. M., & Goss, S. (Eds.). (2010). *The use of technology in mental health: Applications, ethics, and practice*. Springfield, IL: C. C. Thomas

Anttila, M. M., Välimäki, M. M., Koivunen, M. M., Luukkaala, T. T., Kaila, M. M., Pitkänen, A. A., & Kontio, R. R. (2011). Adoption of an Internet-based patient education programme in psychiatric hospitals. *Journal of Psychiatric and Mental Health Nursing, 18*(10), 914-923.

Atanasoff, L. M. (2006). Computer - mediated communication and online counseling relationship development. *Dissertation Abstracts International Section A: Humanities and Social Sciences, 66*(10-A), 3575.

Atkinson, L.K., Denham, A., & Quick, J. (2012). Mobile technologies in education and health care. In L. L'Abate & D. A. Kaiser (Eds.), *Handbook of Technology in Psychology, Psychiatry, and Neurology: Theory, Research, and Practice* (pp. 209-226). New York: Nova Science Publishers.

Atkinson, R. K., Lin, L., & Joseph, S. S. (2012). Animations and multimedia tutorials. In L. L'Abate & D. A. Kaiser (Eds.), *Handbook of Technology in Psychology, Psychiatry, and*

Neurology: Theory, Research, and Practice (pp. 69-90). New York: Nova Science Publishers.

Atkinson, R. K., Sabo, K., & Conley, Q. (2012). The participatory web. In L. L'Abate & D. A. Kaiser (Eds.), *Handbook of Technology in Psychology, Psychiatry, and Neurology: Theory, Research, and Practice* (pp. 59-68). New York: Nova Science Publishers.

Ayoko, O. B., Konrad, A. M., & Boyle, M. V. (2012). Online work: Managing conflict and emotions for performance in virtual teams. *European Management Journal, 30*(2), 156-174.

Baca, C. T., & Manuel, J. K. (2007). Satisfaction with long-distance motivational interviewing for problem drinking. *Addictive Disorders & their Treatment, 6*(1), 39-41.

Backhaus, A., Agha, Z., Maglione, M., L., Repp, A., Ross, B., Zuest, D., Rice-Thorp, N. M., Lohr, J., & Thorp, S. R. (2012). Videoconferencing psychotherapy: A systematic review. *Psychological Services, 9*(2), 111-131.

Bailey, R., Yager, J., & Jenson, J. (2002). The psychiatrist as clinical computerologist in the treatment of adolescents: Old barks in new bytes. *American Journal of Psychiatry, 159,* 1298-1304.

Baker, D. C., & Bufka, L. F. (2011). Preparing for the telehealth world: Navigating legal, regulatory, reimbursement, and ethical issues in an electronic age, *Professional Psychology: Research and Practice,* 42 (6), 405-11.

Bambling, M., King, R., Reid, W., & Wegner, K. (2008). Online counselling: The experience of counsellors providing synchronous single-session counselling to young people. *Counselling & Psychotherapy Research, 8*, 110-116.

Banos, R. M., Botella, C., Guillen, V., Garcia-Palacios, A., Quero, S., Breton-Lopez, J., Alcaniz, M. (2009). An adaptive display to treat stress-related disorders: EMMA's world. *British Journal of Guidance & Counselling, 37*, 347-356.

Barak, A. (1999). Psychological applications on the Internet: A discipline on the threshold of a new millennium. *Applied & Preventive Psychology, 8*, 231-245.

Barak, A. (2003). Ethical and professional issues in career assessment on the internet. *Journal of Career Assessment, 11*, 3-21.

Barak, A. (2007). Emotional support and suicide prevention through the internet: A field project report. *Computers in Human Behavior, 23*, 971-984. doi:10.1016/j.chb.2005.08.001

Barak, A., & Bloch, N. (2006). Factors related to perceived helpfulness in supporting highly distressed individuals through an online support chat. *CyberPsychology & Behavior, 9*(1), 60-68.

Barak, A., Boniel-Nissim, M., & Suler, J. (2008). Fostering empowerment in online support groups. *Computers in Human Behavior, 24*, 1867-1883.

Barak, A., & Grohol, J. M. (2011). Current and future trends in Internet-supported mental health interventions', *Journal of Technology in Human Services,* 29 (3), 155-96.

Barak. A., Hen, L., Boniel-Nissim, M., Shapira, N. (2009). A comprehensive review and meta-analysis of the effectiveness of internet-based psychotherapeutic inter-ventions. *Journal of Technological Human Services*, *26*, 109-160.

Barak, A., Klein, B., & Proudfoot, J. G. (2009). Defining internet-supported therapeutic interventions. *Annals of Behavioral Medicine, 38*(1), 4-17.

Barnett, J. E. (2005). Online counseling: New entity, new challenges. *The Counseling Psychologist, 33*(6), 872-880.

Barnett, J. E., & Shale, A. J. (2012). The integration of Complementary and Alternative Medicine (CAM) into the practice of psychology: A vision for the future. *Professional Psychology: Research and Practice, 43*(6), 576-585.

Baron, J., Bierschwale, D., & Bleiberg, J. R. (2006). Clinical implications of students' use of online communication for college psychotherapy. *Journal of College Student Psychotherapy, 20*, 69-77.

Barnett, J. E. (2005). Online counseling: New entity, new challenges. *The Counseling Psychologist, 33*(6), 872-880.

Barnett, J. S., & Kolmes, K. (2013). Practicing in the era of social media. In G. P. Koocher, J. C. Norcross, & B. A Greene (Eds.), *Psychologist's desk reference. Third Edition* (pp. 700-704). New York: Oxford University Press.

Baron, J., Bierschwale, D., & Bleiberg, J. R. (2006). Clinical implications of students' use of online communication for college psychotherapy. *Journal of College Student Psychotherapy, 20*, 69-77.

Barthelmeus, S. J. (2000). Disclosure of the limitations, risks and benefits by online counseling services: An investigation of the effects of differing amounts of information on perceived desirability. *Dissertation Abstracts International, 60*, 3556B.

Baur, C. (2000). Limiting factors on the transformative powers of e-mail in patient- physician relationships: A critical analysis. *Health Communication, 12*, 239-259.

Bauer, S., Moessner, M., Wolf, M., Haug, S., & Kordy, H. (2009). ESSPRIT-an internet-based programme for the prevention and early intervention of eating disorders in college students. *British Journal of Guidance & Counselling, 37*, 327-336.

Beintner, I., Jacobi, C., & Taylor, C. B. (2012). Effects of an Internet-based prevention programme for eating disorders in the USA and Germany — A meta-analytic review'. *European Eating Disorders Review,* 20 (1), 1-8.

Bell, V. (2007). Online information, extreme communities and internet therapy: Is the internet good for our mental health? *Journal Of Mental Health, 16*, 445-457.

Bendelin, N., Hesser, H., Dahl, J., Carlbring, P., Nelson, K., & Andersson, G. (2011). Experiences of guided Internet-based cognitive-behavioural treatment for depression: A qualitative study. *BMC Psychiatry, 11, 107.*

Bender, J., L., et al. (2011). Can pain be managed through the Internet? A systematic review of randomized controlled trials', *Pain,* 152 (8), 1740-50.

Berger, T., et al. (2011). Internet-based treatment of depression: A randomized control-led trial comparing guided with unguided self-help'. *Cognitive Behaviour Therapy,* 40 (1), 251-66.

Berger, T., Caspar, F., Richardson, R., Kneubühler, B., Sutter, D., & Andersson, G. (2011). Internet-based treatment of social phobia: A randomized controlled trial comparing unguided with two types of guided self-help. *Behaviour Research and Therapy.*

Bessell, T. L., McDonald, S., Silagy, C. A., Anderson, J. N., Hiller, J. E., & Sansom, L. N. (2002). Do internet interventions for consumers cause more harm than good? A systematic review. *Health Expectations, 5*, 28-37.

Bessière, K., Kiesler, S., Kraut, R., & Boneva, B. S. (2008). Effects of Internet use and social resources on changes in depression. *Information, Communication & Society, 11*, 47-70. doi: 10.1080/13691180701858851

Beutler, S. (2008). Introducing students to career exploration. *Techniques: Connecting Education and Careers, 83*, 50-52.

Bhandari, G., Tiessen, B., & Snowdon, A. (2011), 'Meeting community needs through leadership and innovation: A case of virtual psychiatric emergency department (ED)', *Behaviour & Information Technology,* 30 (4), 517-23.

Bickman, L., Kelley, S. D., & Athay, M. (2012). The technology of measurement feedback systems. *Couple and Family Psychology: Research and Practice, 1*, 274 –284. DOI: 10.1037/a0031022.

Bien, T. H., Miller, W. R., & Tonigan, J. S. (1993). Brief interventions for alcohol problems: A review. *British Journal of Addiction, 88*, 315-336.

Biocca, F., & Levy, M.R., (Eds.). (1995). *Communication in the age of virtual reality.* Hillsdale, NJ: Lawrence Erlbaum Associates.

Blake, D. D., Weathers, F. W., Nagy, L. M., & et al. (1995). The development of a Clinician-Administered PTSD Scale. *Journal of Traumatic Stress, 8*:75 –90.

Blanchard, E. B., Jones-Alexander, J., Buckley, T. C., & Forneris, C. A. (1996). Psychometric properties of the PTSD Checklist (PCL). *Behavior Research and Therapy, 34*:669 –73.

Blankers, M., Koeter, M. J., & Schippers, G. M. (2011). Internet therapy versus internet self-help versus no treatment for problematic alcohol use: A randomized controlled trial. *Journal of Consulting and Clinical Psychology*, *79*(3), 330-341.

Bloom, J. W. (1998). The ethical practice of web counseling. *British Journal of Guidance & Counselling, 23*, 53-59.

Bobbitt, B. L., Cate, R. A., Beardsley, S. D., Azocar, F., & McCulloch, J. (2012). Quality improvement and outcomes in the future of professional psychology: Opportunities and challenges. *Professional Psychology: Research and Practice, 43*(6), 551-559. http://psycnet.apa.org/journals/pro/43/6/551/

Bobevski, I., Holgate, A. M., & McLennan, J. (1997). Characteristics of effective telephone counseling skills. *British Journal of Guidance & Counselling, 25*, 239-249.

Bockting, C. L. H., et al. (2011). Disrupting the rhythm of depression using mobile cognitive therapy for recurrent depression: Randomized controlled trial design and protocol', *BMC Psychiatry,* 11.

Boettcher, J., Hasselrot, J., Sund, E., Andersson, G., & Carlbring, P. (2014). Combining attention training with internet-based cognitive-behavioural self-help for social anxiety: A randomised controlled trial. *Cognitive Behaviour Therapy*, *43*(1), 34-48.

Bordnick, P., Copp, H., Traylor, A., Graap, K., Carter, B., Walton, A., Ferrer, M. (2009). Reactivity to cannabis cues in virtual reality environments. *Journal of Psycho-active Drugs, 41*, 105-112.

Bordnick, P., Graap, K., Copp, H. Brooks, J. Ferrer, M. (2005). Virtual reality cue reactivity assessment in cigarette smokers, *Cyber Psychology & Behavior, 8*, 487-492.

Bordnick, P, Traylor, A., Copp, H., Graap, K., Carter, B., Ferrer, M., & Walton, A.(2008). Assessing reactivity to virtual reality alcohol based cues. *Addictive Behaviors, 33*, 743-756.

Borowitz, S. M. & Ritterband, L. M. (2001). Using the Internet to teach parents and children about constipation and encopresis. *Medical Informatics and the Internet in Medicine*, *26*, 283-295. PMID: 11783712.

Botella, C., Gallego, M. J., Garcia-Palacios, A., Banos, R. M., Quero, S., & Alcaniz, M. (2009). The acceptability of an internet-based self-help treatment for fear of public speaking. *British Journal of Guidance & Counselling, 37*, 297-311.

Botella, C., García-Palacios, A., Villa, H., Baños, R. M., Quero, S., Alcañiz, M., & Riva, G. (2007). Virtual reality exposure in the treatment of panic disorder and agoraphobia: A controlled study. *Clinical Psychology & Psychotherapy, 14*, 164-175. doi:10.1002/cpp.524

Bouchard, S., Paquin, B., Payeur, R., & et al. (2004). Delivering cognitive-behavior therapy for panic disorder with agoraphobia in videoconference. *Telemedicine Journal of E-Health, 10*, 13 –25.

Bradford, S., & Rickwood, D. (2014). Adolescent's preferred modes of delivery for mental health services. *Child & Adolescent Mental Health, 19*(1), 39-45.

Bradner, E. (2003). Computer mediated communication among teams: What are "teams" and how are they virtual?. In C. Lueg & D. Fisher (Eds.), *Computer supportive cooperative work* (1st ed., pp. 135-154). Philadelphia: Springer Science.

Brahm, T. & Kunze, F. (2012). The role of trust climate in virtual teams. *Journal of managerial psychology, 27*(6), 595-614.

Brahm, T. & Kunze, F. (2012). *Increasing the performance of virtual teams: The context role of trust climate*. Informally published manuscript, University of St. Gallen, University of St. Gallen, Cary, N.C., Retrieved from https://www.alexandria.unisg.ch/Publikationen/212785/L-it

Brand, J. & D. (2012), 'Telehealth approaches to obsessive-compulsive related disorders'. *Psychotherapy Research,* 22 (3), 306-16.

Brandt, V., England, W., & Ward, S. (2011). Virtual teams: as telecommu-nications technology makes it possible to assemble teams made up of individuals dispersed across the globe, it becomes essential to under-stand how teams function differently when they don't meet face to face. *Research-Technology Management, 54*(6), 62.

Brenes, G. A., Ingram, C.W., & Danhauer, S.C. (2011). Benefits and challenges of conducting psychotherapy by telephone. *Professional Psychology: Research and Practice, 42,* 543-549.

Brock, R. L., Barry, R. A., Lawrence, E., Dey, J., & Rolffs, J. (2012). Internet administration of paper-and-pencil questionnaires used in couple research: Assessing psychometric equivalence. *Assessment, 19*, 226-242.

Brooks, E., et al. (2012). The diffusion of telehealth in rural American Indian communities: A retrospective survey of key stakeholders', *Telemedicine Journal of E-Health,* 18 (1), 60-65.

Brundage, S. B., Graap, K., Gibbons, K. F., Ferrer, M., & Brooks, J. (2006). Frequency of stuttering during challenging and supportive virtual reality job interviews. *Journal of Fluency Disorders, 31*, 325-339.

Burgess, N., Christensen, H., Leach, L. S., Farrer, L., & Griffiths, K. M. (2008). Mental health profile of callers to a telephone counselling service. *Journal of Telemedicine and Telecare, 14*, 42-47.

Burke, M., Kraut, R., & Joyce, E. (2010). Membership claims and requests: Conversation-level newcomer socialization strategies in online groups. *Small Group Research, 4*, 4-40. doi: 10.1177/1046496409351936.

Burns, J. M., Durkin, L. A., & Nicholas, J. (2009). Mental health of young people in the United States: What role can the Internet play in reducing stigma and promoting help seeking? *Journal of Adolescent Health, 45*(1), 95-97.

Bush, N.E., Bosmajian, C.P., Fairall, J.M., McCann, R.A., & Ciulla, R.P. (2011). afterdeployment.org: A web-based multimedia wellness resource for the postdeployment military community. *Professional Psychology: Research and Practice, 42* 455-462.

Butler, S. K., & Constantine, M. G. (2006). Web-based peer supervision, collective self-esteem, and case conceptualization ability in school counselor trainees. *Professional School Counseling, 10*, 146-152.

Button, K. S., et al. (2012), 'Factors associated with differential response to online cognitive behavioural therapy', *Social Psychiatry and Psychiatric Epidemiology,* 47 (5), 827-33.

Cascio, W. F., & Shurygailo, S. (2003). E-Leadership and Virtual Teams. *Organizational Dynamics, 31*(4), 362-376.

Chhay R. V. & Kleiner, B. H. (2013). Effective communication in virtual teams. *Industrial Management, 55*(4), 27-30.

Caffery, L., & Smith, A. C. (2006). The relation between response time and the re-utilization of an email based counselling system. *Journal of Telemedicine and Telecare, 12*(3), 20-22.

Calear, A. L., Christensen, H., Mackinnon, A., Griffiths, K. M., & O'Kearney, R. (2009). The YouthMood project: A cluster randomized controlled trial of an online cognitive behavioral program with adolescents. *Journal of Consulting and Clinical Psychology, 77*, 1021-1032.

Camillus, C. M. (2008). To e- or not to e-: An analogue study of disclosure rates in e-counseling. *Dissertation Abstracts International: Section B: The Sciences and Engineering, 68*(7-B), 4813.

Carlson, L. A., Portman, T. A. A., & Bartlett, J. R. (2006). Professional school counselors' approaches to technology. *Professional School Counseling, 9*(3), 252-256.

Campbell, A. N. C., Miele, G.M., Nunes, E.V., McCrimmon, S., Chitza, U.E. (2012). Web-based, psychosocial treatment for substance use disorders in community treatment settings, *Psychological Services,* 9 (2), 212-14.

Carlbring, P., & Andersson, G. (2006). Internet and psychological treatment. how well can they be combined? *Computers in Human Behavior, 22*, 545-553. doi:10.1016/j.chb.2004.10.009

Carlbring, P., Andersson, G., & Kaldo, V. (2011). State-of-the-art treatment via the internet: An optimistic vision of the future. *Cognitive Behaviour Therapy*, *40*(2), 79-81.

Carlbring, P., Nordgren, L. B., Furmark, T., & Andersson, G. (2009). Long-term outcome of internet-delivered cognitive–behavioural therapy for social phobia: A 30-month follow-up. *Behaviour Research and Therapy, 47*, 848-850. doi: 10.1016/j.brat.2009.06.012

Carlbring, P., Maurin, L., Törngren, C., Linna, E., Eriksson, T., Sparthan, E., & Andersson, G. (2011). Individually-tailored, internet-based treatment for anxiety disorders: A randomized controlled trial. *Behaviour Research and Therapy*, *49*(1), 18-24.

Carlson, L. E., Lounsberry, J.J., Maciejewski, O., Wright, K., Collacutt, V., Taenzer, P. (2012). Telehealth-delivered group smoking cessation for rural and urban participants: feasibility and cessation rates, *Addictive Behaviors,* 37 (1), 108-14.

Carrard, I. I., Crépin, C. C., Rouget, P. P., Lam, T. T., Golay, A. A., & Van der Linden, M. M. (2011). Randomised controlled trial of a guided self-help treatment on the internet for binge eating disorder. *Behaviour Research And Therapy*, *49*(8), 482-491.

Carrard, I. I., Fernandez-Aranda, F. F., Lam, T. T., Nevonen, L. L., Liwowsky, I. I., Volkart, A. C., & Norring, C. C. (2011). Evaluation of a guided internet self-treatment programme for bulimia nervosa in several European countries. *European Eating Disorders Review, 19*(2), 138-149.

Chester, A., & Glass, C. A. (2006). Online counselling: A descriptive analysis of therapy services on the internet. *British Journal of Guidance & Counselling, 34*, 145-160.

Choi, I., Zou, J., Titov, N., Dear, B. F., Li, S., Johnston, L., & Hunt, C. (2012). Culturally attuned Internet treatment for depression amongst Chinese Australians: A randomised controlled trial. *Journal Of Affective Disorders, 136*(3), 459-468.

Christogiorgos, S., Vassilopoulo, V., Florou, A., Xydou, V., Douvou, M., Vgenopoulou, S., Tsiantis, J. (2010). Telephone counselling with adolescents and countertransference phenomena: Particularities and challenges. *British Journal of Guidance & Counselling, 38*(3), 313-325. doi:10.1080/03069885.2010.482394

Chung-Do, J., Helm, S., Fukunda, M., Alicata, D., Nishimura, S., & Else, I. (2012). Rural Mental Health: Implications for Telepsychiatry in Clinical Service, Workforce Development, and Organizational Capacity. Telemedicine and e-Health, 18, 244-246.

Chung, W. W., Vesco, A. T., Resko, S., Schiman, N., & Fristad, M. A. (2012). Psycho-social interventions for youth with bipolar disorders: Combining clinicians' and caregivers' perspectives. *Professional Psychology: Research and Practice, 43*(6), 633-640. http://psycnet.apa.org/journals/pro/43/6/633/

Ciccia, A. H., Whitford, B., Krumm, M., McNeal, K. (2011). Improving the access of young urban children to speech, language and hearing screening via telehealth, *Journal of Telemedicine and Telecare,* 17 (5), 240-44.

Ciemins, E., Coon, P., Peck, R., Holloway, B., Min, S.J. (2011). Using telehealth to provide diabetes care to patients in rural Montana: Findings from the Promoting Realistic Individual Self-Management Program, *Telemedicine and e-Health,* 17 (8), 596-602.

Clancy Dollinger, S., & Chwalisz, K. (2011). Reaching rural caregivers with a multicomponent telehealth intervention: The telehelp line for caregivers. *Professional Psychology: Research and Practice, 42,* 528-534.

Clay, R. A. (2014a). A public health approach to suicide. *Monitor on Psychology, 45*, 40-42.

Clay, R. A. (2014b). Reducing rural suicide. *Monitor on Psychology, 45*, 36-39

Clayton, S., Borzekowski, D., Himelhoch, S., Dixon, L., Potts, W., Medoff, D., Hackman, A., & Balis, D. (2009). Media and Internet ownership and use among mental health outpatients with serious mental illness. *The American Journal of Drug And Alcohol Abuse, 35*(5), 364-367.

Cleary, A. M., & DeLosh, E. L. (2012). Wireless Response Systems: 'Clicker' uses and benefits in and out of the classroom. In L. L'Abate & D. A. Kaiser (Eds.), *Handbook of Technology in Psychology, Psychiatry, and Neurology: Theory, Research, and Practice* (pp. 59-68). New York: Nova Science Publishers.

Cockayne, N. L., Glozier, N., Naismith, S. L., Christensen, H., Neal, B., & Hickie, I. B. (2011). Internet-based treatment for older adults with depression and co-morbid cardiovascular disease: Protocol for a randomised, double-blind, placebo controlled trial. *BMC Psychiatry, 11.*

Comer, J. S., & Barlow, D. H. (2014). The occasional case against broad dissemination and implementation: Retaining the role for specialty care in the delivery of psychological treatments. *American Psychologist, 69*, 1018.

Comer, J. S., Furr, J. M., Cooper-Vince, C. E., Kerns, C. E., Chan, P. T., Edson, A. L., Khanna, M., Franklin, M.E., Gracia, A.M. & Freeman, J. B. (2014). Internet-delivered, family-based treatment for early-onset OCD: A preliminary case series. *Journal of Clinical Child and Adolescent Psychology*, *43*(1), 74-87.

Comfort, J., & Franklin, P. (2014). *The Mindful International Manager: How to Work Effectively Across Cultures.* (2nd. ed.). London: Kogan Page Limited.

Conoley, J. C., & Conoley, C. W. (2010). Why does collaboration work? Linking Positive Psychology and collaboration. *Journal of Educational and Psychological Consultation 20*(1), 75-82.

Cox, D. J., Gonder-Frederick, L., Ritterband, L. M., Patel, K., Schächinger, H., Fehm-Wolfsdorf, G., Hermanns, N., Snoek, F., Zrebiec, J., Polonsky, W., Schlundt, D., Kovatchev, B., & Clarke, W. (2006). Blood Glucose Awareness Training (BGAT): What is it, where is it, and where is it going. *Diabetes Spectrum*, *29,* 467.

Cox, D. J., Ritterband, L., Magee, J., Clarke, W., & Gonder-Frederick, L. (2008). Blood glucose awareness training delivered over the Internet. *Diabetes Care, 31*, 1527-1528.

Cox, N. S., Alison, J.A., Rasekaba, T., Holland, A.E. (2012). Telehealth in cystic fibrosis: a systematic review, *Journal of Telemedicine and Telecare,* 18 (2), 72-8.

Cukor, J., Spitalnick, J. S., Difede, J., Rizzo, A. A., & Rothbaum, B. O. (2009). Emerging treatment for PTSD. *Clinical Psychology Review, 29*, 715-726.

Cunningham, J. A., Humphreys, K., & Koski-Jannes, A. (1999). Providing personalized assessment feedback for problem drinking on the Internet. Paper presented at the 33rd annual convention of the Association for the Advancement of Behavior Therapy, Toronto, Ontario.

Cusinato, M., & L'Abate, L. (Eds.). (2012). *Advances in relational competence theory: With special attention to alexithymia*. New York: Nova Science Publishers.

Daim, T. U., Ha, A., Reutiman, S., Hughes, B., & Pathak, U. (2012). Exploring the communication breakdown in global virtual teams. *International journal of project management, 30*(2), 199-212.

Dallery, J., Raiff, B. R., & Grabinski, M. J. (2013). Internet-based contingency management to promote smoking cessation: A randomized controlled study. *Journal Of Applied Behavior Analysis*, *46*(4), 750-764.

Darcy, J., Brunsden, V., & Hill, R. (2011). Exploring online support: Informal caregivers' usage of a mental health discussion board. *Journal Of Cybertherapy And Rehabilitation, 4*, 477-482.

Davis, M., Guyker, W., & Persky, I. (2012), 'Uniting veterans across distance through a telephone-based reminiscence group therapy intervention', *Psychological Services,* 9 (2), 206-08.

DeAngelis, T. (2014). Thank you for not smoking. *Monitor on Psychology, 45*, 41-53.

Dear, B. F., Titov, N., Schwencke, G., Andrews, G., Johnston, L., Craske, M. G., & McEvoy, P. (2011). An open trial of a brief transdiagnostic internet treatment for anxiety and depression. *Behaviour Research and Therapy*, *49*(12), 830-837.

Delahunt, P. B., Morton, J. B., & Mahncke, H. W. (2012). Computer-based cognitive stimulation programs to remediate age-related cognitive decline: What makes a program effective? In L. L'Abate & D. A. Kaiser (Eds.), *Handbook of Technology in Psychology, Psychiatry, and Neurology: Theory, Research, and Practice* (pp. 121-138). New York: Nova Science Publishers.

De las Cuevas, C. (2012). Telehealth conferencing in the neurosciences. In L. L'Abate & D. A. Kaiser (Eds.), *Handbook of Technology in Psychology, Psychiatry, and Neurology: Theory, Research, and Practice* (pp. 355-374). New York: Nova Science Publishers.

DeMers, S. T., Van Horne, B. A., & Rodolfa, E. R. (2008). Changes in training and practice of psychologists: Current challenges for licensing boards. *Professional Psychology: Research and Practice, 39*(5), 473-479. doi: 10.1037/0735-7028.39.5.473

Demiris, G., Thompson, H., Boquet, J., Le, T., Chaudhuri, S., Chung, J. (2012). 'Older adults' acceptance of a community-based telehealth wellness system', *Informatics for Health and Social Care. 38 (1), 27-36.*

Devereaux, R. L., & Gottlieb, M. C. (2012). Record keeping in the cloud: Ethical considerations. *Professional Psychology: Research and Practice, 43*(6), 627-632. http://psycnet.apa.org/journals/pro/43/6/627/

Difede, J., Cukor, J., Jayasinghe, N., Patt, I., Jedel, S., Spielman, L., Giosan, C., Hoffman, H.G. (2007). Virtual Reality exposure therapy for the treatment of Posttraumatic stress disorder following September 11, 2001. *Journal of Clinical Psychiatry, 68*, 1639-1647.

DiIorio, C., Reisinger, E. L., Yeager, K. A., & McCarty, F. (2009). A telephone-based self-management program for people with epilepsy. *Epilepsy & Behavior, 14*, 232-236. doi:10.1016/j.yebeh.2008.10.016

Doyle, C. (2003). *Work and organizational psychology: An introduction with attitude.* Hove, England: Psychology Press.

Döring, N., & Eichenberg, C. (2007). Klinisch-psychologische interventionen mit mobilmedien. ein neues paxis-und forschungsfeld. / clinical-psychological interventions with mobile media. A new field of practice and research. *Psychotherapeut, 52*, 127-135. doi:10.1007/s00278-006-0523-9.

Drude, K. (2012). Social media use by health care professionals. *The Ohio Psychologist, 59*, 10-11.

Duncan, A. B., Velasquez, S. E., & Nelson. E-L. (2014). Using videoconferencing to provide psychological services to rural children and adolescents: A review and case example. *Journal of Clinical Child and Adolescent Psychology*

Dunne, J. E., Sarvet, B., Lambert, K., & Wertheimer, M. (2012). New risks to confidentiality in the modern era: Strategies that can help maintain patient confidentiality. *Psychiatric Times, Vol.29* (12), 32-34.

Dunstan, D. A., & Tooth, Susan M. (2012), 'Treatment via videoconferencing: A pilot study of delivery by clinical psychology trainees', *The Australian Journal of Rural Health,* 20 (2), 88-94.

Dunne, J. E., Sarvet, B., Lambert, K., & Wertheimer, M. (2012). New risks to confidentiality in the modern era: Strategies that can help maintain patient confidentiality. *Psychiatric Times, Vol.29* (12), 32-34.

Efstathiou, G. (2009). Students' psychological web consulting: Function and outcome evaluation. *British Journal of Guidance & Counselling, 37*, 243-255. doi:10.1080/03069880902956983

Eonta, A M , Christon, L. M., Hourigan, S.E., Ravindran, N., Vrana, S.R., & Southam-Gerow, M.A. (2011). Using everyday technology to enhance evidence-based treatments. *Professional Psychology: Research and Practice, 42,* 513-520.

Essig, T. (2012) The addiction concept and technology: Diagnosis, metaphor, or something else? A psychodynamic point of view. *Journal of Clinical Psychology*, 68 (11), 1175–1184.

Efstathiou, G. (2009). Students' psychological web consulting: Function and outcome evaluation. *British Journal of Guidance & Counselling, 37*, 243-255. doi:10.1080/03069880902956983

Eonta, A.M., Christon, L. M., Hourigan, S.E., Ravindran, N., Vrana, S.R., & Southam-Gerow, M.A. (2011). Using everyday technology to enhance evidence-based treatments. *Professional Psychology: Research and Practice, 42,* 513-520.

Essig, T. (2012) The addiction concept and technology: Diagnosis, metaphor, or something else? A psychodynamic point of view. *Journal of Clinical Psychology*. 68 (11), 1175–1184.

Estabrooks, P. A., Shoup, J. A., Gattshall, M., Dandamudi, P., Shetterly, S., & Xu, S. (2009). Automated telephone counseling for parents of overweight children: A randomized controlled trial. *American Journal of Preventive Medicine, 36*, 35-42. doi:10.1016/j.amepre.2008.09.024

Farber, B. A., Shafron, G., Hamadani, J., Wald, E., & Nitzburg, G. (2012). Children, technology, problems, and preferences. *Journal of Clinical Psychology*, *68* (11), 1225-1229. article first published online: 7 SEP 2012 | DOI: 10.1002/jclp.21922

Farrer, L., Christensen, H., Griffiths, K. M., & Mackinnon, A. (2011). Internet-based CBT for depression with and without telephone tracking in a national helpline: Randomised controlled trial. *Plos ONE*, *6*(11).

Farrell-Carnahan, L., Hettema, J., Jackson, J., Kamalanathan, S., Ritterband, L. M., & Ingersoll, K. S. (2013). Feasibility and promise of a remote-delivered preconception Motivational Interviewing intervention to reduce risk for Alcohol Exposed Pregnancy. *Telemedicine and e-Health, 19*(8): 597-604.

Farrell-Carnahan, L., Ritterband, L. M., Bailey, E. T., Thorndike, F. P., Lord, H. R., & Baum, L. D. (2010). Feasibility and preliminary efficacy of a self-hypnosis intervention available on the web for cancer survivors with insomnia. *E-Journal of Applied Psychology, 6(2),* 10-23.

Farrer, L., Christensen, H., Griffiths, K. M., & Mackinnon, A. (2011). Internet-based CBT for depression with and without telephone tracking in a national helpline: Randomised controlled trial. *Plos ONE*, *6*(11).

Fichter, M.M., Quadflieg, N., Misslmuller, K., Lindner, S., Osen, B., Huber, T., Wunsch-Lieteritz, W. (2012). Does internet-based prevention reduce the risk of relapse for anorexia nervosa? *Behaviour Research and Therapy,* 50 (3), 180-90.

Finn, J. (2006). An exploratory study of email use by direct service social workers. *Journal of Technology in Human Services, 24*(4), 1-20.

Fishkin, R., Fishkin, L., Leli, U., Katz, B., & Snyder, E. (2011). Psychodynamic treatment, training, and supervision using Internet-based technologies. *Journal Of The American Academy Of Psychoanalysis & Dynamic Psychiatry*, *39*(1), 155-168.

Fletcher-Tomenius, L. J., & Vossler, A. (2009). Trust in online therapeutic relationships: The therapist's experience. *Counselling Psychology Review, 24*(2), 24-33.

Forducey, P., Glueckauf, R., Berquist, T., Maheu, M. & Yutsis, M. (2012). Telehealth for persons with severe functional disabilities and their caregivers: Facilitating self-care management in the home setting. *Psychological Services*, 9 (2), 144-62.

Finkelstein, S. M., Speedie, S.M., Zhou, X. Potthoff, S., Ratner, E.R. (2011), Perception, satisfaction and utilization of the VALUE home telehealth service, *Journal of Telemedicine Telecare,* 17 (6), 288-292.

Frasier, L. D., Thraen, I., Kaplan, R., Goede, P. (2012). Development of standardized clinical training cases for diagnosis of sexual abuse using a secure telehealth application, *Child Abuse and Neglect,* 36 (2), 149-55.

Fukkink, R. G., & Hermanns, J. M. A. (2009). Children's experiences with chat support and telephone support. *Journal of Child Psychology and Psychiatry, 50*(6), 759-766. doi:10.1111/j.1469-7610.2008.02024.x.

Furumo, K. & Pearson, J. M. (2007). Gender-Based communication styles, trust, and satisfaction in Virtual Teams. *Journal of Information, Information Technology, and Organizations, 2*, 47+.

Gabriele, J. M. (2009). Effects of nondirective and directive support on weight loss in an e-counseling intervention. Dissertation Abstracts International: Section B: The Sciences and Engineering, 69(9-B), 5777.

Gainsbury, S., & Blaszczynski, A. (2011). A systematic review of Internet-based therapy for the treatment of addictions. *Clinical Psychology Review,* 31 (3), 490-98.

Gallego, M. J., & Emmelkamp, P. M. G. (2012). Effectiveness of internet psychological treatments in mental health disorders. In L. L'Abate & D. Kaiser (Eds.), *Handbook of Technology in Psychology, Psychiatry, and Neurology: Theory, Research, and Practice* (pp. 395-422). New York: Nova Science Publishers.

Gallego, M. J., Emmelkamp, P. M. G., van der Kooij, M., & Mees, H. (2011). The effects of a Dutch version of an Internet-based treatment program for fear of public speaking: A controlled study, *International Journal of Clinical and Health Psychology,* 11 (3), 459-72.

Garrett, N. & Latham, N.K. (2006). An overview and process evaluation of TeleWalk: A telephone-based counseling intervention to encourage walking in older adults. *Health Promotion International*, 21(3), 201-208. doi:10.1093/heapro/dal015

Georgiades, S. D. (2008). A solution-focused intervention with a youth in a domestic violence situation: Longitudinal evidence. *Contemporary Family Therapy, 30*, 141-151.

Gerardi, M., Rothbaum, B. O., Ressler, K., Heekin, M. & Rizzo, A.A. (2008). Virtual Reality Exposure Therapy Using a Virtual Iraq: Case Report. *Journal of Traumatic Stress, 21,* 209-213.

Gerke, S. K., & Berens, L. V. (2003). *Quick Guide to Interaction Styles and Working Remotely: Strategies for Leading and Working in Virtual Teams.* Huntington Beach, CA: Telos Publications.

Greenberg, P. S., Greenberg, R. H., & Antonucci, Y. L. (2007). Creating and sustaining trust in virtual teams. *Business Horizons, 50*(4), 325-333.

Germain, V., Marchand, A., Bouchard, S., Drouin, M.S., & Guay, S. (2009). Effectiveness of cognitive behavioural therapy administered by videoconference for posttraumatic stress disorder. *Cognitive Behavior Therapy, 38*, 42 –53.

Germain, V., Marchand, A., Bouchard, S., Guay, S., & Drouin, M. (2010). Assessment of the therapeutic alliance in face-to-face or videoconference treatment for posttraumatic stress disorder. *Cyberpsychology, Behavior, and Social Networking,* 13(1), 29-35. doi:10.1089= cyber.2009.0139.

Gibson, K., O'Donnell, S., Coulson, H. & Kakepetum-Schultz, T. (2011). Mental health professionals' perspectives of telemental health with remote and rural First Nations communities. *Journal of Telemedicine Telecare,* 17 (5), 263-67.

Glasheen, K., & Campbell, M. (2009). The use of online counselling within an australian secondary school setting: A practitioner's viewpoint. *Counselling Psychology Review, 24,* 42-51.

Glück, T. M., & Maercker, A. (2011). A randomized controlled pilot study of a brief web-based mindfulness training. *BMC Psychiatry*, 11.

Godleski, L. Darkins, A. & Peters, J. (2012). Outcomes of 98,609 U.S. Department of Veterans Affairs patients enrolled in telemental health services, 2006–2010. *Psychiatric Services, 63*(4). 383-385.

Godleski, L., Nieves, J.E., Darkins, A., & Lehmann, L. (2008). VA telemental health: Suicide Assessment. *Behavior Science and Law, 26*, 271-286.

Goss, S., & Anthony, K. (2009). Developments in the use of technology in counselling and psychotherapy. *British Journal of Guidance & Counselling, 37*, 223-230. doi:10.1080/03069880902956967

Grady, B. J., Lever, N., Cunningham, D., Stephan, S. (2011). Telepsychiatry and school mental health. *Child and Adolescent Psychiatric Clinics of North America,* 20 (1), 81-94.

Green, K. E., & Iverson, K. M. (2009). Computerized cognitive–behavioral therapy in a stepped care model of treatment. *Professional Psychology: Research and Practice, 40,* 96-103. doi: 10.1037/a0012847

Griffiths, K. M., & Christensen, H. (2007). Internet-based mental health programs: A powerful tool in the rural medical kit. *The Australian Journal of Rural Health, 15*(2), 81-87.

Griffith, T. L., Mannix, E. A., & Neale, M. A. (2003). Conflict and Virtual Teams. In Gibson, Cristina, B & Cohen, Susan, G (Eds.), *Virtual Teams That Work Creating Conditions for Virtual Team Effectiveness* (335-352). San Francisco: Jossey-Bass.

Grisham, T. (2006). Metaphor, poetry, storytelling and cross-cultural leadership. *Management Decision*, *44*(4), 486.

Gros, D. F., Strachan, M., Ruggiero, K.J., Knapp, R.G., Frueh, B.C., Egede, L.E., Lejuez, C.W., Tuerk, P.W., & Acierno, R. (2011). Innovative service delivery for secondary prevention of PTSD in at-risk OIF-OEF service men and women. *Contemporary Clinical Trials, 32*, 122 –128.

Gros, D. F., Veronee, K., Strachan, M., Ruggerio, K.J., & Acierno, R. (2011). Managing suicidality in home-based telehealth. *Journal of Telemedicine and Telecare, 17*, 332-335.

Gros, D.F., Yoder, M., Tuerk, P.W., Lozano, B.E., & Acierno, R. (2011). Exposure therapy for PTSD delivered to veterans via telehealth: predictors of treatment completion and outcome and comparison to treatment delivered in person. *Behavior Therapy, 42*(2), 276-83.

Grosch, M., C., Gottlieb, M. C., & Cullum, C. M. (2011). Initial practice recommendations for teleneuropsychology, *The Clinical Neuropsychologist,* 25 (7), 1119-33.

Grover, M., Naumann, U., Mohammad-Dar, L., Glennon, D., Ringwood, S., Eisler, I., Williams, C., Treasure, J., & Schmidt, U. (2011), A randomized controlled trial of an Internet-based cognitive-behavioural skills package for carers of people with anorexia nervosa, *Psychological Medicine: A Journal of Research in Psychiatry and the Allied Sciences,* 41 (12), 2581-91.

Gulec, H., Moessner, M., Mezei, A., Kohls, E., Túry, F., & Bauer, S. (2011). Internet-based maintenance treatment for patients with eating disorders. *Professional Psychology: Research and Practice, 42*(6), 479-486.

Gun, S., Titov, N., & Andrews, G. (2011). Acceptability of Internet treatment of anxiety and depression. *Australasian Psychiatry, 19*(3), 259-264.

Haberstroh, S., Parr, G., Bradley, L., Morgan-Fleming, B., & Gee, R. (2008). Facilitating online counseling: Perspectives from counselors in training. *Journal of Counseling & Development, 86,* 460-470.

Hadjistavropoulos, H. D., Thompson, M., Ivanov, M., Drost, C., Butz, C.J., Klein, B., & Austin, D.W. (2011). Considerations in the development of a therapist-assisted internet cognitive behavior therapy service. *Professional Psychology: Research and Practice, 42,* 463-471.

Han, S. (2008). Cyber counseling in the U.S.A. and south Korea: Attitudes and needs of the millennial generation and the net generation on campus. *Dissertation Abstracts International Section A: Humanities and Social Sciences, 69*(1-A), 109.

Hanley, T. (2006). Developing youth-friendly online counselling services in the United Kingdom: A small scale investigation into the views of practitioners. *Counselling & Psychotherapy Research, 6*(3), 182-185. doi:10.1080/14733140600857535

Hanley, T. (2009). The working alliance in online therapy with young people: Preliminary findings. *British Journal of Guidance & Counselling, 37*, 257-269. doi:10.1080/03069880902956991

Hanley, T., & Reynolds, D. J., Jr. (2009). Counselling psychology and the internet: A review of the quantitative research into online outcomes and alliances within text-based therapy. *Counselling Psychology Review, 24*, 4-13.

Haozous, E., Doorenbos, A.Z., Demiris, G., Eaton, L.H., Towle, C., Kundu, A., & Buchwald, D. (2012). Role of telehealth/videoconferencing in managing cancer pain in rural American Indian communities, *Psychooncology,* 21 (2), 219-23.

Harris, E., & Younggren, J. N. (2011). Risk management in the digital world, *Professioal Psychology: Research and Practice,* 42 (6), 412-18.

Harvard. (2010). *Leading virtual teams.* (1st ed.). Boston: Harvard Business Press.

Hettinger, L. J., & Haas, M. W. (Ed.). (2003). *Virtual and adaptive environments: Applications, implications, and human performance issues.* Mahwah, NJ: Erlbaum.

Hine, C. (Ed.). (2005). *Virtual Methods: Issues in Social Research on the Internet.* New York: Berg.

Hoch, J. E., & Kozlowski, S. W. (2012). Leading Virtual Teams: Hierarchical Leadership, Structural Supports, and Shared Team Leadership. *Journal of applied psychology.*

Harwood, T. M., & L'Abate, L. (2010). *Self-help in mental health: A critical evaluation.* New York: Springer-Science.

Harwood, T. M., Pratt, D., Beutler, L. E., Bongar, B. M., Lenore, S., & Forrester, B. T. (2011). Technology, telehealth, treatment enhancement, and selection. *Professional Psychology: Research and Practice, 42,* 448-454.

Hassija, C., & Gray, M. J. (2011). The effectiveness and feasibility of videoconferencing technology to provide evidence-based treatment to rural domestic violence and sexual assault populations. *Telemedicine and e-Health,* 17 (4), 309-15.

Haug, S., Meyer, C., & John, U. (2011). Efficacy of an internet program for smoking cessation during and after inpatient rehabilitation treatment: A quasi-randomized controlled trial. *Addictive Behaviors, 36*(12), 1369-1372.

Havas, J., de Nooijer, J., Crutzen, R., & Feron, F. (2011). Adolescents' views about an Internet platform for adolescents with mental health problems. Health Education, 111(3), 164-176.

Hayden, L. J., Glenn, S.M., Hahn, T.J., Randall, F., & Randolph, E. (2012), The use of Internet technology for psychoeducation and support with dementia caregivers, *Psychological Services,* 9 (2), 215-18.

Heather, N. (1995). Brief intervention strategies. In R. K. Hester & W. R. Miller (Eds.), *Handbook of alcoholism treatment approaches: Effective alternatives*, Second edition (pp. 105-122). Needham Heights, MA: Allyn & Bacon.

Hedman, E., Andersson, E., Ljotsson, B., Andersson, G., Ruck, C. & Lindefors, N. (2011), Cost-effectiveness of Internet-based cognitive behavior therapy vs. cognitive behavioral group therapy for social anxiety disorder: Results from a randomized controlled trial, *Behaviour Research and Therapy,* 49 (11), 729-36.

Hedman, E., Andersson, G., Andersson, E., Ljotsson, B., Ruck, C., Asmundson, G.J. & Lindefors, N. (2011), Internet-based cognitive-behavioural therapy for severe health anxiety: Randomised controlled trial. *British Journal of Psychiatry,* 198 (3), 230-36.

Hedman, E., Andersson, G., Ljotsson, B., Andersson, E., Ruck, C., Mortberg, E. & Lindefors, N. (2011). Internet-based cognitive behavior therapy vs. cognitive behavioral group therapy for social anxiety disorder: A randomized controlled non-inferiority trial, *PLoS ONE,* 6 (3).

Hedman, E., Furmark, T., Carlbring, P., Ljotsson, B., Ruck, C., Lindefors, N. & Andersson, G. (2011). A 5-year follow-up of internet-based cognitive behavior therapy for a social anxiety disorder'. *Journal of Medical Internet Research,* 13 (2), 34-43.

Hedman, E., Ljótsson, B. B., Rück, C. C., Bergström, J. J., Andersson, G. G., Kaldo, V. V., & Jansson, L., Andersson, E., Andersson, E., Blom, K., El Alaoiu, S., Falk, L., Ivarsson, J., Nasri, B., Rydh, S., & Lindefors, N. N. (2013). Effectiveness of Internet-based cognitive behaviour therapy for panic disorder in routine psychiatric care. *Acta Psychiatrica Scandinavica, 128*(6), 457-467.

Heintzelman, A., Murdock, N. L., Krycak, R. C., & Seay. L. (2014). Recovery from infidelity: Differentiation of self, trauma, forgiveness, and posttraumatic growth among couples in continuing relationships. *Couple and Family Psychology: Research and Practice, 3*, 13-29.

Helgadottir, F. A., & Fairburn, C. G. (2014). Web-centered training in psychological treatments: A study of therapist preferences. *Behaviour Research and Therapy,* 52, 61-63.

Henderson, S. J. (2009). Assessment of personal goals: An online tool for personal counseling, coaching, and business consulting. *Measurement and Evaluation in Counseling and Development, 41,* 244-249.

Hertlein, K. M., & Blumer, M. L. C. (2014). *The couple and family technology framework.* New York: Routledge.

Hester, R. K. & Delaney, H. D. (1997). Behavioral Self-Control Program for Windows: Results of a controlled clinical trial. *Journal of Consulting and Clinical Psychology, 65,* 685-693.

Hester, R. K., Delaney, H. D., & Campbell, W. (2011). Moderatedrinking.com and Moderation Management: 12-month outcomes of a randomized clinical trial. *Journal of Consulting and Clinical Psychology, 79*, 215-224, doi: 10.1037/a0022487.

Hester, R. K., Delaney, H.D., & Campbell, W. (2012). The College Drinker's Check-up: Outcomes of two randomized clinical trials of a computer-based brief motivational intervention. *Psychology of Addictive Behaviors, 26*, 1-12. doi:10.1037/a0024753.

Hester, R.K., Delaney, H.D., Campbell, W., & Handmaker, N.(2009). A web application for moderation training: Initial results of a randomized clinical trial. *Journal of Substance Abuse Treatment, 37*, 266-276, doi: 10.1016/j.jsat.2009.03.001.

Hester, R. K., Lenberg, K. L., Campbell, W., & Delaney, H. D. D. (2013). Overcoming addictions, a web-based application, and SMART Recovery, an online and in-person mutual help group for problem drinkers Part 1: Three-month outcomes of a randomized controlled trial. *Journal of Medical Internet Research, 15(7):*e134.

Hester, R. K., Squires, D. D., & Delaney, H.D. (2005). The Computer-based Drinker's Check-up: 12 month outcomes of a controlled clinical trial with problem drinkers. *Journal of Substance Abuse Treatment, 28*, 159-169.

Herman, S. (2010). Career HOPES: An internet-delivered career development intervention. *Computers in Human Behavior, 26,* 339-344.doi:10.1016/j.chb.2009.11.003

Hesser, H., Gustafsson, T., Lundén, C., Henrikson, O., Fattahi, K., Johnsson, E., Westin, V.Z., Carlbring, P., Maki-Torkko, E., Kaldo, V. & Andersson, G. (2012). A randomized controlled trial of internet-delivered cognitive behavior therapy and acceptance and commitment therapy in the treatment of tinnitus. *Journal of Consulting and Clinical Psychology, 80*(4), 649-661.

Hilgart, M. M., Ritterband, L. M., Thorndike, F. P., & Kinzie, M. B. (2012). Using Instructional Design process to improve design and development of Internet interventions. *Journal of Medical Internet Research.* 14(3), e89.URL: http://www.jmir.org/2012/3/e89/. PMCID:PMC3414906.

Himle, J.A., Fischer, D.J., Muroff, J.R., Van Etten, M.L., Lokers, L.M., Abelson, J.L. & Hanna, G.L. (2006). Videoconferencing-based cognitive-behavioral therapy for obsessive-compulsive disorder. *Behavior Research Therapy, 44,* 1821–1829.

Hoefling, T. (2001). *Working virtually*. (1st ed.). Sterling, VA: Stylus. 2003.

Hogan, T. P., Wakefield, B., Nazi, K.M., Houston, T.K. & Weaver, F.M. (2011). Promoting access through complementary eHealth technologies: Recommendations for VA's home telehealth and personal health record programs, *Journal of General Internal Medicine,* 26 (Suppl 2), 628-35.

Holländare, F., Johnsson, S., Randestad, M., Tillfors, M., Carlbring, P., Andersson, G. & Engstrom, I. (2011), Randomized trial of internet-based relapse prevention for partially remitted depression, *Acta Psychiatrica Scandinavica,* 124 (4), 285-2

Holmes, D. (2001). *Virtual globalization: Virtual spaces/tourist spaces*. London, England: Routledge.

Hooper, L. M., L'Abate, L., Sweeney, L. G., Gianesini, G., & Jankowski, P. J. (2014). *Models of psychopathology: Generational processes and relational roles*. New York: Springer-Science.

Horgan, A. A., & Sweeney, J. J. (2010). Young students' use of the Internet for mental health information and support. *Journal Of Psychiatric and Mental Health Nursing, 17*(2), 117-123.

Hovey, L., Kaylor, M.B., Alwan, M., & Resnick, H. (2011), Community-based telemonitoring for hypertension management: Practical challenges and potential solutions. *Telemedicine and e-Health,* 17 (8), 645-51.

Hughes, B. M. (2008). How should clinical psychologists approach complementary and alternative medicine: Empirical, epistemological, an ethical considerations. *Clinical Psychology Review, 28*, 657-675.

Isabelle, C., Christelle, C., Patrick, R., Tony, L., Van der Linden, M., & Alain, G. (2011). Acceptance and efficacy of a guided Internet self-help treatment program for obese patients with binge eating disorder. Clinical Practice And Epidemiology In Mental Health, 7.

Isaacs, L. (2012). Creating Successful Virtual Teams in a New Age. *Information Management Journal*, *46*(2), 44+.

Jackson, P. J., & Wielen, J. (2002). *Teleworking: International perspectives: from telecommuting to the virtual organisation*. London: Routledge.

Jacobi, C., Volker, U., Trockel, M.T., & Taylor, C.B. (2012). Effects of an internet-based intervention for subthreshold eating disorders: A randomized controlled trial, *Behaviour Research and Therapy,* 50 (2), 93-99.

Jain, S. (2011). Treating posttraumatic stress disorder via the Internet does therapeutic alliance matter? *JAMA: Journal of the American Medical Association,* 306 (5), 543-44.

Jang, J., Dixon, D. R., Tarbox, J., Granpeesheh, D., Kornack, J., & de Nocker, Y. (2012). Randomized trial of an eLearning program for training family members of children with autism in the principles and procedures of applied behavior analysis. *Research In Autism Spectrum Disorders, 6(*2), 852-856.

Jaques, D., & Salmon, G. (2007). *Learning in groups: A handbook for face-to-face and online environments* (32-44). London: Routledge.

Jencius, M., & Rainey, S., (2009). Current online career counseling practices and future trends. *Career Planning and Adult Development Journal, 25*, 17-28.

Johnsen, J. A. K., Vambheim, S. M., Wynn, R., & Wangberg, S. C. (2014). Language of motivation and emotion in an Internet support group for smoking cessation: Exploratory use of automated content analysis to measure regulatory focus. *Psychology Research and Behavior Management, 7*, 19-29.

Johnston, B., Kidd, L., Wengstrom, Y., & Kearney, N. (2012), An evaluation of the use of Telehealth within palliative care settings across Scotland, *Palliative Medicine,* 26 (2), 152-61.

Johnston, L., Titov, N., Andrews, G., Spence, J., & Dear, B. F. (2011). A RCT of a transdiagnostic Internet-delivered treatment for three anxiety disorders: Examination of support roles and disorder-specific outcomes. *Plos ONE, 6*(11).

Joint Task Force for the Development of Telepsychology Guidelines for Psychologists (2013). Guidelines for the Practice of telepsychology. *American Psychologist, 68*, 791-800.

Jones, L. M., & McCabe, M. P. (2011). The effectiveness of an Internet-based psychological treatment program for female sexual dysfunction, *Journal of Sexual Medicine,* 8 (10), 2781-2792.

Jones, M. D., Etherage, J.R., Harmon, S.C. & Okiishi, J.C.(2012). Acceptability and cost-effectiveness of military telehealth mental health screening, *Psychological Services,* 9 (2), 132-43.

Joseph, V., West, R.M., Shickle, D., Keen, J. & Clamp, S. (2011). Key challenges in the development and implementation of telehealth projects'. *Journal of Telemedicine Telecare,* 17 (2), 71-77.

Joyce, E., & Kraut, R. E. (2006). Predicting continued participation in newsgroups. *Journal of Computer-Mediated Communication, 11,* 723-747. doi:10.1111/j.1083-6101. 2006.00033.x

Kaliebe, K. E., Heneghan, James, and Kim, Thomas J. (2011). Telepsychiatry in juvenile justice settings. *Child and Adolescent Psychiatric Clinics of North America,* 20 (1), 113-23.

Kalman, Y. M., Raban, D. R., & Rafaeli, S. (2013). Netified: Social cognition in crowds and clouds. In Y. Amichai-Hamburger (Ed.), *The social net: Understanding our online behavior*. Oxford: Oxford University Press.

Kazantzis, N., Deane, N. F. P., Ronan, K. R., & L'Abate, L. (Eds*).* (2005). *Using homework assignments in cognitive behavior therapy*. New York; Rutledge.

Kazantzis, N., & L'Abate, L. (Eds.). (2007). *Handbook of homework assignments in psychotherapy: Theory, research, and prevention.* New York: Springer-Science.

Kelly, J. F., & Coons, H. L. (2012). Integrated health care and professional psychology: Is the setting right for you? *Professional Psychology: Research and Practice, 43*(6), 586-595. http://psycnet.apa.org/journals/pro/43/6/586/

Kenardy, J., McCafferty, K., & Rosa, V. (2006). Internet-delivered indicated prevention for anxiety disorders: Six-month follow-up. *Clinical Psychologist*, 10, 39-42. doi:10.1080/13284200500378746

Kersting, A., Kroker, K., Schlicht, S., Baust, K., & Wagner, B. (2011). Efficacy of cognitive behavioral internet-based therapy in parents after the loss of a child during pregnancy: Pilot data from a randomized controlled trial. *Archives of Women's Mental Health*, 14(6), 465-477.

Kersting, A., Kroker, K., Schlicht, S., & Wagner, B. (2011). Internet-based treatment after pregnancy loss: Concept and case study. *Journal of Psychosomatic Obstetrics & Gynecology*, 32(2), 72-78.

King, B. (2012). How much is too much? Limit setting and sexual acting out in a digital era. *Journal of Clinical Psychology*, *68*(11), 1196–1204). Article first published online: 19 SEP 2012 DOI: 10.1002/jclp.21919

King, D. L., Defabbro, P. H., Griffith, M. S., & Gradisar, M. (2012). Cognitive-behavioral approaches to outpatient treatment of internet addiction in children and adolescents. *Journal of Clinical Psychology*, 68(11), 1185–1195. Article first published online: 13 SEP 2012 | DOI: 10.1002/jclp.21918

King, R., Bambling, M., Lloyd, C., Gomurra, R., Smith, S., Reid, W. & Wegner, K. (2006). Online counselling: The motives and experiences of young people who choose the internet instead of face to face or telephone counselling. *Counselling & Psychotherapy Research*, 6, 169-174. doi:10.1080/14733140600848179

King, R., Bambling, M., Reid, W., & Thomas, I. (2006). Telephone and online counselling for young people: A naturalistic comparison of session outcome, session impact and therapeutic alliance. *Counselling & Psychotherapy Research*, 6, 175-181. doi:10.1080/14733140600874084

King, V. L., Stoller, K. B., Kidorf, M., Kindbom, K., Hursh, S., Brady, T., Brooner, R. K. (2009). Assessing the effectiveness of an internet-based videoconferencing platform for delivering intensified substance abuse counseling. *Journal of Substance Abuse Treatment*, 36, 331-338. doi:10.1016/j.jsat.2008.06.011.

Kirkman, B. L., Rosen, B., Gibson, C. B., Tesluk, P. E., & McPherson, S. O. (2002). Five challenges to virtual team success: lessons from Sabre Inc. *Academy of Executive Management, 16*(3), 67-79.

Kiropoulos, L. A., Klein, B., Austin, D. W., Gilson, K., Pier, C., Mitchell, J., Ciechomski, face CBT? *Journal of Anxiety Disorders, 22*(8), 1273-1284. doi: 10.1016/ j.janxdis.2008.01.008

Kiropoulos, L. A., Cannard, G. & Redman, T. (2010). A therapist-assisted cognitive behavior therapy internet intervention for posttraumatic stress disorder: Pre-, post- and 3-month follow-up results from an open trial. *Journal of Anxiety Disorders, 24,* 635-644. doi:10.1016/j.janxdis.2010.04.005

Kleespies, P. M. (2014). *Decision making in behavioral emergencies: Acquiring skill in evaluating and managing high-risk patients*. Washington, DC: American Psychological Association.

Klein, B., Meyer, D., Austin, D.W. & Kyrios, M. (2011). Anxiety online—A virtual clinic: Preliminary outcomes following completion of five fully automated treatment programs for anxiety disorders and symptoms, *Journal of Medical Internet Research,* 13 (4), 353-72.

Klein, B., Mitchell, J., Abbott, J., Shandley, K., Austin, D., Gilson, K., Kiropoulos, L., Cannard, G. & Redman, T. (2010). A therapist-assisted cognitive behavior therapy internet intervention for posttraumatic stress disorder: Pre-, post- and 3-month follow-up results from an open trial. *Journal of Anxiety Disorders, 24*, 635-644. doi:10.1016/j.janxdis.2010.04.005

Kliegl, R., & Bates, D. (2011). International collaboration in psychology is on the rise. *Scientometrics, 87*(1), 149.

Klomp, R.W., Spitalnick, J. S., & Reissman, D. B. (2011). Virtual Classroom Immersion Training: Safeguarding the Health, Safety, and Resiliency of Emergency Responders. *Training and Development*, 65, 38-43.

Knaevelsrud, C., & Maercker, A. (2006). Does the quality of the working alliance predict treatment outcome in online psychotherapy for traumatized patients? *Journal of Medical Internet Research*, 8(4), e31. doi:doi:10.2196/jmir.8.4.e31

Knaevelsrud, C., & Maercker, A. (2007). Internet-based treatment for PTSD reduces distress and facilitates the development of a strong therapeutic alliance: A randomized controlled clinical trial. *BMC Psychiatry,* 7(13). Retrieved October 29, 2008, from http://www.biomedcentral.com/1471-244X/7/13

Kobak, et al. (1997). A computer-administered telephone interview to identify mental disorders. *Journal of the American Medical Association, 278*(11) 905-910.

Koch, E. F. (2012), The VA Maryland Health Care System's telemental health program, *Psychological Services,* 9 (2), 203-205.

Kolmes, K. (2012). Social media in the future of professional psychology. *Professional Psychology: Research and Practice*, *43*(6), 606-612. http://psycnet.apa.org/journals/ pro/43/6/606/

Kolmes, K., & Taube, D. O. (2014). Seeking and finding our clients on the Internet: Boundary considerations in cyberspace. *Professional Psychology: Research and Practice*, *45*(1), 3-10.

Kolt, G., Oliver, M., & Schofield, G., Kerse, N., Garrett, N. & Latham, N.K. (2006). An overview and process evaluation of TeleWalk: A telephone-based counseling intervention to encourage walking in older adults. *Health Promotion International*, 21(3), 201-208. doi:10.1093/heapro/dal015

Koocher, G. P. (2007). Twenty-first century ethical challenges for psychology. *American Psychologist, 62*, 375-384. doi:10.1037/0003-066X.62.5.375

Koocher, G. P. (2009). Any minute now but far far away: Electronically mediated mental health. *Clinical Psychology: Science and Practice, 16,* 339-342.

Kozlov, M. D., & Johansen, M. K. (2010). Real behavior in Virtual Environments: Psychology experiments in a simple virtual-reality paradigm using video games. *Cyberpsychology, Behavior, and Social Networking, 13*(6), 711.

Krukowski, R. A., Tilfor, J.M, Harvey-Berino, J. & West, D.S. (2011). Comparing behavioral weight loss modalities: Incremental cost-effectiveness of an Internet-based versus an in-person condition, *Obesity,* 19 (8), 1629-35.

Kurki, M. M., Kovivunen, M. M., Anttila, M. M., Hätönen, H. H., & Välimäki, M. M. (2011). Usefulness of Internet in adolescent mental health outpatient care. *Journal of Psychiatric and Mental Health Nursing*, *18*(3), 265-273.

L'Abate, L. (1977). *Enrichment: Structured interventions with couples, families, and groups.* Washington, D. C.: University Press of America.

L'Abate, L. (1986). *Systematic family therapy*. New York: Brunner/Mazel.

L'Abate, L. (1987). *Family psychology II: Theory, therapy, enrichment, and training* Washington, DC: University Press of America. (Pp. 1-289).

L'Abate, L. 1990). *Building family competence: Primary and secondary prevention strategies*. Newbury Park, CA: Sage.

L'Abate, L. (1992). *Programmed writing: A self-administered approach for interventions with individuals, couples, and families*. Pacific Grove, CA: Brooks/Cole.

L'Abate, L. (Ed.). (2001). *Distance writing and computer-assisted interventions in psychiatry and mental health*. Westport, CT: Ablex.

L'Abate, L. (2002). *Beyond psychotherapy: Programmed writing and structured computer-assisted interventions.* Westport, CT: Ablex.

L'Abate, L. (2004a). *A guide to self-help mental health workbooks for clinicians and researchers*. Binghamton, NY: Haworth.

L'Abate, L. (Ed.). (2004b). *Using workbooks in prevention, psychotherapy, and rehabilitation: A resource for clinicians and researchers*. Binghamton, NY: Haworth.

L'Abate, L. (Ed.). (2007). *Low-cost interventions to promote physical and mental health: Theory, research, and practice,* New York: Springer.

L'Abate, L. (2008a). A proposal for including distance writing in couple therapy. *Journal of Couple and Relationship Therapy, 7,* 337-362.

L'Abate, L. (Ed.). (2008b). *Toward a science of clinical psychology: Laboratory evaluations and interventions.* New York: Nova Science Publishers.

L'Abate, L. (2011a). *Hurt feelings in intimate relationships: Theory, research, and applications*. New York: Cambridge University Press.

L'Abate, L (2011b). *Sourcebook of interactive exercises in mental health.* New York: Springer Science.

L'Abate, L. (2012). Workbooks: Programmed Interactive Practice Exercises. In L. L'Abate & D. A. Kaiser (Eds.), *Handbook of Technology in Psychology, Psychiatry, and Neurology: Theory, Research, and Practice* (pp. 375-394). New York: Nova Science Publishers.

L'Abate, L. (2013a). *Beyond the systems paradigm: Emerging constructs in family and personality psychology*. New York: Springer-Science.

L'Abate, L (2013b). *Clinical psychology and psychotherapy as a science: An iconoclastic perspective.* New York: Springer-Science.

L'Abate, L. (2013c). *Research about pre-para-post therapeutic activities in mental health: Prevention, promotion, psychotherapy, and rehabilitation.* New York: Nova Science Publishers.

L'Abate, L., Cusinato, M., Maino, E., Colesso, W., & Scilletta, C. (2010): *Relational competence theory: Research and applications in mental health*. New York: Springer-Science.

L'Abate, L., & De Giacomo, P. (2003). *Improving intimate relationships: Integration of theoretical models with preventions and psychotherapy applications*. Westport, CT: Praeger.

L'Abate, L, & Kaiser, D. A. (Eds.). (2012). *Handbook of technology in psychology, psychiatry, and neurology: Theory, research, and practice*. New York: Nova Science Publishers.

L'Abate, L., & McMahan, O. (2001). Programmed distance writing with seminarian couples. In L. L'Abate (Ed.), *Distance writing and computer-assisted interventions in psychiatry and mental heath* (pp. 137-156). Westport, CT: Ablex.

L'Abate, L., Reed, R., & McMahan, O. (2001). Workbooks and with incarcerated felons. In L. L'Abate(Ed.), *Distance writing and computer-assisted interventions in psychiatry and mental heath* (pp. 157-167). Westport, CT: Ablex.

L'Abate, L., & Milan, M. (Eds.). (1985). *Handbook of social skills training and research.* New York: Wiley.

L'Abate, L., & Rupp, G. (1981). *Enrichment: Skill training for family life*. Washington, DC. University Press of America.

L'Abate, L., & Sweeney, L. G. (Eds.). (2011). *Research on writing approaches in Mental health.* Leiden, BE: Brill Group Publications Limited.

L'Abate, L., & Weinstein, S. E. (1987). *Structured enrichment programs for couples and families.* New York: Brunner/Mazel.

L'Abate, L., & Young, L. (1987). *Casebook of structured enrichment programs for couples and families.* New York: Brunner/Mazel.

Lal, S., & Adair, C. E. (2014). E-Mental Health: A Rapid Review of the Literature. *Psychiatric Services*, *65*(1), 24.

Lam-Po-Tang, J., & Mckay, D. (2010). Dr Google, MD: A survey of mental health-related internet use in a private practice sample. *Australasian Psychiatry*, *18*(2), 130-133.

Lancee, J., van den Bout, J., van Straten, A., & Spoormaker, V. I. (2012). Internet-delivered or mailed self-help treatment for insomnia? A randomized waiting-list controlled trial. *Behaviour Research and Therapy, 50*(1), 22-29.

Lannin, D. G., & Scott, N. A. (2014). Best practices for an online world. *Monitor-on-Psychology,* February, 56-61.

Lara, D. R., Ottoni, G. L., Brunstein, M. G., Frozi, J., de Carvalho, H. W., & Bisol, L. W. (2012). Development and validity data of the Brazilian Internet Study on Temperament and Psychopathology (BRAINSTEP). *Journal of Affective Disorders, 141*(2-3), 390-398.

Latalova, K., Prasko, J., Kamaradova, D., Jelenova, D., Ociskova, M., & Sedlackova, Z. (2013). Internet psychoeducation for bipolar affective disorder: Basis for preparation and first experiences. *Psychiatric Quarterly*, 84 (4).

Lawlor, E., Breslin, J. G., Renwick, L., Foley, S., Mulkerrin, U., Kinsella, A., Turner, N., & O'Callaghan, E. (2008). Mental health literacy among Internet users. *Early Intervention In Psychiatry,* 2(4), 247-255.

Lazzari, C., Egan, S. J., & Rees, C. S. (2011). Behavioral activation treatment for depression in older adults delivered via videoconferencing: A pilot study. *Cognitive and Behavioral Practice,* 18 (4), 555-65.

Leach, L. S., & Christensen, H. (2006). A systematic review of telephone-based interventions for mental disorders. *Journal of Telemedicine and Telecare, 12*, 122-129. doi:10.1258/135763306776738558

Lee, D., Helal, S., Anton, S., DeDeugd, S. & Smith, A. (2012). Participatory and persuasive telehealth, *Gerontology,* 58(3), 269-81.

Lehavot, K., Barnett, J. E., & Powers, D. (2010). Psychotherapy, professional relationships, and ethical considerations in the MySpace generation. *Professional Psychology: Research and Practice, 41*(2), 160-166. doi:10.1037/a0018709

Leibert, T., Archer, J. Jr., Munson, J., & York, G. (2006). An exploratory study of client perceptions of Internet counseling and the therapeutic alliance. Journal of Mental Health Counseling, 28(1), 69-83.

Lekushoff, A. (2012). Lifestyle-driven virtual teams: A new paradigm for professional services firms. *Ivey Business Journal, 76*(5), 24.

Lester, D. (2006). E-therapy: Caveats from experiences with telephone therapy. *Psychological Reports, 99*, 894-896. doi:10.2466/PR0.99.7.894-896.

Levy-Warren, M. H. (2012). Press pause before send: A case in point. *Journal of Clinical Psychology, 68*(11), 1164–1174.

Lewis, J., & Coursol, D. (2007). Addressing career issues online: Perceptions of counselor education professionals. *Journal of Employment Counseling, 44*, 146-153.

Lewis, M. (2014). *The rise of consciousness and the development of emotional life*. New York: Guilford.

Li, W., Chen, C., & Wang, C. (2008). Agreements on working alliance and session impact in cybercounseling and interview counseling. *Bulletin of Educational Psychology, 40*, 1-22.

Lillevoll, K. R., Vangberg, H. B., Griffiths, K. M., Waterloo, K., & Eisemann, M. R. (2014). Uptake and adherence of a self-directed internet-based mental health intervention with tailored e-mail reminders in senior high schools in Norway. *BMC Psychiatry, 14*(1), 1-21.

Linn, A. J., Vervloet, M., van Dijk, L., Smith, E.G., van Weert, J.C.M. (2011), Effects of eHealth interventions on medication adherence: A systematic review of the literature. *Journal of Medical Internet Research,* 13 (4), 203-17.

Lipnak, J., & Stamps, J. (2000). *Virtual teams: People working across boundaries with technology*. (2nd ed.). New York: John Wiley & Sons.

Lipnak, J., & Stamps, J. (2010). *Leading virtual teams: expert solutions to everyday challenges*. (14th ed.). Boston: Harvard Business School Publishing.

Litz, B. T., Engel, C. C., Bryant, R. A., & Papa, A. (2007). A randomized, controlled proof-of-concept trial of an internet-based, therapist-assisted self-management treatment for posttraumatic stress disorder. *The American Journal of Psychiatry, 164,* 1676-1683.

Liu, W-L., Zhang, K., Locatis, C. & Ackerman, M. (2011). Internet-based videoconferencing coder/decoders and tools for telemedicine, *Telemedicine and e-Health,* 17 (5), 358-62.

Ljótsson, B., Falk, L., Vesterlund, A. W., Hedman, E., Lindfors, P., Rück, C., Hursti, T., Andréewitch, S., Jansson, L., Lindefors, N., & Andersson, G. (2010). Internet-delivered exposure and mindfulness based therapy for irritable bowel syndrome – A randomized controlled trial. *Behaviour Research and Therapy, 48*(6), 531-539. doi: 10.1016/j.brat.2010.03.003

Ljótsson, B., Hedman, E., Lindfors, P., Hursti, T., Lindefors, N., Andersson, G., & Rück, C. (2011). Long-term follow-up of internet-delivered exposure and mindfulness based treatment for irritable bowel syndrome. *Behaviour Research And Therapy, 49*(1), 58-61.

Ljotsson, B., Lundin, C., Mitsell, K., Carlbring, P., Ramklint, M., & Ghaderi, A. (2007). Remote treatment of bulimia nervosa and binge eating disorder: A randomized trial of internet-assisted cognitive behavioural therapy. *Behaviour Research and Therapy, 45,* 649-661. doi: 10.1016/j.brat.2006.06.010

Lohr, H. D., Rosenvinge, J. H., & Wynn, R. (2011). Integrating psychoeducation in a basic computer skills course for people suffering from social anxiety: Participants' experiences. *Journal of Multidisciplinary Healthcare, 4,* 311-319.

Lorian, C. N., Titov, N., & Grisham, J. R. (2012). Changes in risk-taking over the course of an internet-delivered cognitive behavioral therapy treatment for generalized anxiety disorder. *Journal of Anxiety Disorders, 26*(1), 140-149.

Lovejoy, T. I., Demireva, P. D., Grayson, J. L., & McNamara, J. R. (2009). Advancing the practice of online psychotherapy: An application of Rogers' diffusion of innovations theory. *Psychotherapy: Theory, Research, Practice, Training, 46*(1), 112-124. doi:10.1037/a001515.

Luo, J. S. (2007). Virtual reality therapy: On your desktop today. *Primary Psychiatry, 14*(4), 20-22.

Luxton, D. D., June, J. D., & Kinn, J. T. (2011). Technology-based suicide prevention: Current applications and future directions. *Telemedicine and e-Health, 17,* 50-54.

Lynch, J., & Gay, S. (2012). A survey of telehealth coordinators in Canada, *Journal of Telemedicine and Telecare,* 18 (4), 231-4.

Magee, J. C., Ritterband, L. M., Thorndike, F. P., Cox, D. J., & Borowitz, S. (2008) Exploring the relationship between parental worry about their child's health and usage of an Internet intervention for pediatric encopresis. *Journal of Pediatric Psychology, 34(5),* 530-538.

Mahar, S. M., & Mahar, J. (2009). *The unofficial guide to building your business in the Second Life virtual world: Marketing and selling your product, services, and brand in-world.* New York: AMACOM.

Maheu, M. M., McMenamin, J., & Pulier, M. L. (213). Optimizing the use of technology in psychology with best practice principles. In G. P. Koocher, J. C. Norcross, & B. A Greene (Eds.), *Psychologist's desk reference. Third Edition* (pp. 695-699). New York: Oxford University Press.

Maheu, M. M., Pulier, M. L., McMenamin, J., & Posen, L. (2012). The future of telepsychology, telehealth, and various technologies in psychological research and practice. *Professional Psychology: Research and Practice, 43*(6), 613-621.

Maheu, M. M., Pulier, M. L., & Roy, S. (2013). Finding, evaluating, and using smartphone applications. In G. P. Koocher, J. C. Norcross, & B. A Greene (Eds.), *Psychologist's desk reference. Third Edition* (pp. 704-708). New York: Oxford University Press.

Mailey, E. L., Wójcicki, T. R., Motl, R. W., Hu, L., Strauser, D. R., Collins, K. D., & McAuley, E. (2010). Internet-delivered physical activity intervention for college students with mental health disorders: A randomized pilot trial. *Psychology, Health & Medicine, 15*(6), 646-659.

Mallen, M. J. (2006). Online counseling: Dynamics of process and assessment. *Dissertation Abstracts International: Section B: The Sciences and Engineering,* 66(8-B), 4490.

Manzoni, G.M., Pagnini, F., Corti, S., Molinari, E., & Castelnuovo, G. (2011). Internet-based behavioral interventions for obesity: An updated systematic review, *Clinical Practice and Epidemiology in Mental Health,* 7, 19-28.

Maples, M. F., & Han, S. (2008). Cybercounseling in the United States and south Korea: Implications for counseling college students of the millennial generation and the networked generation. *Journal of Counseling & Development, 86*, 178-183.

Marchand, A., Beaulieu-Prevost, D., Guay, S., Bouchard, S., Drouin, M.S., & Germain, V. (2011). Relative efficacy of cognitive-behavioral therapy administered by videoconference for posttraumatic stress disorder: A six-month follow-up, *Journal of Aggression, Maltreatment & Trauma,* 20 (3), 304-21.

Marcus, M. A., Westra, H. A., Eastwood, J. D., & Barnes, K. L. (2012). What are young adults saying about mental health? An analysis of Internet blogs. *Journal of Medical Internet Research, 14*(1), 303-317.

Marin, R. A., Christensen, A., & Atkins, D. C. (2014). Infidelity and behavioral couple therapy: Relationships outcomes over 5 years following therapy. *Couple and Family Psychology: Research and Practice, 3,* 1-12.

Marks, I. M., & Cavanah. K. (2009). Computer-aided psychological treatments: Evolving issues. *Annual Review of Clinical Psychology, 5,* 121-141.

Marks, I. M., Cavanah. K., & Geca, L. (2007). *Hands-on help: Computer-aided psychotherapy.* New York: Psychology Press.

Martin-Khan, M., Wootton, R., Whited, J, & Gray, L.C. (2011). A systematic review of studies concerning observer agreement during medical specialist diagnosis using videoconferencing, *Journal of Telemedicine Telecare,* 17 (7), 350-57.

Marziali, E., & Garcia, L. J. (2011). Dementia caregivers' responses to 2 Internet-based intervention programs, *American Journal of Alzheimer's Disease and Other Dementias,* 26 (1), 36-43.

Matthews, M., Doherty, G., Sharry, J., & Fitzpatrick, C. (2008). Mobile phone mood charting for adolescents. *British Journal of Guidance & Counselling, 36*, 113-129. doi: 10.1080/03069880801926400

McAdams, C. R., III, & Wyatt, K. L. (2010). The regulation of technology-assisted distance counseling and supervision in the United States: An analysis of current extent, trends, and implications. *Counselor Education and Supervision, 49*, 179-192.

McCord, C.E., Elliott, T. R., Wendel, M.L., Brossart, D.F., Cano, M.A., Gonzalez, G.E., & Burdine, J.N. (2011). Community capacity and teleconference counseling in rural Texas. *Professional Psychology: Research and Practice, 42*, 521-527.

McDaniel, A. M., & Stratton, R. M. (2006). Internet-based smoking cessation initiatives: Availability, varieties, and likely effects on outcomes. *Disease Management & Health Outcomes, 14*(5), 275-285. doi: 10.2165/00115677-200614050-00003

McGeary, D. D., McGeary, C. A., & Gatchel, R. J. (2012). A comprehensive review of telehealth for pain management: Where we are and the way ahead. *Pain Practice, 12*, 570-577.

McGraw, P. B. (2009, December 21). Seeding meetings morph into virtual reality. *Daily Herald* [Arlington Heights, IL].

McKelley, R. A., & Rochlen, A. B. (2007). The practice of coaching: Exploring alternatives to therapy for counseling-resistant men. Psychology of Men and Masculinity, 8, 53-65. doi: 10.1037/1524-9220.8.1.53

McKinney, C., & Morse, M. (2012). Assessment of disruptive behavior disorders: Tools and recommendations. *Professional Psychology: Research and Practice, 43*(6), 641-649. http://psycnet.apa.org/journals/pro/43/6/641/.

McLeod, K. C. (2008). Online counseling: A non-experimental descriptive correlation of attitudes and knowledge of professional counselors. *Dissertation Abstracts International: Section B: The Sciences and Engineering, 68*(9-B), 6319.

McMillen, P. S., & Pehrsson, D. (2009). Improving a counselor education web site through usability testing: The bibliotherapy education project. Counselor Education and Supervision, 49, 122-136.

Megan, B., Irby, K. A., Boles, C. J., & Skelton, J. A. (2012). TeleFIT: Adapting a multidisciplinary, tertiary-care pediatric obesity clinic to rural populations. *Telemedicine and e-Health, 18*, 247-249.

Mehta, S., & Chalhoub, N. (2006). An e-mail for your thoughts. *Child and Adolescent Mental Health, 11*(3), 168-170.

Nelson, E-L., & Lillis, T. A. (2013)> Managing real-time telepsychology practice. In G. P. Koocher, J. C. Norcross, & B. A Greene (Eds.), *Psychologist's desk reference. Third Edition* (pp. 690-694). New York: Oxford University Press.

Melville, K. M., Casey, L. M., & Kavanagh, D. J. (2010). Dropout from Internet-based treatment for psychological disorders. *British Journal of Clinical Psychology, 49*(4), 455-471.

Menon, G. M., & Rubin, M. (2011). A survey of online practitioners: Implications for education and practice. *Journal of Technology in Human Services,* 29 (2), 133-41.

Mermelstein, R., & Turner, L. (2006). Web-based support as an adjunct to group-based smoking cessation for adolescents. *Nicotine & Tobacco Research, 8*(1), S69-S76. doi: 10.1080/14622200601039949

Meropol, N. J., Daly, M.B., Vig, H.S., Manion, F.J., Manne, S.L., Mazar, C., Murphy, C., Solarino, N., & Zubarev, V. (2011). Delivery of internet-based cancer genetic counselling services to patients' homes: A feasibility study. *Journal of Telemedicine Telecare,* 17 (1), 36-40.

Mewton, L., Smith, J., Rossouw, P. & Andrews, G. (2014). Current pespectives on Internet delivered cognitive behavioral therapy for adults with anxiety and related disorders. *Psychology Research and Behavior Management, 7*, 37-46.

Midkiff, D.M., & Wyatt, W.J. (2008). Ethical issues in the provision of online mental health services (etherapy). *Journal of Technology in Human Services, 26*(2/4), 310-332.

Mileham, B. L. A. (2007). Online infidelity in internet chat rooms: An ethnographic exploration. *Computers in Human Behavior, 23*, 11-31. doi: 10.1016/j.chb.2004.03.033

Miller, B. C. (2010). *Nice teams finish last: The secret to unleashing your team's maximum potential.* New York: American Management Association.

Miller, E. T., Neal, D. J., Roberts, L.J., Baer, J.S., Cressler, S.O., Metrik, J., & Marlatt, G.A. (2002). Test-retest reliability of alcohol measures: Is there a difference between internet-based assessment and traditional methods? *Psychology of Addictive Behaviors, 16*, 56-63.

Miller, T. W. (2006). Telehealth issues in consulting psychology practice. *Consulting Psychology Journal: Practice and Research, 58*, 82-90. doi:10.1037/1065-9293.58.2.82

Miller, W. R., Leckman, A.L., Delaney, H.D., & Tinkcom, M. (1992). Long-term follow-up of behavioral self-control training. *Journal of Studies on Alcohol, 53,* 249-261.

Miller, W. R. & Pechacek, T. F. (1987). New Roads: Assessing and treating alcohol dependence. *Journal of Substance Abuse Treatment, 4*, 73-77.

Miller, W. R., & Rollnick, S. (2002). *Motivational interviewing.* (2nd ed.). New York: Guilford Press.

Miller, W. R., & Sanchez, V. C. (1994). Motivating young adults for treatment and lifestyle change. In G. Howard (Ed.), *Issues in alcohol use and misuse by young adults* (pp. 55-81). Notre Dame, IN: University of Notre Dame Press.

Mills, S. (2006). When humans need humans: The lack of use of computer-based ICT in distance pastoral care. *Interacting with Computers, 18*, 556-567. doi:10.1016/j.intcom.2006.01.006

Mitchell, J., Stanimirovic, R., Klein, B., & Vella-Brodrick, D. (2009). A randomised controlled trial of a self-guided internet intervention promoting well-being. *Computers in Human Behavior, 25*, 749-760. doi:10.1016/j.chb.2009.02.003

Mitchell, J., Vella-Brodrick, D., & Klein, B. (2010). Positive psychology and the internet: A mental health opportunity. *E-Journal of Applied Psychology*, *6*(2), 30-41.

Mitchell, K. J., & Wells, M. (2007). Problematic internet experiences: Primary or secondary presenting problems in persons seeking mental health care? *Social Science & Medicine, 65*(6), 1136-1141.

Mohr, D. C. (2009). Telemental health: Reflections on how to move the field forward. *Clinical Psychology: Science and Practice, 16,* 343-347.

Mohr, D.C., Burns, M.N., Schueller, S.M., Clarke, G., Klinkman, M. (2013). Behavioral intervention technologies: Evidence review and recommendations for future research in mental health. *General Hospital Psychiatry, 35*(4), 332-338.

Moore, D., & Ayers, S. (2011). A review of postnatal mental health websites: Help for health-care professionals and patients. *Archives of Women's Mental Health, 14*(6), 443-452.

Mora, L., Nevid, J., & Chaplin, W. (2008). Psychologist treatment recommendations for internet-based therapeutic interventions. *Computers in Human Behavior, 24*, 3052-3062. doi:10.1016/j.chb.2008.05.011

Morgan, D. G., Crossley, M., Kirk, A., McBain, L., Stewart, N.J., D'arcy, C., Forbes, D., Harder, S., Dal Bello-Haas, V., & Basran, J. (2011), Evaluation of telehealth for preclinic assessment and follow-up in an interprofessional rural and remote memory clinic, *Journal of Applied Gerontology,* 30 (3), 304-31.

Morland, L. A., Greene, C.J., Grubbs, K., Kloezman, K., Mackintosh, M.-A., Rosen, C., & Frueh, B.C. (2011), Therapist adherence to manualized cognitive-behavioral therapy for anger management delivered to veterans with PTSD via videoconferencing, *Journal of Clinical Psychology,* 67 (6), 629-38.

Morland, L. A., Hynes, A.K., Mackintosh, M-A., Resnick, P.A., Chard, K.M. (2011), Group cognitive processing therapy delivered to veterans via telehealth: A pilot cohort, *Journal of Traumatic Stress,* 24 (4), 465-69.

Morris, M. E., & Aguilera, A. (2012). Mobile, social, and wearable computing and the evolution of psychological practice. *Professional Psychology: Research and Practice, 43*(6), 622-626. http://psycnet.apa.org/journals/pro/43/6/622/

Moskowitz, D. A., Melton, D., & Owczarzak, J. (2009). PowerON: The use of instant message counseling and the internet to facilitate HIV/STD education and prevention. *Patient Education and Counseling, 77,* 20-26. doi:10.1016/j.pec.2009.01.00

Mouthaan, J., Sijbrandij, M., Reitsma, J.B., Luitse, J.S.K., Goslings, J.C., & Olff, M.(2011). Trauma tips: An Internet-based intervention to prevent posttraumatic stress disorder in injured trauma patients. *Journal of CyberTherapy and Rehabilitation,* 4 (3), 331-40.

Mukherjee, D. (2012). Leading virtual teams: How do social, cognitive, and behavioral capabilities matter? *Management Decision, 50*(2), 273-290.

Mulvaney, S. A., Ritterband, L. M., & Bosslet, L. (2011). Mobile intervention design in diabetes: Review and recommendations. *Current Diabetes Reports, 11(6),* 486-493.

Mulvaney, S. A., Rothman, R. L, Wallston, K. A., Lybarger, C., & Dietrich, M. S. (2010). An internet-based program to improve self-management in adolescents with type 1 diabetes. *Diabetes Care, 33*, 602-604.

Muroff, J., Steketee, G., Himle, J., & Frost, R. (2010). Delivery of internet treatment for compulsive hoarding (D.I.T.C.H.). *Behaviour Research and Therapy, 48*, 79-85. doi: 10.1016/j.brat.2009.09.006

Murphy, L., Parnass, P., Mitchell, D. L., Hallett, R., Cayley, P., & Seagram, S. (2009). Client satisfaction and outcome comparisons of online and face-to-face counselling methods. *British Journal of Social Work, 39*(4), 627-640. doi:10.1093/bjsw/bcp041

Murphy, L., MacFadden, R., & Mitchell, D. (2008). Cybercounseling online: The development of a university-based training program for e-mail counseling. *Journal of Technology in Human Services, 26* (2/4), 447-469.

Murray, C. D., Pettifer, S., Howard, T., Patchick, E. L., Cailette, F., Kulkarni, J., & Bamford, C. (2007). The treatment of phantom limb pain using immersive virtual reality: Three case studies. *Disability and Rehabilitation, 29*, 1465-1469.

Nelson, E-L., Bui, T. N., & Velasquez, S. E. (2011). Telepsychology: Research and practice overview, *Child and Adolescent Psychiatric Clinics of North America,* 20 (1), 67-79.

Nelson, E-L., & Velasquez, S. E. (2011). Implementing psychological services over televideo, *Professional Psychology: Research and Practice,* 42 (6), 535-42.

Nemoto, K., Tachikawa, H., Sodeyama, N., Endo, G., Hashimoto, K., Mizukami, K., & Asada, T. (2007). Quality of Internet information referring to mental health and mental disorders in Japan. *Psychiatry and Clinical Neurosciences, 61*, 243-248.

Newman, M. G., Szkodny, L. E., Llera, S. J., & Przeworski, A. (2011). A review of technology-assisted self-help and minimal contact therapies for anxiety and depression: Is human contact necessary for therapeutic efficacy? *Clinical Psychology Review, 31*, 89-103. doi:10.1016/j.cpr.2010.09.008

Newman, M. G., Szkodny, L. E., Llera, S. J., & Przeworski, A. (2011). A review of technology-assisted self-help and minimal contact therapies for drug and alcohol abuse and smoking addiction: Is human contact necessary for therapeutic efficacy? *Clinical Psychology Review, 31*, 178-186. doi:10.1016/j.cpr.2010.10.002

Neylon, C. (2009). Stitching science together. *Nature, 461*(7266), 881.

Nijhof, S. L., Bleijenberg, G., Uiterwaal, C., Kimpen, J., & van de Putte, E. (2012), Effectiveness of internet-based cognitive behavioural treatment for adolescents with chronic fatigue syndrome (FITNET): A randomised controlled trial, *The Lancet,* 379 (9824), 1412-18.

Niles, B. L., Klunk-Gillis, J., Ryngala, D., Silberbogen, A., Pasynick, A., & Wolf, E. (2011), Comparing mindfulness and psychoeducation treatments for combat-related ptsd using a telehealth approach, *Psychological Trauma: Theory, Research, Practice, and Policy,* 4(5), 538-547.

Nordal, K. C. (2012). Healthcare reform: Implications for independent practice, *Professional Psychology: Research and Practice, 43*(6), 535-544.

Nordgreen, T., Standal, B., Mannes, H., Haug, T., Sivertsen, B., Carlbring, P., Andersson, G., Heiervang, E. &Havik, O. E. (2010). Guided self-help via internet for panic disorder: Dissemination across countries. *Computers in Human Behavior, 26*(4), 592-596. doi: 10.1016/j.chb.2009.12.011

Novotney, A. (2014). An all-out anti-bullying focus. *Monitor on Psychology, 45*, 63-65.

Ocker, R. J. (2007). A Balancing Act: The Interplay of Status Effects on Dominance in Virtual Teams. *IEEE Transactions on Professional Communication, 50*(3), 204.

O'Neal, M. (2014). Campus psychological counseling goes online for students at the U of Florida. *The Chronicle of Higher Education Technology*, January Issue.

Oraegbunam, N. M. (2009). Applying information and communication technology in counselling practice. *Procedia - Social and Behavioral Sciences, 1*(1), 1749-1752. doi: 10.1016/j.sbspro.2009.01.309

Pabian, Y. L., Welfel, E., & Beebe, R.S. (2009). Psychologists' knowledge of their state laws pertaining to Tarasoff-type situations. *Professional Psychology: Research and Practice, 40*: 8-14.

Palermo, T. M., Wilson, A. C., Peters, M., Lewandowski, A., & Somhegyi, H. (2009). Randomized controlled trial of an internet-delivered family cognitive–behavioral therapy intervention for children and adolescents with chronic pain. *Pain, 146*(1-2), 205-213. doi: 10.1016/j.pain.2009.07.034

Palyo, S. A., Schopmeyer, K. A., & McQuaid, J. R. (2012). Tele-pain management: Use of videoconferencing technology in the delivery of an integrated cognitive–behavioral and physical therapy group intervention, *Psychological Services,* 9 (2), 200-02.

Parikh, R., TouVelle, M., Wang, H., Zallak, S.N (2011). Sleep telemedicine: Patient satisfaction and treatment adherence, *Telemedicine and e-Health,* 17 (8), 609-14.

Parr, J. M., Kavanaugh, D. J., Young, R., Mitchell, G. (2011). Acceptability of cognitive-behaviour therapy via the internet for cessation of benzodiazepine use, *Drug and Alcohol Review,* 30 (3), 306-14

Parsons, T. D., & Rizzo, A. A. (2008). Affective outcomes of Virtual Reality Exposure Therapy for anxiety and specific phobias: A Meta-Analysis. *Journal of Behavior Therapy and Experimental Psychiatry, 39*, 250-261.

Pemberton, M.R., Williams, J., Herman-Stahl, M., Calvin, S.L., Bradshaw, M.R., Bray, R.M., Ridenhour, J.L., Cook, R., Hersch, R., Hester, R.K., & Mitchell, G. (2011). Behavioral effects of two web-based alcohol interventions in the United States military. *Journal of Studies on Alcohol and Drugs, 72*, 480-489.

Pollock, S.L. (2006). Internet counseling and its feasibility for marriage and family counseling. *The Family Journal: Counseling and Therapy for Couples and Families, 14*(1), 65-70.

Pornsakulvanich, V., Haridakis, P., & Rubin, A. M. (2008). The influence of dispositions and internet motivation on online communication satisfaction and relationship closeness. *Computers in Human Behavior, 24*, 2292-2310. doi: 10.1016/j.chb.2007.11.003

Possemato, K., Ouimette, P., and Knowlton, P. (2011). A brief self-guided telehealth intervention for post-traumatic stress disorder in combat veterans: A pilot study, *Journal Telemedicine Telecare,* 17 (5), 245-50.

Powell, B. J., Proctor, E. K., & Glass, J. E. (2014). A systematic review of strategies for implementing empirically supported mental health interventions. *Research On Social Work Practice*, *24*(2), 192-212.

Powell, J., & Clarke, A. (2006). Internet information-seeking in mental health: Population survey. *British Journal of Psychiatry, 189*(3), 273-277.

Pretorius, N., Arcelus, J., Beecham, J., Dawson, H., Doherty, F., Eisler, I., Gallagher, C., Gowers, S., Isaacs, G., Johnson-Sabine, E., Jones, A., Newell, C., Morris, J., Richards, L., Ringwood, S., Rowlands, L., Simic., M., Treasure, J., Waller, G., Williams, C., Yi, I., Yoshioka, M., & Schmidt, U. (2009). Cognitive-behavioural therapy for adolescents with bulimic symptomatology: The acceptability and effectiveness of internet-based delivery. *Behaviour Research and Therapy, 47*, 729-736. doi:10.1016/j.brat.2009.05.006

Preschl, Barbara, Maercker, Andreas, and Wagner, Birgit (2011). The working alliance in a randomized controlled trial comparing online with face-to-face cognitive-behavioral therapy for depression, *BMC Psychiatry,* 11.

Preziosa, A., Grassi, A., Gaggioli, A., & Riva, G. (2009). Therapeutic applications of the mobile phone. *British Journal of Guidance & Counselling, 37*, 313-325. doi:10.1080/03069880902957031

Price, E. L., Perez-Stable, E.J., Nickleach, D., Lopez, M., & Karliner, L.S. (2012), Interpreter perspectives of in-person, telephonic, and videoconferencing medical interpretation in clinical encounters, *Patient Education and Counseling,* 87 (2), 226-232.

Prochaska, J. J., Reyes, R. S., Schroeder, S. A., Daniels, A. S., Doederlein, A., & Bergeson, B. (2011). An online survey of tobacco use, intentions to quit, and cessation strategies among people living with bipolar disorder. *Bipolar Disorders*, *13*(5-6), 466-473.

Proudfoot, J. (2012). The future is in our hands: The role of mobile phones in the pevention and management of mental disorders. *Australian & New Zealand Journal of Psychiatry, 47*, 111-113,

Proudfoot, J., Klein, B., Barak, A., Carlbring, P., Cuijpers, P., Lange, A., Ritterband, L.& Andersson, G. (2011). Establishing guidelines for executing and reporting internet intervention research. *Cognitive Behaviour Therapy*, *40*(2), 82-97.

Project MATCH Research Group. (1997). Matching alcoholism treatments to client heterogeneity: Project MATCH posttreatment drinking outcomes. *Journal of Studies on Alcohol, 58,* 7-29.

Project MATCH Research Group. (1998). Matching alcoholism treatments to client heterogeneity: Project MATCH three-year drinking outcomes. *Alcoholism: Clinical and Experimental Research, 22,* 1300-1311.

Radostina, K. P. (2014). Face-to-face versus virtual teams: What have we really learned? *The Psychologist-Manager Journal, 17*(1), 2-29.

Rains, S. A. (2005). Leveling the Organizational Playing Field—Virtually: A Meta-Analysis of Experimental Research Assessing the Impact of Group Support System Use on Member Influence Behaviors. *Communication Research, 32*, 193-234.

Reed, G. M., McLaughlin, C. J., (in press). Ten interdisciplinary principles for professional practice in telehealth: Implications for psychology. *Professional Psychology: Research and Practice.*

Reese, R. J., Conoley, C. W., & Brossart, D. F. (2006). The attractiveness of telephone counseling: An empirical investigation of client perceptions. *Journal of Counseling & Development, 84*, 54-60.

Reger, G. M., & Gahm, G. (2008). Virtual Reality Exposure Therapy for active duty soldiers. *Journal of Clinical Psychology, 64,* 940-946.

Reger, G. M., Gahm, G., Rizzo, A.A., Swanson, R., & Duma, S. (2008). Soldier Evaluation of the Virtual reality Iraq. *Telemedicine and e-HEALTH, 15*, 101-104.

Reger, G. M., Holloway, K. M., Candy, C., Rothbaum, B. O., Difede, J., Rizzo, A. A., & Gahm, G.(2011). Effectiveness of Virtual Reality Exposure Therapy for Active Duty Soldiers in a Military Mental Health Clinic. *Journal of Traumatic Stress, 24*, 93-96.

Renninger, K. A., & Shumar, W. (Ed.). (2002). *Building virtual communities: Learning and change in cyberspace*. New York: Cambridge University Press.

Richards, D. (2009). Features and benefits of online counselling: Trinity college online mental health community. *British Journal of Guidance & Counselling, 37*, 231-242. doi:10.1080/03069880902956975

Richardson, L. K., Frueh, B. C., Grubaugh, A. L., Egede, L., & Elhai, J. D. (2009). Current directions in videoconferencing tele-mental health research. *Clinical Psychology: Science and Practice,16,* 323-338.

Ritterband, L. M. (2010). Commentary: Can cognitive behavioral therapy of insomnia be effectively provided via an Internet-based program? *Best of Sleep Medicine 2010: An Annual Collection of Scientific Literature,* 91-93.

Ritterband, L. M., Andersson, G., Christensen, H. M., Carlbring, P., & Cuijpers, P. (2006). Directions for the International Society for Research on Internet Interventions (ISRII). *Journal of Medical Internet Research, 8(3)*: e23. http://www.jmir.org/2006/3/e23/. PMID: 17032639

Ritterband, L. M., Bailey, E. T., Thorndike, F. P., Lord, H. R., Farrell-Camahan, L., & Baum, L. D. (2012). Initial evaluation of an Internet intervention to improve the sleep of cancer survivors with insomnia. *Psycho-Oncology, 21(7),* 695-705. DOI:10.1002/pon. 1969.

Ritterband, L. M., Borowitz, S. M., Cox, D. J., Kovatchev, B., Walker, L. S., Lucas, V., & Sutphen, J. (2005). Using the Internet to provide information prescriptions. *Pediatrics, 116*, e643-e647

Ritterband, L. M., Cox, D. J., Gordon, T., Borowitz, S. M., Kovatchev, B., Walker, L. S., & Sutphen, J. (2006). Examining the added value of audio, graphics, and interactivity in an Internet intervention for pediatric encopresis. *Children's Health Care, 35(1)*, 47-59.

Ritterband, L. M., Cox, D. C., Kovatchev, B. P., Borowitz, S. M., Ling, W. D., & Marshall, B. (2001). A Telecommunication Monitoring System (TMS) for clinical and research practice. *Professional Psychology: Research and Practice, 32(6)*, 636-641.

Ritterband, L. M., Cox, D. J., Kovatchev, B. P., McKnight, L., Walker, L. S., Patel, K., Borowitz, S., & Sutphen, J. (2000). An Internet intervention as adjunctive therapy for pediatric encopresis. *Journal of Consulting and Clinical Psychology, 71,* 910-917.

Ritterband, L. M., Cox, D. C., Walker, L. S., Kovatchev, B., et al. (2003). An Intenet intervention as adjuncting therapy for pediatric encopresis. *Journal of Consulting & Clinical Psychology, 71,* 910-917.

Ritterband, L. M., Gonder-Frederick. L. A., Cox, D. J., Clifton, A. D., West, R. W., & Borwitz, S. M. (2003). Internet interventions: In review, in use, and into the future. *Professional Psychology: Research and Practice, 34,* 527-534.

Ritterband, L. M., & Palermo, T. M. (2009). eHealth in Pediatric Psychology. *Journal of Pediatric Psychology*, *34*, 453-456.

Ritterband, L. M., & Tate, D. K. (2009). The science of Internet interventions. *Annuals of Behavioral Medicine, 38*, 1-3.

Ritterband, L. M., & Thorndike, F. P. (2006). Internet interventions or patient education websites? *Journal of Medical Internet Research, 8(3)*: e18. PMID: 17032634

Ritterband, L. M. & Thorndike, F. P. (2012). The further rise of Internet interventions: Commentary on Espie et al., A randomized, placebo-controlled, trial of online Cognitive Behavioral Therapy for chronic Insomnia Disorder delivered via an automated media-rich web application. *Sleep*, 35(6), 737-8.

Ritterband, L. M., Thorndike, F. P., Cox, D. J., Kovatchev, B. P., & Gonder-Frederick. L. A. (2009). A behavior change model for Internet interventions. *Annuals of Behavioral Medicine, 38*, 18-27.

Ritterband, L. M., Thorndike, F. P., Gonder-Frederick. L. A., Magee, J. C., Bailey, E. T., Saylor, D. K., & Morin, C. M. (2009). Efficacy of an Internet-based behavioral intervention for adults with insomnia. *Archives of General Psychiatry, 66*, 692-698.

Ritterband, L. M., Thorndike, F. P., Lord, H. R., Borowitz, S., Walker, L. S., Ingersoll, K. S., Sutphen, J., & Cox, D. J. (2013). An RCT of an internet intervention for pediatric encopresis with one year follow-up. *Clinical Practice in Pediatric Psychology, 1(1)*, 68-80.

Riva, G. (2009). Virtual reality: An experiential tool for clinical psychology. *British Journal of Guidance & Counselling, 37*, 337-345. doi:10.1080/03069880902957056

Riva, G., Alcaniz, M., Anolli, L., Bacchetta, M., Banos, R., Beltrame, F., . . . Troiani, R. (2001). The VEPSY Updated Project: Virtual Reality in Clinical Psychology. *Cyberpsychology & Behavior, 4*(4), 449.

Rizzo, A. S., Difede, J., Rothbaum, B.O., Reger, G., Spitalnick, J.S., Cukor, J., & Mclay, R. (2010). Development and early evaluation of the Virtual Iraq/Afghanistan exposure therapy system for combat-related PTSD. *Annals of the New York Academy of Science, 1208*, 114-125.

Rizzo, A. S., Parsons, T. D., Kenny, P., & Buckwalter, J. G. (2012). Using Virtual Reality for clinical assessment and interventions. In L. L'Abate & D. A. Kaiser (Eds.), *Handbook of Technology in Psychology, Psychiatry, and Neurology: Theory, Research, and Practice* (pp. 277-318). New York: Nova Science Publishers.

Robinson, P. H., & Serfaty, M. A. (2008). Getting better byte by byte: A pilot randomized controlled trial of email therapy for bulimia nervosa and binge eating disorder. *European Eating Disorders Review, 16*, 84-93.

Robinson, S., Perkins, S., Bauer, S., Hammond, N., Treasure, J., & Schmidt, U. (2006). Aftercare intervention through text messaging in the treatment of bulimia nervosa – Feasibility pilot. International Journal of Eating Disorders, 39(8), 633-638.

Rogers, M. (2007). Four resources create "virtual" look at Civil War; psychology database and first-person narratives also provide human touch. *Library Journal* (1976), *132*(15), 21.

Rollman, B., Belnap, B., & LeMenager, M. (2009). Telephone-delivered collaborative care for treating post-CABG depression: A randomized controlled trial. *JAMA, 302*(19), 2095-2103. doi:10.1001/jama.2009.1670

Rooke, S. E., Gates, P. J., Norberg, M. M., & Copeland, J. (2014). Applying technology to the treatment of cannabis use disorder: Comparing telephone versus internet delivery using data from two completed trials. *Journal of Substance Abuse Treatment, 46*(1), 78-84.

Rosegrant. J. (2012). Introduction: Clinicians respond to their clients' technology. *Journal of Clinical Psychology, 68*(11),1161-1163.

Rosmarin, D. H., Pargament, K. I., Pirutinsky, S., & Mahoney, A. (2010). A randomized controlled evaluation of a spiritually integrated treatment for subclinical anxiety in the Jewish community, delivered via the Internet. *Journal Of Anxiety Disorders, 24*(7), 799-808.

Rothwell, E., Ellington, L., Planalp, S., & Crouch, B. (2012). Exploring challenges to telehealth communication by specialists in poison information, *Quality Health Research,* 22 (1), 67-75.

Roy, H. & Gillett, T. (2008). E-mail: A new technique for forming a therapeutic alliance with high-risk young people failing to engage with mental health services? A case study. *Clinical Child Psychology and Psychiatry, 13*(1), 95-103.

Ruggiero, K. J., Resnick, H. S., Acierno, R., Coffey, S. F., Carpenter, M. J., Ruscio, A. M., Stephens, R.S., Kilpatrick, D.G., Stasiewicz, P.R., Roffman, R.A., Bucuvalas, M. & Galea, S. (2006). Internet-based intervention for mental health and substance use problems in disaster-affected populations: A pilot feasibility study. *Behavior Therapy, 37*, 190-205. doi:10.1016/j.beth.2005.12.001

Sabella, R. A., Poynton, T. A., & Isaacs, M. L. (2010). School counselors perceived importance of counseling technology competencies. *Computers in Human Behavior, 26*(4), 609-617. doi:10.1016/j.chb.2009.12.014

Sánchez-Ortiz, V. C., House, J. J., Munro, C. C., Treasure, J. J., Startup, H. H., Williams, C. C., & Schmidt, U. U. (2011). 'A computer isn't gonna judge you': A qualitative study of users' views of an internet-based cognitive behavioural guided self-care treatment package for bulimia nervosa and related disorders. *Eating And Weight Disorders, 16*(2), 93-101.

Sánchez-Ortiz, V. C., Munro, C., Startup, H., Treasure, J., & Schmidt, U. (2011). The role of email guidance in internet-based cognitive-behavioural self-care treatment for bulimia nervosa. *European Eating Disorders Review, 19*(4), 342-348.

Sánchez-Ortiz, V. C., Munro, C., Stahl, D., House, J., Startup, H., Treasure, J., Williams, C. & Schmidt, U. (2011), A randomized controlled trial of internet-based cognitive-behavioural therapy for bulimia nervosa or related disorders in a student population, *Psychological Medicine: A Journal of Research in Psychiatry and the Allied Sciences,* 41 (2), 407-417.

Santa Ana, E. J., Stallings, D.L., Rounsaville, B.J. & Martino, S. (2011). Development of an in-home telehealth program for outpatient veterans with substance use disorders', *Psychological Services, 10*(3), 304-314.

Santor, D. A., & Bagnell, A. (2008). Enhancing the effectiveness and sustainability of school-based mental health programs: Maximizing program participation, knowledge uptake and ongoing evaluation using internet-based resources. *Advances In School Mental Health Promotion, 1*(2), 17-28.

Savin, D., Glueck, D.A., Chardavoyne, J., & Novins, D.K. (2011). Bridging cultures: Child psychiatry via videoconferencing', *Child and Adolescent Psychiatric Clinics of North America,* 20 (1), 125-34.

Schmalzi, L., Thomke, E., Ragno, C., Nilseryd, M., Stockselius, A., & Ehrsson, H. H. (2011). Puling telescoped phantom out of the stump: Manipulating the perceived position of phantom limbs using a full-body illusion. *Frontiers in Human Neuroscience, 5,* Article 121. Doi.10.3389/fahum.2011.000121.

Schroeder, R. (1996). *Possible worlds: The social dynamic of virtual reality technology.* Boulder, CO: Westview Press.

Schruijer, S. G. (2006). Research on Collaboration in Action. *International Journal of Action Research, 2*(2), 222+.

Schweitzer, L., & Duxbury, L. (2010). Conceptualizing and measuring the virtuality of teams. *Information Systems Journal, 20*(3), 267-295. Doi: 10.1111/j.1365-2575.2009.00326.x

Schultze, N. (2006). Rapid communication: Success factors in internet-based psychological counseling. *CyberPsychology & Behavior, 9*(5), 623-626. doi:10.1089/cpb.2006.9.623

Schwartz, T. J., & Lonborg, S.D. (2011). Security management in telepsychology. *Professional Psychology: Research and Practice, 42,* 419-425.

Shachaf, P. (2008). Cultural diversity and information and communication technology impacts on global virtual teams: An exploratory study. *Information & Management, 45*(2), 131-142.

Sharma, R. C. (2011). Online Communication and Collaboration. Donelan, H., et al. (Eds.). *British Journal of Educational Technology*, 42 (1), p. E10.

Shields, R. (2003). *The virtual.* London: Routledge.

Short, J. C., Piccolo, G., Powell, A., & Ives, B. (2005). Investigating Multilevel Relationships in Information Systems Research: An Application to Virtual Teams Research Using Hierarchical Linear Modeling. *JITTA : Journal of Information Technology Theory and Application, 7*(3), 1+.

Siebdrat, F., Hoegl, M., & Ernst, H. (2009). How to Manage Virtual Teams. *MIT Sloan Management Review, 50*(4), 63-68.

Seligman, M. E. P., Rashid, T., & Parks, A. C. (2006). Positive psychotherapy. *American Psychologist, 61*, 774-788. doi:10.1037/0003-066X.61.8.774

Setoyama, Y., Yamazaki, Y., & Namayama, K. (2011). Benefits of peer support in online Japanese breast cancer communities: Differences between lurkers and posters. *Journal Of Medical Internet Research, 13*(4), 510-522.

Shaikh, U., Nettiksimmons, J., & Romano, P. (2011). Pediatric obesity management in rural clinics in California and the role of telehealth in distance education, *The Journal of Rural Health,* 27 (3), 263-69.

Shandley, K., Klein, B, Kyrios, M., Austin, D., Ciechomski, L. & Murray, G. (2011). Training postgraduate psychology students to deliver psycho-logical services online, *Australian Psychologist,* 46 (2), 120-25.

Sharp, I. R., Kobak, K. A., & Osman, D. A. (2011). The use of videoconferencing with patients with psychosis: A review of the literature, *Annals of General Psychiatry,* 10.

Shaw, H. E., & Shaw, S. F. (2006). Critical ethical issues in online counseling: Assessing current practices with an ethical intent checklist. *Journal of Counseling & Development, 84*, 41-53.

Sheeran, T., Rabinowitz, R., Lotterman, J., Reilley, C.F., Brown, S., Donehower, P., Ellsworth, E., Amour, J.L., & Bruce, M.L.. (2011), Feasibility and impact of telemonitor-based depression care management for geriatric homecare patients, *Telemedicine and e-Health,* 17 (8), 620-26.

Shore, J.H., Hilty, D.M., & Yellowlees, P. (2007). Emergency management guidelines for tele-psychiatry. *General Hospital Psychiatry, 29*: 199-206.

Sieben, B. (2007). Doing research on emotion and virtual work: A compass to assist orientation. *Sage Publications*, *60*(4), 561-580.

Silberbogen, A.K., Ulloa, E., Mori, D.L., & Brown, K. (2012). A telehealth intervention for veterans on antiviral treatment for the hepatitis C virus. *Psychological Services, 9* (2), 163-73.

Simms, D. C., Gibson, K., & O'Donnell, S. (2011). To use or not to use: Clinicians' perceptions of telemental health, *Canadian Psychology/Psychologie canadienne,* 52 (1), 41-51.

Simpson, S. (2009). Psychotherapy via videoconferencing: A review. *British Journal of Guidance & Counselling, 37*, 271-286. doi:10.1080/03069880902957007

Skinner, A. E. G., & Latchford, G. (2006). Attitudes to counseling via the internet: A comparison between in-person counselling clients and internet support group users. *Counselling & Psychotherapy Research, 6*(3), 158-163. doi:10.1080/14733140600853641

Skinner, H. A. (1994). *Computerized lifestyle assessment*. Toronto, Ontario: Multi-Health Systems, Inc.

Sloan, D. M., Gallagher, M.W., Feinstein, B.A., Lee, D.J., & Pruneau, G.M.. (2011). Efficacy of telehealth treatments for posttraumatic stress-related symptoms: A meta-analysis, *Cognitive Behaviour Therapy,* 40 (2), 111-25.

Smith, D. J., Griffiths, E., Poole, R., di Florio, A., Barnes, E., Kelly, M. J., Craddock, N., Hood, K. & Simpson, S. (2011). Beating Bipolar: Exploratory trial of a novel internet-based psychoeducational treatment for bipolar disorder. *Bipolar Disorders*, *13*(5-6), 571-577.

Smith-Jentsch, K. A., Scielzo, S. A., Yarbrough, C. S., & Rosopa, P. J. (2008). A comparison of face-to-face and electronic peer-mentoring: Interactions with mentor gender. *Journal of Vocational Behavior, 72*(2), 193-206. doi:10.1016/j.jvb.2007.11.004

Smith, R.E., Fagan, C., Wilson, N. L., Chen, J., Corona, M., Nguyen, H., Racz, S., & Shoda, Y. (2011). Internet-based approaches to collaborative therapeutic assessment: New opportunities for professional psychologists. *Professional Psychology: Research and Practice, 42,* 494-504.

Solomon, O. (2012). The use of technology for and with children with Autism Spectrum Disorder. In L. L'Abate & D. A. Kaiser (Eds.), *Handbook of Technology in Psychology, Psychiatry, and Neurology: Theory, Research, and Practice* (pp. 155-178). New York: Nova Science Publishers.

South, M., Wolf, J. M.& Herlihy, L. E. (2012). Future dimensions: Neuroscience applications to practice in child and adolescent psychology. *Professional Psychology: Research and Practice, 43*(6), 560-567. http://psycnet.apa.org/journals/pro/43/6/560/

Spates, C. R., Kalata, A. H., Ozeki, S., Stanton, C. E., & Peters, S. (2012). Initial open trial of a computerized behavioral activation treatment for depression. *Behavior Modification, 37,* 259-297.

Spaulding, R., Cain, S., & Sonnenschein, K. (2011). Urban telepsychiatry: Uncommon service for a common need', *Child and Adolescent Psychiatric Clinics of North America,* 20 (1), 29-39.

Spaulding, R., Stevens, D., & Velasquez, S. E. (2011). Experience with telehealth for sleep monitoring and sleep laboratory management, *Journal of Telemedicine & Telecare,* 17 (7), 346-49.

Spek, V., Cuijpers, P., Nyklicek, I., Riper, H., Keyzer, J., & Pop, V. (2006). Internet-based cognitive behaviour therapy for symptoms of depression and anxiety: A meta-analysis. Psychological Medicine, 37, 319-328.

Spence, J., Titov, N., Dear, B.F., Johnston, L., Solley, K., Lorian, C., Wootton, B., Zou, J., & Schwenke, G. (2011). Randomized controlled trial of Internet-delivered cognitive behavioral therapy for posttraumatic stress disorder, *Depression and Anxiety,* 28 (7), 541-50.

Spence, S. H., Holmes, J. M., March, S., & Lipp, O. V. (2006). The feasibility and outcome of clinic plus internet delivery of Cognitive–Behavior therapy for childhood anxiety. *Journal of Consulting and Clinical Psychology, 74*(3), 614-621. doi:DOI: 10.1037/0022-006X.74.3.614

Spigelman, C., Reiter, S., & Weiss, P. L. (2009). A conceptual framework for electronic socio-emotional support for people with special needs. *International Journal of Rehabilitation Research, 32*(4), 301-308. doi:10.1097/MRR.0b013e32831e4519

Stain, H. J., Payne, K., Thienel, R., Michie, P., Carr, V. & Kelly, B. (2011), The feasibility of videoconferencing for neuropsychological assessments of rural youth experiencing early psychosis, *Journal of Telemedicine Telecare,* 17 (6), 328-31.

Steinfeld, B.I., & Keyes, J.A. (2011). Electronic medical records in a multidisciplinary health care setting: A clinical perspective. *Professional Psychology: Research and Practice, 42* 426-432.

Stevenson, D. R.(2011). Tertiary-level telehealth: A media space application, *Computer Supported Cooperative Work (CSCW),* 20 (1-2), 61-92.

Stice, E., Rohde, P., Durant, S., & Shaw, H. (2012). A Preliminary trial of a prototype Internet dissonance-based eating disorder prevention program for young women with body image concerns. *Journal of Consulting and Clinical Psychology, 80,* 907-916.

Strachan, M., Gros, D. F., Yuen, E., Ruggiero, K. J., Foa, E. B., & Acierno, R. (2012), Home-based telehealth to deliver evidence-based psychotherapy in veterans with PTSD, *Contemporary Clinical Trials,* 33 (2), 402-9.

Strickland, D., McAllister, D., Coles, C.D., & Osborne, S. (2007). An evolution of virtual reality training designs for children with autism and fetal alcohol spectrum disorders. *Topics in Language Disorders, 27*, 226-241.

Stummer, G. (2009). Client contact styles in online therapeutic work via e-mail. *Counselling Psychology Review, 24*, 14-23.

Su, W., Fang, X., Miller, J. K., & Wang, Y. (2011). Internet-based intervention for the treatment of online addiction for college students in China: A pilot study of the Healthy Online Self-Helping Center. *Cyberpsychology, Behavior, And Social Networking, 14*(9), 497-503.

Sutton, S., & Gilbert, H. (2007). Effectiveness of individually tailored smoking cessation advice letters as an adjunct to telephone counselling and generic self-help materials: Randomized controlled trial. *Addiction, 102*, 994-1000. doi:10.1111/j.1360-0443.2007.01831.x

Squires, D.D., & Hester, R.K. (2002). Development of a computer-based brief intervention for drinkers: The increasing role for computers in the assessment and treatment of addictive behaviors. *The Behavior Therapist, 25,* (3), 59-65.

Squires, D.D., & Hester, R.K. (2004). Utilizing technical innovations in clinical practice: The Drinker's Check-up software program. *IN SESSION: Journal of Clinical Psychology, 60,* 159-170.

Stayer, S. M., Pelletier, S. L., Rollins, L. K., Heim, S. W., Ingersoll, K. S., Ritterband, L. M., Schorling, J. B. (2012). Evaluating a web-based tool to increase physician screening and counseling for alcohol misuse: A Virginia Practice Support Research Network Trial. *The Journal of the American Board of Family Medicine*, 25(5), 605-13.

Takriti, Y., El-Sayeh, H. G., & Adams, C. E. (2005). Internet-based search of randomised trials relevant to mental health originating in the Arab world. *BMC Psychiatry, 5.*

Tate, D. F. (2011). A series of studies examining internet treatment of obesity to inform internet interventions for substance use and misuse. *Substance Use & Misuse, 46*(1), 57-65.

Tercyak, K. P., O'Neill, S. C.; Roter, D. L., & McBride, C. M. (2012). Bridging the communication divide: A role for health psychology in the genomic era. *Professional Psychology: Research and Practice, 43*(6), 568-575. http://psycnet.apa.org/journals/pro/43/6/568/

Thorndike, F. P., Carlbring, P., Smyth, F. L., Magee, J. C., Gonder-Frederick, L., Ost, L., Ritterband, L. M. (2009). Web-based measurement: Effect of completing single or multiple items per webpage. *Computers in Human Behavior, 25(2),* 393-401.

Thorndike, F. P., Ritterband. L., Gonder-Frederick, L., Lord, H., Ingersoll, K., & Morin, C. (2013). A randomized controlled trial of an Internet intervention for adults with insomnia: Effects on comorbid psychological and fatigue symptoms. *Journal of Clinical Psychology, 69*(10), 1078-1093.

Thorndike, F. P., Ritterband, L. M., Saylor, D. K., Magee, J. C., Gonder-Frederick, L. A., & Morin, C. M. (2011). Validation of the Insomnia Severity Index as a Web-based measure. *Behavioral Sleep Medicine, 9(4),* 216-223.

Thorndike, F. P., Saylor, D. K., Bailey, E. T., Gonder-Frederick, L., Morin, C.M., & Ritterband, L. M. (2008). Development and perceived utility and impact of an Internet intervention for insomnia. *E-journal of Applied Psychology, 4*, 32-42.

Thorp, S. R., Fidler, J., Moreno, L., Floto, E. & Agha, Z.. (2012). Lessons learned from studies of psychotherapy for posttraumatic stress disorder via video teleconferencing, *Psychological Services,* 9 (2), 197-99.

Tiffin, J., & Terashima, N. (2001). *HyperReality: Paradigm for the third millennium.* London: Routledge.

Tillfors, M., Andersson, G., Ekselius, L., Furmark, T., Lewenhaupt, S., Karlsson, A., & Carlbring, P. (2011). A randomized trial of internet-delivered treatment for social anxiety disorder in high school students. *Cognitive Behaviour Therapy*, *40*(2), 147-157.

Titov, N., Andrews, G., Schwencke, G., Robinson, E., Peters, L., & Spence, J. (2010). Randomized controlled trial of internet cognitive behavioural treatment for social phobia with and without motivational enhancement strategies. *Australian And New Zealand Journal Of Psychiatry*, *44*(10), 938-945.

Titov, N., Dear, B. F., Schwencke, G., Andrews, G., Johnston, L., Craske, M. G., & McEvoy, P. (2011). Transdiagnostic internet treatment for anxiety and depression: A randomised controlled trial. *Behaviour Research And Therapy*, *49*(8), 441-452.

Toseland, R. W., Naccarato, T., & Wray, L. O. (2007). Telephone groups for older persons and family caregivers: Key implementation and process issues. *Clinical Gerontologist: The Journal of Aging and Mental Health, 31*, 59-76. doi:10.1300/J018v31n01_05

Trapp, R. (2001, March 11). Enterprise: 'I See What You Say' - Video Conferencing Comes of Age. *The Independent (London, England).*

Trepal, H., Haberstroh, S., Duffey, T., & Evans, M. (2007). Considerations and strategies for teaching online counseling skills: Establishing relationships in cyberspace. *Counselor Education and Supervision, 46*, 266-279.

Tsai, H-H., & Tsai, Y-F. (2011). Changes in depressive symptoms, social support, and loneliness over 1 year after a minimum 3-month videoconference program for older nursing home resident', *Journal of Medical Internet Research,* 13 (4), 373-84.

Tsan, J. Y., & Day, S. X. (2007). Personality and gender as predictors of online counseling use. *Journal of Technology in Human Services, 25*, 39-55. doi:10.1300/J017v25n03_03

Tu, C. H. (2004). *Online collaborative learning communities: Twenty-one designs to building an online collaborative learning community*. Westport, Conn: Libraries Unlimited.

Tuber, S., & Seckin, B. (2012). A tape recorder as a therapeutic "witness" in the treatment of an 8-year-old girl. *Journal of Clinical Psychology,66,* 1216-1224.

Tuerk, P.J., Yoder, M., Ruggiero, K.J., Gros, D.F., & Acierno, R. (2010). A pilot study of prolonged exposure for posttraumatic stress disorder delivered via telehealth technology. *Journal of Traumatic Stress, 23*,116 –23.

Tunick, R.A., Mednick, L., & Conroy, C. (2011). A snapshot of child psychologists' social media activity: Professional and ethical practice implications and recommendations. *Professional Psychology: Research and Practice, 42,* 440-447.

Turvey, C.L., Willyard, D., Hickman, D.H., Klein, D.M., & Kukoyi, O. (2007). Telehealth screen for depression in a chronic illness care management program. *Telemedicine and Ehealth, 13*, 51-56.

Van Allen, J., Davis, A-M., & Lassen, S. (2011). 'The use of telemedicine in pediatric psychology: Research review and current applications. *Child and Adolescent Psychiatric Clinics of North America,* 20 (1), 55-66.

Van Allen, J., & Roberts, M. C. (2011). Critical incidents in the marriage of psychology and technology: A discussion of potential ethical issues in practice, education, and policy. *Professional Psychology: Research and Practice, 42,* 433-439.

Van der Houwen, K., Schut, H., van den Bout, J., Stroebe, M., & Stroebe, W. (2010). The efficacy of a brief internet-based self-help intervention for the bereaved. *Behaviour Research and Therapy, 48*, 359-367. doi: 10.1016/j.brat.2009.12.009

van der Krieke, L., Wunderink, L., Emerencia, A. C., de Jonge, P., & Sytema, S. (2014). E--mental health self-management for psychotic disorders: State of the art and future perspectives. *Psychiatric Services, 65*(1), 33.

Vanderslice, J. L. (2009). TechnoEthics in counseling practice: Knowledge, attitudes, and usage of ethical precautions for electronic communication by texas professional counselors. *Dissertation Abstracts International Section A: Humanities and Social Sciences, 69*(9-A), 3466.

Vecchione, M., Alessandri, G., & Barbaranelli, C. (2012). Paper-and-pencil and web-based testing: The measurement invariance of the Big Five personality tests in applied settings. *Assessment, 19*, 243-246.

Venter, A., Burns, R., Hefford, M., & Ehrenberg, N.(2012), Results of a telehealth-enabled chronic care management service to support people with long-term conditions at home, *Journal of Telemedidine and Telecare, 18* (3), 172-5.

Vernmark, K., Lenndin, J., Bjärehed, J., Carlsson, M., Karlsson, J., Öberg, J., Carlbring, P., Eriksson, T., & Andersson, G. (2010). Internet administered guided self-help versus individualized e-mail therapy: A randomized trial of two versions of CBT for major depression. *Behaviour Research and Therapy, 48*, 368-376. doi: 10.1016/ j.brat.2010.01.005

Vigerland, S., Thulin, U., Ljótsson, B., Svirsky, L., Öst, L., Lindefors, N., & Andersson, G. & Serlachius, E. (2013). Internet-delivered CBT for children with specific phobia: A pilot study. *Cognitive Behaviour Therapy, 42*(4), 303-314.

Vogel, P. A., Launes, G., Moen, E. M., Solem, S., Hansen, B., Haland, A.T. & Himle, J.A. (2012), 'Videoconference- and cell phone-based cognitive-behavioral therapy of obsessive-compulsive disorder: A case series', *Journal of Anxiety Disorders,* 26 (1), 158-64.

Wade, R., Cartwright, C., & Shaw, K. (2012). Factors relating to home telehealth acceptance and usage compliance. *Risk Management and Healthcare Policy,* 5, 25-33.

Wade, S. L., Waltz, N. C. Carey, J. C., and Williams, K. M. (2009). Brief report: Description of feasibility and satisfaction findings from an innovative online family problem-solving intervention for adolescents following traumatic brain injury. *Journal of Pediatric Psychology, 34,* 517-522.

Wade, R., Shaw, K., and Cartwright, C. (2012), Factors affecting provision of successful monitoring in home telehealth', *Gerontology, 58*, 371-377.

Wade, S. L., Oberjohn, K., Conaway, K., Osinska, P. & Bangert, L.. (2011), Live coaching of parenting skills using the internet: Implications for clinical practice, *Professional Psychology: Research and Practice,* 42 (6), 487-93.

Wade, S. L., Waltz, N. C. Carey, J. C., and Williams, K. M. (2008). Preliminary efficacy of a Web-based family problem-solving treatment program for adolescents with traumatic brain injury. *Journal of Head Trauma Rehabilitation, 23,* 367-377.

Wade, S. L., Walz, N. C., Carey, J-A, Williams, K. M., Cass, J., Herren, L., Mark, E., & Yeates, K. O. (2010). A randomized trial of teen online problem solving for improving executive function deficits following brain pediatric traumatic injury. *Journal of Head Injury Rehabilitation, 25,* 1-7.

Wade, V. A., Elliott, J. A., & Hiller, J. E. (2012). A qualitative study of ethical, medico-legal and clinical governance matters in Australian telehealth services, *Journal of Telemedicine and Telecare,* 18 (2), 109-14.

Wagner, B., Knaevelsrud, C., & Maercker, A. (2006). Internet-based cognitive-behavioral therapy for complicated grief: A randomized controlled trial. *Death Studies, 30*(5), 429-453.

Wagner, B., Schulz, W., & Knaevelsrud, C. (2012). Efficacy of an internet-based intervention for posttraumatic stress disorder in Iraq: A pilot study. *Psychiatry Research, 195*(1-2), 85-88.

Wainfan, L., & Davis, P. K. (2004). *Challenges in virtual collaboration: Videoconferencing, audioconferencing, and computer-mediated communications.* Santa Monica: Rand.

Waldron, H. B., & Brody, J. L. (2010). Functional family therapy for adolescent substance use disorders. In J. R., Weisz & A. E. Kasdin (Eds.), *Evidence-based psychotherapies for children and adolescents* (2nd ed., pp 401-415). New York, NY: Guilford.

Wang, F. (2011). Economic evaluations of the effects of longevity on telemedicine and conventional healthcare provision. *Telemedicine and e-Health,* 17 (6), 431-34.

Wangberg, S.C., Gammon, D., & Spitznogle, K. (2007). In the eyes of the beholder: Exploring psychologists' attitudes towards and use of e-therapy in Norway. *CyberPsychology & Behavior, 10*(3), 418-423.

Ward-Zimmerman, B., & Cannata, E. (2012). Partnering with pediatric primary care: Lessons learned through collaborative colocation. *Professional Psychology: Research and Practice, 43*(6), 596-605. http://psycnet.apa.org/journals/pro/43/6/596/

Watts, A. G., & Dent, G. (2008). The evolution of a national distance guidance service: Trends and challenges. *British Journal of Guidance & Counselling, 36*, 455-465. doi: 10.1080/03069880802334505

Weinerman, B. H., Barnett, J., Loyola, M., den Duyf, J., Robertson, S., Ashworth, V., Apland, L., & Kazanjian, A. (2012), Telehealth-A Change in a Practice Model in Oncology, *Telemedicine Journal and E-Health, 18*, 391-393.

Wells, M., & Mitchell, K. J. (2007). Youth sexual exploitation on the Internet: DSM-IV diagnoses and gender differences in co-occurring mental health issues. *Child & Adolescent Social Work Journal*, *24*(3), 235-260.

Wells, M., Mitchell, K.J., Finkelhor, D., & Becker-Blease, K.A. (2007). Online mental health treatment: Concerns and considerations. *CyberPsychology & Behavior, 10*(3), 453-459.

Wells, M., Mitchell, K. J., Finkelhor, D., & Blease, K. (2006). Mental health professionals' exposure to clients with problematic Internet experiences. *Journal of Technology In Human Services*, *24*(4), 35-52.

Wendel, M. L., Brossart, D.F., Elliott, T.R., McCord, C., & Diaz, M.A. (2011). Use of technology to increase access to mental health services in a rural Texas community. *Family & Community Health: The Journal of Health Promotion & Maintenance, 34* (2), 134-40.

Whiteside, U., Lungu, A., Richards, J., Simon, G., Clingan, S., Siler, J., Snyder, L. & Ludman, E. (2014). Designing messaging to engage patients in an online suicide prevention intervention: Survey results from patients with current suicidal ideation. *Journal Of Medical Internet Research, 16*(2), e42.

Wilkinson, N., Ang, R.P., & Goh, D.H. (2008). Online video game therapy for mental health concerns: A review. *International Journal of Social Psychiatry, 54*, 370-382.

Wilsie, C. C., & Brestan-Knight, E. (2012). Using an online viewing system for parent–child interaction therapy consulting with professionals. *Psychological Services,* 9 (2), 224-26.

Wilson, S. R., & Cram, P. (2012). Another sobering result for home telehealth--and where we might go next: Comment on "A Randomized Controlled Trial of Telemonitoring in Older Adults With Multiple Health Issues to Prevent Hospitalizations and Emergency Department Visits". *Archives of Internal Medicine*, 172(10), 779-780.

Wilczenski, F. L., & Coomey, S. M. (2006). Cyber-communication: Finding its place in school counseling practice, education, and professional development. *Professional School Counseling, 9*, 327-331.

Williams, R., Bambling, M., King, R., & Abbott, Q. (2009). In-session processes in online counselling with young people: An exploratory approach. *Counselling & Psychotherapy Research, 9*(2), 93-100. doi: 10.1080/14733140802490606

Wood, A. F., & Smith, M. J. (2005). *Online communication: Linking technology, identity, and culture* (2nd ed.). Mahwah, NJ: L. Erlbaum.

Wood, R. T. A., & Griffiths, M. D. (2007). Online guidance, advice, and support for problem gamblers and concerned relatives and friends: An evaluation of the "GamAid" pilot service. *British Journal of Guidance & Counselling, 35*, 373-389. doi: 10.1080/03069880701593540.

Woolgar, M., & Scott, S. (2014). The negative consequences of over-diagnosing attachment disorders in adopted children: The importance of comprehensive formulations. *Clinical Child Psychology and Psychiatry, 19*, 355-366.

Wootton, B. M., Titov, N., Dear, B. F., Spence, J., Andrews, G., Johnston, L., & Solley, K. (2011). An internet administered treatment program for obsessive–compulsive disorder: A feasibility study. *Journal Of Anxiety Disorders, 25*(8), 1102-1107.

Wootton, B. M., Titov, N., Dear, B. F., Spence, J., & Kemp, A. (2011). The acceptability of internet-based treatment and characteristics of an adult sample with obsessive compulsive disorder: An internet survey. *Plos ONE, 6*(6).

Wright, J. H. & Bloom, A.S. (1997). Computer assisted psychotherapy. *The Journal of Psychotherapy Practice and Research, 6*, 315-329.

Wynn, S. D., & Sherrod, R. A. (2012). Providing mental health care to veterans in rural areas: Using Telehealth in mobile clinics, *Journal of Psychosocial Nursing Mental Health Services, 50*, 22-28.

Yablon, Y. B. (2008). Internet as a source of help in dealing with school violence. *Journal of Educational Computing Research, 39*, 205-220. doi:10.2190/EC.39.3.a

Yuen, E. K., Goetter, E.M., Herbert, J.D, & Forman, E.M. (2012). Challenges and opportunities in internet-mediated telemental health. *Professional Psychology: Research and Practice,* 43 (1), 1-8.

Zack, J. S. (2008). How sturdy is that digital couch? Legal considerations for mental health professionals who deliver clinical services via the internet. *Journal of Technology in Human Services. Special Issue: Internet-Delivered Therapeutic Interventions in Human Services: Methods, Issues, and Evaluation, 26*(2-4), 333-359. doi: 10.1080/ 15228830802097083

Zilliacus, E., Meiser, B., Lobb, E., Dudding, T. E., Barlow-Stewart, K., & Tucker, K. (2010). The virtual consultation: Practitioners' experiences of genetic counseling by videoconferencing in Australia. *Telemedicine and e-Health, 16,* 350-357. doi:10.1089/tmj.2009.0108.

Zofi, Y. S. (2012). *A manager's guide to virtual teams*. New York: American Management Association.

Zur, O., Williams, M. H., Lehavot, K., & Knapp, S. (2009). Psychotherapist self-disclosure and transparency in the internet age. *Professional Psychology: Research and Practice, 40,* 22-30. doi: 10.1037/a0014745

Zyromski, B., Bryant, A., Jr., Deese, B. D., & Gerler, E. R., Jr. (2008). Succeeding in school: A qualitative study of primarily American Indian students' use of an online intervention. *Professional School Counseling. Special Issue: Strengths-Based School Counseling, 12,* 119-122.

INDEX

B

C

D

E

F

G

H

I

N

Q

R

S

T